FAST FORWARD THINKING

40 Rules for Entrepreneurs and Investors in Medicine, Science, and Biotech

Luis Pareras, MD, PhD

American Association for
PHYSICIAN
LEADERSHIP

978-1-960762-13-9 Paperback
978-1-960762-14-6 eBook

Published by **American Association for Physician Leadership, Inc.**
PO Box 96503 | BMB 97493 | Washington, DC 20090-6503

Website: www.physicianleaders.org

13 8 7 6 5 4 3 2 1

Copyedited, typeset, indexed, and printed in the United States of America

PUBLISHER
Nancy Collins

PRODUCTION MANAGER
Jennifer Weiss

DESIGN & PRODUCTION
Carter Publishing Studio
Nancy Collins
Luis Pareras

COPYEDITOR
Pat George

To the scientists who dare to dream big and try bold and extraordinary things.

The only people for me are the mad ones, the ones who are mad to live, mad to talk, mad to be saved, desirous of everything at the same time, the ones who never yawn or say a commonplace thing, but burn, burn, burn like fabulous yellow roman candles exploding like spiders across the stars and in the middle you see the blue centerlight pop and everybody goes "Awww!"

JACK KEROUAC

Table of Contents

I. Knowledge

Rule #1
Understand What "Cutting-Edge" Really Means | 3

Rule #2
You Are Always Six Months Late | 25

Rule #3
See Both the Forest and the Trees | 33

Rule #4
Map the Landscape and Connect the Dots | 41

Rule #5
If Everybody Likes the Idea, It Is Too Late | 47

Rule #6
There Will Be Constant Changes of Wind Direction | 53

Rule #7
Strategic Positioning Matters | 59

Rule #8
Leverage Exponentials, Emergence, Luck, and Truth | 75

Rule #9
Prioritize Your Critical Path | 87

Rule #10
The Gap Analysis | 97

Rule #11
Take the Right Initial Steps to Make It Happen | 107

Rule #12
There Is Not a Right Time to Start | 119

Rule #13
How Much Is an Idea Worth? | 125

Rule #14
Understand What Happens in the First Meeting with a Venture Capitalist | 133

RULE #15
Types of Mistakes a Venture Capitalist Can Make | 153

RULE #16
Every Investment Is a Story | 163

RULE #17
Identify Your "Wow" Slide | 169

RULE #18
Use the Right Pitch Structure | 175

RULE #19
The Anatomy of a Term Sheet in Science-Driven Companies | 181

RULE #20
Pre-money Valuation Is Important, but Not as Important as the Equity Story | 199

RULE #21
You Will Need a Different Kind of Board of Directors | 207

RULE #22
The Team! | 215

RULE #23
Hire the Right People | 225

RULE #24
Become a Chief Networking Officer | 233

RULE #25
On Negotiation Skills | 239

RULE #26
On Communication Skills | 259

RULE #27
On Leadership at the Cutting Edge: 25 Pearls of Management Wisdom | 269

II. Mindset

RULE #28
Forecasting in Science: The Right Mindset | 297

RULE #29
Game Theory in Emerging Fields | 303

RULE #30
You Don't Want to Lie with Statistics | 319
RULE #31
On Bayesian Thinking | 357
RULE #32
On Probabilistic Thinking | 367
RULE #33
On Algorithmic Thinking | 381
RULE #34
On Visual Thinking | 407

III. Choosing the Future

RULE #35
Sourcing Deal Flow | 419
RULE #36
Choosing the Future | 429

IV. Epilogue: Science, Curiosity, Ethics, and Happiness

RULE #37
Understand Why Science Matters | 467
RULE #38
Surround Yourself with Curiosity-Driven Minds | 475
RULE #39
You Will Face Ethical Dilemmas | 481
RULE #40
On Happiness in Science: Finding Joy in Learning and Growth | 489

List of Figures

FIGURE 1. Science-Driven Companies and Deep Tech | 6
FIGURE 2. AI + Synthetic Biology: Two Cutting-Edge Fields Collide | 22
FIGURE 3. Speed and Mortality | 28
FIGURE 4. The Forest, the Tree, the Weather, and the Fire | 36
FIGURE 5. Example: Mapping the Landscape of Oncology | 43
FIGURE 6. Example: Mapping the Landscape of Pancreatic Cancer | 45
FIGURE 7. Gene Editing and Synthetic Biology | 64
FIGURE 8. Strategic Positioning | 68
FIGURE 9. Positioning While Investing in SynBio | 72
FIGURE 10. Emergence in Large Language Models | 79
FIGURE 11. Mycoplasma Laboratorium | 81
FIGURE 12. Understanding Bias | 84
FIGURE 13. A Typical Gantt Chart | 98
FIGURE 14. Example of Gap Analysis in Biotech: CMC Checklist | 102
FIGURE 15. Things to Consider When Starting-Up: Part 1 | 110
FIGURE 16. Things to Consider When Starting-Up: Part 2 | 112
FIGURE 17. Research Versus Innovation | 128
FIGURE 18. The First Meeting | 135
FIGURE 19. How Big Is the Problem Is Not Its Market Size: The Special Case of Rare Diseases | 138
FIGURE 20. Strategies to Solve Rare Diseases | 142
FIGURE 21. Are the Endpoints Clear Enough? | 146
FIGURE 22. Is There a Chance of Accelerated Pathway? | 150
FIGURE 23. What Goes Through the Investor's Mind? | 152
FIGURE 24. Error Matrix | 155
FIGURE 25. A Solid Proof of Concept in Biotech | 172
FIGURE 26. Structure of a Compelling Pitch | 178
FIGURE 27. Anatomy of a Term Sheet | 194
FIGURE 28. Equity Story | 202
FIGURE 29. How a Board of Directors Works | 212
FIGURE 30. Things a CEO Needs to Oversee | 218
FIGURE 31. On Negotiation | 256
FIGURE 32. On Communication | 266
FIGURE 33. Decision-Making Guidelines | 294

FIGURE 34. A Different Way of Thinking | 300
FIGURE 35. Game Theory Basic Tools | 306
FIGURE 36. What Is *p*? | 321
FIGURE 37. The Base Rate Fallacy | 326
FIGURE 38. Type I and Type II Errors | 328
FIGURES 39-40. How to Quickly Approximate N | 332
FIGURE 41. Understanding Sensitivity and Specificity | 334
FIGURE 42. A Look at the Stock Market Right Distributions | 338
FIGURE 43. Regression Analysis | 343
FIGURE 44. Finding Trends in Nasdaq-Listed Biotech Companies: Part 1 | 346
FIGURE 45. Finding Trends in Nasdaq-Listed Biotech Companies: Part 2 | 348
FIGURE 46. Deep Neural Networks | 352
FIGURE 47. Understanding Bayesian Reasoning | 359
FIGURE 48. A Simple Data Request | 385
FIGURE 49. IPO Trends | 386
FIGURE 50. Can the Stock Market Be Predicted? | 390
FIGURE 51. Value Creation Steps That Can Be Fed to AI | 392
FIGURE 52. Deep Neural Networks Predictive Analysis | 394
FIGURE 53. My Own Quant Architecture | 396
FIGURE 54. AI Reports | 400
FIGURE 55. AIA (Artificial Intelligence Analyst) | 402
FIGURE 56. An Example of a Mind Map | 409
FIGURE 57. Visual Thinking for Future Anti-Ageing Therapies | 412
FIGURE 58. Visual Thinking for Guiding Investment Decisions | 414
FIGURE 59. Factors Affecting How Easy It Will Be to Prove | 438
FIGURE 60. Choosing the Right Indications | 442
FIGURE 61. The S-Shaped Curve of Value | 450
FIGURE 62. Investments, Information, and Liquidity Events | 456
FIGURE 63. How to Teach Science | 470
FIGURE 64. Ethical Dilemmas in Genome Editing | 484

ABOUT THE AUTHOR

Luis Pareras, MD, PhD, stands at the forefront of innovation, embodying a rare combination of the clinical, academic, and entrepreneurial realms. With a transition from the operating room, where he impacted one patient at a time, to the fascinating world of venture capital, impacting millions, Pareras's journey is one of curiosity.

Leading Invivo Ventures, he oversees several venture capital funds dedicated to groundbreaking advancements in life sciences and healthcare. Each investment, each decision reflects more than just business acumen — it encapsulates lessons from over 25 years in the science-driven ecosystem. Under his leadership, the fund has sculpted the future of numerous life sciences companies, reflecting Pareras's passion for merging business strategies with transformative science.

In addition to his many accomplishments, Pareras has been an instrumental figure on the boards of numerous biotech startups, bringing with him a wealth of experience in the governance of companies. Each of these companies stands at the leading edge of their respective fields, driven by a shared mission to ultimately benefit patients. His deep understanding of corporate governance, coupled with his expertise in leading investment strategies and guiding transaction processes, has made him a valued venture capital investor in this challenging field.

Pareras has a background as a neurosurgeon with expertise in disruptive technologies such as gene therapy, cell therapy, synthetic biology, and artificial intelligence. He is also an esteemed academic with a Global Executive MBA from IESE and teaching positions at several business schools. His unique vantage point stems from his immersive experiences in science, allowing him to engage with brilliant minds that are shaping our future.

Beyond his business endeavors, Pareras is a celebrated author. His former works, including *Innovation and Entrepreneurship in Healthcare,* are testaments to his deep knowledge and commitment to the sector, as well as his ability to simplify complex concepts for readers of all backgrounds. This book, *Fast Forward Thinking,* is his tribute to the mesmerizing world of science and venture capital. Drawing from his firsthand experiences, it's a reflection of someone utterly captivated by the realms of science and venture capital. He hopes to inspire the spirit of curiosity and discovery in all, whether investors, entrepreneurs, scientists, or merely those driven by the thirst for knowledge.

As an active participant and advisor for myriad healthcare innovation organizations, Pareras not only bridges the gap between idea and execution but also emphasizes the importance of visual thinking in grasping our unpredictable future. Through his writings and his professional endeavors, he offers insights into harnessing the transformative power of curiosity in the world of deep tech.

Whether in the boardroom, the operating theater, or the classroom, Luis Pareras is a name synonymous with the cutting-edge of progress and a spirit that constantly seeks to understand, predict, and shape the future.

Contact Luis Pareras, MD, PhD
luis.pareras@invivo.partners
Twitter: @pareras
LinkedIn: Luis Pareras

Preface

If you're trying to find your way in the exciting but sometimes confusing world of science-driven companies and emerging technologies, this book is for you. It's a collection of lessons I've picked up over more than 25 years in this exciting ecosystem of investment and entrepreneurship. These lessons aren't always neat or orderly, just like the cutting-edge space itself, but they're close to my heart. I'm sharing them with you in the hope that they can guide you on your own journey of investing and help you better predict the future.

And let's be clear: The insights in this book aren't absolute truths. I offer them to help you form your own strategies and tools. Every adventurer in this field, whether they are scientists, entrepreneurs, or young investors, must create their own path and develop their personal style.

The chapters in this book explain how science becomes business. We discuss a diverse array of topics, some of which may feel unorthodox or come as a surprise. However, each of these themes, irrespective of how unconventional they might seem, contributes to a mindset that has been my compass in choosing promising companies in which to invest.

Every piece of wisdom in this book, every concept explored and every lesson shared, leads us to a vital destination: the chapter on choosing. In the world of the cutting-edge and science-driven ventures, knowing how to select the best projects is both an art and a science. This crucial chapter on choosing represents the heart of the book, a culmination of all preceding insights. Here, I explain my framework for peering into the future of a company, for making the educated predictions that are so pivotal in my role. Essentially, this book is my attempt to articulate simply how I choose companies.

Over the years, I've gained perspective, which helps me separate what's truly important from what isn't. As an investor, my task is akin to that of a futurist: piecing together signals from the present, constructing plausible scenarios, and making decisions based on these incomplete forecasts. So, as we embark on this journey, remember that our ultimate goal is to understand the intricacies of choice, to acquire the ability to make informed predictions about the future.

I used to be a neurosurgeon, working in the operating room and helping one patient at a time. Then, I moved into venture capital where I could impact millions of lives through investments in therapies and synthetic biology. This amazing journey, from medicine to investing, is the backbone of this book. The words in this book are based on more than two decades of exploration and learning. It feels as if I've been crafting this book during every decision, triumph, failure, and hurdle I've faced.

While many examples are drawn from the field of biotech, a realm I'm particularly familiar with, do not be put off if that isn't your area of expertise or interest. We're living in an extraordinary science-driven era where everything is at the frontier of everything. The boundaries of biotech and other scientific disciplines are blurring, and a more holistic movement is emerging.

This wider movement encompasses cutting-edge, science-driven companies often referred to as "deep tech" or "STEM." Regardless of their particular focus, these companies share common characteristics and challenges. Consequently, many of these experiences and lessons from biotech are highly applicable to other sectors within deep tech.

In this book, I keep things simple. It is deliberately not too technical in order to make it more a casual read than a study book. There won't be lengthy discussions or complicated jargon. Instead, you'll find a clear, straightforward guide that prioritizes concepts over complexity. As a scientist, I approach each situation with humility, acknowledging that there's always more to learn.

This isn't a how-to manual. It's an invitation for you to join in a dynamic process of learning and discovery, understanding that there's no single "right" way to do things. I've distilled my experiences, lessons, and knowledge into clear, easy-to-digest, and impactful "pills" that will inspire thought, encourage action, and help you develop your own strategies.

I've taken care to lay out my thinking visually, using schematic figures as maps to order ideas and offer a clear pathway through complex thoughts. These "Quick Notes" are not essential for understanding the content, as all their information is also detailed in the side text accompanying each figure. They are, however, an integral part of the book's landscape. I've included them to encourage and facilitate a habit of visual thinking.

As we venture into the complexities of tomorrow, this ability to mentally structure and visualize ideas will become increasingly valuable. It's a skill that helps organize thoughts, capture relationships, and grasp patterns that may not be readily apparent in text form. This knack for visualization is one of our most potent tools for understanding — and attempting to predict — the future, which is, in essence, the underlying goal of this book. So, while these figures aren't crucial for your reading comprehension, they serve as a gateway to a mode of thought that could prove essential in your journey towards foreseeing what lies ahead.

This book is organized in four sections:

I. **Knowledge:** This first part of the book will help you understand the basics of innovation and venture capital in science-driven companies. We'll explain what "cutting-edge" means and how quickly things change in this area. You'll understand the ecosystem, the rules and the tools that are essential to navigate it, from the first spark of an idea to assembling a winning team.

II. **Mindset:** This section may seem a bit unusual and unconventional, but it's essential in equipping you with the mindset needed to navigate to the heart of the book, the third part. We'll explore game theory, discuss why understanding statistics is crucial, and demonstrate how probabilistic, algorithmic, and visual thinking can aid your journey.

III. **Choosing the Future:** Here's where everything we've discussed so far will come together. We will take a deep dive into sourcing deal flow and the art of choosing the future. Regardless of whether you are a scientist, an entrepreneur, or an investor, the rules here will guide you in learning to identify potential breakthroughs and evaluate their potential impact, setting you on the path to making transformative choices.

IV. **Epilogue (Science, Curiosity, Ethics, and Happiness):** In this final section, we'll delve into why science matters, the significance of curiosity, and the ethical dilemmas we might encounter. We'll also pay tribute to a unique form of happiness, a "scientific" happiness that springs from struggle, effort, and meaning. This section is a philosophical reflection on our journey, grounding our exploration within the broader human context. It reminds us of the driving forces behind our pursuit of the cutting-edge: a quest for truth, dedication to ethical behavior, and a profound love for science.

This book is not meant to be read linearly, from cover to cover. Each chapter stands on its own, a unique piece of the investment puzzle, illuminated from a distinct angle. While certain concepts may resurface across chapters, rest assured, this is not a mere repetition. Rather, it's an opportunity to examine these ideas under a different light, to dig deeper, and to see how they intertwine with various facets of the venture capital ecosystem.

As we delve into these subjects, you might notice a thread of familiarity, an echo of something we've previously discussed. But just as a prism refracts light to reveal the spectrum of colors, each chapter refracts these common concepts to reveal the many hues of their significance in different contexts. Each iteration is a reinforcement, a layering of knowledge and an opportunity for deeper understanding.

The repetition, far from being redundant, aims to fortify the reader's grasp of the core principles, providing the chance to see how they operate within different frames of reference.

While there's a logical thread that binds these chapters, you're free to chart your own course through this book, diving into the topics that spark your curiosity or align with your current interests. No matter the order in which you choose to read, each chapter will make sense in its own right while adding depth and richness to your understanding of science-driven companies.

You'll encounter a few unfamiliar creatures here — concepts like emergence, game theory, algorithmic thinking, and more generally the whole fast-forward thinking approach. Everything is meant to give you the foundations to think about the future in a smarter way. Each section, each "building block," can be read independently, giving you the freedom to explore the topics that resonate with you most strongly at any given moment. As I've learned over the years, the world of emerging investments is anything but linear, and so is the journey through this book.

For a unique reading experience, you could begin by delving into Section III on "Choosing the Future." This pivotal chapter, focusing on the selection of the most promising projects, sets the stage for the rest of the book. Once you've gotten a taste of this central concept, you can rewind to the start of the book, understanding the various tools, strategies, and mindsets that lead to this crucial point. Then, return to "Choosing the Future" for a second read, this time equipped with a fresh perspective and new insights gleaned from the preceding chapters.

But, again, don't hesitate to read it in any order you want. Trust your instinct and let your curiosity guide you, it usually is the best way to learn.

As a personal note and to add a touch of inspiration and reflection, you'll notice that each chapter begins with a quote about art. You might wonder why art in a book about venture capital and science. My answer is simple: Art brings balance. I've always found solace in art, particularly in painting. It offers an escape from the pressure of the daily grind, providing a space for contemplation and creativity. In times of ups and downs, art gives me a steady ground to stand on.

Each quote has been chosen to resonate with the theme of the chapter it prefaces, adding another dimension to the ideas we explore. It's a slight detour from the main subject, I agree. But I hope you'll find it a welcome diversion, as it is meant to enhance our journey, offering both wisdom and a breath of fresh air.

Finally, in this journey of life, I've been incredibly fortunate and privileged. I can tell you firsthand that investing in companies is extraordinarily gratifying. It is also incredibly hard. I've had the chance to delve into the fascinating realm of science, to be involved in groundbreaking ventures, and to engage with the minds that are shaping our future.

This book is my humble attempt at contributing back to the community that has fostered my growth and shaped my journey. This book is a tribute to the mesmerizing world of science and venture capital, written from the perspective of someone utterly captivated by it. It aims to celebrate and inspire the spirit of curiosity and discovery that resides in all of us — investors, entrepreneurs, scientists, or anyone who finds joy in the pursuit of knowledge. My hope is that it will provide both an understanding of the transformative power of curiosity and a guide on how to harness it in the realm of deep tech. May the insights within these pages light your way.

Luis Pareras, MD, PhD
Founder & Managing Partner
Invivo Capital

I

Knowledge

Rule #1

Understand What "Cutting-Edge" Really Means

"The role of the artist is to not look away."
Akira Kurosawa

In 1947, an artist named Jackson Pollock embarked on a revolutionary journey, one that would forever change the landscape of painting. Alone in his studio, he laid an unstretched canvas on the floor, a blank canvas just waiting to be filled. Pollock began to drip paint onto this canvas, allowing gravity, velocity, and pure improvisation to guide his hand. The result was a new style that defied traditional confines. These creations, later known as "drip paintings," were the harbingers of the New York Abstract Expressionism movement.

But let's not get ahead of ourselves. When he was done, Pollock called upon his wife, Lee Krasner, to contemplate the work with him. Krasner, an abstract expressionist painter in her own right, was not met with the usual questions seeking approval or critique, such as "Do you like it?" or "Is it good?" Instead, she faced a question that was far more profound.

"Lee... is this a painting?" Pollock asked.

This question resonates deeply with me. Pollock was so far ahead of his time, so deep in uncharted territory, so "on the leading edge" so to speak, that he was unsure about the nature of his creation. His painting defied conventional boundaries; it was not "a window" showing something, but an action space; it had no discernable motif, no clear beginning or end. It was a painting that was not just seen but felt.

This story is a poignant reminder of how difficult it is to identify or to classify "the new." I'm often asked a simple question: "How does it feel when you first see something truly new and groundbreaking? How do you know it when you see it?" These questions touch the core of what I do. They ask about that exciting moment when I come across a new idea with the potential to change everything. And they wonder how I can recognize such a special moment when it happens. Pollock's story sums up exactly how I feel when I encounter a truly revolutionary innovation.

When I see a disruptive idea for the first time, it's like a jigsaw puzzle with some pieces missing. I might be confused at first, but then my curiosity kicks in. The idea might not align with what I've known or expected. It pushes my thinking, making me question what I thought was certain. Like Pollock pondering his painting, I often ask myself, "Is this possible? Can this become a company?" It feels like immediate skepticism — a very healthy and scientific reaction — immediately followed by an "imagine if" sense of wonder in case it were true.

So, the initial reaction is often one of astonishment, sometimes bordering on disbelief. I never completely understand at first. This is largely due to the fact that disruptive innovations fundamentally challenge our existing understanding of what's possible. Once the initial shock subsides, curiosity tends to kick in. You might start asking questions about how it works, why it works, and what its implications could be.

Just like the abstract painting from our opening story ignited inquiries about the nature of art, new, groundbreaking ideas spark curiosity about the possible transformation of established norms. This curiosity extends far beyond simple fascination; it forms the basis for a deep desire to understand, to dissect the novelty, and to envision its broader implications.

Learn how to identify these feelings because it is important. As an entrepreneur, they serve as your internal compass, guiding your decision-making and steering your focus toward the projects that are worth pursuing. For investors, these feelings act as an intuition, a sixth sense, if you will, helping you find those ventures that hold the most promise and are worth exploring further. Embrace the discomfort and uncertainty now; you'll turn them into your allies later. Learn to harness them.

Defining Science-Driven Startups

Today, the boundaries of scientific disciplines are becoming increasingly blurred. This is because several fields of science are now intermingling and cross-pollinating, creating a fresh wave of innovation that's as exciting as it is unpredictable. Cross-disciplinary collaboration has achieved an unprecedented volume and speed, and it's making our scientific future fascinatingly complex.

Take biotech, for instance. It's no longer the isolated field it once was; now it's inextricably interwoven with other new disciplines. In this field, it's hard to tell where biology ends and where engineering or math or computer science begins. Today, there's artificial intelligence already designing biological circuits, and biology and engineering principles are used interchangeably.

This cross-pollination is leading to an extraordinary moment in human history. Our technological and scientific advancement is moving at such a rapid pace that it's almost impossible to keep up with or predict. As the frontiers of traditional scientific areas merge and meld, we're unlocking incredible potential for innovation and growth.

Therefore, for clarity and to prevent potential confusion as we progress through the book, I will be using three terms interchangeably: "science-driven company," "STEM company," and "deep tech." These terms might seem distinct at first glance, but in the context of our discussion, they all point to the same idea. They refer to a "cutting-edge" organization or initiative where science is at the forefront of its value creation. They represent ventures that lean heavily on scientific knowledge, technological expertise, engineering skills, or advanced mathematical principles to create and deliver their products or services.

Just as a reminder, a "science-driven company" emphasizes the role of scientific inquiry and innovation in guiding the company's direction and defining its offerings. A "STEM company," short for science, technology, engineering, and mathematics, implies a broader reliance on these critical fields in driving the company's operations and product development. Lastly, "deep tech" is a term often used to describe companies that are based on substantial scientific advances and high-tech engineering innovation. Throughout this book, when I mention any of these three terms, understand that I am referring to companies

Figure 1. Science-Driven Companies and Deep Tech

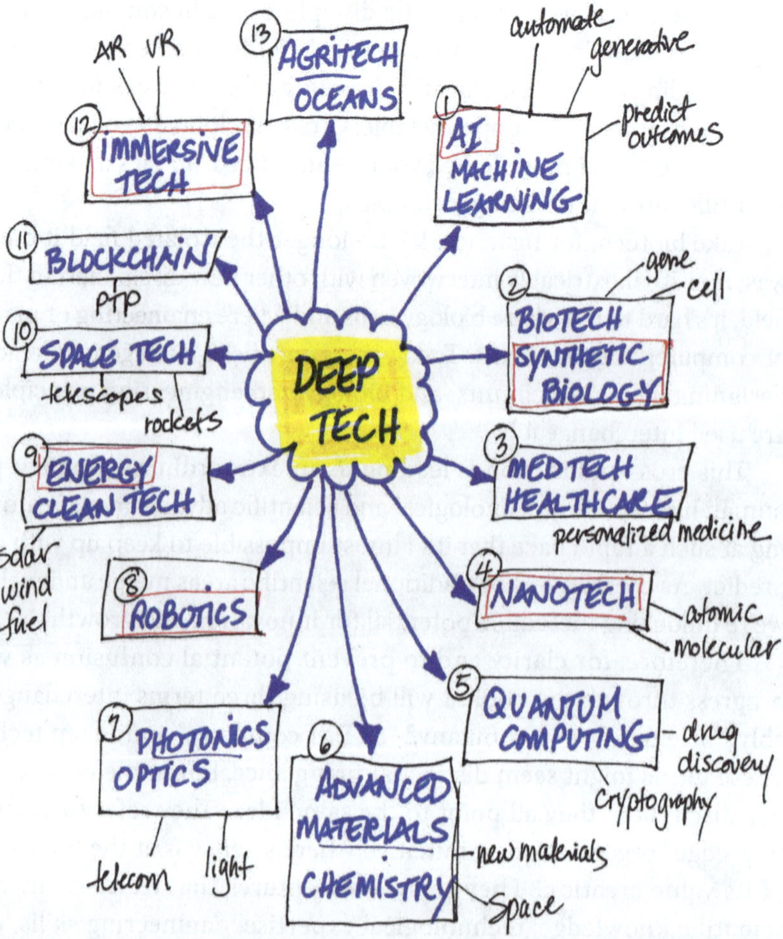

Deep-tech, or science-driven entrepreneurship, represents an expansive and diverse array of fields, each brimming with potential for revolutionary advancements. It's important to note that many of these fields overlap and intersect, and ground-breaking work often happens at the intersections. Innovation in these areas requires a deep understanding of the underlying science, making them a crucial part of the deep-tech landscape.

- **Artificial Intelligence and Machine Learning:** AI and ML provide the means to analyze massive amounts of data and draw insights, predict outcomes, and automate tasks.
- **Biotechnology:** Biotech is the use of living systems and organisms to develop or create products. This includes drug development, genetic engineering, cell and tissue culture technologies, personalized medicine, gene therapy, and more.

- **Synthetic Biology:** This is an interdisciplinary field that involves the design and construction of new biological parts, devices, and systems. It has potential applications in areas like agriculture, medicine, and energy.
- **Nanotechnology:** Nanotech involves manipulating matter at the atomic and molecular scale. It holds immense potential for breakthroughs in materials science, medicine, electronics, and energy production.
- **Quantum Computing:** This field leverages principles of quantum mechanics to process information. Quantum computing could revolutionize fields like cryptography, optimization problems, and drug discovery, where traditional computing struggles.
- **Advanced Materials and Chemistry:** This discipline involves the design and discovery of new materials with exceptional properties. It affects a wide range of sectors, from electronics and clean energy to medicine and aerospace.
- **Neuroscience:** The study of the nervous system, particularly the brain, is leading to advances in our understanding of cognition, behavior, and brain-based disorders. It's also spurring progress in brain-computer interfaces and mental health treatments.
- **Photonics and Optics:** This discipline includes the generation, manipulation, and detection of light. It has applications in telecommunications, imaging, and healthcare.
- **Robotics and Autonomous Systems:** This field involves the design and implementation of robots and autonomous systems to automate physical tasks. Applications range from manufacturing and agriculture to healthcare and space exploration.
- **Energy and CleanTech:** Innovations in this field aim to improve the efficiency of energy use and develop sustainable and clean sources of energy. This includes advancements in solar power, wind energy, fuel cells, and nuclear energy.
- **Space Technologies:** This field is concerned with the development of technologies for space exploration and utilization, including satellite technology, rocket propulsion, space telescopes, and more.
- **Immersive Technologies:** This includes augmented reality (AR), virtual reality (VR), and mixed reality (MR) and has applications in gaming, education, healthcare, and more.
- **Blockchain:** This allows data to be stored and exchanged on a peer-to-peer network, with potential applications ranging from cryptocurrencies to supply chain management.
- **Health Tech:** This encompasses various technologies designed to improve healthcare delivery and outcomes, including telemedicine, wearable devices, and digital therapeutics.
- **AgriTech:** This field involves the application of technology to agriculture, aiming to improve yields and sustainability. It includes precision farming, automation, and genetic modifications

where science is king, the core driving force. I believe this uniformity of language will help simplify our discussion.

How Science Creates Value

The beginning of the 21st century will be remembered as the Cambrian explosion of cooperative innovation, an era in which all sorts of scientists and creative people connected from anywhere and collaborated in the creation of the next big thing — a "flattening" of the world, so to speak. Scientists are suddenly engaging in rapid dialogue all over the planet, leveling the playing field as never before.

The speed at which we move forward makes it virtually impossible to keep track of all developments. Does this mean the world is moving too fast for us to adjust? For entrepreneurs and investors alike, it is more important than ever to understand the new rules of science-driven entrepreneurship.

In this hyperconnected world, collaboration is critical. Indeed, knowledge and expertise are no longer confined to a select few. Anyone, from any part of the world, can contribute to the global conversation, challenging established ideas and pushing the boundaries of what's possible. This democratization of innovation is not just beneficial, it's essential. In a world that's changing at surprising speed, we need all the creativity and talent we can muster.

But even as we celebrate the opportunities that this new era brings, we must also acknowledge its challenges. The speed of change can be overwhelming, and the sheer volume of information can make it hard to separate the signal from the noise. Navigating this landscape requires a new set of skills. Critical thinking, adaptability, and a willingness to take calculated risks are more important than ever.

Science-driven innovations are unique in their genesis and manifestation. Unlike incremental improvements or market-driven advancements, these innovations are often a product of fundamental scientific research. They emerge from laboratories and research institutions, often after rigorous experimentation, testing, and validation.

The rules governing science-driven innovations differ greatly from those of traditional business or market-driven innovations. They are shaped by a complex interplay of factors such as scientific principles, regulatory guidelines, ethical considerations, and societal impact. They require a deep understanding of the underlying science, an ability to navigate the intricate landscape of intellectual property rights, and a keen foresight to anticipate the implications of these technologies on society and the environment.

Furthermore, science-driven innovations often have a high degree of uncertainty and risk, given their pioneering nature. They demand a high tolerance for failure, as they push the boundaries of what is known and possible. Yet, they also offer immense potential for transformative change, carrying the promise of breakthrough solutions to some of the world's most pressing challenges.

Deep tech, as I understand and interpret it, encompasses a broad array of technologies that are fundamentally rooted in scientific advancements and innovation. It is a term that encapsulates dozens of disciplines, including but not limited to artificial intelligence (AI), energy, biotechnology, synthetic biology, quantum computing, and more.

Deeptech ventures are not just science-driven companies; they operate at the cutting edge. The distinction here is crucial. The game here is about capitalizing on groundbreaking scientific discoveries and advancements to create new products, services, or technologies that can significantly impact society and industries.

For instance, in AI, researchers are developing advanced algorithms and models based on complex mathematical and statistical principles. In energy, scientists and engineers are leveraging physics to develop clean nuclear fusion. Biotech and synthetic biology companies are using principles from biology, genetics, and chemistry to develop innovative therapeutics, addressing health challenges that were once considered impossible to overcome.

Let's summarize here some of the defining characteristics that science-driven companies have:

- They operate with **high levels of technical risk**. Their work is often rooted in the latest science, which involves a lot of unknowns.
- They tend to be in fields with **high regulatory oversight**. Since many of these companies are in sectors like biotechnology, artificial intelligence, and aerospace, they often have to navigate a web of government regulations and compliance requirements.
- Their innovations often **outpace regulatory frameworks**. Because deep-tech companies operate at the forefront of

scientific and technological progress, they frequently confront legal and regulatory systems that are not equipped to manage the novel issues they raise. This can pose unique challenges in terms of compliance, risk management, and policy engagement.

- They usually possess **patents** or other types of intellectual property rights. Often, they've spent a considerable amount of time on lab or field research before trying to turn their technology into a commercial product.
- Investing in deep-tech companies often demands **more funding and a longer commitment.** They are capital-intensive because these companies need extensive research and development.
- The team's skills and expertise are paramount. These companies typically emerge from **highly skilled technical teams** whose members often have advanced degrees and extensive industry or research experience.
- In addition, their leadership teams frequently include **specialized roles** like chief technology officers (CTOs), chief science officers (CSOs), and chief medical officers (CMOs), in addition to chief executive officers (CEOs). This reflects the central role that science and technology play in these businesses.
- Their boards require not just strategic or financial acumen, but also **significant hands-on attitude** and benefit from the presence of **independent directors**. These individuals, who are not linked to the company's day-to-day operations or its financial stakeholders, bring an additional layer of technical knowledge to the table. These independent directors often come with top-notch expertise in the field and provide an impartial perspective on the board's decisions.
- They engage with a **broad range of stakeholders**. From collaborating with academic researchers to negotiating with policymakers, to educating the public about their technologies, deep-tech companies need to communicate effectively with a diverse array of stakeholders. This calls for skills in advocacy, education, and diplomacy in addition to technical expertise.
- They are inherently **disruptive**. Deep-tech companies aim to fundamentally change the status quo with their technologies, often targeting large markets or creating new ones.

- **Partnerships and collaborations** play a crucial role. Given the complexity of the technology and the cost associated with development and market entry, deep-tech companies often rely on strategic partnerships and collaborations to accelerate their growth.
- **Long development cycles** are the norm. The development of groundbreaking technology takes time, patience, and resilience. The path from concept to commercialization is often a long and winding one, with many potential hurdles along the way.
- The field is defined less by financial profit than by the pursuit of knowledge and the drive to make an impactful contribution. While it is undeniable that financial success is an important aspect, the true currency for entrepreneurs within this space is **intellectual influence** and prestige.
- To fully understand them is a task that demands not only a robust technical knowledge but also a **commitment to continuous learning** about the field. Consequently, a significant proportion of investors in this space possess a PhD or equivalent high-level training in the fields they invest in.
- They often **tackle "big" or "hard" problems**. They are frequently focused on addressing major societal or industrial challenges — from climate change to disease diagnosis and treatment, to space exploration.
- They face an **intense competitive landscape**. These companies must not only strive to solve complex problems, but to do so in a way that's more efficient, effective, and innovative than their rivals. The nature of deep-tech competition often hinges on who can solve the problem better and faster, and who can adapt quickest to changing circumstances or new discoveries.

Exploring the Cutting-Edge

As you've probably noticed, the principles governing biotech and science-driven companies set them apart from conventional entrepreneurship. It's time we explore some of these distinct characteristics, plus some new ones, in more depth.

The cutting-edge has no rules, no mentors.

In an emerging field or a cutting-edge sector, the usual constraints and guidelines that govern established disciplines are noticeably absent. It is akin to a wilderness with no defined paths, no set rules. Be advised: It is a mess, it is chaotic, you can never be certain about anything.

This is both a challenge and an opportunity. Venturing into the cutting- or leading-edge is like building a road as we travel across it. We are not merely traversing a path laid out by those who came before us; we are creating the path as we move forward. This requires us to be both the traveler and the roadbuilder, the explorer and the cartographer. It requires us to anticipate and adapt to the challenges that arise, using our creativity and initiative to overcome them. It is indeed an industry for creative people.

Traditional fields have their gurus, their masters who have traversed the path before us and can guide us along the way. However, in the leading-edge space, by definition, no one knows enough about it. Every field here is so novel that no one has yet become a master. This lack of mentors necessitates self-teaching and advice from external key opinion leaders (KOLs). Those who venture into the leading-edge must become comfortable with uncertainty and be willing to learn, unlearn, and relearn in real-time.

So, the leading edge, by its nature, is a perpetually expanding frontier. As we push the boundaries of our knowledge and capabilities, the frontier recedes, revealing new landscapes for us to explore. In contrast to traditional fields, which can become saturated or static over time, the leading edge is a dynamic and fluid space that always has room for fresh ideas and novel approaches. The cutting-edge never ends — it will perpetually amaze you. Let that sink in.

The cutting-edge is contrarian by nature.

I contend that frontier innovation funds are best led by contrarian investors, those who swim against the tide of prevailing market sentiments. Science-driven companies often require substantial upfront resources. They usually receive first funding through public channels or grants and are typically stationed within academic or research institutions. Instead of being driven by a tight-knit group of entrepreneur peers, these ventures could be steered by postdoctoral researchers collaborating with international teams.

To thrive in the deep-tech investment realm, investors need to revisit their original investment philosophy and have a more deliberate focus on the problems these investments seek to address. This implies embracing a problem-solving orientation: an inclination to assist in addressing venture-associated challenges rather than hastily moving on to the next investment opportunity.

So, we all roll up our sleeves and get deeply involved with the company, especially at the early stages. These challenges are extensive enough to facilitate ecosystem creation (involving co-investors, universities, public authorities, and corporate groups) dedicated to their resolution. Let me summarize: I invest in problems, not in solutions, precisely because the solution has not been found yet.

Here, investors should not idly wait for deal flow. Instead, they should proactively identify and select ventures. The result would be a curated portfolio of projects with well-defined problems and a strong appeal capable of attracting additional resources and collaborators. Here, more than in other sectors, necessity indeed begets innovation.

The cutting-edge moves at unprecedented speed.

The world is currently experiencing an acceleration like never before. This phenomenon of acceleration is not entirely new; throughout history, there have always been periods marked by rapid progress and evolution, whether in the realm of scientific discoveries, technological innovations, cultural shifts, or societal transformations. However, what sets our epoch apart is the sheer scale and ubiquity of this acceleration, as well as its compounding nature.

This acceleration is observable across virtually every domain of human endeavor. From artificial intelligence and synthetic biology to climate change mitigation and space exploration, we are pushing the boundaries of knowledge and capabilities at a pace that is unprecedented. Several factors contribute to this unique acceleration.

Technological advancements, particularly in computing power and data prediction (AI), have created a fertile ground for accelerated growth and progress. The increasing interconnectedness of the world means ideas and innovations spread faster, contributing to this sense of acceleration. The number of highly intelligent individuals dedicated to solving these problems is on the rise. Just a few decades ago, there were only a handful of true experts in specific fields. Consider the field of AI today, where we now have thousands of exceptional scientists and mathematicians excelling in every discipline.

Furthermore, the acceleration itself fuels more acceleration! As advancements are made, they provide the foundation upon which new innovations are built, creating a positive feedback loop that propels us forward at an ever-increasing speed. The innovations of today are built on the advancements of yesterday, and so the cycle continues, driving us into a future that we can barely comprehend.

The cutting-edge thrives on modularity and emergence.

This cycle of acceleration, the building of new innovations atop previous advancements, manifests strikingly within my domain of expertise: synthetic biology. One of the most telling examples of this progression is the development and use of BioBricks. BioBricks, simply put, are standardized sequences of DNA, sensors, logic circuits, etc., that can be used and combined as modular building blocks for creating new biological systems.

The concept of BioBricks is inspired by principles from engineering and computer science, particularly the idea of modularity. Each BioBrick is designed to perform a specific function and can be easily connected to other BioBricks to form larger, more complex systems. This allows for easy assembly, modification, and sharing of genetic "code" among researchers.

BioBricks are part of an open-source philosophy in synthetic biology, where the aim is to create a universal toolkit of standardized biological parts that can be shared and used by anyone, much like Lego blocks in the world of toys or open-source software in computing. This idea has greatly facilitated the development of synthetic biology, enabling researchers to build upon each other's work and accelerate innovation.

As more and more contributors join the field, we see an increasing number of these BioBricks, each a new tool authored by a different mind. But the resulting collection of BioBricks is more than just an arithmetic sum of individual parts. Every new tool not only expands the pool of resources available to us but also enriches the entire field. The combined potential of these BioBricks significantly outstrips their individual capabilities, leading to a phenomenon where the whole is much more than the sum of its parts.

The phenomenon of modularity is not limited to synthetic biology; it can be seen in the world of artificial intelligence (AI) as well. From the intricate operations of algorithms to the novel discoveries in mathematics, each breakthrough contributes to the foundation upon which the next innovation is built. The evolution of AI showcases this beautifully: from the simplicity of recurrent neural networks (RNNs) we moved on to the sophistication of long short-term memory networks (LSTMs), and then to the sheer power and versatility of transformers. Each development, though valuable on its own, gains an added dimension of utility when integrated with its predecessors. Together, they form a holistic system that is exponentially more efficient and potent than the sum of its individual parts.

Consider this as a form of "intellectual modularity" wherein each algorithm, each mathematical model, is like a piece of a larger puzzle. These modular units, just like BioBricks in synthetic biology, can be combined, interchanged, and optimized to create complex systems capable of groundbreaking tasks. It's an accelerating cycle of innovation, a layered cake of progress, where each layer, while powerful on its own, contributes to a power much greater and much more intricate than it could ever achieve solo. As we continue to evolve in our understanding and creation of AI, this cycle of modularity and integration persistently pushes the boundaries of what's possible, ultimately shaping the future of AI.

All this brings us to what we call "emergence." Emergence is when complex systems and patterns form out of relatively simple interactions, creating new properties and capabilities that weren't apparent in the individual components.

Consider ants, for instance. An isolated ant or even a small group of ants might seem to wander randomly, lacking any noticeable purpose or coordination. However, once their numbers increase, a striking transformation occurs. The ants begin to display coordinated behavior, such as bridge building or nest maintenance, that wasn't evident in smaller numbers. The fascinating part of this process is that this coordinated behavior doesn't require a central controlling authority. Instead, it naturally "emerges" from the interactions among the ants themselves.

Emergence means that simple rules are able to generate very complex behaviors. And this concept of emergence isn't limited to a particular field. In fact, it can be generalized to encompass the entire landscape of cutting-edge innovation. Modular tools that appear little by little — new technological advances, new science discoveries — cease to be incremental and start compounding, becoming transformative. In the leading edge, progress is marked by a steady stream of advancements, each new development building upon those that came before.

In this way, the leading-edge space becomes a dynamic and ever-evolving ecosystem, characterized by a continuous feedback loop of discovery, innovation, and growth. Each advancement fuels the next, and the resulting acceleration drives us further into uncharted territory. And while the pace can sometimes be overwhelming, there's also an undeniable excitement in being part of something that is continually evolving and growing.

The cutting-edge is driven by iconoclasts and "scientists of interest."

One of the biggest strengths of the intersection of science and entrepreneurship today is the community forming around it. The energy and talent entering this era is special. The people who are coming into the game — the creativity, the intelligence — is unparalleled right now. Engaging with these innovative individuals, being in constant dialogue with them, is one of the most rewarding aspects of working in the leading-edge. It is an exchange of ideas and perspectives that is as stimulating as it is enlightening.

These dialogues serve as a constant source of inspiration and learning, pushing us to think outside the box and challenge our assumptions. They foster a culture of continuous improvement and mutual growth, driving us to strive for excellence in our pursuits.

In our team, we've affectionately coined some of these trailblazers — the ones that we follow more closely due to their potential — as scientists of interest, or SOIs. This term, now fondly embedded in our own fund culture, signifies individuals who embody a spirit of relentless curiosity, a passion for exploration, and an unwavering dedication to advancing the frontiers of knowledge. They are the ones who continually question, innovate, and inspire, fostering an atmosphere of relentless learning and growth. By remaining in perpetual dialogue with these SOIs — what a privilege — we ensure that we remain on the cutting-edge of discovery, constantly spurred by their unique insights and fresh perspectives.

The cutting-edge is relentlessly changing.

To encapsulate the essence of the contemporary *zeitgeist*, I include in this chapter a beloved anecdote involving none other than the legendary physicist Albert Einstein. The year was 1942, and Einstein was teaching at Oxford University. As the academic year neared its end, it was time to set the final examination. With his characteristic calm, Einstein began dictating the questions. Suddenly, his aide approached him, a look of utter panic on his face. "Mr. Einstein, these are the same questions you asked last year!" he exclaimed. "The students will have the answers prepared. They will cheat!" Einstein looked at his aide, unflustered. "Oh, but don't worry," he responded, his voice steady and sure, "the answers have changed."

This anecdote is much more than a whimsical tale about a renowned scientist. It encapsulates the dynamism and fluidity of the leading-edge. Einstein understood that in fields of intense science and rapid development, the answers are rarely static. As we continue to explore, experiment, and push boundaries, we continually redefine our understanding of the world. What was true yesterday might not be true today, and what is true today might not be true tomorrow. Indeed, we may even say that the answers are changing every year, every month, every day.

This is the realm of the leading-edge, a realm in which we must perpetually adapt, learn, and rethink. Yet, it is in this realm that we find the most exciting opportunities for discovery, for innovation, and for progress. As we journey into the uncharted territories of the leading-edge, we must remember to embrace this dynamism, to question our assumptions, and to always be ready to learn and adapt. For, in the words of Einstein, the answers are always changing. We must be bold enough to change with them.

The cutting-edge aims for big impact.

The impact of deep tech and science-driven companies on our society is unprecedented. These organizations stand at the forefront of technological advancement, wielding the latest breakthroughs in science and technology to confront the myriad challenges humanity faces today. They are relentlessly pushing the boundaries of knowledge and capacity, not only to advance technology but also to improve the human condition, protect our planet, and ensure a sustainable future.

So, in the 21st century, science and its ultimate output, truth, are emerging as major forces shaping our world. The pursuit of truth through rigorous scientific inquiry has the power to unveil the fundamental laws governing our universe and illuminate the path toward progress. Science provides a solid foundation for evidence-based decision-making and policy formulation.

In an era of fake news and misinformation, the objective pursuit of truth becomes paramount. It allows us to distinguish fact from fiction, enabling us to make informed choices that affect our lives and the future of our planet. Scientific discoveries serve as guideposts, directing us toward effective solutions and sustainable practices.

The scope of problems these science-driven companies are striving to solve is vast and varied. Here are just a few examples:

1. **Understanding Consciousness and Intelligence:** How can a physical entity like the brain give rise to subjective experiences and cognition? Deep-tech companies in the field of artificial intelligence, like OpenAI and DeepMind, are pioneering research into this enigma, providing us with fresh insights into the workings of intelligence.
2. **Addressing Aging and Age-Related Diseases:** Aging and the diseases that come with it remain a significant challenge. However, biotech and synthetic biology companies are making remarkable strides in this arena, exploring the roles of telomeres and genetic mutations, and developing therapies that could potentially slow, stop, or even reverse the aging process.
3. **Targeting Cancer and Genetic Diseases:** Despite significant advancements, cancer and genetic diseases continue to pose substantial medical challenges. But the advent of gene-editing tools like CRISPR, and the evolution of personalized medicine are ushering in a new era of targeted, potentially curative treatments.
4. **Understanding Reality and Quantum Physics:** Quantum physics stands at the frontier of our understanding of reality, yet there is much we still don't know. Companies dedicated to quantum computing and research are working tirelessly to unlock the secrets of the quantum world, potentially revolutionizing our understanding of the universe.

5. **Fighting Climate Change and Environmental Degradation:** Deep-tech companies are also actively working toward solutions to combat climate change and environmental degradation. From developing clean and efficient energy solutions to innovating in the field of waste management and recycling, these companies are instrumental in our fight to preserve the planet.
6. **Combating Infectious Diseases:** The COVID-19 pandemic emphasized the urgent need for quick response to emerging infectious diseases. Biotech companies, utilizing advanced platforms like mRNA technology, are working on more rapid vaccine development and scalable production techniques, potentially revolutionizing our approach to future pandemics.
7. **Mitigating Antibiotic Resistance:** Antibiotic resistance poses a significant threat to global health. Deep-tech companies are developing innovative solutions, such as new classes of antibiotics, chimeric endolysins, and bacteriophage therapy, to combat this growing problem.
8. **Promoting Food Security and Sustainable Agriculture:** With the global population predicted to keep on growing, the demand for food will rise significantly. Companies specializing in agritech and synthetic biology are addressing this issue, developing sustainable farming practices and lab-grown food alternatives.
9. **Advancing Energy Efficiency and Renewable Energy Sources:** The quest for clean, renewable energy sources is crucial in our fight against climate change. From advanced solar technologies to nuclear fusion and hydrogen fuel cells, deep-tech companies are revolutionizing the way we generate and consume energy.
10. **Guiding AI Ethics and Security:** As artificial intelligence becomes more integrated into our daily lives, ensuring its ethical use and security is paramount. Companies in the AI space are developing guidelines for ethical AI use, improving transparency, and safeguarding AI systems against misuse.

These are just a handful of the problems deep-tech companies are addressing. They are leveraging cutting-edge science and technology to not only propel us into the future but also ensure that this future is a brighter, safer, and healthier one.

Final Words About the Future

"Computational" is the key word here.

It is 2023 as I'm writing this book, and the recent news about the progress in both AI and synthetic biology has everyone in wonder. At the heart of this transformative moment is a profound realization: Life and physics are a computational process.

The essence of biology, for example, lies in information storage, retrieval, and processing mechanisms, akin to what we see in computation. Our DNA, RNA, and proteins — the fundamental components of data processing in life — are essentially biological codes and the machinery to read and execute them. The advent of computational biology has enabled us to understand and manipulate these codes in unprecedented ways, paralleling our advances in manipulating and understanding human language through AI. Soon, the term "biology" may not be sufficient without its preceding qualifier — "computational." This phenomenon is reshaping the scientific landscape as we speak.

In the world of AI, large language models like ChatGPT, Bard, and Claude have demonstrated remarkable proficiency in understanding and generating human language. These models can learn the statistical patterns of language (as long as there is a structure to learn) and can then generate new text that aligns with these patterns, essentially "speaking" the language in a synthetic manner.

Now, a parallel revolution is taking place in biology. As I mentioned, the computational structure of life allows us to treat biological processes like a language, the language of life, so to speak. AI models can be trained to understand these biological "languages," leading to breakthroughs like DeepMind's AlphaFold, which can predict protein structures with remarkable accuracy. AlphaFold is effectively a large "language model" for proteins, and this is just the tip of the iceberg.

Please allow me to take a small detour to reflect on why large language models (LLMs) like GPT-4 fascinate and surprise us so profoundly. The key, as I see it, lies in their uncanny resemblance to our own mental processes. I can vouch that our brains, while in the act of constructing language, are constantly engaged in predicting the next word, much like LLMs. As I write these words, my brain tirelessly navigates the linguistic landscape, focusing asymmetric "attention" to words already written and words yet to be chosen.

Yet, the brain, with its staggering complexity, often confounds us, leading us to believe it to be an impossible organ to replicate. It is no longer just the perspective of an investor that I bring to this discussion, but also my background in neuroscience. But here is where I propose an unconventional perspective.

I contend that the brain's complexity is not so much a prerequisite for its functionality, but more a byproduct of the irreversible nature of evolution. Consider this: Evolution does not operate in reverse. It does not "undo" or "rewind"; instead, it adds layers upon layers of control, constantly adding on to what already exists without removing anything. Therefore, the brain, as we see it today, is a cumulative outcome of such iterative layering, comprising numerous forward and feedback mechanisms, ceaselessly interacting with each other.

But, when you peel back these intricate layers, what lies at the heart of our brain's operations is pure math. Every neuron in our brains functions as a mathematical operator of sorts, listening to the "pings" or signals from its fellow neurons. When the cumulative input reaches a certain threshold, the neuron "fires" or sends out its own ping, very much like how artificial neurons in a deep neural network operate.

So, in essence, beneath the ostensible chaos and complexity, our brains are mathematical marvels. They continuously compute and calibrate, embodying the elegance and precision of mathematics in their workings. And it is this underlying principle of mathematical computation that large language models successfully emulate, thereby making them a powerful tool in our quest to understand and leverage the mysteries of the brain.

Let's get back on track and dive into our main topic again. I think the word "computational" will no longer be confined to the realm of computer science. It is becoming central to many fields, especially those at the frontier of science and technology.

As biology becomes more computational, and as our AI models become better at understanding and generating biological "languages," we are poised to witness extraordinary advancements in synthetic biology, AI, and other related fields. It's a testament to the computational nature of many aspects of our reality, including the very fabric of life. This revolution is just beginning, and its influence will extend far and wide, from synthetic biology to AI, and beyond. It will project science-driven companies into the future at an unprecedented speed, a fantastic field to invest in.

Figure 2. AI + Synthetic Biology: Two Cutting-Edge Fields Collide

This figure illustrates the process of mapping the landscape of artificial intelligence and synthetic biology, focusing on the key questions and promising developments in the field. As distinct as these two areas may seem, they are increasingly intersecting in ways that offer unprecedented opportunities for innovation and growth. This confluence is creating a seismic shift that is fundamentally changing life as we know it, stimulating a flurry of startup activity.

- **From Genes to Morphology:** The interface between AI and synthetic biology brings about a unique approach to understanding the complex process of morphogenesis — how the genotype gives rise to phenotype. AI's capacity for pattern recognition and prediction can decode the complicated genetic and cellular interactions that culminate in the formation of an organism's form and structure.

- **AI-Guided Evolutionary Design:** AI's ability to simulate and optimize evolutionary processes has opened the door to the guided design of biological systems. By applying machine learning algorithms, we can drive the evolution of microbes to develop novel, optimized biological solutions. The potential applications are far-reaching, from environmental to industrial and medical.
- **Data Analysis and Pattern Recognition:** The genomic and proteomic data being generated in biological research is vast and complex. AI, with its robust capabilities in data analysis and pattern recognition, can aid in discerning the subtle patterns hidden within this biological data deluge, making significant contributions to our understanding of biological systems.
- **Computational Design of Biological Systems:** AI is revolutionizing the design of biological systems. By applying AI algorithms, researchers can now optimize the design of genetic circuits and proteins, expediting the creation of synthetic life forms and tailored biological products.
- **Drug Discovery:** AI and synthetic biology can accelerate the traditionally slow, expensive process of drug discovery. AI algorithms can sift through vast datasets to identify promising drug candidates, while synthetic biology techniques can rapidly prototype these drugs.
- **Logic Gates and Optimal Design of Circuits:** By analogy to electronic circuits, synthetic biology seeks to build biological circuits to control cellular behavior. AI is used to design these circuits optimally, implementing biological equivalents of logic gates, and devising regulatory mechanisms that precisely control gene expression.
- **Genome Editing:** The synergy of AI and synthetic biology has significant implications for genome editing technologies, such as CRISPR. AI can enhance the efficiency, precision, and safety of genome editing, paving the way for new therapeutic avenues and opportunities in genetic engineering.
- **Brain-Cortex Signal Translation:** The integration of AI with synthetic biology is also paving the way for advances in neurobiology, particularly in translating brain-cortex signals. This could potentially lead to revolutionary developments in neuroprosthetics and brain-computer interfaces.
- **AI-driven Manufacturing:** AI's ability to optimize processes and predict outcomes, combined with synthetic biology's power to engineer biological systems, could reinvent manufacturing. The potential for creating sustainable, biology-driven manufacturing processes is enormous.
- **Brain/Computer Interfaces:** The interface between AI and the human brain is becoming increasingly tangible. By decoding neural signals using AI, we are moving closer to creating direct communication pathways between the human brain and computers, opening up incredible possibilities in computing, communication, and even thought control.

Rule #2

You Are Always Six Months Late

"I'm late, I'm late! For a very important date! No time to say hello, goodbye! I'm late, I'm late, I'm late!"

The White Rabbit in Lewis Carroll's Alice in Wonderland

The leading edge is much like a relentless river, its forceful current rushing forward. There's no room for hesitation; the moment you hesitate or stall, you're swept away by the strong tide of progress. Competition is always close behind, urging you to not just keep up, but outpace others.

A bold reminder of the importance of speed hangs in my office, a poster with the stark words, "You are six months late." This poster serves as a metaphorical warning and its message underlines the crucial need to stay perpetually ahead of the curve, to not just keep up with innovation, but to be the one setting the pace.

This is true for all leading-edge fields. To illustrate, let's consider the field of synthetic biology, where developing new drugs is a race against time itself. Each day, numerous potential treatments are being explored, each hoping to be the one that outshines all others. It's not just an academic pursuit, but a race to save lives, a race against time and disease.

The price of delay in leading-edge fields reaches far beyond just financial losses. It ripples through our society and stalls scientific progress. Being six months late in this field isn't just about losing potential profit or market share; it means delaying life-saving solutions and breakthroughs that could revolutionize industries, save lives, or even reshape our understanding of the world.

This is not just a singular tale but a recurring story across the competitive landscape of the biotech industry. To grasp the severity of the issue, imagine a Kaplan-Meier curve, a popular tool in medical and health research for estimating and illustrating the survival probabilities of a population in the presence of censored observations. The steps drop down at each event time and the size of the drop corresponds to the number of events at that time point. The curve starts at a survival of 1 (or 100%) and declines over time towards zero, with steeper slopes indicating quicker drops in survival probability.

In this scenario, the curve represents the failure rate of initiatives that started too late. The drop-off is sharp and brutal. Initiatives that don't start swiftly from the get-go are likely to fail, unable to recover from their initial tardiness.

This highlights the value of being proactive and preemptive rather than reactive. Lost time cannot be recovered, and missed opportunities rarely come around again. In the world of leading-edge investment, the early bird not only gets the worm but also shapes the future. In this context, "six months late" could very well be a lifetime.

Fostering a Culture of Urgency

Fostering a culture of urgency in any organization, particularly those operating at the leading edge, is a delicate balance. It's about creating an environment where everyone recognizes the value of time and the importance of swift action without instigating a sense of panic or promoting reckless haste. This urgency is not about frenzied activity or indiscriminate speed, but rather an understanding of the criticality of time and a commitment to purposeful, deliberate action.

A successful culture of urgency begins with leadership. Leaders must set the tone, communicate the importance of time, and demonstrate urgency in their actions. This involves clearly communicating objectives, defining timelines, and holding themselves and their teams accountable for meeting these timelines. It's not enough to simply state that time is of the essence; leaders must embody this principle in their decision-making and daily activities.

However, urgency should not be mistaken for a relentless, breakneck pace that could lead to burnout or compromise the quality of work. Instead, it's about instilling a mindset of efficiency and effectiveness. It's about creating an environment where people understand that "busy" does not always equate to "productive," and that working smarter, not just harder, is key. In a culture of urgency, every team member understands the significance of their role and the impact of their work on the larger goals of the organization. This understanding often results in higher levels of engagement and commitment, as individuals recognize the value they bring and the difference they make. Moreover, fostering a culture of urgency necessitates cultivating an atmosphere of trust and transparency.

When people understand the "why" behind the urgency, they are more likely to buy into it and support it. This is where open communication comes into play, ensuring everyone understands the project's goals, the stakes involved. In essence, fostering a culture of urgency is about igniting a collective commitment to efficient action, instilling a sense of purpose, and nurturing an environment where everyone is motivated to act swiftly and effectively to achieve the shared goals. When done right, it can be a potent force in driving an organization's success and maintaining its position at the leading edge.

Regulatory Bodies Usually Lag Behind Us

Being perpetually six months late is the norm, a fact that we've learned to accept and manage. However, an interesting paradox exists in this fast-paced world: While we rush, pivot, and innovate to stay ahead of the curve, our regulatory counterparts often lag behind us, bound by stringent procedures and protocols. Regulatory bodies, designed to ensure the safety, efficacy, and ethics of new technologies, are often slower to adapt to rapid technological changes. They face the daunting task of reviewing and approving cutting-edge innovations while maintaining robust oversight. Their cautious pace is justified, given their mandate to protect public interest. Yet, this asymmetry of speeds between deep-tech firms and regulators presents unique opportunities.

For instance, regulatory bodies are more open to accelerated approvals for ground-breaking technologies, especially when these offer substantial improvements over existing solutions or fill unmet needs. This trend is particularly noticeable in areas like biotech, where expedited approvals can mean bringing life-saving drugs or therapies to

Figure 3. Speed and Mortality

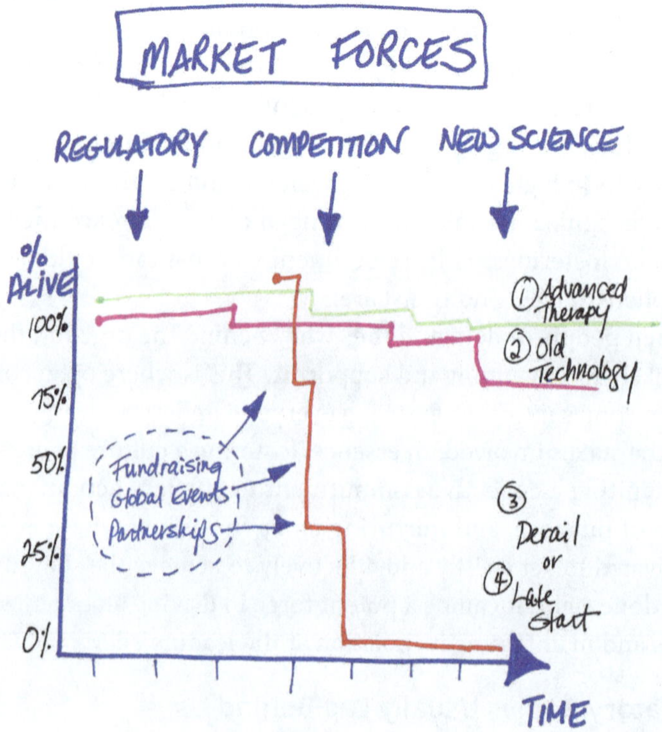

The relentless river of progress characterizes the cutting edge of innovation, where hesitation can mean being swept away by the strong tide. In Figure 3, we envision a graphical depiction of the urgency and the competitive nature of leading-edge fields, such as synthetic biology. Using the metaphor of a Kaplan-Meier survival curve, we depict the failure rate of initiatives that start too late. The "survival" in this context represents successful projects, while "time" on the x-axis symbolizes the speed of project initiation and implementation.

- In this figure, the y-axis represents the "survival rate" or the success rate of initiatives, and the x-axis represents "time" or speed of project initiation. The curve starts at the top left of the graph, indicating a higher success rate for projects that start immediately (time zero). As we start rightwards along the x-axis (indicating delays in project initiation), the curve drops sharply. This sharp drop illustrates the brutal reality: Initiatives that don't start swiftly from the get-go are likely to fail, unable to recover from their initial tardiness.
- To lend further depth to this graphical narrative, points of interest are annotated along the curve, each marking significant events or factors that have impacted the success rate. For instance, a point could be annotated to signify the emergence of a competitive product, a development that could seriously jeopardize the success of the slower initiatives. Another point could mark a significant regulatory change that either stymies or propels the pace of innovation in the industry. Yet another annotation could highlight a major breakthrough or finding in research, which could dramatically change the course for some initiatives.

- Additionally, other influential elements could be as important:
  - **Funding and Investment Impact:** The amount and timeliness of funding often play a decisive role in determining an initiative's success. Therefore, sufficient and timely funding, represented by specific markers, can propel the curve upwards, indicating improved survival prospects.
  - **Effect of Global Events:** Global events such as pandemics, economic crises, or geopolitical changes can cause major shifts in the survival rate.
  - **Role of Key Partnerships and Alliances:** Such alliances can significantly expedite initiatives and enhance their success rate, thereby potentially elevating the position of the curve.
- These annotations not only enhance our understanding of the factors that influence success but also underline how these events can dramatically alter the survival rate. They underscore the inherent volatility of these leading-edge fields, where progress is rapid and the landscape can change drastically in a short span of time.
- Overall, this figure serves to reiterate a fundamental truth of the leading-edge ecosystem: Time is of the essence. Delays can be devastating, and the ability to swiftly seize opportunities is crucial for survival. The pace of progress waits for no one; the early bird not only gets the worm but also shapes the future. The stark, graphical depiction emphasizes the value of being proactive and preemptive rather than reactive in the world of leading-edge investment and paints a vivid picture of the competitive landscape of these fields.

The Kaplan-Meier curve is a simple yet powerful statistical tool often used in fields like medical and social sciences to visualize the "survival" rates over time. In this context, "survival" can refer to the actual survival of patients in medical studies, the duration of time until a particular event occurs, or the persistence of a certain condition. The curve displays how the probability of "survival" changes over time, with time plotted on the X-axis and the probability of survival on the Y-axis. Its widespread use in science is due to its ability to present complex statistical data in a manner that is easy to understand and interpret, making it a vital tool for researchers and scientists across disciplines.

market faster. Harnessing this opportunity requires us to work closely with these bodies, demonstrating the urgency and potential of our solutions and promoting transparency and collaboration.

A faster approval doesn't only mean we can bring our product to market sooner. It also opens the door for quicker liquidity events. We can accelerate our timelines, not just in terms of product development, but also for potential exits, mergers, or public offerings. This speed, however, should never compromise ethical considerations or the quality of our products.

Furthermore, leveraging this pace disparity can lead to reduced development times. We can work with regulatory bodies early on, seeking their input and guidance to streamline our development processes, effectively reducing time-to-market. Engaging with regulators early can also help us anticipate potential roadblocks and plan accordingly.

Ultimately, this asymmetry of speeds is a peculiar aspect of the deep-tech world. Rather than viewing it as a hurdle, we can see it as an opportunity. By maintaining open lines of communication with regulators, being proactive, and embracing a spirit of cooperation, we can navigate this dynamic landscape effectively. As we do so, we must remember our fundamental goal: to bring impactful, safe, and ethical solutions to the world faster.

Be Aware: A Derailed Company Is Difficult to Get Back on Track

Derailments, meaning situations where the company is facing a problem that takes way too much time to solve, are not only costly but can be exceedingly difficult to rectify. Companies that encounter setbacks and find themselves off course often face an uphill battle to regain momentum and credibility. The critical need for speed, coupled with the intricate complexities of scientific innovation, makes these enterprises particularly vulnerable to derailment.

When a company slows down due to problems that require extended periods to resolve, it tends to lose its pace within the industry's rapidly advancing frontier. This loss of momentum can lead to a cascade of difficulties. Investors may hesitate to provide further funding, questioning the company's capability to overcome setbacks and deliver on its promises. Moreover, the company might struggle to advance its technology or product, further impeding progress.

Every company and every situation is indeed unique, but the common thread running through them is the need for optimal speed and a focused path. It's not about rushing mindlessly, but about constantly maintaining forward momentum and ensuring that all efforts are channeled in the right direction.

As we shall explore in later chapters, focusing on the "critical path" is vital to steer clear of losing time or of potential derailments. The critical path is a sequence of activities that must be completed on time for the project to create value. Any delay in these tasks directly impacts the project timeline. Identifying this path helps the team understand which tasks are crucial and where their efforts should be concentrated.

Moreover, fostering a culture of agility and openness to change, often termed a "pivot culture," is key to avoiding and managing setbacks. In this context, "pivoting" means altering the strategic course based on new insights, feedback, or changes in the market or technology landscape. This ability to adapt quickly allows companies to respond to challenges, seize emerging opportunities, and maintain their speed without compromising on the quality of their work.

Remember, a delayed company is a compromised one, and regaining lost ground is no small feat.

Rule #3

See Both the Forest and the Trees

"I am getting so far out one day I won't come back at all."
William S. Burroughs

In the dynamic world of investment, particularly within the realm of leading-edge innovations, an informed vision of the landscape is important. To fully grasp this notion, consider the metaphor of a forest. Traditional investors may view a company as a tree — studying its roots for scientific boldness, its trunk for robust operational structure, its branches for growth potential, and its leaves for signs of vitality. Indeed, these elements are crucial. However, to make investment decisions solely based on the characteristics of the "tree" is to overlook the broader and equally important "forest": the technology or scientific field in which the company operates.

Investing in the realm of disruptive innovation calls for an expansion of the usual scope of analysis, going beyond the individual company to include its positioning within the dynamic technological ecosystem. Is the tree planted on the sunny side of the mountain or does it languish in the shadows? Does it have access to a vital water source or is it perched atop an arid hill? Is the soil fertile enough?

The forest represents the current landscape of technologies/options. In biotech for example, the questions should include "Will this field/technology be in the future of medicine? Is this something solid and trendy enough for key opinion leaders (KOLs)? Are these types of companies raising good investment rounds in our ecosystem, again, not per their qualities themselves but precisely because the space is a hot field? How is the deal activity in this particular field? Do we see a lot of acquisitions or IPOs?

Seeing Beyond the Tree

To move beyond the singular perspective of the "tree," we must first establish a deep understanding of the current technological or scientific landscape and its projected future developments — the "forest." This task involves a careful examination of the current trends in the industry, as well as a cultivated instinct for detecting future shifts. This often includes drawing a "map" of the different competing technologies trying to solve a specific problem of our interest. The next chapter is devoted to the particularities of how to draw that map.

One way to navigate this landscape is to engage in dialogue with fellow venture capitalists investing in similar spaces. These discussions can provide crucial insights into potential growth areas, thereby building a comprehensive and informed view of the field. The collective wisdom and behavior of other investors, paired with one's own analysis, can illuminate the path toward promising investment opportunities.

KOLs also provide an invaluable resource. Renowned for their expertise and influence, KOLs can offer unique insights into trends, emerging technologies, and potential disruptions. Establishing relationships with KOLs within your investment field can provide an additional layer of understanding, enabling you to anticipate future developments in the market.

However, conversing with peers and experts is only a part of the equation. A deeper, more intimate understanding of the "forest" is possible through diligent and continuous study. Reading a breadth of scientific papers, industry news, and market analysis reports can enrich your understanding of the industry and its potential growth areas.

Technological tools can also provide substantial assistance in this quest. For instance, monitoring recent initial public offering (IPO) performances and deal activity can reveal market trends and the investment community's sentiments toward certain technologies or sectors. Predictive technologies and data analytics can also serve as a guiding compass, offering empirical evidence to support or challenge your instincts.

Through this amalgamation of dialogue, continuous learning, and technological assistance, an investor can begin to view not just the "tree," but also the broader "forest." It is this broadened perspective that allows an investor to see beyond the superficial allure of a promising "tree" and discern whether it is rooted in fertile ground within the forest of future technologies.

The Weather Matters Too: Understanding Market Trends

Just as a forester reads the signs of the changing seasons, predicting rainfall and temperature shifts to understand how the forest will respond, an investor must learn to decipher the subtle signs of shifting market trends. In the grand forest of the industry, the "weather" comes in the form of socio-economic factors, regulatory changes, technological advancements, and consumer behavior patterns. Much like the way weather can drastically affect a forest's health and growth, these market trends can profoundly influence the trajectory of companies and entire sectors.

Understanding these trends is like having a barometer to gauge the health and vitality of the market, predicting storms on the horizon or identifying the conditions ripe for growth. Just as every species in a forest thrives in certain weather conditions, every company has a set of market conditions in which it can truly flourish. A rainy season may be disastrous for certain trees, yet bring prosperity to others. Similarly, a certain market trend might be detrimental to one company but create a golden opportunity for another.

For instance, an upswing in environmental consciousness among consumers may act like a summer rain, enabling green-tech companies to thrive while leaving those less eco-friendly to weather a difficult season. Changes in regulations might be akin to a sudden frost, making the environment challenging for companies in specific sectors. On the other hand, advancements in technology might be likened to a long-awaited spring, creating an atmosphere of growth and opportunity for tech-driven companies.

Being attuned to these market trends enables an investor to anticipate changes and make strategic investment decisions. It's not just about seeing the health of the "trees" in the present moment, but also understanding the "weather" conditions that will shape the "forest" in

Figure 4. The Forest, the Tree, the Weather, and the Fire

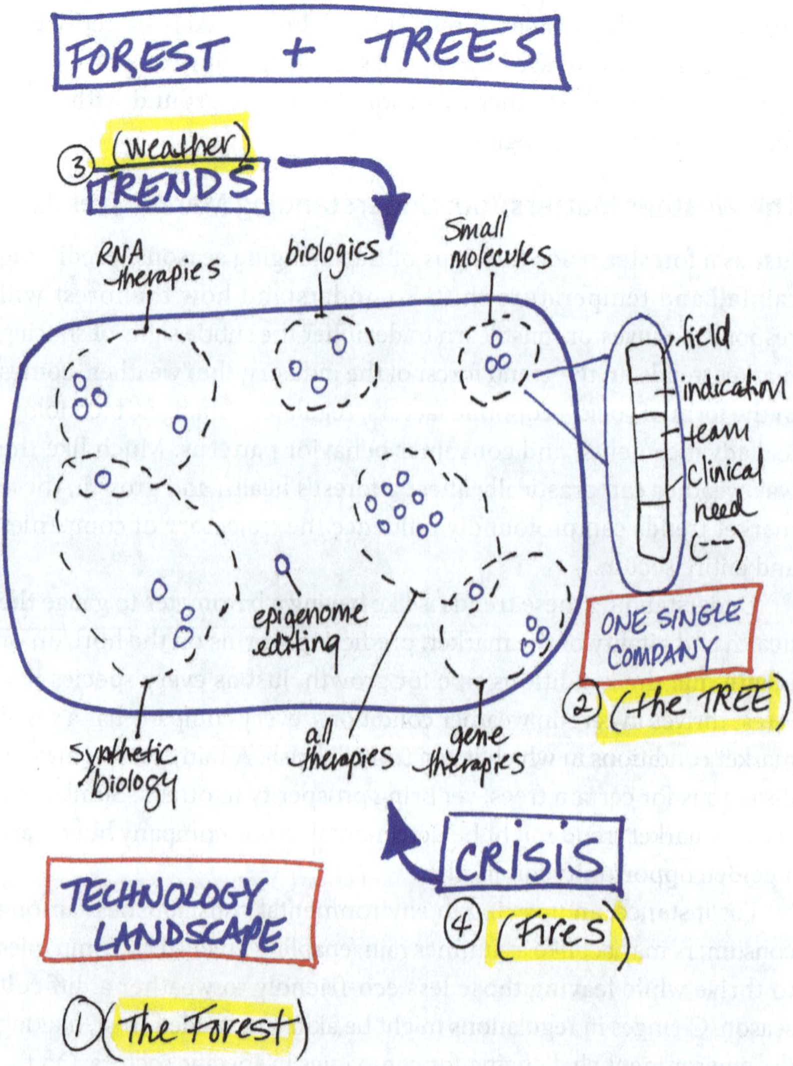

This figure represents a metaphorical exploration of the investment landscape, likening it to a dynamic forest ecosystem. This holistic view incorporates the individual "tree" (the company), the "forest" (the industry or technology landscape), the "weather" (market trends), and "fires" (industry crises), providing a comprehensive understanding of the investment environment. By visualizing these interrelated factors, the figure allows us to grasp the complexities of investing in disruptive innovation sectors.

Rule #3: See Both the Forest and the Trees

- For the sake of clarity, let's visualize this metaphor within the context of oncology. This forest stands for the landscape of oncological indications, where different technologies coexist like trees in a forest. These include, but are not limited to, RNA therapies, synthetic biology, epigenome editing, biologics, cell therapies, gene therapies, and small molecules.
- The "sunlight" or popularity that each technology receives is not evenly distributed across the forest. For instance, RNA therapies, being quite trendy now, may be seen as located in the sunlit part of the forest. In contrast, certain technologies such as small molecules, which might be considered less significant for the near future, could be perceived as being in a less sunny, more obscure part of the forest. Every investor will have their own perceptions about which parts of the forest are flourishing and which are not.
- In this forest, we can also single out a specific company, represented as a tree. Each tree or company has numerous characteristics that we examine when making investment decisions, including the field of operation, indication, team, and clinical need. These characteristics are discussed throughout this book.
- However, within this forest, the winds or trends blow in various directions. These include regulatory changes, government policies, and public opinion. It is important to determine which way the wind is blowing, which in our metaphor is represented as the weather. The forest might also be susceptible to crises, represented as fires. For example, a significant setback in an RNA therapy clinical trial could instigate a fire, affecting a portion of the forest. Such a fire might occur in either the sunlit or obscure parts of the forest, underscoring the need to consider all factors.
- Our final conclusion drawn from this metaphor is the importance of considering all factors at play when identifying the best projects for investment or development. We should not focus solely on the individual tree or company but also consider where in the forest the company is situated, the conditions of this location, how the weather or trends are impacting this specific part of the forest and the company, and to be vigilant about potential crises that could reshape the forest's geography.
- Understanding the forest metaphor gives an investor a robust perspective on investment landscape. Yet, this is just a part of the larger investment journey. In addition to these macro-level considerations, micro-level factors like the company's leadership, its financial health, its competitive positioning, and its ability to innovate and adapt, are equally vital to determine whether it has the potential to grow into a sturdy tree.
- Another important factor is time. The "seasons" within the forest may shift, with some technologies becoming more prominent while others lose their luster. A prudent investor needs to keep an eye on how these seasons are changing and how this could impact their investments. Risk management is another crucial aspect. Just like a forester who keeps an eye out for potential forest fires, an investor needs to be vigilant for signs of market instability or regulatory shifts that could cause their investments to stumble.
- In the end, investing in a company is not only about choosing the tallest, most robust tree. It is also about understanding the complex interplay of factors within the forest that could influence that tree's future growth. By maintaining a balanced view of both the forest and the tree, investors can make more informed decisions and enhance their chances of investment success.

the future. It allows for prudent investments in the "trees" best suited to weather the storms and bask in the sunshine of favorable conditions.

Forest Fires and Renewal: Navigating Industry Crises

The image of a forest fire often evokes thoughts of destruction and devastation. However, within nature's cycle, these fires can also play a vital role in forest renewal, clearing away the old and making room for new growth. Similarly, in the economic landscape, crises can reshape industries, sweeping away outmoded systems and sparking new opportunities.

When crisis strikes an industry, like a forest fire, it can feel sudden and destructive. The environment may appear hostile and forbidding, with companies struggling to survive. However, just as certain species have adapted to not only withstand forest fires but even thrive in their aftermath, so too can businesses and investors navigate these challenges to emerge stronger.

First, crises can expose weaknesses in companies. Companies with robust structures, sound business models, and effective leadership — the hardy trees with deep roots — can endure. The crisis effectively stress-tests companies, separating those built to withstand shocks from those less prepared.

Second, crises can stimulate innovation. When the old ways of doing things are swept away, companies are prompted to find new ways to adapt and survive. Out of necessity, they may develop new products, streamline processes, or discover new markets, much like the way a forest ecosystem may evolve and diversify after a fire.

Finally, just as a forest fire can clear the ground for new growth, a crisis can open up new investment opportunities. Companies that have weathered the storm may emerge as industry leaders, while startups may see a gap in the market left by businesses that couldn't adapt. As an investor, being aware of these changes allows you to invest in these emerging opportunities, planting the seeds for future growth.

However, navigating industry crises requires the right balance of patience, insight, and decisive action. Just as a forester needs to understand the forest's natural cycles, including the role of fire, an investor needs to comprehend the industry's dynamics and the transformative power of crises. Only then can one truly navigate these industry fires, seizing the opportunities they bring for renewal and growth.

Anticipating the Future and Harnessing Opportunities

The ability to see both the forest and the tree is not merely an advantage — it's a necessity. A careful, thorough analysis of a company's potential — the tree — is vital. However, an understanding of the broader technological landscape — the forest — is equally, if not more, critical. The weather and the fires matter as well.

Investors who can view the investment landscape from all these perspectives are better equipped to discern real opportunities from mere distractions. They can navigate the volatile world of disruptive innovation with greater confidence, anticipating future shifts and making timely, informed decisions.

Therefore, adopt a future-forward, holistic approach to your investment strategy. Cultivate the ability to anticipate, understand the broader landscape, and look beyond the surface. Whether you are navigating the turbulent world of biotech or any leading-edge field, remember: It's about discerning the potential of today's innovation within the context of tomorrow's possibilities. And for that, mapping the landscape is of great importance.

Rule #4

Map the Landscape and Connect the Dots

"In the depth of winter, I finally learned that within me there lay an invincible summer."
Albert Camus

Visual thinking forms the backbone of my investment strategy. In the complex and shifting terrain of leading-edge investment, it provides a means to navigate, to connect the dots, and to comprehend the wider context in which we operate. Whether you're an investor considering a new venture or an entrepreneur looking to steer your startup in a potentially profitable direction, understanding the landscape of your field is paramount.

Imagine you're considering founding a synthetic biology company that leverages a particular technology or scientific approach. To succeed, you must first comprehend the dozens of alternative technologies that could address the same problem. It's essential to map out these alternatives, understanding their strengths and weaknesses, and identify the open, unanswered questions within the field. These unresolved queries, once answered, will propel the industry forward.

Consider the analogy of technologies positioned on a chessboard. Each piece, or technology, has its role, capabilities, and limitations. Your technology is one such player, and your understanding of the role it can play in this grand strategy is crucial. But, you cannot play the game if you don't know how the other pieces (technologies) move. The same principle applies if you are not analyzing a technology but rather an indication, such as pancreatic cancer or pulmonary fibrosis.

Once again, understanding the chessboard becomes vital. You need to know who else is striving to solve the same problem and with what technologies.

Connecting the dots is not a one-time event, but an ongoing process. The landscape isn't a static entity; it's in constant flux, evolving and shifting as new technologies emerge, scientific breakthroughs occur, and market trends change. Thus, your understanding of it must also be dynamic.

Remember, in the world of leading-edge investment, you are not merely a bystander observing the ebb and flow of the landscape. You're an active participant, shaping and being shaped by the landscape as you traverse it. You, as an investor or entrepreneur, are both the chess player and a piece on the board, influencing and responding to the ever-evolving game of industry dynamics.

On the Methodology

Every investor has their own style and methodologies. I don't claim mine is better than anyone else's. Mine has a very distinctive visual-driven approach. Visual thinking enables me to distill complex data into simple, digestible formats, helping me see patterns, relationships, and trends that might otherwise go unnoticed. It helps me turn abstract concepts and heaps of data into tangible, understandable visuals that can inform strategic decisions and foster a more effective communication with the team of entrepreneurs who are leading the company.

Diving into the methodology of landscape analysis, it's important to understand the breadth and depth of tools available to us. This toolbox, if you will, comprises several techniques, each with its distinct purpose and utility. This process is not merely academic — it is an active, hands-on practice of gathering and analyzing data from a variety of sources.

- **Data Collection:** The foundation of any analysis is the data. In landscape analysis, this can come from multiple sources, including academic articles, industry reports, company websites, patent databases, and news articles. It's essential to leverage both quantitative data (e.g., market sizes, growth rates, patent counts) and qualitative data (e.g., industry trends, technology descriptions, expert opinions).

Figure 5. Example: Mapping the Landscape of Oncology

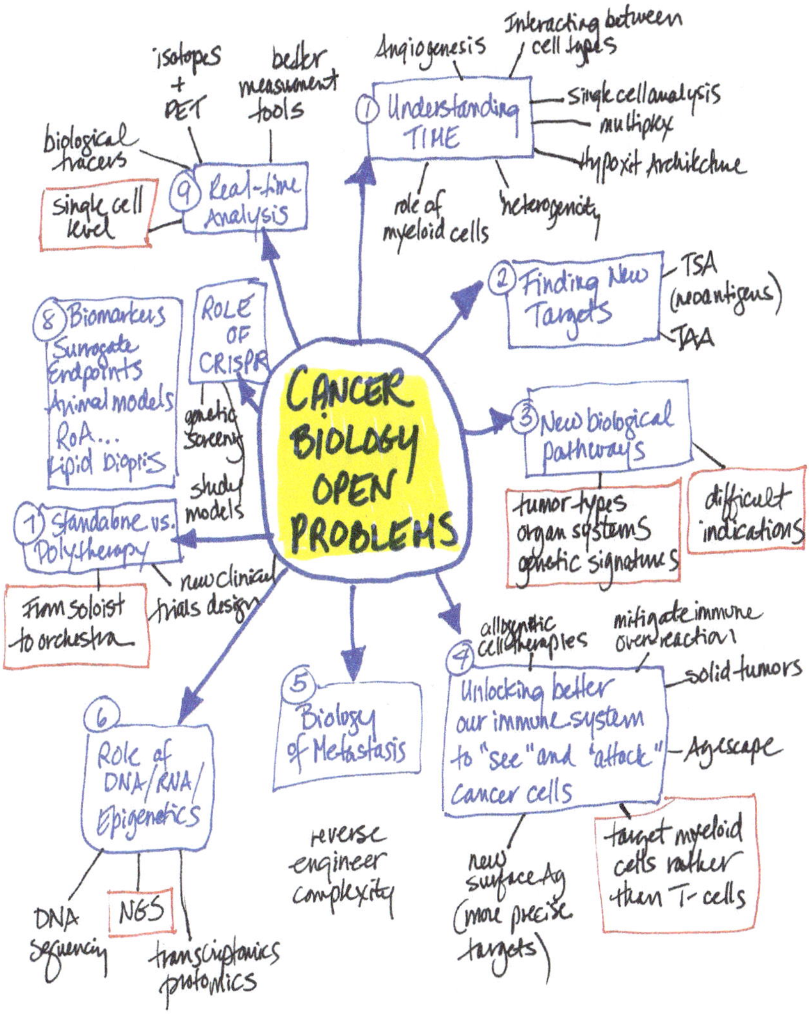

Figure 5 illustrates a map on the landscape of oncology, focusing on the key unanswered questions in the field. The figure is divided into several sections, each corresponding to a significant open question in oncology.

This graphic shows the main issues in cancer research, including studying how cancer spreads, the impact of epigenetics on cancer growth, and new ways to use our immune system to find cancer cells. Each issue and the methods used to address them are shown as nodes and sub-nodes in the figure. It's a visual guide to what's happening in cancer research now and where it might go in the future. Understanding these issues and approaches can help investors and business founders find opportunities for investment and innovation.

- **Competitor Analysis:** This involves identifying and assessing your competitors, their products, strategies, strengths, and weaknesses. A comprehensive competitor analysis will give you insights into market trends, potential threats, and opportunities for differentiation.
- **Patent Mapping:** Patents are a treasure trove of information, and their analysis can give you insights into technology trends, innovation hotspots, key players, and potential collaborators or competitors. Patent mapping involves identifying relevant patents, analyzing their content (e.g., technology, application), and visualizing the relationships and trends.
- **Technology Assessment:** This is an evaluation of the technological capabilities, potential, and implications of the technologies in your landscape. It involves understanding the technical details, maturity level, limitations, associated risks, and potential applications and impacts of the technologies.
- **Market Research:** This includes knowing the size, growth, trends, parts, and customer needs and actions of your target market. For example, in analyzing deal activity in a specific technology, you'd look at the number of deals, the total volume, and the size of the deals. You can learn this through surveys, talks, focus groups, and review of other data.

The sources of information for landscape analysis are diverse. Read, read, read! Scientific literature can provide insights into the latest research and developments. Patent databases, such as the USPTO, EPO, and WIPO, can reveal trends in innovation, key players, and technology hotspots. Market reports, often available from market research firms, can offer data and insights into market sizes, growth rates, and trends. Industry conferences, webinars, and seminars are excellent sources for the latest industry news and trends. And finally, talking to key opinion leaders and relevant scientists around the world will help you keep the pace with this rapidly evolving ecosystem.

Landscape analysis is a multi-faceted and iterative process. It involves collecting and analyzing data from a variety of sources, employing multiple tools and techniques, and continually updating and refining your understanding as new data and insights emerge.

Figure 6. Example: Mapping the Landscape of Pancreatic Cancer

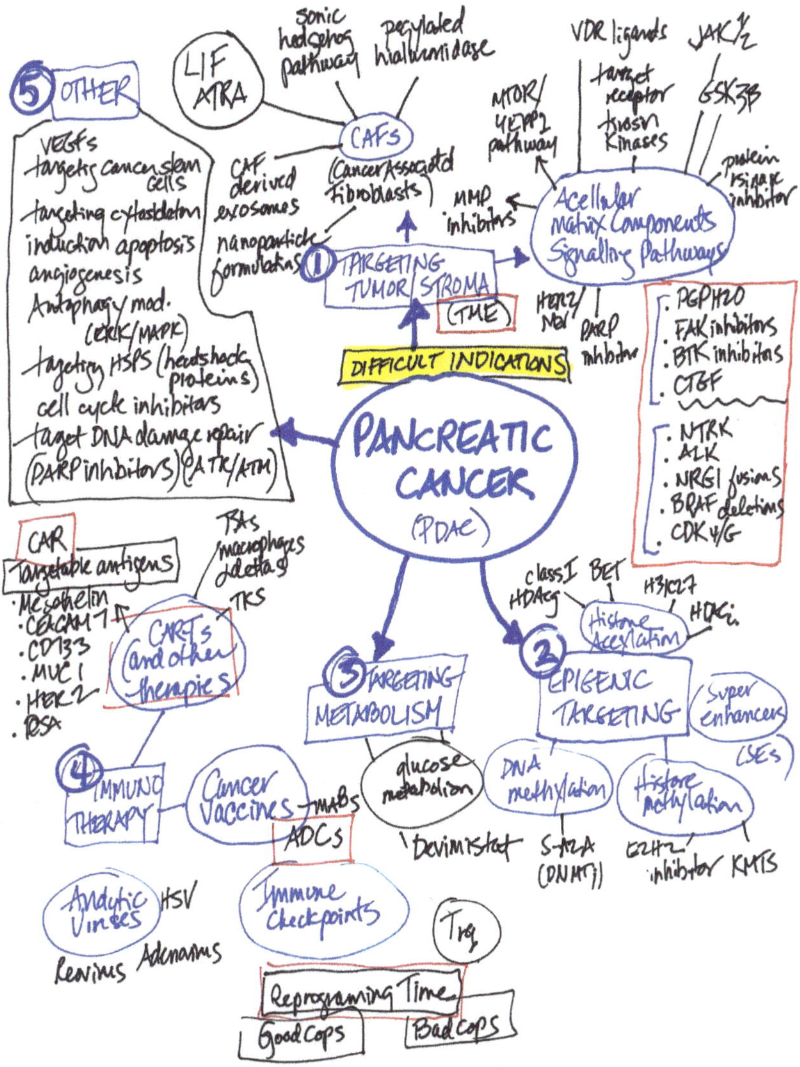

This figure reflects current treatments for pancreatic cancer at the time of this writing.

The biotech field changes quickly, with new methods and tech emerging all the time. Consequently, the figure might already be out of date. It shows different ways to treat pancreatic cancer, such as chemotherapy, targeted therapy, immunotherapy, cell therapy, and gene therapy. Keeping the figure updated is key to understanding the topic.

Rule #5

If Everybody Likes the Idea, It Is Too Late

"Whenever you find yourself on the side of the majority, it is time to pause and reflect."

Mark Twain

Investing is an art, a science, and perhaps most importantly, a game of anticipation. The allure of "popular" investments is undeniable. They are tried, tested, and often deliver predictable results. But, are they always the best choice for an investor who is looking to maximize returns and impact? Not necessarily.

Let's start by acknowledging that the investment world is prone to trends. When a particular sector or type of technology is "hot," there can be a rush of investors looking to get in on the action, leading to inflated valuations and a potential overlook of fundamental flaws. In science-driven investing, staying independent, doing your due diligence, and not getting swayed by the herd is essential.

When everyone is rushing toward a particular field or technology, chances are its peak potential has been recognized, and it may no longer offer the best value or the most significant impact. When I'm thinking about investing in a company, I test its potential. I do this by explaining the investment to my team and to people outside our fund. This helps me see if the investment story holds up and how people react to it.

Here's my rule: If everyone says it's a great idea, I don't invest. It is already too late. This might sound strange, but it works for me. If everybody understands it, it is not really leading edge and I am already too late.

Let's go a bit deeper. Predicting the past is easy; it's a mere exercise in pattern recognition. But the future does not necessarily conform to the patterns of the past. You cannot predict the future by merely extrapolating the trends of today. The true opportunity lies in discerning the trends of tomorrow, in seeing what others cannot see, in daring to venture where others fear to tread.

Hence, the path to success in the world of leading-edge investments involves embracing the discomfort of uncertainty, courting controversy, and being willing to stand apart from the crowd. It is about having the courage to bet on the unconventional, the unproven, the unpopular. It's about being bold enough to embrace the technologies that still don't work today, but everyone will love tomorrow.

A sense of discomfort also is often an indicator that we are truly on the precipice of change. When evaluating potential investments, if I feel too comfortable, it typically suggests that the idea is not at the leading edge of its respective field. Remember, in the realm of groundbreaking innovation, comfort may suggest familiarity, which often means that the idea has already permeated the industry. In such a case, we might be arriving late to the party, and therefore, the potential for exceptional returns may be diminished.

The essence of leading-edge investment lies in venturing into the unexplored, in embracing the uncertainty of the unknown. Therefore, I use my comfort level as a proxy to gauge the potential of an investment opportunity. If an idea makes me feel uneasy, it's usually a good sign that we are dealing with something truly transformative.

Understanding Disruption and Its Value

Disruption is the game-changer. It's the introduction of a new technology, a novel approach, or a revolutionary idea that challenges and changes the status quo. Disruptive innovations have the potential to redefine the boundaries of science, medicine and technology, leading to advancements that can transform lives and industries. They also hold the potential for substantial returns on investment, especially when recognized and capitalized on early.

The biotech landscape, for example, is dotted with "me-too" ventures — companies that follow in the footsteps of successful businesses, reproducing similar technologies or business models.

While these companies may seem like safe bets, they often lack the disruptive potential that can lead to significant returns, especially if you are investing at an early stage because there are still many years to get to the market. By the time a "me-too" company has made its mark, the truly disruptive opportunities have often moved elsewhere.

Recognizing and investing in disruptive potential early can yield exponential returns. That is what we call "the early bird advantage." It requires keen insight, foresight, and a willingness to take calculated risks. The ability to anticipate the future trajectory of a novel technology, therapeutic approach, or business model can put you ahead of the investment curve, positioning you to capitalize on opportunities before they become mainstream.

The Power of Contrarian Thinking

On top of all this, in the realm of science-driven companies, contrarian thinking becomes particularly potent. The pace of scientific discovery and technological advancement is breathtaking, and new opportunities are constantly emerging, often in unexpected places. Here, more than anywhere, the ability to see what others don't and the courage to act on it can lead to remarkable results.

As the landscape of scientific advancement is incredibly diverse and rapidly changing, it is not uncommon for groundbreaking innovations to be initially misunderstood or underestimated. They may defy conventional wisdom or challenge established practices, and thus may not fit neatly into traditional investment frameworks. This is where the contrarian investor thrives.

Consider the rise of biotech, genomics, and personalized medicine. These fields were once on the fringe of the healthcare industry, viewed by many investors as too risky or speculative. Contrarian investors, however, recognized the potential for these disruptive technologies to redefine healthcare and made early investments that have since yielded substantial returns.

But, of course, contrarian thinking is not simply about being different for the sake of being different. It's about rigorous due diligence, deep understanding of the science, and the ability to foresee its potential applications and implications. It requires, as we saw in the last chapter, a comprehensive assessment of the technology, the market, the regulatory environment, and the team behind the company. When these elements come together, contrarian investments can realize extraordinary value.

All this becomes critical in managing the risks inherent in science-driven investments. With the rapid pace of scientific discovery, today's cutting-edge technology can become obsolete tomorrow. Contrarian investors, with their focus on overlooked or underestimated opportunities, are often well-positioned to pivot and adapt when the winds of scientific change shift.

Ultimately, the power of contrarian thinking in science-driven companies lies in its ability to uncover hidden gems and seize opportunities before they become mainstream. It's about having the vision to see the potential in the unconventional and the courage to act on that conviction, even in the face of skepticism and doubt. It's about the audacity to believe in the power of science to reshape the world.

Timing Is of the Essence

An anecdote from my own experience provides a striking illustration of the importance of timing and understanding the landscape's evolution in investment. Just last year, our venture capital fund exited three companies. It's not that these ventures were unsuccessful— in fact, they were industry leaders, leveraging cutting-edge technologies that were ahead of their time. Their contributions were remarkable, their technologies pioneering.

However, if these very same companies were considered for an investment today, they wouldn't pass even the first meeting. Not because they've lost their edge, but because the technological landscape has evolved so swiftly and dramatically that what was once "leading-edge" has now become "routine." The rapid pace of scientific discovery and technological innovation has made their once-groundbreaking technologies seem almost commonplace now.

This is a testament to the astonishing pace at which innovation propels industries forward. Yesterday's "revolutionary" becomes today's "standard," and today's "innovative" becomes tomorrow's "outdated."

Hence, it's crucial to understand that an investment opportunity's attractiveness is transient, heavily influenced by the dynamics of the market and the pace of innovation. It's not merely about identifying great companies or groundbreaking technologies; it's also about the "when."

Leading-Edge Is a Moving Target

Wrapping up, investing in or starting a company is like trying to hit a moving target: You're not merely assessing the potential of a venture based on its current standing, but on where it will stand in the future — typically between 1 and 5 years from now. You are, in essence, trying to anticipate where the sector will be, not where it currently is.

It's a delicate balancing act of foresight and intuition, coupled with rigorous analysis. We shoot where the target will be in the future, not where the target is today. Yet, it is this very challenge that makes the endeavor so intriguing, so rewarding. If everyone agrees with your investment idea, if it's universally lauded as "great," then you're likely playing it safe, perhaps too safe.

This doesn't mean that every "unpopular" or "risky" investment is a guaranteed success. Far from it. It simply means that the biggest rewards often come from taking calculated risks, from daring to venture where others have not. It's about having the courage to back an unconventional idea, the conviction to stand by it, and the resilience to weather the inevitable storms. As a leading-edge investor, you're not just investing in companies or technologies; you're investing in possibilities, in potential.

Rule #6

There Will Be Constant Changes of Wind Direction

"The answer, my friend, is blowin' in the wind,
the answer is blowin' in the wind."
Bob Dylan

Science is a field characterized by constant change, but in recent years, the rate of change has exponentially increased. As scientific knowledge expands, so does the pace of its growth. Each day, new papers are published, revealing novel insights, groundbreaking discoveries, and innovative techniques that have the potential to fundamentally shift the landscape of various industries. This continual evolution is the wind that alters the course of science-driven companies.

One such discovery can be bad news for your venture. A new paper might introduce a more efficient method, an improved technological platform, or a revolutionary approach that could render your current trajectory obsolete. Indeed, in the highly competitive landscape of scientific industries, staying abreast of the latest research is not merely beneficial — it is imperative. Therefore, in the realm of science-driven businesses, we must expect, prepare for, and embrace the inevitability of swift wind shifts.

This is not to say that change should induce fear or apprehension. Instead, it underscores the importance of maintaining a flexible strategy, a keen awareness of the evolving landscape, and the readiness to adapt when necessary. This approach is encapsulated in the concept of "pivoting," a strategic redirection in response to new information or changes in the business environment.

Pivoting is not a sign of failure but rather an indication of a company's agility and responsiveness to the rapid advancements in science. By continually realigning your venture with the latest scientific progress, you not only ensure relevance but also enhance the potential for success. It's about viewing each gust of wind not as a threat but as an opportunity — a chance to leverage the very forces of change to propel your business forward.

This is also the reason VC investments are typically staged in tranches, or portions, at different milestones. This practice helps manage the inherent risks associated with investing in these dynamic fields.

The tranche system in VC investments allows for funding to be released at various stages of a company's development rather than in a single lump sum. Each tranche is tied to specific milestones, which can range from technical achievements, such as the successful completion of a product prototype, to scientific targets like seeing new data on a particular experiment or successfully completing a specific phase in a clinical trial.

Harnessing Collective Intelligence

Be advised: As an abundance of new information is continuously generated with countless papers, patents, and findings, it becomes impossible for any one person, or even a single organization, to keep pace with this influx of knowledge. Hence, the necessity of harnessing collective intelligence arises — utilizing the pooled knowledge and insights from a community to navigate the swiftly changing landscape.

Collective intelligence isn't a new phenomenon. It has its roots in the ancient human practice of sharing knowledge, a practice that enabled us to progress as a species. In the context of modern science-driven industries, it translates into active engagement with the broader scientific community. The benefits of this engagement are manifold.

First, the scientific community acts as an early warning system. If a new paper threatens your current technological platform, you will hear the echoes through the community. If a promising new discovery has been made, it will cause ripples of discussion. Staying closely connected to these discussions allows companies to anticipate changes and respond swiftly.

Second, the collaborative problem-solving capacity of the scientific community is an invaluable resource. Open-source projects, community hackathons, and collaborative research initiatives demonstrate the power of collective minds working toward shared goals. Tapping into this collective problem-solving capacity can help companies overcome challenges, innovate, and adapt to changes more effectively.

Third, networking plays a crucial role in harnessing collective intelligence. By building strong relationships within the scientific community, companies can gain access to a broader range of ideas, perspectives, and expertise. This diversity of thought is a significant driving force for innovation, equipping companies with the creative solutions needed to pivot in response to the shifting winds of change.

Finally, collective intelligence promotes a culture of continuous learning. In the face of rapid change, the ability to learn and adapt becomes a company's most vital competency. A dynamic engagement with the scientific community fosters a learning mindset, keeping teams on their toes and always ready to evolve.

Balancing Short-Term Adaptability and Long-Term Vision

Science-driven companies find themselves in a complex dichotomy. On one hand, they must remain adaptable to the rapidly evolving scientific landscape, ready to pivot at a moment's notice as new discoveries and technologies emerge. On the other hand, they must maintain focus and a clear long-term vision, a guiding star that gives direction to their efforts and decisions.

Balancing these contrasting demands is akin to a tightrope walk. A misstep in either direction could lead to disaster: Excessive adaptability may result in strategic instability, while an unyielding commitment to a long-term vision may render a company blind to critical developments. Understanding this balancing act is crucial, and several strategies can help companies navigate this challenge effectively:

- **Creating a Flexible Strategic Plan:** Strategic planning need not be a rigid process. By creating a flexible strategic plan that accounts for potential changes in the scientific landscape, companies can build adaptability into their long-term vision. This could involve setting broad strategic objectives that can be achieved through multiple pathways, allowing for changes in tactics without a shift in strategy.

- **Building an Agile Organization:** Organizational agility refers to the ability of a company to respond quickly and effectively to changes. By building an agile organization, companies can ensure their adaptability. This might involve fostering a culture of continuous learning, encouraging cross-functional collaboration, and investing in technologies that facilitate rapid decision-making and information-sharing. These are characteristics that usually apply in early-stage startups.
- **Fostering Foresight Capabilities:** Foresight involves the ability to anticipate and prepare for future changes. Companies can foster this capability by staying closely connected to the scientific community, investing in research and development, getting into early business development deals, and using predictive analytics and other foresight tools. By building strong foresight capabilities, companies can ensure that their long-term vision remains relevant and informed by the latest scientific developments.

Scenario Planning

Scenario planning is an invaluable strategic tool, particularly in sectors where the "winds of change" blow strong and often. This technique involves constructing multiple plausible future scenarios and formulating strategic responses for each.

At its core, scenario planning acknowledges the uncertainty and complexity of the future. Rather than attempting to predict what will happen, it aims to explore what could happen. Each scenario is a narrative, rich and detailed, that describes a potential future state. The scenarios are not intended to be exhaustive or predictive; instead, they provide a structured way to consider diverse outcomes, challenging assumptions and stimulating strategic thinking.

Scenario planning typically involves several key steps. It begins with identifying the focal issue or decision. Then, the critical forces in the environment are recognized. These might include scientific advancements, regulatory changes, or shifts in consumer behavior. Subsequently, these forces are used to create a set of varied and challenging scenarios. For each scenario, the implications and potential strategic responses are explored. Finally, the learnings are translated into strategic decisions in the present, with an eye on adaptability for the future.

The Role of Regulatory Bodies: Navigating the Winds of Change

The high-speed pace of scientific innovation is a significant factor, but it's not the only force driving change. Regulatory bodies and the policies they enforce play a pivotal role in shaping the landscape these companies navigate.

Regulatory bodies, such as the Food and Drug Administration (FDA) in the United States and the European Medicines Agency (EMA) in Europe, set the rules of the game in many biotech science-driven initiatives. These agencies determine what is safe, effective, and ethical, significantly impacting how science-driven companies conduct their operations, research, and development.

The influence of regulatory bodies can extend beyond compliance. They can stimulate innovation by setting new standards that require creative, scientific solutions. Conversely, they can limit the viability of certain products or technologies due to safety, ethical, or other concerns.

Given their critical role, staying abreast of regulatory changes is crucial for science-driven companies. Just like scientific breakthroughs, changes in regulations can necessitate significant shifts in a company's direction. Regulatory changes might mean stricter safety standards, changes in approval processes, or new requirements for clinical trials. The best companies view regulatory bodies as partners rather than obstacles, working with them to ensure their innovative solutions meet regulatory standards. Staying informed about regulatory changes, anticipating their impact, and adapting accordingly are essential strategies for navigating the ever-changing winds in these fields.

Rule #7
Strategic Positioning Matters

"Art is not what you see, but what you make others see."
Edgar Degas

In the world of innovation, disruption is a term that is often used liberally. But what does it truly mean to disrupt? In essence, disruption signifies a profound shift — a change that significantly reshapes an existing market or industry, or perhaps even creates a new one. However, not all disruption is created equal. It's essential to understand that disruption occurs in varying degrees. Some innovations refine and enhance, while others redefine and recreate. The distinction is critical. It influences everything from investment decisions to competitive strategies. To truly appreciate the depth and breadth of disruption, one must understand its different degrees.

Here we will explore the varying degrees of disruption, borrowing concepts from the world of biotech — best in class, first in class, first in modality — and extrapolating them to a broader context. We will then touch upon a rare, yet profound form of disruption, one that transcends modality to create entirely new categories. These degrees of disruption will offer a lens through which we can view and appreciate the magnitude of change that leading-edge innovation brings about, not just in biotech, but across all fields of science.

We'll discuss them in depth a bit later, but for now you just need to know that the terms "first in class," "best in class," and "first in modality" are used to describe different types of therapeutic drugs. Here's what each of them means:

- **Best in Class:** This refers to a drug that is considered the most effective or has the best safety profile among all drugs in the same class (i.e., drugs that target the same pathway or mechanism). While a best-in-class drug isn't necessarily the first of its kind, it generally offers some advantages over the first-in-class drug, such as improved efficacy, fewer side effects, or more convenient dosing.

- **First in Class:** This refers to the first drug that targets a specific biological pathway or mechanism. Such a drug is often the first to demonstrate that modulating a new target or pathway can have therapeutic effects. Once a first-in-class drug is approved, it opens the door for other drugs that target the same pathway or mechanism.
- **First in Modality:** This refers to the first therapeutic developed using a new technology or approach. For example, the first RNA interference drug or the first gene therapy would be considered first in modality. This term is less commonly used than "first in class" or "best in class," but it's used to highlight groundbreaking innovations in drug development.

This exploration is not merely academic; it carries practical implications. For entrepreneurs, understanding these degrees of disruption can shape their innovation strategies and articulate their value proposition. For investors, it offers a framework to assess potential co-investors in the future, expected return, and expected time to liquidity event in an investment.

As we navigate this journey of understanding the degrees of disruption, remember that these are not rigid classifications but more of a spectrum. Innovations may blur the lines, embodying aspects of multiple degrees at once. This fluidity is part of what makes the realm of disruption so exciting and so unpredictable. The only constant in this world of disruption is change itself.

Best in Class

"Best in class" is the first stage on the ladder of disruption. This term refers to solutions or products that significantly enhance or improve upon an existing approach or technology. The distinguishing feature here is that these innovations operate within an established framework or modality. They don't redefine the game; instead, they play it better. In the realm of biotech, best-in-class disruptions might involve a new drug that leverages established methodologies but achieves superior results. For instance, it might treat a particular disease more effectively, reduce side effects, or offer a more favorable administration regimen. In essence, it takes the familiar and makes it better.

I must mention here that the intersection of best-in-class innovations and personalization is a potent concept in the field of precision medicine. It represents the advancement of solutions that not only leverage superior science and technology, but also cater to the unique needs of specific patient groups.

This approach transcends the "one-drug-fits-all" methodology and moves toward tailored treatments, thereby delivering greater efficacy and impact. By refining best-in-class solutions to fit specific genetic profiles or patient demographics, we can magnify the potential of these innovations, further enhancing healthcare outcomes.

Of course, "best-in-class" disruption is a concept that can apply across industries and sectors as well. In the realm of software, a best-in-class innovation might take the form of a tool that performs familiar functions but does so more efficiently, more intuitively, or more powerfully. So, "better" is the keyword when we talk about best-in-class innovations.

These disruptions don't rewrite the rules; they follow them more effectively. They present a significant step forward, but within the boundaries of an existing paradigm. However, as we ascend the ladder of disruption, we'll see that some innovations don't just play the game better — they change the game entirely.

First in Class

As we climb the disruption ladder, we reach the "first-in-class" level. This tier involves innovations that aren't just better — they're pioneering. First in class refers to products or solutions that initiate an entirely new class of technologies or products. They don't just improve upon the old — they break new ground.

In the biotech world, a first-in-class disruption might involve a novel class of drug that treats a disease in a way that has never been done before. For example, monoclonal antibodies for autoimmune diseases represented a first-in-class breakthrough when they first emerged. These biological drugs harnessed the body's own immune system to fight these diseases in a way that no other treatments had done before, fundamentally transforming the landscape of therapeutic strategies in that field. In this particular example, they were not new because they had been used before in oncology.

Regulatory hurdles arise largely due to the novel and often disruptive nature of first-in-class innovations. Existing laws and regulations might not fully anticipate or account for the implications of these new technologies, resulting in potential regulatory gray areas.

Here, it is imperative for companies to maintain an ongoing dialogue with relevant regulatory authorities throughout the development and deployment process. Involving regulatory experts early on, conducting pre-submission consultations, and obtaining clarity on the required evidence for approval can facilitate a smoother regulatory journey.

Also, ethical challenges are intrinsically linked to the breakthrough nature of first-in-class innovations. Novel technologies can profoundly impact societies and individuals, raising questions around privacy, consent, security, equity, and more.

Being "first in class" comes with both substantial opportunities and significant challenges. On the one hand, being a pioneer allows you to shape the market, establish the standards, and enjoy a period of limited competition. On the other hand, it also involves the challenge of trailblazing, convincing consumers or users to adopt a novel product or technology, and establishing a new market where none existed before. It also can give you a better liquidity event in terms of valuation.

Lastly, pricing for first-in-class products can be challenging. Since there's no direct competition or comparable product in the market, setting a price that accurately reflects the value of the innovation while also being acceptable to consumers, insurers, and other stakeholders can be tricky.

First in Modality

A step above "first in class" is "first in modality," which signifies an even higher degree of innovation. These are innovations that introduce an entirely new modality or method for achieving a particular outcome. These innovations are not just about creating a new product or technology within an existing framework, but rather about fundamentally altering the framework itself.

In the realm of biotech, a clear example of a first-in-modality disruption is represented by gene-editing technologies such as CRISPR. Before the advent of gene editing, genetic diseases were treated for the most part by managing symptoms or slowing the progression of the disease. With CRISPR, we have the potential to cure genetic diseases by editing the faulty genes directly. This is more than just a new class of treatment; it's an entirely new approach or modality for treating diseases.

Allow me a brief detour to expand on this. Picture a vast library filled with books. Each book, just like a gene in our body, has a critical role to play in the overall narrative of the library. It's a living, evolving ecosystem where information is stored and passed down through generations. However, occasionally, there might be a misprint, a typo, or a wrong paragraph in one of these books, much like a genetic mutation that leads to disease in an organism.

Gene therapy is akin to realizing that there is a problematic paragraph in a book — a sequence that doesn't make sense or is causing a misunderstanding for those who read it. Rather than replacing the entire book, we "simply" add a new book that has the correct paragraph. This newly added book offers the right information even though the original book with the error still sits on the shelf. In biological terms, gene therapy introduces a new, functional gene into a person's cells to compensate for a dysfunctional one, allowing the body to carry out the correct function without altering the original, faulty gene.

Now, imagine the advancement to a more direct solution. Editing genes, like utilizing a sophisticated word processor, enables us to correct the error right in the original book. We open the book, locate the paragraph with the error, and replace it with the correct text. Similarly, techniques like CRISPR-Cas9 allow scientists to cut out a faulty gene and replace it with a healthy one, rectifying the problem at its source.

Finally, we delve into the realm of synthetic biology, an extension of the metaphorical library. It's now not merely about correcting errors in the existing books; it's about writing new chapters, constructing entirely new narratives. These new narratives might create capabilities that were previously unimaginable. In the biological context, synthetic biology enables scientists to create new biological parts, devices, and systems, or to redesign systems that already exist in nature. It pushes the boundaries of what's possible, enabling cells to perform things

Figure 7. Gene Editing and Synthetic Biology

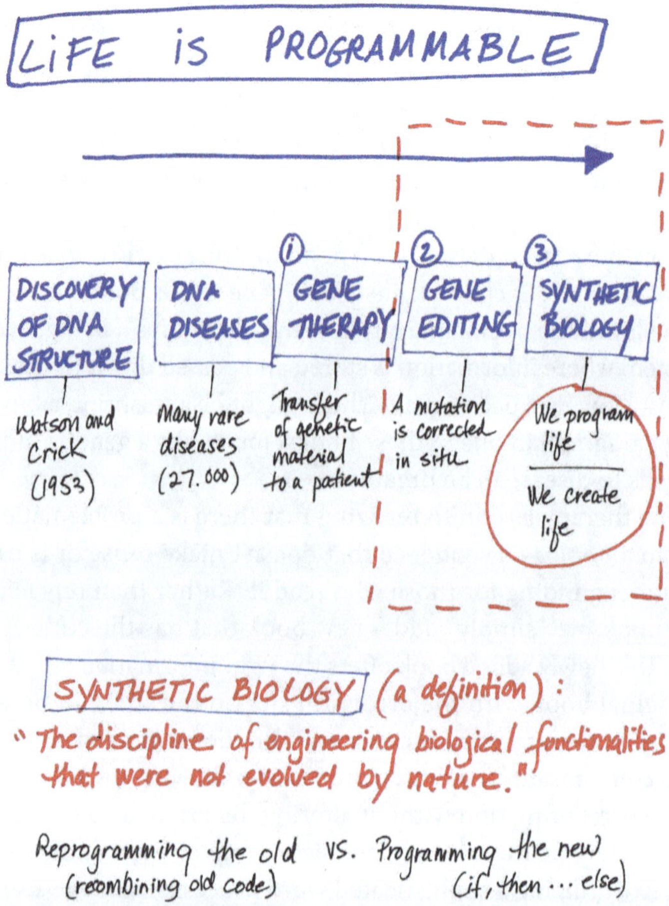

The underpinning assumption of synthetic biology is a radical yet captivating concept: Life is programmable. This idea harks back to the mid-20th century, specifically 1953, when James Watson and Francis Crick unveiled the double helix structure of DNA, our genetic blueprint. Understanding DNA was akin to obtaining a master key, a critical tool that would unlock countless mysteries of biology and disease.

In the wake of Watson and Crick's discovery, medical professionals and researchers around the world began to draw connections between alterations in the genome and specific diseases. Today, we're aware of over 7,000 rare diseases, many of which are tied to genetic aberrations and could potentially be addressed through modifications of our DNA.

The trajectory of genetic intervention technologies mirrors our increasing comprehension and manipulation of life's code. Initially, we developed gene therapy, a technique that involves transferring genetic material to a patient. This is somewhat like adding a new book to the library; it doesn't alter the original "misprinted" book but supplements it with a correct version. Following gene therapy, gene editing technologies emerged, offering a more direct solution to genetic disorders. Techniques such as CRISPR-Cas9 serve as precise word processors, allowing scientists to cut out faulty genes and replace them with healthy ones. Instead of merely adding a new book to the library, we're now editing the error in the original book.

Our understanding of life's code has now reached an unprecedented level, giving birth to the discipline of synthetic biology. This cutting-edge field goes beyond editing or correcting life's code; it's about programming it as if it were a computer, giving us the ability to create life or modify it in ways we never thought possible.

- To comprehend the complexities and potential of synthetic biology, envision a ladder of increasing coding sophistication. On the first rung, we have the ability to program cells to perform tasks that nature had never conceived. For example, we can modify cells to express a specific protein in a particular organ to combat a disease.
- As we climb the ladder, we reach the second stage, where we can code sensors within the cells. These sensors allow the cell to perceive its environment and regulate its protein expression. For instance, if a cancerous environment is detected due to hypoxia (low oxygen levels), the cell could be programmed to respond by expressing an immune checkpoint.
- Progressing to the third stage, we add a feedback loop, allowing the cell not only to sense but also to react to its environment. It becomes akin to an "if/then" statement in computer programming. Here, the cell can sense the proteins it produces and control its release, reducing the risk of overproduction and ensuring a more precise therapeutic response.
- Finally, on the highest rung of synthetic biology, we introduce computing power into biological systems. This is equivalent to an "if/then/else" statement in coding, giving cells the ability to execute complex operations like Boolean logic, memory recall, oscillation, amplification, and more. This advanced capability could enable us to achieve feats that were inconceivable just a few years ago.

In summary, our ability to decipher and manipulate life's code has evolved significantly, from simply adding correct versions to faulty genes, to editing errors right at the source, to reprogramming cells with unprecedented sophistication. As we ascend this ladder of complexity in synthetic biology, we are pushing the boundaries of what's possible, unlocking a future that holds unimaginable potentials.

they were never programmed by nature to do — in a way, the end of Darwinism.

Back from our detour... Being first in modality means a potential for vast market opportunities but also the challenge of establishing and growing a market that is fundamentally different than what existed before. It requires not only technical innovation but also a vision for how this new modality can reshape the world.

First-in-modality innovations often have the potential to transform healthcare, but they also carry the risk of exacerbating existing inequalities. How can we ensure that these revolutionary treatments are accessible and affordable for all who need them? How do we balance the drive for profit, which often fuels innovation, with the ethical obligation to provide healthcare equitably?

Moreover, "first in modality" also introduces new considerations for intellectual property and competitive positioning. With an entirely new modality, there's likely to be a flurry of patent applications, strategic partnerships, and perhaps even legal disputes, as different players seek to carve out their niches in this new landscape.

For investors, first-in-modality innovations might be seen as high-risk, high-reward ventures. They offer potentially huge returns if they succeed, but they also carry substantial risks, given their novelty and the uncertainties associated with developing and commercializing a completely new approach.

A Special Category: Frontier Innovations

The pinnacle of disruptive innovation lies in what I like to call "frontier innovations." This degree of disruption goes beyond introducing a new product, a new class, or even a new modality. It involves creating an entirely new category of technologies or products that didn't exist before, introducing novel concepts that redefine the landscape of industries and markets.

Artificial intelligence (AI) serves as a quintessential example of this degree of disruption. Before AI, the concept of a machine that could learn, make decisions, and evolve on its own was the stuff of science fiction. However, with the advent of AI, not only has this become a reality, it has also given birth to a whole new category of technology. AI isn't just a new product or a new class of software; it represents a new category of intelligence and decision-making mechanism, and it will reshape everything.

AI has also proved to be a cross-cutting innovation, transforming multiple industries across the board. In healthcare, AI is used to predict diseases, personalize treatments, and even assist in surgeries. In finance, it powers algorithmic trading, fraud detection, and robo-advisors. In entertainment, AI drives recommendation algorithms, game design, and virtual reality experiences. Each of these applications can be seen as a sub-category within the broader category of AI.

Creating a new category is the epitome of disruptive innovation. It involves profound transformations that redefine the status quo and create enormous potential for growth. However, it also presents immense challenges, from technological hurdles to market acceptance, regulatory issues, and ethical considerations. It requires a visionary approach, persistence, and a high tolerance for risk and uncertainty. Nonetheless, the potential rewards of creating a new category are immense, and such disruptions often form the basis of the next generation of leading companies.

Making Sense of It All

One of the essential aspects of science-driven entrepreneurship is understanding the positioning of a company or technology in terms of its uniqueness and the strategies it employs to capture value. This positioning often falls within a matrix that involves (1) degrees of innovation and (2) the primary value capture approach. The innovation dimension ranges from best in class to first in modality, while the value capture strategy lies on a spectrum from being a technological platform to being a product pipeline. "Technological platform-driven value" refers to situations where the core technology in itself is the primary source of value. Such a platform can often be leveraged across various products or services, potentially across different market segments or even industries. In contrast, "pipeline-driven value" refers to scenarios where value is primarily derived from specific products developed using the technology. Here, the focus is more on the application of the technology in creating specific, marketable drugs that address a particular problem or need.

In this matrix, four unique quadrants emerge: Best in Class & Technological Platform, Best in Class & Pipeline, First in Modality

Figure 8. Strategic Positioning

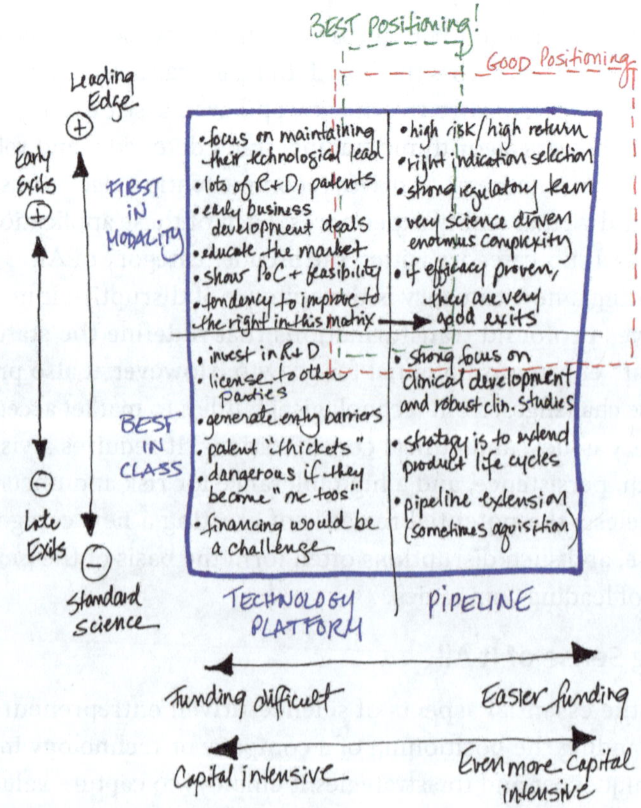

This figure offers an insightful breakdown of four distinct strategic quadrants, each representing a different type of biotech company. The position of a company within this matrix is determined by its strategic focus and core capabilities, and each quadrant presents its unique challenges, considerations, and paths to success. By understanding this figure, we can better comprehend the diverse strategies employed by biotech companies, as well as the intricate landscape of potential risks and opportunities they navigate.

- **Best in Class & Technological Platform:** Companies in this quadrant need to focus on commercializing their technology and achieving this "best" status, as it is dangerous for them to become a simple "me-too" product and be out of the market. They need to continuously invest in R&D and potentially develop new upgraded versions of their technology in an interactive way. The primary business strategy here would be to license the technology to as many users or sectors as possible to maximize its value. Creating barriers to change could be useful if possible. If a new best in class shows up they will probably disappear, sometimes very quicky. They need to have a solid patent thicket to further layers of protection. Being a platform in an already known class, even if the best one, they may struggle to get financing, as many investors are focused in the leading edge space which would correspond to First in modality.

- **Best in Class & Pipeline:** In this quadrant, companies need strong product development and strong clinical studies. They also need to worry about product life cycles and developing new products to replace those that become obsolete. Intellectual property extension strategies are important, and acquiring new IP to further expand their products. Extending the company's product pipeline, either by developing new drugs or by finding new indications for existing drugs, is crucial for adding value and establishing a more robust market position. This strategy helps ensure sustainability and competitiveness, as it diversifies the company's portfolio and reduces reliance on a single product. At the end of the day, the introduction of new drugs that are superior to existing ones in the market can pose significant challenges to those older drugs. If a competitor develops a new "best in class" drug, it can quickly overshadow the company's treatment candidates, making it difficult for them to maintain their potential and succeed. Therefore, continual innovation and adaptation are key.
- **First in Modality & Technological Platform:** Companies in this quadrant are breaking new ground, so they need to be prepared to face significant uncertainties and risks. They need to focus on maintaining their technological lead, as they are in a race with other companies trying to develop similar technologies. They need to continuously invest in R&D and patent protection to keep their competitive advantage. They must focus on educating the market about the potential of their technology and on demonstrating its feasibility through proofs of concept and pilot projects. The main business strategy here is to establish partnerships with other companies or institutions that can help them develop applications for their technology. Research and Development (R&D) is crucial here, along with robust and clear intellectual property (IP) protection. Developing their own diverse drug pipeline is essential to mitigate risks. When companies rely solely on a specific technological platform, they are vulnerable to competition from new technologies that could offer better results. This risk is especially pronounced if a competitor introduces a more effective or efficient solution. Therefore, by investing in their own R&D and expanding their pipeline with a variety of products or solutions, companies can safeguard against the potential obsolescence of their core technology and maintain a competitive edge in the market.
- **First in Modality & Pipeline:** These companies are high-risk, high-return. They face considerable uncertainties, but their focus is on product development rather than on the technology itself. They need to find the right indications for their therapies and develop products that can meet customer needs. They face regulatory uncertainty, as being first in modality means nobody has done it before and the regulator does not have a clear picture of how to regulate it. This might be an advantage in itself, as typically they have faster routes to authorization. They are extremely science driven; often, their science is complex and highly sophisticated. If they prove efficacy in trials, they typically have the best offers and are sold quickly, allowing for a great value capture in terms of money and time. (They are sold earlier than best in class pipeline-based companies.)

In terms of worries, all companies in this matrix should be concerned about technological obsolescence and competitive threats. Companies in the best-of-class quadrants should worry about other companies that are developing better technologies, while those in the first-in-modality quadrants need to worry about regulatory uncertainty and careful indication selection. Companies with a technological platform strategy should worry about finding the right partners and users for their technology, while those with a pipeline strategy need to worry about solving a specific clinical need ensuring that clinical need is important, and diversifying their risk by extending their pipelines.

& Technological Platform, and First in Modality & Pipeline. Each quadrant carries its own strategic focus, associated challenges, and particular considerations for companies operating within these realms.

A careful analysis of these quadrants can provide insightful guidance to entrepreneurs, investors, and business strategists in crafting an optimal path for their ventures. By analyzing the quadrants, we gain insights into the diverse strategies biotech firms adopt and understand the complex landscape of risks and opportunities they must navigate. Please refer to Figure 8 for a more in-depth understanding.

Key insights from this strategy-matrix include (see Figure 8):

- **Best in Class & Technological Platform:** These companies need to avoid becoming a "me too" company by continuously investing in R&D, developing patent protections, and licensing their technology to multiple parties. However, they may struggle to get financing due to the high technological risk (a new better technology might kill them) and investors' focus on the leading-edge space.
- **Best in Class & Pipeline:** Firms in this quadrant must focus on product development and strong clinical studies, manage product life cycles, and pursue IP extension strategies. They should also look to expand their product offerings or indications to remain competitive.
- **First in Modality & Technological Platform:** These trailblazers face significant uncertainties and risks. Their success hinges on continuous R&D investment, patent protection, market education, and establishing partnerships to develop applications for their technology.
- **First in Modality & Pipeline**: Characterized by high risk and high return, these companies must focus on product development and finding the right indications for their therapies. Regulatory uncertainties present both challenges and potential advantages, with faster routes to authorization often possible.

All firms must remain vigilant about technological obsolescence and competitive threats. Regulatory uncertainties, partnership dynamics, and the need to solve specific clinical needs are key considerations across the matrix.

The Best Positioning?

Indeed, there's no such thing as "the best positioning." Every company should be guided by its unique technology and target the area where it can genuinely create value. It's important to note that everything we've discussed in this chapter is not absolute but rather a general framework to understand strategic positioning. Each company carries its own distinctive characteristics and specific circumstances that influence its journey. Therefore, while this framework offers valuable insights, it should be adapted and interpreted in the light of a company's individual context and goals.

However, a field that is very dear to me is the combination of a cutting-edge technological platform with a diversified pipeline of first-in-modality innovations. This unique positioning allows companies to continually leverage their technology for new product development while spreading risk across a variety of applications.

Companies employing this strategy develop a core technology, often involving a novel approach to disease treatment or a unique diagnostic tool. This technology then serves as the foundation upon which they build their product pipeline. The technology itself can be a significant value proposition. It's not only the foundation for the company's current products but also has the potential for future products. It can demonstrate the scalability and versatility of the company's proprietary technology, effectively serving as a proof-of-concept.

Having a diverse pipeline built on a unique technological platform provides the company with the chance to prove the platform's worth across multiple indications or modalities. This can reinforce investor confidence, bolster the company's credibility in the market, and even provide opportunities for partnership or licensing deals. The advantages of this approach include the potential for significant value creation, a spread of risk across multiple projects, and the opportunity to establish a company as a leader in its field.

This strategy, while being a potential value-creation powerhouse, also has challenges. It requires hefty financial resources, a high level of technical expertise, and a team that can oversee the development of multiple projects while advancing the core technology platform. Companies need to be strategic in prioritizing their pipeline development and mindful of the possible cannibalization of their products.

Figure 9. Positioning While Investing in SynBio

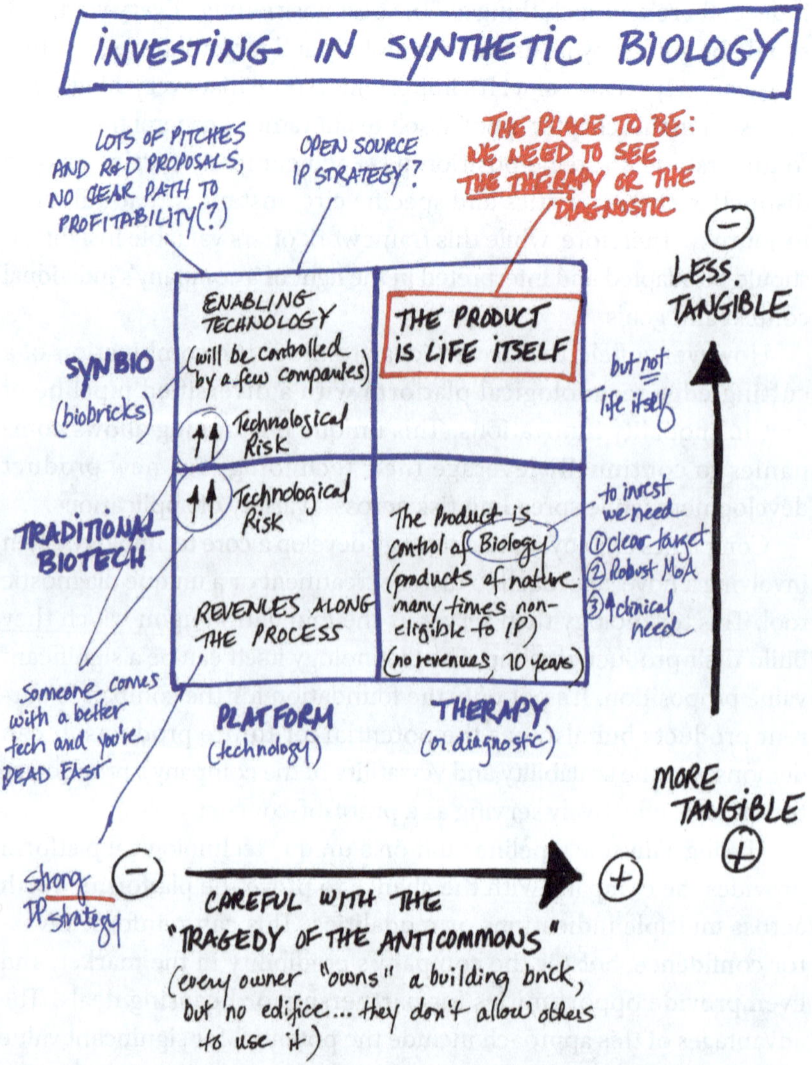

Each field brings with it unique characteristics and considerations that investors must take into account. Synthetic biology, arguably the most leading-edge field in biotech today, is no exception. The field is pioneering in nature, bridging the gaps between biology, engineering, and computing, and thus requires unique considerations for potential investors.

- **Synthetic biology** is a multidisciplinary area of research that combines the principles of biology, engineering, and computer science to create or redesign biological systems and organisms that do not naturally exist in the world. It seeks to make the design, construction, and modification of biological systems more predictable and systematic. The primary goal of synthetic biology is to improve and simplify the process of engineering biological systems, which is traditionally complex and time-consuming. This often in volves the use of genetic engineering techniques to create synthetic DNA sequences that can be inserted into the genome of an organism to confer new or improved functions.

- This field is still relatively young and its ethical, safety, and regulatory aspects are subjects of ongoing discussion, as the full potential of this technology has yet to be realized and its implications are vast.
- To encapsulate the complex investment landscape within synthetic biology, it can be helpful to construct a **2x2 matrix.** The y-axis of this matrix represents the range from traditional biotech at the bottom, characterized by biologics and small molecules, to the advanced synthetic biology at the top, encompassing everything from cell therapy and gene therapy to more well-defined synthetic biology. The x-axis, on the other hand, denotes the focus of the company, either as a technology platform or as a therapeutic company.
- If we consider this matrix, the journey from the bottom to the top on the y-axis represents a transition **from tangible to intangible assets**, reflecting the increasingly abstract and complex nature of synthetic biology. On the other hand, moving from left to right along the x-axis, we encounter a unique problem: **the tragedy of the anti-commons.** The concept of the anti-commons refers to a situation where multiple entities own pieces of a larger whole, and the lack of coordination or cooperation among these owners can lead to underutilization of resources or impede progress. In the context of synthetic biology, this issue arises due to the fact that the field relies heavily on
- BioBricks, chunks of intellectual property, similar to Lego blocks. Each owner controls a piece of the puzzle, but nobody owns the whole.
- **The two left quadrants of the matrix represent a high degree of technological risk.** In traditional biotech, represented by the bottom-left quadrant, revenues can be earned through the sale of technologies. In the context of synthetic biology, these become enabling technologies that are necessary to construct more complex biological systems. The IP strategy is crucial in this upper-left quadrant, as the open-source nature of many BioBricks adds a layer of complexity. It is imperative to recognize that new BioBricks are continuously being developed, and investors should see a clear path to profitability.
- **On the right side of the matrix, the quadrants represent a more stable investment landscape.** The upper right quadrant, where specific synthetic biology technologies are applied for a specific indication, whether therapeutic or diagnostic, is particularly interesting. Here, the product, in a sense, is life itself.
- Finally, the bottom-right quadrant represents the traditional biotech investment land-scape. Here, the focus is on **harnessing and controlling the power of biology**. In this quadrant, the investment decision would heavily rely on a clear target, a robust mechanism of action, and a high clinical need. The investment would need to demonstrate a viable path to profitability, considering the various clinical and market-related challenges that may arise.
- Navigating the synthetic biology investment landscape requires a unique blend of understanding of the complex biological systems, the dynamics of intellectual property, and the trends in the biotech sector. The 2x2 matrix represents a tool that investors can use to understand the unique characteristics of the field and to make informed decisions.

They need to ensure that each new product adds value to the company without undermining the potential success of existing products. The success in this quadrant can be remarkable, but is predicated on maintaining focus and effectively managing the inherent challenges.

Rule #8
Leverage Exponentials, Emergence, Luck, and Truth

"I am a great believer in luck, and I find the harder I work, the more I have of it."
Thomas Jefferson

The dynamic landscape of disruptive innovation and investing requires an understanding of four key concepts that underpin the realms of science, business, and decision-making: exponentials, emergence, luck, and truth. These four concepts, though seemingly distinct, are intricately intertwined and exert profound influence on investment strategies and the trajectory of innovative ventures.

The concept of exponentials is fundamental to grasping the scale and pace of breakthroughs in various scientific and technological domains. It serves as a key to deciphering the potential of innovative technologies and startups. Exponential growth, characterized by an increasing rate of change over time, can lead to outcomes far surpassing linear projections. A deep understanding of this concept can help investors anticipate the future, manage opportunities early, and make informed decisions that yield significant returns.

Emergence is an intriguing concept. It refers to the phenomenon where new properties, behaviors, or complexities arise spontaneously from simple components as they interact, leading to outcomes that are not predictable from the individual parts alone. It is often characterized as "the whole is greater than the sum of its parts." This concept is fundamental in the realms of biology, complex systems, artificial intelligence, and indeed, in the science-driven startup ecosystem.

Luck, often dismissed as an uncontrollable and unpredictable force, plays an undeniable role in investment. However, it is not simply a matter of chance but rather an intricate interplay of probabilities and outcomes. Recognizing and capitalizing on this aspect can be instrumental in navigating the uncertainties of investment scenarios and can mean the difference between missed opportunities and successful ventures.

The pursuit of truth forms the bedrock of any scientific endeavor and, by extension, any science-driven startup. Navigating the delicate balance between confidence in one's ideas and maintaining an openness to contradicting evidence is a crucial challenge. Confirmation bias, the human propensity to seek out and favor information that confirms pre-existing beliefs, can be a significant obstacle in this pursuit. By actively acknowledging and combatting this bias, science-driven startups can stay aligned with their fundamental mission: the pursuit of scientific truth.

This chapter aims to delve into these concepts, elucidating their significance and offering insights into how they can be harnessed to shape successful investment strategies and innovative ventures.

Understanding Exponentials

Exponential growth represents a pattern of data that sharpens over time, accelerating in the quantity or the sum of the subject at hand. It is a fundamental concept in various fields, including biology, physics, economics, and more pertinently, investing. Unlike linear growth, which progresses at a constant rate, exponential growth involves a variable — often time — being raised to a power.

In the context of investments in science-driven companies, this growth model bears significant implications. It helps depict how investments can evolve, especially investments in fast-growing industries. However, our cognitive makeup often inclines us toward linear thinking — projecting the future based on the immediate past. This mental model, though adequate in many scenarios, fails to capture the dynamism inherent in exponential growth. Understanding the power of exponentials is instrumental in making insightful predictions and decisions, especially in disruptive scientific initiatives and investing.

Consider the comparison between 1.00^365 and 1.01^365. The former is 1.00, but if you were to increment one unit by a mere 1%

every day for a year, that unit would not increase just by 365% (as linear thinking would suggest) but would grow over a multiple of 37 times the original (3600%). This small, consistent change compounded over time can lead to a profound difference, demonstrating the non-intuitive nature of exponential growth.

Disruptive scientific initiatives often embody exponential growth. For instance, advances in technologies like artificial intelligence (AI), genomics, or quantum computing are on exponential trajectories, with their development doubling in speed or halving in cost at consistent intervals. Therefore, an investor or innovator versed in exponential thinking is well-positioned to anticipate these rapid advancements and the potential opportunities they present.

Anticipating exponential growth enables the identification of high-potential investments and sectors poised for rapid expansion. A sector's growth pattern can often signal underlying technological developments and market dynamics. By understanding these patterns, investors can strategically position themselves in industries on the cusp of exponential growth, leading to significant returns on investment.

Understanding Emergence

Emergence, at its core, is a phenomenon that underscores the unexpected complexity arising from simple components. When applied broadly, it refers to instances where the total characteristics and behaviors of a system are significantly more intricate and unpredictable than the sum of its individual parts.

This principle is deeply entrenched within numerous disciplines such as physics, biology, and social sciences, each demonstrating the remarkable capacity of components to collectively manifest properties that would have been inconceivable in isolation. The concept of emergence, thus, has profound implications for science-driven startups, demanding an alternative lens to perceive and evaluate their potential.

Transposing the principle of emergence to the realm of science-driven startups reveals fascinating insights. It allows for the recognition that the combined value and impact of a startup's technology often eclipse the linear sum of its individual elements. This amplification, characteristic of emergence, can propel startups toward disruptive innovation.

For example, in the field of artificial intelligence, the convergence of machine-learning algorithms, computational power, and vast datasets can result in unexpected levels of performance.

A case in point is the apparent emergence of advanced reasoning capabilities in language models once the number of parameters exceeds 100 billion. This phenomenon has been extensively documented and is not a programmed feature but seems to "emerge" as a result of training these large models on extensive text corpus. Those models suddenly "understand" the world and we don't know how. The models start to generate responses that demonstrate an understanding of context, can infer meaning, make logical deductions, and even exhibit creativity. This emergent ability signifies an impressive milestone in the AI field, showing that under certain conditions, artificial systems can generate outputs that seemingly go beyond the capacity of their individual components.

Similarly, a compelling example in the realm of synthetic biology comes from the work of pioneering geneticist Craig Venter. Venter and his team constructed a synthetic, minimal genome consisting only of the essential genes required for life. They then implanted this genome into a recipient cell, effectively creating the first organism whose entire genetic makeup was designed in vitro. This engineered organism, termed Mycoplasma Laboratorium, exhibits all the key characteristics of life: It can grow, metabolize nutrients, and reproduce, all directed by the artificial genome.

This instance of life "emerging" from the most fundamental biological building blocks is remarkable and represents a landmark achievement in the field of synthetic biology. It is a potent illustration of emergence, as the complexity of life — growth, metabolism, reproduction — has spontaneously arisen from a simple, synthetic genome. This feat underscores the profound possibilities of synthetic biology, as the combinatorial interplay of genes, proteins, and cellular machinery can give rise to living systems with novel, potentially valuable traits.

Each of these examples underscores the extraordinary power and potential of emergence in the landscape of science-driven startups, compelling investors to reconsider how they perceive, evaluate, and harness the latent potential of these ventures.

The understanding and anticipation of emergent phenomena offer significant strategic advantages for investors in science- driven startups.

Figure 10. Emergence in Large Language Models

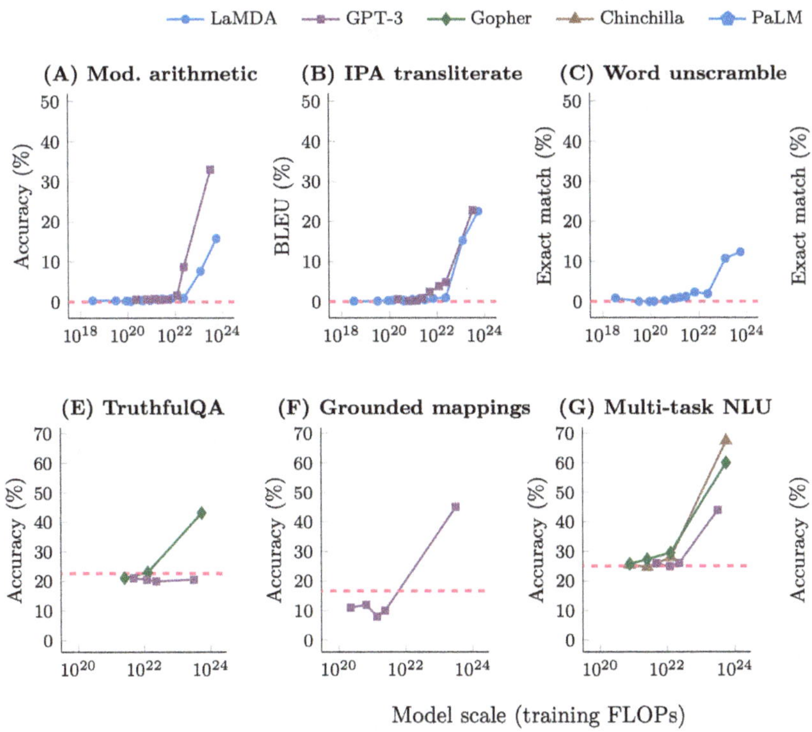

Source: Emergent Abilities of Large Language Models, Wei et al. (2022)

Here, an ability is considered emergent if it is absent in smaller models but becomes apparent in larger ones. Emergent abilities are not easily predictable by simply extrapolating a scaling law (which implies consistent performance enhancements) based on smaller models.

When we visualize these abilities on a scaling curve, where the x-axis represents model scale and the y-axis indicates performance, a distinctive pattern becomes evident. The performance is almost random until the model reaches a critical scale, at that point it significantly improves. This abrupt change in behavior, also known as a phase transition, is not foreseeable when we only observe smaller-scale systems. Modern language models scale primarily based on three factors: computational capacity, number of model parameters, and the size of the training dataset. In this figure, the performance of different models is analyzed using scaling curves, plotting the performance against training compute (measured in FLOPs) on the x-axis.

The concealed potential for exponential growth often lies within these emergent properties, thereby transforming this understanding into a powerful tool for the discerning investor.

Recognizing the signs of emergence in early-stage startups and industries is an art, as it necessitates a deep comprehension of the integrated system, not merely its isolated components. Investors must cultivate a vision that transcends linear extrapolation, appreciating the dynamics of complex systems and the unpredictable results they can produce. Strategies may involve identifying synergistic interactions between technologies, recognizing transformative potential in seemingly nascent trends, and understanding how diverse fields might intersect to create unprecedented value.

The concept of emergence aligns seamlessly with the central theme of this book. It stands as a testament to the vast possibilities inherent in the art of anticipation, the value of early management of opportunities, and the significance of making informed, successful decisions. Emergence, with its inherent complexity and unpredictability, embodies the very essence of disruptive innovation.

Understanding Luck

Luck, in the context of investing, is often perceived as the favorable turn of events that an investor neither anticipates nor directly influences. However, this definition simplifies the complex and nuanced interplay between decision-making, risk management, and randomness in the world of investing. As such, it's critical to recognize that what seems like pure luck often results from understanding and navigating uncertainties, probabilities, and outcomes.

A quote that resonates deeply with me is that "what is observed is at most a combination of probabilities and outcomes, not merely outcomes." This perspective underscores the importance of understanding the role of luck in investments, encapsulated in probabilistic outcomes.

Often, successful investors are those who have mastered the art of managing uncertainties, making calculated risks, and optimizing for probabilistic outcomes. We will go deeper into that concept in the chapter about probabilistic thinking, but for now, understand that what is perceived as "luck" is often the byproduct of a meticulous process of identifying and capitalizing on potential opportunities within the realm of probabilities.

Figure 11. Mycoplasma Laboratorium

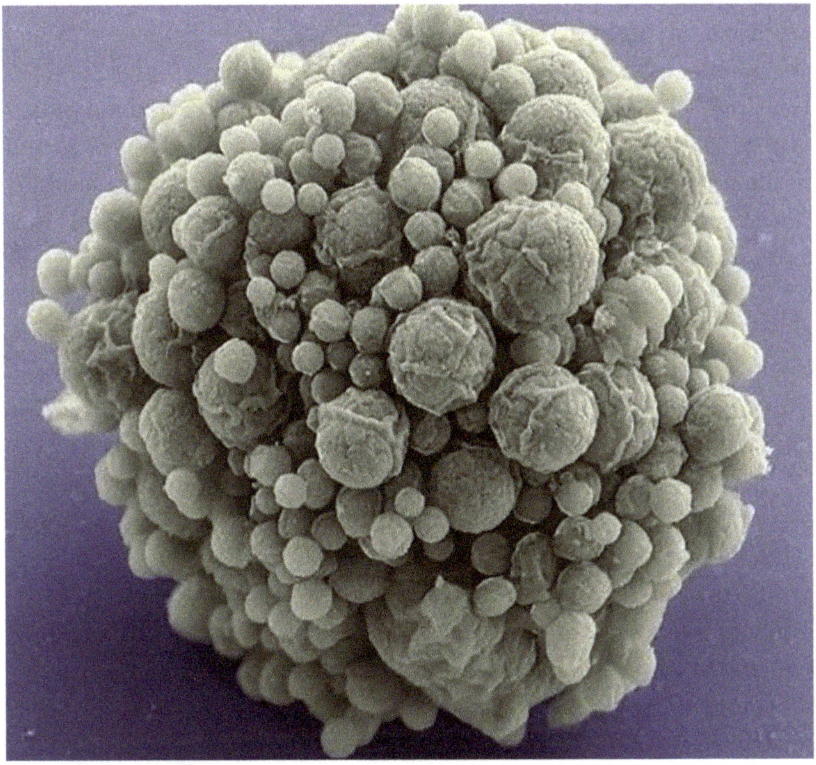

Source: Essential Genes of a Minimal Bacterium. Venter et al. (2006)

The story of Mycoplasma laboratorium marks a critical milestone in the field of synthetic biology. Spearheaded by Craig Venter, a renowned biochemist and geneticist, this ground-breaking project sought to create synthetic life in a laboratory for the first time.

- In the early 2000s, Venter and his team set out on a mission to synthesize a bacterium from scratch. The path to synthetic life was anything but straightforward. This synthetic bacterium had a genome designed entirely by a computer and built in the lab. For the first time, an organism existed whose parent was a computer.
- This unprecedented achievement sparked both excitement and controversy. On one hand, the ability to create synthetic life could potentially revolutionize fields such as medicine, energy, and environmental conservation. For instance, custom-built microorganisms could be designed to clean up oil spills or produce biofuels. On the other hand, ethical concerns have been raised about the potential for misuse, such as the creation of harmful pathogens. All this underscores the immense potential of synthetic biology, paving the way for a future where synthetic organisms could become commonplace, potentially transforming numerous sectors and aspects of human life.

Enhancing one's "luck" in investing does not rely on hoping for a better roll of the dice. Instead, it depends on the investor's ability to optimize for probabilities. The "Luck Razor" principle says: "When choosing between two paths, chose the path that has a larger luck surface area." This optimization involves a comprehensive understanding of risk-reward ratios, extensive knowledge of market dynamics, and prudent investment strategies. By mastering these aspects, an investor can improve the odds of success, turning what seems like "luck" into a product of skill and strategy.

In the investing world, separating the effects of skill and luck — signal and noise — can often be challenging. The success of an investment might come down to fortuitous timing or a stroke of luck, such as a sudden market shift or an unexpected technological breakthrough. At the same time, the investor's acumen, strategic planning, and thoughtful risk management play a significant role in the long-term trajectory of their investment portfolio. In considering luck, it's crucial to understand its role as an equalizer and a differentiator. In the short term, luck can be the deciding factor between two similar investment opportunities. However, over the long term, the effects of luck tend to average out, and skill becomes a more dominant factor. This principle underscores the importance of patience and diversification in investment strategies. If you have a larger "N" of investments, luck will probably play a less important role.

The paradox of skill states that in activities where both skill and luck contribute to outcomes, as skill level increases, luck becomes more important in determining results. This paradox is particularly pertinent in the investment landscape, where many players possess high skill levels, and the competition is intense. As more players gain access to advanced investment tools, analytical capabilities, and knowledge, the differential skill level decreases, and the role of luck in securing superior returns becomes more prominent. Understanding this paradox can guide investors in refining their strategies, tempering their expectations, and maintaining humility amid success or failure.

So, acknowledging the role of luck doesn't imply relinquishing control or adopting a passive investment strategy. Instead, investors can build strategies that maximize potential returns under varying scenarios, hedging against risks while remaining open to fortuitous opportunities. Diversification, hedging, scenario planning and stress testing can be useful tools in this endeavor, allowing investors to anticipate a range of potential outcomes and understand how their investments would fare in different situations. Montecarlo analysis might be useful as well, and I urge the reader to note the concept in the chapters about algorithmic thinking.

Understanding and embracing the role of luck in investing also encourages a flexible and adaptive mindset, crucial in the rapidly changing, complex field of investing. By staying nimble, investors can quickly capitalize on unexpected opportunities and mitigate unforeseen risks, ultimately steering their own luck in the investing world.

Understanding Truth: The Keystone of Decision-Making

Truth can often be a malleable concept, influenced by personal beliefs, biases, market sentiments, and even hype. However, seeking objectivity and truth is paramount to developing clear, informed strategies. This pursuit of truth involves a critical assessment of data, rigorous verification of facts, and a continual reevaluation of assumptions.

In scientific and technological innovations, the notion of truth takes on an additional layer of complexity. It is not merely about market dynamics or financial metrics; it delves into the laws of nature, the principles of science, and the feasibility of technological advances. Truth here is inextricably tied to empirical evidence and scientific rigor.

Confirmation bias refers to the human tendency to seek, interpret, and recall information in a way that validates preexisting beliefs or hypotheses. It is a pervasive cognitive bias that can significantly skew our understanding of reality and our decision-making process. This bias manifests in various forms in the investment domain: The types of research papers read, the quotes underlined in a book, the advice sought from others, even the data points considered in an analysis can all be influenced by one's preconceptions. An investor might be more prone to acknowledging information that supports their investment thesis and dismissing contradictory evidence.

We get now to the importance of seeking truth. Science-driven startups operate at the nexus of business and scientific research. They are tasked not only with creating viable business models but also with pushing the boundaries of scientific knowledge. To be successful, these startups must instill a culture of rigorous truth-seeking, which

Figure 12. Understanding Bias

Here's a list of several types of bias that can affect scientific research and a brief description of how they work:

1. **Confirmation Bias:** This bias is the tendency to seek, interpret, and remember information in a way that confirms pre-existing beliefs or theories, thereby ignoring contrary evidence. This can lead to skewed results in scientific studies and hamper the discovery of true underlying phenomena.
2. **Selection Bias:** This refers to the inappropriate selection of individuals, groups, or data for analysis in such a way that proper randomization is not achieved. It can result in findings that are not representative of the population intended to be analyzed, thus leading to incorrect conclusions.
3. **Publication Bias:** This is the tendency for researchers, editors, and pharmaceutical companies to handle the reporting of experimental results that are positive (i.e., showing a significant finding) differently from results that are negative (i.e., supporting the null hypothesis) or inconclusive, leading to a bias in the available literature.
4. **Observer Bias:** Also known as "experimenter bias," this is the tendency for observers or researchers to unconsciously influence the results of a study due to cognitive biases, expectations, or knowledge about the hypothesis. This bias can lead to inaccurate data collection and interpretation.
5. **Sampling Bias:** This occurs when the data collected or chosen for research does not accurately represent the intended population. It can lead to results that are systematically biased, as they are based on a non-representative sample.
6. **Hindsight Bias:** Also known as the "knew-it-all-along" effect, this is the tendency to perceive past events as having been predictable. In science, it can affect the interpretation of results and the formulation of future hypotheses.
7. **Funding Bias:** This occurs when the source of funding for the research can influence the outcomes, consciously or unconsciously. Research funded by entities with vested interests may be more likely to report results favorable to their product or position.

All these biases can significantly affect the results of scientific studies, demonstrating the importance of rigor, transparency, and adherence to the scientific method to minimize their impact.

involves questioning assumptions, scrutinizing data, and rigorously testing hypotheses.

Practices to actively counter confirmation bias may include rigorous peer review processes, structured debates, and decision-making frameworks that ensure diverse perspectives are considered. They also foster a culture where changing one's mind in the face of new evidence is valued over clinging to outdated beliefs. They are important here, believe me. Understanding and actively seeking truth is not only a scientific necessity but a competitive advantage in the innovation economy.

Rule #9

Prioritize Your Critical Path

"I will not follow where the path may lead, but will go where there is no path, and I will leave a trail."
Muriel Strode's "Wind-Wafted Wild Flowers"

The critical path is a strategic concept that encapsulates the sequence of necessary and interdependent steps that must be completed to achieve a specific goal, usually tied to creating value within an organization or a project. This concept originates from project management, where it is used to schedule and manage complex tasks. However, its utility extends beyond project timelines; it is also instrumental in developing a company's strategic direction, allocating resources, and evaluating progress.

Understanding the critical path is crucial in the complex and often unpredictable world of science-driven entrepreneurship. It provides entrepreneurs with clarity on what needs to be done and when, and, more importantly, what adds great value and what adds less meaningful value, helping them prioritize tasks that contribute directly to their goals.

For investors, recognizing the critical path offers a lens through which to evaluate potential investments, monitor progress, and identify potential roadblocks or opportunities. Tranches in an investment, for example, tend to be linked to the critical path.

In this chapter, we will delve deeper into the concept of the critical path, exploring its importance in different settings and illustrating its application through practical examples. We'll differentiate between a technology platform and a pipeline platform — a distinction vital to understanding the unique critical paths in the biotech industry. We'll also discuss tasks outside the critical path and the role of flexibility in navigating this strategic roadmap. Through these discussions, I aim to provide readers with a comprehensive understanding of the critical path and its pivotal role in value creation.

The Concept of the Critical Path

Investors and entrepreneurs alike must be able to identify, articulate, and navigate the critical path to effectively pursue their goals, so you need to start training your eye to recognize the critical path of any company. That means visualizing all the necessary steps — and none of the unnecessary ones — to reaching a specific predefined and important milestone.

To define a critical path, we need to know where we want to go. Investors use the critical path as a lens to evaluate what is important in potential investments. A clear critical path provides a roadmap that demonstrates how an entrepreneur or business intends to convert resources into value. It outlines the milestones to be achieved and sets a timeline for each, making it an effective tool for monitoring progress and managing expectations. A well-defined critical path can significantly enhance an investor's confidence; a fuzzy or unrealistic critical path can be a red flag signaling potential issues down the line.

Entrepreneurs, on the other hand, use the critical path as a strategic planning tool. It helps them prioritize tasks, allocate resources effectively, and keep their team focused on the steps that are most important for reaching their goals. Understanding and articulating the critical path can also be crucial in securing investment, as it demonstrates the entrepreneur's strategic thinking and plan for creating value.

In science-driven sectors such as biotech, the critical path often depends on whether the company operates as a technology platform or a pipeline platform. As we discussed earlier, a technology platform company leverages its scientific or technological expertise as a product in itself. The critical path for such a company would typically involve steps like advancing the technology, protecting intellectual property, finding market applications, and applying the very same technology to see it shine in the form of a proof of concept (PoC).

Conversely, a pipeline platform employs a specific technology or tool to address a range of distinct clinical or practical needs. For such companies, the critical path usually involves a series of scientific and regulatory milestones, like preclinical studies, regulatory approval, and clinical trials. Thus, the concept of the critical path, while universally applicable, can take on different forms depending on the specific context.

To better understand the concept of the critical path in the context of a science-driven company, let's consider a hypothetical case study of a biotech firm that utilizes a specific genome editing tool to develop treatments for diverse genetic disorders. Here's a simple perspective of the major areas to pay attention to in its clinical path:

Preclinical Studies: The critical path begins with preclinical studies, during which the firm tests the effectiveness of their genome editing tool on disease models in the laboratory. These studies are designed to provide preliminary evidence of the technology's potential for therapeutic application (PoC in animal models). Failure at this stage could send the firm back to the drawing board for modifications to their therapy candidate.

Regulatory Approval for Clinical Trials: If the preclinical studies show positive results, the next critical step involves completing the "regulatory" preclinical with all the required mandatory studies to prove safety, efficacy, drug formulation and stability, manufacturing information, and many other things, submitting the findings to regulatory bodies, such as the FDA or the EMA, for approval to proceed with clinical trials on human subjects. This stage can involve meticulous preparation of documentation and rigorous scrutiny by regulatory authorities. Approval signifies that the authorities are satisfied with the evidence of safety and potential efficacy presented in the preclinical data.

Clinical Trials: Upon receiving regulatory approval, the firm can initiate clinical trials. Clinical trials are usually divided into three phases:

- **Phase 1 trials** test the safety and dosage of the therapy in a small group of healthy volunteers.
- **Phase 2 trials** further investigate safety and start to evaluate efficacy in a homogeneous and controlled small group of patients.

- **Phase 3 trials** confirm efficacy and monitor side effects in heterogeneous large groups of patients.

Each phase presents its own challenges and requires successful completion before moving on to the next. Failure to show safety or efficacy at any stage can halt the entire process.

Market Approval and Commercialization: If the therapy proves safe and effective in clinical trials, the firm will seek final market approval from regulatory bodies. Upon approval, the firm can start manufacturing and distributing the therapy, marking the final critical step in this path.

In this sequence of crucial steps, it's worth highlighting the multiple intricate components that contribute directly to the final value. Certain steps will be essential (and fall within the critical path), while others will not. Understanding regulatory requirements, the specific condition being treated, and the technology's characteristics is crucial to distinguish between the two. For instance, in the preclinical stage, a multitude of detailed toxicology and safety studies may play a significant role. They include:

Acute Toxicity Studies: These studies evaluate the adverse effects of a single exposure to the drug. The study is designed to help establish a safe starting dose for the first-in-human clinical trials.

Toxicity Studies: These studies assess the adverse effects of repeated exposures to the drug over a longer period. They help identify any potential long-term effects that might not be evident after a single dose.

Genotoxicity Studies: These studies test whether the drug could damage the genetic information within a cell, causing mutations that might lead to cancer.

Carcinogenicity Studies: These studies are carried out to assess whether the drug has the potential to cause cancer after long-term exposure.

Reproductive and Developmental Toxicity Studies: These studies are conducted to determine potential adverse effects on reproductive capability and the developing embryo or fetus.

Safety Pharmacology Studies: These studies aim to assess whether the drug could adversely affect physiological functions such as the cardiovascular, nervous, and respiratory systems.

Immunotoxicity Studies: These studies examine the potential of the drug to affect the immune system, either by suppressing it, which could increase susceptibility to infections and cancers, or overstimulating it, which could lead to allergic or autoimmune diseases.

All these studies (by all means not a comprehensive list) are designed to ascertain if the therapy is safe for human trials, identifying possible side effects, and determining safe dosage levels. Positive results from these studies not only boost investor confidence but also pave the way for regulatory approval — both significant value-drivers for the firm.

Yet, it is important to note that not everything that appears interesting or meaningful is directly tied to the outcome. For example, exploring additional applications of the genome editing tool beyond the targeted genetic disorders might be scientifically exciting, but may not necessarily contribute directly to the critical path of bringing a specific therapy to market.

In an ideal world, we would love to explore every single detail and leave no stone unturned. However, capital is not infinite, and investors and entrepreneurs need to strike a delicate balance. They must determine what to incorporate into the plan even if some elements do not directly contribute to the critical path. Sometimes, these elements could bring unexpected positive externalities that could significantly affect the final outcome.

The tug of war between the necessity of thorough scientific exploration and the constraints of finite resources is a common one in science-driven startups. Scientists are curious; investors are pragmatic. Balancing these opposing forces is more of an art than a science, and those who master it can often uncover efficiencies, mitigate risks, and maximize the value potential of their efforts. Thus, a balanced approach that optimizes the allocation of resources and efforts toward the most impactful areas while allowing some room for exploring additional possibilities, often results in the most favorable outcomes.

Tasks Outside the Critical Path: Opportunities and Pitfalls

Let's go deeper, then. As we just discussed, while the primary focus of a science-driven company should be on the activities that constitute its critical path, other tasks and opportunities, although they don't directly contribute to the current path, can still have significant benefits for the company. These tasks fall outside the critical path and can include a wide range of activities, such as partnership discussions, auxiliary research projects, or even side ventures.

These additional concepts and terminology might help readers understanding the required mindset:

Beneficial or Desirable Tasks: These tasks may not be strictly necessary for the company to achieve its immediate goals but can provide additional value or advantages. For example, an early-stage business development deal with a pharmaceutical company may not expedite regulatory approval but could provide additional funding, broaden the company's network, or offer opportunities for future collaborations.

Externalities: Tasks outside the critical path can sometimes change the course of a company's trajectory. For instance, a side research project, although not part of the initial plan, could yield a breakthrough that significantly enhances the company's value proposition or opens up new markets. This potential for unexpected value makes these tasks worth considering.

Balancing Act: Managing tasks outside the critical path is a delicate balancing act. On one hand, they can offer the chance to explore new opportunities or create additional value. On the other hand, they can also distract from the primary mission and drain resources. This is the eternal problem of focus. These types of tension underscore the need for careful decision-making and prioritization.

Risk Management: An essential part of this process involves evaluating the potential risks associated with tasks outside the critical path. While they can provide unique opportunities, they also can lead to setbacks if not managed properly. Consider, for example, what happens if our results in some research outside the critical path, or even worse, in a collaboration with a third party, show poor results. That indeed may damage the company's reputation.

The ability to be flexible and adaptable is a significant strategic advantage. Many successful science-driven companies have used flexibility to their advantage. They've pursued tasks outside their critical path, which led to breakthroughs, effective partnerships, or new market opportunities. While these tasks required resources and attention that could have been used on immediate goals, the resulting rewards often justified the investment.

Strategic Partnerships and Collaborations Shape the Critical Path in Cutting-Edge Fields

As we tread deeper into the era of rapid technological evolution, one principle stands out in the business realm: No organization can thrive in isolation. The complexities of today's challenges demand integrated solutions, often beyond the capacities of a single entity. This holds particularly true for fields like biotech, where the intersection of multiple disciplines is intrinsic to progress. Strategic partnerships and collaborations have thus become not just beneficial but essential in shaping the critical path toward value creation.

Strategic partnerships enable organizations to pool resources, share expertise, and drive innovation. They provide the unique opportunity to leverage complementary skills and capabilities, providing an impetus to the overall progression along the critical path. In biotech, these partnerships often involve collaborations with research institutions, pharmaceutical companies, tech companies, or even other biotech firms.

For instance, a biotech startup might partner with a research institution to access special enabling technology, state-of-the-art laboratories, specialized equipment, or experienced researchers. These resources can expedite preclinical studies and early-stage research, vital steps on the critical path of a pipeline platform company. Without such a partnership, the company might face significant delays or financial burdens in arranging these resources independently.

Collaborations with pharmaceutical companies can also play a crucial role in the later stages of the critical path. Pharmaceutical companies can offer financial support, regulatory expertise, established distribution networks for clinical trials, or even "build-to-buy" deals opening the window for a liquidity event.

For a biotech firm aiming to bring a novel therapy to market, these partnerships can significantly accelerate progress and reduce risks. Yet, while the potential benefits are substantial, forming and managing strategic partnerships is a complex process that requires careful planning and execution. Effective partnerships are founded on mutual benefits, shared objectives, clear communication, and a robust legal framework. Trust and transparency are the bedrocks of these relationships. It's also vital to maintain a balance between dependence on partners and maintaining organizational autonomy, to ensure the company can adapt to changes in the market or the partnership.

Moreover, collaborations can have implications on the company's intellectual property (IP) rights. When two or more entities work together, issues like ownership of new IP, sharing of existing IP, and protection of proprietary information must be addressed upfront. A well-drafted collaboration agreement can help delineate these issues and prevent future disputes.

Interdisciplinary Integration in the Critical Path

Innovative and cutting-edge fields often require a convergence of disciplines to drive breakthroughs and advancements. Biotech, for instance, relies heavily on insights and methods from biology, chemistry, physics, engineering, computer science, and even artificial intelligence. As a result, a critical path in these fields often involves integrating multiple areas of expertise. This integration, while crucial for innovation, comes with its own set of challenges and requires strategic coordination.

The first challenge in interdisciplinary integration lies in the diversity of knowledge and terminology. Every discipline has its own specialized jargon and methodologies that may not be readily understood by individuals from another field. Miscommunication or misunderstanding can result in lost time, effort, and resources.

One strategy to tackle this challenge is to facilitate regular knowledge-sharing sessions and promote an environment of learning within the team. Encouraging team members to explain concepts in accessible language can help build a shared understanding.

The second challenge is in bridging different perspectives and approaches to problem-solving. Each discipline brings its unique viewpoint and sometimes, these different perspectives can lead to conflict. However, these diverse viewpoints can also be of course an asset if harnessed effectively. Developing a culture of open dialogue, mutual respect, and collaboration can help in leveraging these diverse perspectives to drive innovation.

Another challenge is the distribution of resources among different disciplines. Some fields may require more resources than others, leading to potential imbalance and conflict. To manage this challenge, leaders should ensure transparent and equitable resource allocation, justified by clearly defined roles and objectives within the critical path.

Lastly, the pace of advancements in different disciplines can vary, which can affect the overall timeline and progress. A delay in one field can hold back progress in others. Coordinating these timelines requires effective project management and flexibility. The use of project management tools and regular progress updates can help in synchronizing these diverse timelines.

A Guiding Compass

As we conclude this exploration of the critical path concept, it becomes apparent that the significance of this tool extends beyond merely charting a course for a project or a business venture. The critical path acts as a compass, guiding resource allocation, driving strategic decisions, and ultimately, propelling value creation.

- **Balance and Judgment:** Not all tasks on the critical path hold equal weight, and not all tasks outside of it are extraneous. It's a leader's judgment that determines which tasks are indispensable for the business's present goals and which ones have potential for future growth, even if they currently seem tangential.
- **Strategic Agility:** The real value of understanding the critical path comes with the ability to demonstrate strategic agility. It is the capacity to adapt and respond to changes while keeping the company aligned with its core objectives and mission. This involves acknowledging the potential impact of tasks outside the critical path without losing focus on the primary goals.
- **The Path to Innovation:** It's worth noting that the flexibility to explore tasks outside of the critical path often leads to innovation. Many groundbreaking discoveries have been made in the pursuit of seemingly peripheral projects. So, while maintaining focus on the critical path, a degree of exploratory freedom can yield unexpected dividends.
- **The Bigger Picture:** Finally, understanding and implementing the critical path is not only about reaching a particular end point successfully. It's about navigating the ever-changing landscapes of science.

Rule #10

The Gap Analysis

"Art is not freedom from discipline, but disciplined freedom."
Father Edward Catich

Even though this chapter may appear similar to the previous chapter on the critical path, it is quite different. The critical path is about identifying the steps that are crucial for value creation; gap analysis involves training our minds to identify the things that are missing and could stall us or even derail us.

At its core, gap analysis is a tool widely used by analysts and partners at a venture capital fund to pinpoint what is missing or could be improved in a business strategy. It assesses the difference between the current state of the business and where they want it to be, essentially highlighting the "gaps."

For investors, a gap analysis is an invaluable asset, particularly when considering early-stage companies. Why? Because it unveils not just what's present in a business plan but also what's absent. It's like having a checklist where you're not only ticking off what's there, you're also adding things that ought to be there.

Far from being a one-and-done exercise, gap analysis is a recurring process. As a business adapts to changes in the market, technology, or regulatory requirements, new gaps can appear while old ones may close. A gap analysis, therefore, must be revisited regularly as it serves as a constant feedback mechanism to ensure that a business keeps moving toward its objectives.

Identifying gaps is just one part of the equation. The real value of gap analysis comes from what you do after you identify the gaps. Many

Figure 13. A Typical Gantt Chart

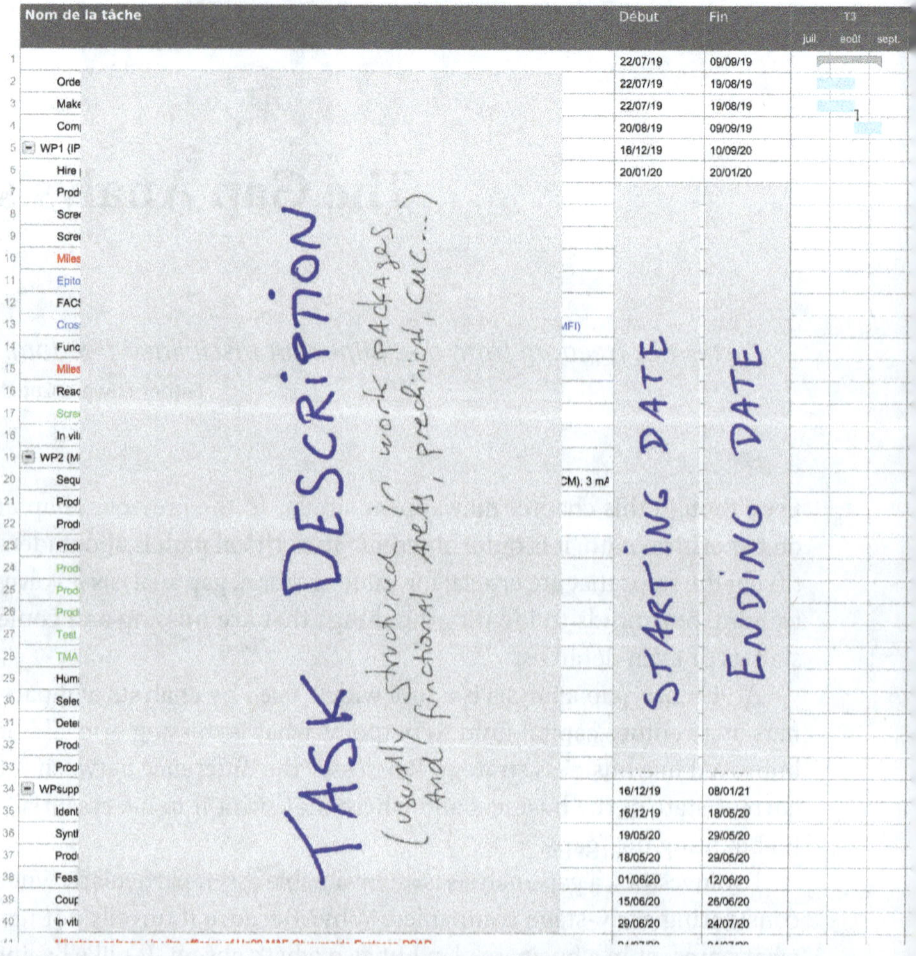

This figure presents a typical Gantt chart, with specific names and sections altered or concealed to preserve confidentiality. The arrangement of the tasks on the chart makes their dependencies on one another visually clear, offering a comprehensive view of how the various tasks interconnect. Moreover, Gantt charts often incorporate cost estimates for each task, giving a bird's eye view of the project's financial landscape.

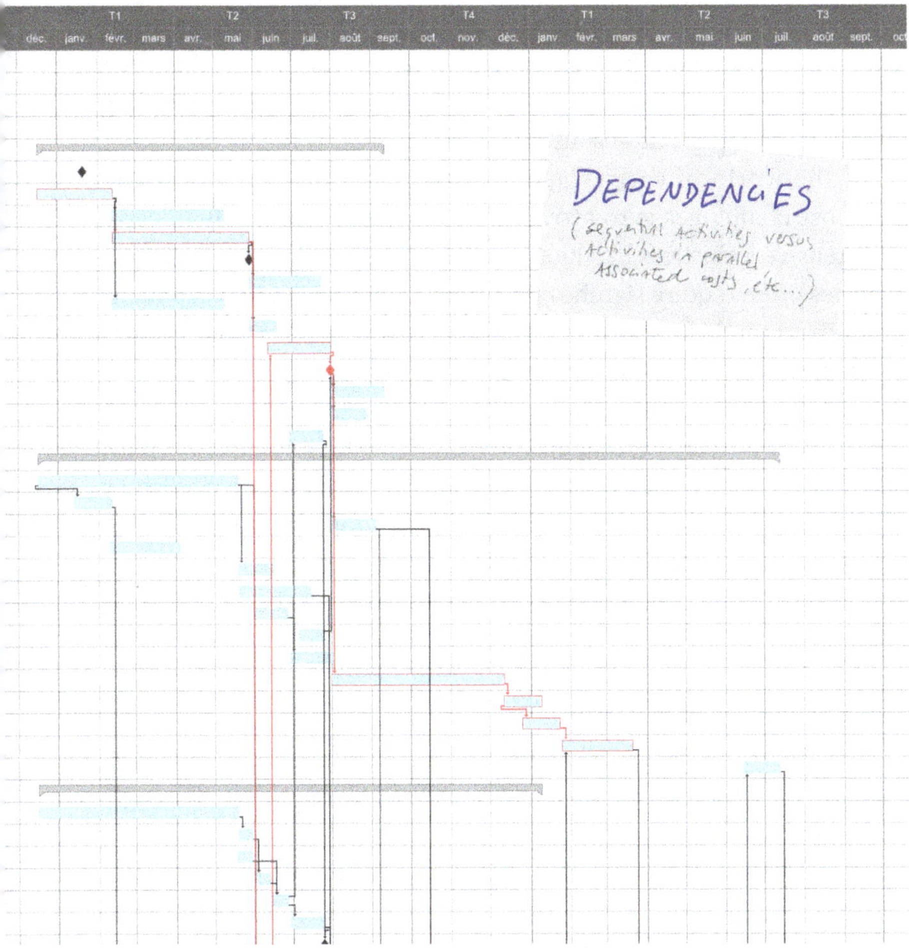

The tasks or activities, which are the critical steps of the development path and CMC processes, are listed on the vertical axis. They are usually broken down into more granular steps. For instance, preclinical proof of concept may be divided into experimental design, execution, data analysis, and report writing. The horizontal axis represents time, with the length of each bar corresponding to the estimated duration of each task. This provides a clear overview of the sequence and overlap of tasks, helping us to understand the interdependencies and the critical path that can't be delayed without affecting the overall timeline.

In an even more sophisticated version of this Gantt chart, each task would also be associated with its estimated costs, providing a powerful tool for budgeting and capital needs forecasting. With this information, we can visually conceptualize how altering timelines, streamlining processes, or renegotiating contracts could potentially impact the overall budget and financing needs.

investors typically add a lot of value here. It's like knowing where the destination is, but without a roadmap or directions you will get stopped before you get where you wanted to go. That's where actionable strategies come into play. These strategies, informed by the insights from the gap analysis, lay out clear steps for bridging the gaps, providing direction for teams and resources.

In the world of early-stage investments, one of the first and foremost challenges is to attract new investors, especially in capital-intensive industries like biotech or AI. The reason is simple: Such ventures often require significant upfront capital to develop products, conduct research, or scale operations. At this stage, a company might not have a track record of success or substantial revenue to back it up. What it does have is potential.

This is where attracting all the right investors comes into play. Investors with a keen eye for potential can provide the necessary capital, as well as guidance and networking opportunities. In such a scenario, a comprehensive gap analysis becomes an even more important tools to guarantee the company will do a good job at their next pitch.

The Concept of a Gantt Chart

In the realm of project management, critical paths, and gap analysis, a Gantt chart serves as an invaluable visual aid. It's akin to having a bird's-eye view of your project.

Named after its inventor, Henry Gantt, a Gantt chart is a horizontal bar chart that graphically represents a project timeline. Each task in the project is represented by a bar; the position and length of the bar reflect the start date, duration, and end date of the task.

In the context of biotech, which often involves complex, long-term projects such as clinical trials or drug development, a Gantt chart can provide a clear, visual representation of the entire project lifecycle.

One of the primary benefits of a Gantt chart is its ability to highlight task dependencies. In the complex world of biotech, where a single project might involve numerous tasks spread across multiple teams, understanding dependencies — which tasks rely on others for their completion — is vital. A delay in a single task can cascade down the dependency chain, affecting the entire project. Similarly, a Gantt chart can highlight the sequence of tasks that must be completed on time for the project to finish on schedule. By visually mapping these dependencies, a Gantt chart can help manage and mitigate potential delays, aiding in efficient project execution.

A Broader View: Gap Analysis in Biotech

In the field of biotech entrepreneurship, the importance of regulatory compliance cannot be overstated. Regulations provide a framework of safety and efficacy standards that biotech companies must meet in their research, development, and manufacturing processes. These standards protect public health and assure the quality and reliability of biotech products. Failure to meet these regulations can result in halted development and severe penalties, including fines, product recalls, and loss of public trust.

Moreover, regulatory compliance is often a key criterion for investors, who are keen to avoid the risks of a halted program associated with regulatory non-compliance.

A gap analysis serves as an essential tool for achieving and maintaining regulatory compliance. It provides a systematic way to compare a company's current practices against the required regulatory standards. By identifying gaps in compliance, it allows a company to rectify them before they lead to problems.

However, it's not just about whether the study is being conducted or not, but also about whether it's being done correctly. A gap analysis should identify missing but also poorly performed experiments. This could involve determining the need for additional animal models, different endpoints to detect an effect, varied timepoints, or different arms in the analysis.

It can also be instrumental in revising the production steps of a drug, checking for any oversights or errors in CMC (chemistry, manufacturing and control) processes that ensure the drug's quality.

Biotech is an industry where intellectual property (IP) and human capital can make or break a company. A gap analysis also can reveal critical mistakes in the IP strategy, such as insufficient patent protection.

Moreover, by reviewing the company's current providers, a gap analysis may suggest the need for higher stature providers, which

Figure 14. Example of Gap Analysis in Biotech: CMC Checklist

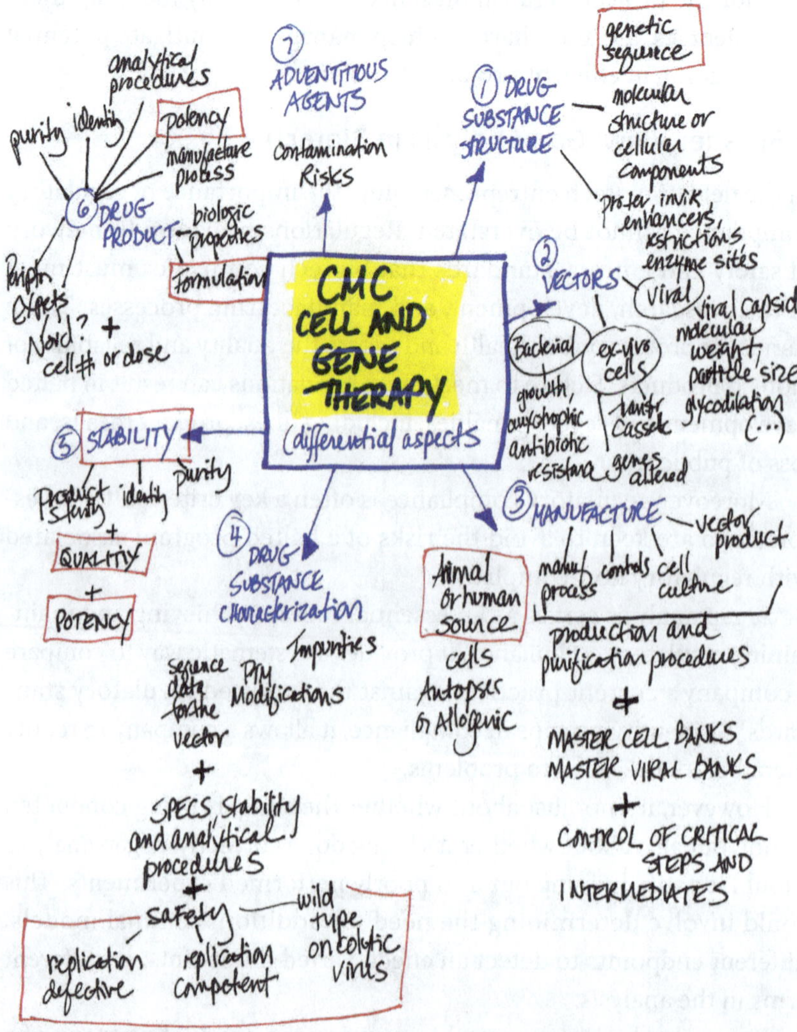

As investors in the cutting-edge field of biotech, two primary areas demand our intense scrutiny when conducting a gap analysis: the development critical path and the chemistry, manufacturing, and control (CMC) processes.

It's in these stages that we assess the scientific validity, regulatory alignment, and potential effectiveness of the drug under investigation. Equally critical is the CMC process, where the quality of the drug intended for patient trials is tested. This process scrutinizes the drug's manufacture to ensure that it's made in a way that meets rigorous quality standards. Together, a thorough analysis of these processes helps us make informed investment decisions in the rapidly evolving world of biotech.

This figure offers a detailed breakdown of a typical checklist used when performing a gap analysis for CMC in cell and gene therapy. The analysis is divided into seven key components, each representing a distinct part of the process.

- **Drug Substance Structure:** This section involves a meticulous inspection of the molecular structure or the cellular components of the drug. The checklist may include items like promoter, introns, enhancers, restriction enzyme sites, and the genetic sequence.
- **Vectors:** Here, specific characteristics of the vector used are considered. Whether it's viral, involving elements such as viral capsid, molecular weight, particle size, and glyco- sylation; or ex vivo cells, checking the transgene cassette, altered genes, and more. For bacterial vectors, growth, auxotrophic issues, antibiotic resistance, and inserted foreign genes are checked.
- **Manufacturing:** This section assesses the source of the drug (animal or human), with further examination if the cells are autologous or allogeneic. Manufacturing processes, controls, cell cultures, vector production, along with any master cell or viral banks, are closely scrutinized.
- **Drug Substance Characterization:** In this stage, data related to the drug substance's sequence, specifications, stability, and analytical procedures are gathered. Safety parameters, such as the drug's replication defectiveness or competence, are examined.
- **Stability:** An evaluation of the product's sterility, identity, purity, quality, and potency is undertaken in this section.
- **Drug Product:** A continuation from the previous stage, it further investigates the purity, identity, analytical procedures, and potency of the drug product. This stage also includes checks on the manufacturing process, biological properties, formulation, and excipients, evaluating their novelty.
- **Adventitious Agents:** The final part of the checklist involves a review for adventitious agents to assess any potential contamination risk.

This outlined checklist serves as an illustrative guide, emphasizing a structured, logical approach towards a gap analysis for CMC in cell and gene therapy. It is by no means exhaustive but aims to provide the reader with an overview of the mindset required for conducting this kind of rigorous analysis.

can enhance the credibility, reliability, and success of the company's operations.

One of the key benefits of gap analysis used in combination with critical path analysis is its ability to streamline processes, thereby saving time and increasing chances of success. For instance, gap analysis can shorten the time needed to get an authorization for first-in-human (FIH) trials, a critical milestone in drug development. Likewise, it can help accelerate the various phases of clinical trials by identifying potential efficiencies, eliminating unnecessary steps, or suggesting parallel workflows.

Through its ability to highlight gaps and provide insights on how to address them, gap analysis can enhance the efficiency and effectiveness of a biotech company's operations, ultimately leading to a higher probability of success.

A Broader View: Gap Analysis in AI

In the rapidly evolving world of artificial intelligence (AI), gap analysis plays a pivotal role in optimizing processes and ensuring robust, safe deployment of AI models. As in any other field, AI development involves a series of steps, from data collection and preprocessing to model training, validation, red-taping and deployment.

A gap analysis in this context could identify potential improvements in each of these steps. For example, it could reveal opportunities to shorten the time for training a model through more efficient algorithms or parallel processing. Similarly, it could suggest strategies for more robust model validation, reducing the risk of overfitting or underfitting.

Furthermore, gap analysis could propose measures for safe and robust deployment, such as better error handling, fail-safe mechanisms, or system redundancy.

AI, with its transformative potential, also will bring in the near future a host of regulatory and ethical considerations. From data privacy and algorithmic bias to the potential misuse of AI, these challenges require careful thought and proactive oversight.

A gap analysis can play a crucial role here by identifying discrepancies between a company's current AI practices and the regulatory and ethical standards it will need to meet. It might reveal gaps in data privacy measures, such as inadequate anonymization or data protection protocols. Alternatively, it could highlight what is missing to achieve a more transparent and explainable AI models to combat algorithmic bias.

By addressing these gaps, companies will not only ensure regulatory compliance but also build trust with their customers and the broader public, ultimately contributing to the responsible and beneficial development of AI.

Rule #11

Take the Right Initial Steps to Make It Happen

"The most important thing in art is The Frame.... Because without this humble appliance, you can't know where The Art stops and The Real World begins. You have to put a 'box' around it because otherwise, what is that shit on the wall?"

Frank Zappa

Venturing into the world of biotech — or any other science-driven discipline for that matter — can be akin to embarking on an expedition into unknown territories. The terrain is challenging, the competition is fierce, and the stakes are high. However, with the right preparation and mindset, this journey can yield groundbreaking innovations and considerable rewards. For scientists poised to make this leap, here are six critical factors to consider.

1. Understand the Biotech Ecosystem and Its Rules

The biotechnology sector is a vast and complex landscape of scientific research, product development, financial investments, and governmental regulation. It is a field where ground-breaking ideas come to fruition and have the potential to drastically alter human life for the better.

If you're considering embarking on a journey into this exciting sector, the first step in your journey is to familiarize yourself with the broader biotech ecosystem. Understanding what creates and destroys value within this space is essential. It's crucial to recognize why venture capitalists (VCs) prefer certain types of problems. They favor solutions addressing significant clinical needs, those that follow accelerated regulatory pathways, and propositions that offer a substantial improvement in patient outcomes. Understanding these preferences will guide your positioning strategy within the industry.

Value within the biotech sector is largely derived from the ability to innovate and deliver solutions that address significant clinical needs. As you delve deeper into the ecosystem, you'll discover that the industry thrives on novel ideas that have the potential to revolutionize healthcare. For instance, the advent of personalized medicine, gene therapies, and digital health technologies have shifted paradigms and ushered in new possibilities for patient care. Value creation also goes hand in hand with the ability to navigate complex regulatory pathways.

Understanding the specific regulations that govern your area of interest, be it drug discovery, diagnostics, medical devices, or digital health, can significantly expedite the process of translating an idea into a viable product or service. Moreover, being aware of potential accelerations in these regulatory pathways, like the FDA's Fast Track, Breakthrough Therapy, and Priority Review designations, can potentially bring your solutions to the market more quickly, thereby increasing value.

VCs prefer problems that are ambitious yet grounded in rigorous science and have a clear path to clinical application. The nature of the problem should also lend itself to the development of a proprietary solution, as this can provide a significant competitive advantage and a potential source of value creation. However, the risk associated with innovation is high, making the scientific rigor of your approach a crucial factor in attracting VC investment.

Additionally, the biotech ecosystem is inherently collaborative. A startup might not have all the resources or expertise needed to bring a product to market, so partnerships and collaborations can be instrumental. Successful biotech entrepreneurs often form strategic partnerships with universities for research, established pharma companies for development and marketing, and contract research organizations for clinical trials. Understanding the dynamics and benefits of these partnerships is another key aspect of comprehending the biotech ecosystem.

To effectively position your venture within the industry, you must understand the market you're entering, identify your unique selling proposition, and communicate this effectively to stakeholders. This involves conducting comprehensive market research, understanding the competitive landscape, and being able to clearly articulate your value proposition.

2. Understand Your Company

Understanding the intricacies of your own venture is a crucial next step in your journey within the biotech industry. This involves several key areas:

First, your venture should be rooted in a deep understanding of the science underlying your specific area of focus. This necessitates identifying the key unresolved questions within your field that could potentially yield transformative clinical solutions. Whether your focus is on novel drug discovery, developing innovative medical devices, or leveraging AI for diagnosis, your project's foundation should address an unmet clinical need. Ensuring that your venture's mission aligns with answering these key questions could guide your research and development efforts more effectively.

Once you've identified the fundamental scientific question driving your venture, you must thoroughly comprehend the current strategies being employed to tackle your specific clinical need. What technologies, therapies, or interventions are currently being used or developed? Where do the gaps lie, and what are the limitations of existing solutions? Conducting a thorough review of the current landscape not only helps you understand your competition but also enables you to identify opportunities for innovation.

The third aspect involves introspection — assessing your company's unique value proposition. What sets you apart from other players in the field? It could be your team's unique expertise, proprietary technology, a novel approach to problem-solving, or access to a specific patient population. It's essential to clearly articulate this uniqueness and leverage it to your advantage.

In the world of biotech, your value proposition often goes hand-in-hand with your intellectual property (IP) strategy. A well-defined IP strategy can provide a strong competitive edge and act as a shield

Figure 15. Things to Consider When Starting-Up: Part 1

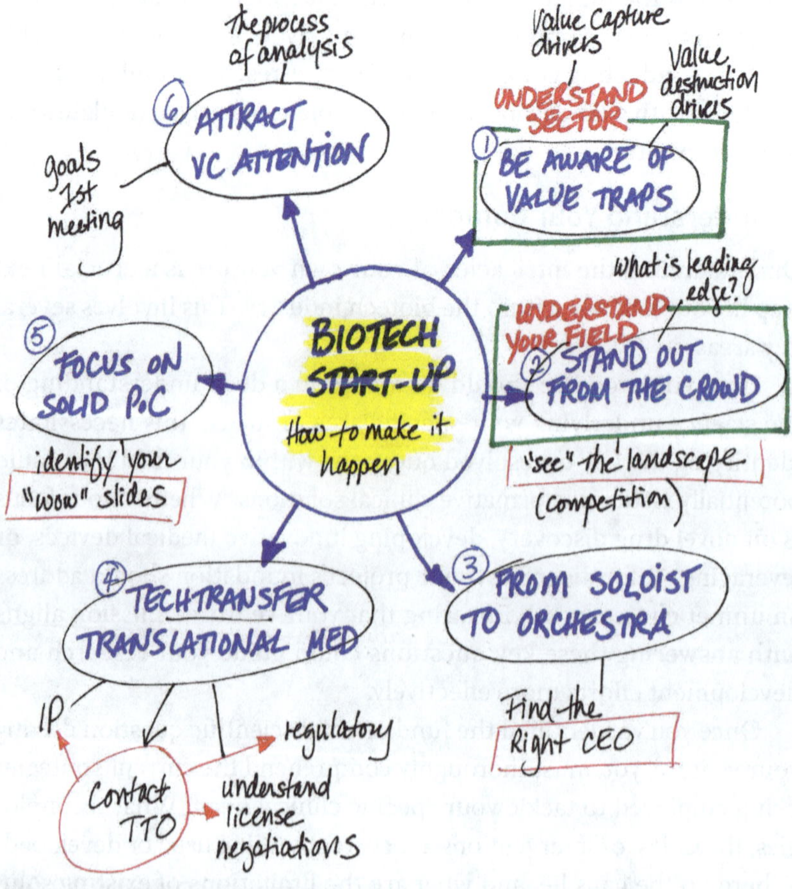

When embarking on a new project in science-driven companies, keep several key considerations in mind. These considerations are not merely checkpoints to cross off a list; rather, they are pivotal components that can influence the trajectory and eventual outcome of your venture. Whether you're attempting to capture value while avoiding pitfalls, distinguishing your venture from competitors, assembling the right team, navigating intellectual property rights, demonstrating a convincing proof of concept, or attracting venture capital attention, these considerations can serve as guideposts to steer your journey.

1. **Be Aware of Value Traps:** Developing a thorough understanding of your sector, including its value traps, is fundamental. Value traps refer to attractive-looking investments that may not actually yield a good return. Identify the factors that create value and those that erode it. This will arm you with insights that could shape discussions with venture capitalists. Knowing what brings them profits and what causes losses is key to building a compelling case for your project. This awareness also guides you in decision-making, helping you avoid pitfalls and directing investments toward more fruitful areas.

2. **Stand Out From the Crowd:** Understanding your field isn't enough; you need to differentiate yourself from competitors. Take time to study the landscape, pinpoint your competitors, and assess how you stand out. Perhaps you have a unique approach, superior technology, or an innovative solution to a problem. Use these points of differentiation to emphasize the unique value that you bring and how it could disrupt the market.
3. **From Soloist to Orchestra:** Building the right team is critical to the success of any venture. Gather a group of individuals who not only have the skills and expertise necessary to push the project forward but also complement each other's abilities. Diverse backgrounds and perspectives often lead to more creative problem-solving and robust decision-making. Remember that a successful venture isn't a solo performance — it's an orchestrated effort by a dedicated, synergistic team.
4. **Engage with Your Institution's Technology Transfer Office**: If you're operating within a scientific environment, your institution's Technology Transfer Office can be a significant asset. They can help you navigate complex intellectual property issues, understand regulatory requirements, and even assist with licensing negotiations. Leveraging this support can safeguard your innovations, optimize technology commercialization, and facilitate smoother transitions from laboratory to market.
5. **Develop a Solid Proof of Concept:** Facts and data need to be aligned with a compelling story that resonates with anyone listening to your vision. It's crucial to identify and highlight the "wow" factors in your project — those elements that are likely to leave an impression and captivate potential investors. investors, is also of paramount importance. These elements can range from groundbreaking technology to a unique business model. They serve as key selling points that help your venture stand out in a competitive landscape. However, your venture's nature may influence how you go about this. If your company operates as a technology platform, your focus might be on showcasing the platform's versatility, scalability, and the various applications it can cater to.

   If, on the other hand, your company runs on a pipeline of products, your emphasis should be on demonstrating the potential success of these products, their unique selling points, and how they address unmet needs in the market. In addition, the rigor of science underpinning your venture is crucial. In a field where credibility is key, your venture's foundation should be deeply rooted in sound scientific principles. Clear and accurate data, meticulous research methodology, and stringent adherence to ethical guidelines are just a few aspects that lend credibility to your scientific venture. Not only does this solid scientific foundation increase trust among potential investors, but it also ensures that your venture is positioned for sustainable, long-term success.
6. **Actively Seek Venture Capital Attention:** Reach out to VCs and make your project's strengths known. Be well-prepared for initial meetings. Present a persuasive case that succinctly communicates the value proposition and the potential return on investment. Show them not only why your venture is worth investing in but also how it aligns with their investment strategy. The right investors can provide not only capital but also invaluable guidance and network connections.

Figure 16. Things to Consider When Starting-Up: Part 2

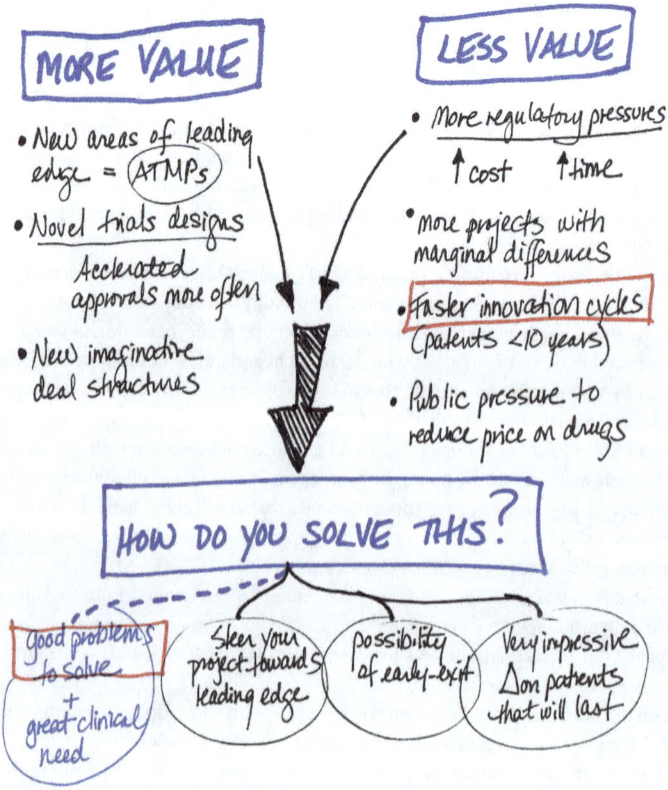

To truly understand value traps, it is crucial to comprehend the mindset of venture capitalists and how they approach the selection of companies. This understanding is essential because certain factors contribute to diminishing value over time. Conversely, some factors can generate increasing value year after year.

Diminishing Value: The biotechnology industry faces a plethora of challenges in the current market scenario. Regulatory pressures, increased development costs, the rapid pace of innovation, a glut of similar projects, and public pressure to reduce drug prices all converge to create an environment that's fraught with difficulties. Let's explore each of these contributing factors in depth.

1. **Regulatory pressures** play a significant role in the value diminishment of new drug development. Regulatory bodies like the U.S. Food and Drug Administration (FDA), European Medicines Agency (EMA), and other international counterparts require rigorous and extensive clinical trials to demonstrate the safety and efficacy of new drugs. The costs associated with these trials are astronomical, as they require extensive data collection, careful patient monitoring, and thorough documentation. The timeline to bring a new drug to market has also lengthened significantly due to increased scrutiny and oversight from regulatory authorities. This lengthy process erodes the period of exclusivity a new drug can enjoy, thereby reducing its potential return on investment. Next, there's the issue of market saturation. The

biotech landscape is rife with myriad projects, many of which bear striking similarities to one another. This clutter makes it increasingly challenging for any single project to stand out and garner the attention and funding it needs to progress. Investors are often presented with an array of options, with only marginal differences between them, that can lead to hesitation and, potentially, a reluctance to invest. This heightened competition reduces the overall value proposition for individual projects.

2. **The rapid pace of innovation** is another crucial factor contributing to the reduction in value. Historically, patents have been a primary mechanism to secure and. maintain value in the biotech and pharmaceutical sectors. They granted exclusive rights to the inventor for a period of 20 years, ensuring a monopoly over the product. However, with the current pace of innovation, a patent's effective lifespan is significantly reduced. In today's innovation landscape, new players continuously enter the market with novel and more valuable solutions, making existing patents obsolete in a much shorter timeframe. This scenario adds to the risk and uncertainty associated with drug development and further diminishes value.
3. Lastly, **public pressure to reduce drug prices** is another significant factor that undermines value. As healthcare costs continue to rise globally, there's growing public and political scrutiny over the high price of new drugs. This pressure often results in price reductions or constraints, which directly impact the return on investment for the pharmaceutical companies and their investors.

Increasing Value:

1. We are currently witnessing the **emergence of new frontiers** in areas like advanced therapies, gene therapy, and cell therapy.
2. Additionally, the **new design of clinical trials** is evolving to keep pace with the rapid development of these advanced therapies. We're seeing an increase in novel trial designs that aim to speed up the regulatory approval process, such as adaptive trials and the use of real-world evidence. These designs allow for more flexibility and faster adaptation to emerging results, reducing the time and cost of drug development. This accelerates the availability of innovative therapies to patients and consequently increases their value.
3. Furthermore, we are seeing an evolution in **deal structures** within the industry. These new and imaginative structures are designed to share risk, maximize the value of assets, and accommodate the high levels of uncertainty. Examples include risk-sharing agreements, outcome-based reimbursement models, and milestone-based payments.

Considering the combination of factors that both diminish and increase value, it is crucial to present a compelling problem to solve, demonstrating a significant clinical need in the industry. Additionally, steering the project towards the cutting edge is vital to maximize its value. Creating the potential for an early exit opportunity can attract investors, and finally, aiming for a substantial and lasting advantage over competitors is essential for long-term success.

against competitors. It is crucial to understand the patent landscape around your technology or therapy and strategize accordingly to protect your unique selling points.

Next, understanding the market dynamics specific to your target therapeutic areas is critical. This entails a deep understanding of the patient populations, the limitations of existing treatment options, and the potential impact of new therapies. It includes factors such as disease prevalence and incidence, patient demographics, the clinical journey of a patient, the cost-effectiveness of existing therapies, and the current standard of care. Also, consider the trends and future directions in the therapeutic area, such as the emergence of personalized medicine or the use of digital health interventions.

Grasping these market dynamics can provide you with valuable insights into your potential customers' needs and wants. It also can help you better position your product or service within the market. Understanding the market dynamics can guide you in making informed decisions about clinical development, regulatory strategy, and marketing and sales strategy.

3. Change Your Mindset from Soloist to Orchestra

Entrepreneurship is not a solo endeavor. The right team can make the difference between success and failure. Initially, your team might be small, but remember that you're building an orchestra, not a one-man band. From identifying the ideal CEO to enlisting seasoned team members with complementary skills and roles, each step in constructing your team is instrumental in navigating the unpredictable waters of entrepreneurship.

Embarking on your venture, one of the first critical decisions involves identifying the ideal CEO. It's crucial to appreciate that the best person for this role might not always be yourself. The most effective CEOs are those who can bring to bear a deep understanding of the biotech landscape, an ability to articulate a compelling vision for the company, and the capacity to motivate and guide a team toward this vision. These individuals ideally should have the tenacity to withstand the inevitable hurdles that accompany the biotech journey, coupled with a successful track record.

Having established strong leadership, the next step involves building the remainder of the team. It's important to remember that a startup's success isn't solely determined by its leadership but also by the collective capabilities and cohesion of its team members. A balanced team composition should involve a diverse mix of roles, including scientific experts, business strategists, operations managers, regulatory specialists, and more. Doers, the individuals who excel in execution, play a crucial role in transforming strategic visions and solutions into tangible outcomes.

In the early stages of your startup, having all required expertise in-house might not be feasible, and this is where strategic outsourcing comes into play. Recognize which aspects of your operations can be effectively outsourced. Tasks such as regulatory affairs, certain research and development functions, and legal services often lend themselves well to this model.

Outsourcing enables startups to access a wealth of expertise and services on an as-needed basis, without the financial commitment and logistical considerations of full-time hires. As your venture evolves and scales, you can gradually shift these outsourced roles in-house as warranted.

4. Engage Early with Your Technology Transfer Office

One critical, yet often overlooked step in this journey is early engagement with your institution's Technology Transfer Office (TTO). TTOs play a crucial role in facilitating the translation of academic research into commercial products, offering valuable guidance and support in navigating the complex landscape of intellectual property (IP) rights, regulatory pathways, and licensing negotiations.

TTOs can help you understand the necessary regulations, guide you through the licensing negotiation process, and facilitate access to resources and connections within the industry. Consulting professionals well-versed in the biotech startup landscape can offer additional support, providing industry- specific advice and helping you make informed decisions. A key part of these initial stages is securing your intellectual property rights.

Before launching your technology into the market, it is crucial to establish robust IP protection. This typically involves applying for patents to safeguard your technology from competitive infringement. The process of applying for and obtaining patents can be complex and time-consuming, requiring a deep understanding of the technology in question, as well as the intricacies of the patent system.

Patent attorneys specialize in the preparation and filing of patent applications. They understand the technical aspects of your invention, the legal requirements for patentability, and the strategic considerations for maximizing the protection and value of your IP. Engaging these professionals early in the process can streamline the patenting process and enhance the strength of your patent portfolio.

Developing a robust IP strategy is not just about securing protection for your technology; it also plays a crucial role in giving you a competitive edge in the market. A well-thought-out IP strategy can help position your startup for success, attracting investors and potential partners, while also serving as a deterrent to competitors. It can provide a clear roadmap for the future development and protection of your technology, aligning with your overall business strategy and goals.

5. Fine-Tune Your Proof of Concept

You need to identify and refine your "wow" slide — the compelling experimental evidence that convinces everyone that your solution is worth pursuing (see Chapter 17).

The heart of your presentation to investors, collaborators, or other stakeholders is often what is colloquially termed the "wow" slide. This is a slide showcasing your most compelling experimental evidence, the key data or results that convincingly demonstrate the efficacy or potential of your solution. Fine-tuning this slide is crucial as it can serve as a beacon that highlights the potential of your scientific approach or technological innovation.

The "wow" slide should be clear, concise, and impactful. It should visually represent the crux of your technology or solution, demonstrating its validity and potential in a convincing and easily digestible way. Quality, rather than quantity, is the key here; it is about presenting the most compelling evidence rather than overwhelming the viewer with data.

However, it is not enough to simply have a striking "wow" slide. Your presentation should also weave a compelling narrative that encapsulates the journey of your idea from its inception to its potential future impact. This story should be clear, coherent, and engaging, clearly explaining the problem you are trying to solve, why it matters, and how your solution addresses it effectively. The narrative should capture the unique value proposition of your technology or approach, aligning with the evidence presented in the "wow" slide. This story, if told well, sets the tone for the entire pitch, creating a memorable narrative that resonates with your audience and enhances their understanding of and engagement with your proposal.

In addition to the "wow" slide and the narrative, the identification of clear, defined milestones is crucial. These milestones offer tangible evidence of your team's ability to execute and move the project forward. They provide a roadmap of the project, showcasing its progress and potential future trajectory. Clear milestones can be a powerful motivator for potential investors, providing them with concrete markers of progress and success.

6. Fundraise

Finally, your venture needs fuel — capital. Fundraising, the act of securing this capital, is a multi-faceted and ongoing process that requires an understanding of venture capital dynamics, the development of enduring investor relationships, strategic planning, and the resilience to navigate potential rejections.

Venture capitalists (VCs) play an instrumental role in the biotech ecosystem, often providing the substantial funding required to bring innovative solutions from the lab to the market. Securing this funding, however, is no easy feat. It requires a keen understanding of how VCs analyze and evaluate projects.

Entrepreneurs must master the art of pitching, presenting their venture in a way that not only demonstrates its scientific potential but also its commercial viability. This includes highlighting significant clinical needs the project addresses, outlining its potential for substantial improvement in patient outcomes, and illuminating its projected return on investment.

Yet, fundraising is not just a transaction — it's about building relationships. VCs are not merely sources of capital; they are partners who can offer valuable insights, industry connections, and mentorship. Cultivating these relationships necessitates open and transparent communication, viewing investors as collaborators in the venture's journey.

Treating VCs as partners, rather than simply fund providers, can open doors to resources that extend beyond financial backing, further propelling the venture towards success.

However, it's important to remember that fundraising is not a one-off event — it's a continuous process. Even after securing the initial round of funding, ventures must plan for future rounds. This necessitates the development of a comprehensive capital strategy that outlines the financial requirements at each stage of the venture's growth. Identifying potential funding sources and understanding when and how to access them is a critical part of this strategy, ensuring the venture remains financially prepared as it progresses.

Finally, it's imperative to acknowledge that the fundraising journey often includes rejection. Not all VCs will see the potential in a particular venture, and rejections are a common part of the process. However, these rejections should not be seen as dead ends. Instead, they offer opportunities for learning and refinement. Feedback, whether positive or negative, can be utilized to improve the pitch and approach, increasing the chances of success in future fundraising attempts.

Wrapping Up

Embarking on a journey in the realm of science-driven companies, be it a biotech startup or a life sciences venture, requires more than just innovative ideas. It calls for a harmonious fusion of those six integral elements that work in unison to orchestrate a successful venture.

Understanding the nuances of the biotech ecosystem is akin to decoding the rules of a game before stepping onto the field. This knowledge not only illuminates the path of value creation, it also navigates you away from value-destroying pitfalls. By mastering the sector's dynamics and the preferences of venture capitalists, you can fine-tune your value proposition to match the sector's rhythm. However, in the complex and diverse world of biotech entrepreneurship, there isn't a one-size-fits-all blueprint for success. By adopting this mindset and approach, entrepreneurs can uncover the unique set of factors that will drive success in their specific situation.

Rule #12

There Is Not a Right Time to Start

"The only time for action is now. It's never too late to do something."
Antoine de Saint-Exupéry

As a scientist entrepreneur, you may find yourself pondering the question: When is the right time to start a company? The answer, irrespective of the intricacies of your situation, is simple and quite straightforward: The time is now. Delay can often be the most costly mistake in the realm of science-driven business, especially when we talk about companies that operate in this ecosystem characterized by fierce competition and rapid evolution. If you do not begin your run toward the future with utmost immediacy, you risk being outpaced by other keen minds working tirelessly on the same problem. It is a race against time and the first to cross the finish line with a viable solution will claim the spoils.

For example, consider the macroeconomic environment as a factor but not as a deterrent. Traditional wisdom often cautions against starting ventures during times of economic crises. However, this view lacks the nuanced understanding of the potential opportunities that crises present.

While the economy might seem like it's in a downturn, it could be an opportune moment to introduce an innovative product or service. It is during these periods that good management shines through, turning economic challenges into profitable outcomes. Crises shake up the status quo, creating room for new players to emerge and capture the market.

Crisis as a Catalyst

There exists a common misconception that economic downturns or crises present unfavorable conditions for initiating a business. This line of thinking, however, is more of an oversimplification than an absolute truth. Crises invariably disrupt existing market structures, unsettle established players, and create voids in the supply and demand equilibrium. They challenge the status quo, and in doing so, they often unveil previously unseen opportunities or untapped markets. For instance, a decline in a particular industry could lead to the availability of skilled scientific PhDs, lower costs of resources, or a reduction in competition.

Thus, during these periods, effective and agile management comes to the fore, where it can navigate through the uncertainties, seize these unique opportunities, and create a niche for the organization. An economic crisis, through the lens of an adept entrepreneur, can be transformed from a potential hazard into a tool for carving out unique market positions, innovating new products, or simply challenging and surpassing competition.

In other words, a crisis can be seen as a litmus test for entrepreneurial acumen, sorting out the merely competent from the truly innovative. The key lies not in avoiding crises, but in leveraging them as catalysts for growth and opportunity.

One of the chief apprehensions that potential entrepreneurs grapple with during periods of economic instability is the perceived scarcity of funding. It is certainly true that during such times, investors may become more cautious, and the overall availability of funds may appear to dwindle. However, this should not deter determined entrepreneurs. Why? Because good companies — those with robust models and competent leadership that address pressing problems — always have avenues for financing. Every time somebody tells me there's no money in the market, I answer: "Not for the bad companies, certainly."

Indeed, while the financial landscape may be more challenging, it does not become barren. The crucial factor lies in demonstrating the merit of your venture to potential investors. A company that solves a significant problem, that exhibits a sustainable business model, and is helmed by a capable and visionary leader, will always be viewed as an attractive investment proposition.

The Imperative of Authenticity

In many entrepreneurial arenas, the mantra "Fake it till you make it" is often thrown around, suggesting that portraying an image of success, even if premature, can lead to actual success. While this approach might hold some water in certain sectors, when it comes to science-driven ventures, particularly biotech, it falls dangerously short. In these sectors, the stakes are extremely high. Often, it's not merely about business success or failure, but about the health and lives of individuals.

Pretending to have a solution or claiming efficacy without solid evidence can lead to disastrous outcomes. This is why the mantra needs to be modified to "Make it till you break it." In essence, strive to make your project a success, but be prepared to break it off if it becomes clear it isn't viable.

One key strategy to adopt here is the concept of "killer experiments." These are early-stage tests designed to challenge your project's core assumptions. The purpose is not to prove that your project will succeed, but rather to determine as early as possible whether it will fail.

I have a very Darwinian bias here, I must admit. Sometimes keeping companies alive through private capital or grants is just delaying their end a few months down the line. The sooner a non-viable project is identified, the sooner resources can be redirected toward more promising ventures. In a sense, it's a mechanism for minimizing wasted time, effort, and resources on doomed projects, thus allowing for a leaner, more efficient approach to innovation.

The field of biotechnology is unique and sobering in its purpose and implications. While other industries also impact people's lives in various ways, the immediacy and directness of biotech's impact is of a different magnitude altogether. We are dealing with the predicament of life itself. It's a field where our work could mean the difference between life and death, health and sickness, hope and despair for the individuals we aim to serve.

Working within the biotech industry imbues us with an extraordinary responsibility. The powerful technologies we develop, the drugs we create, and the therapies we pioneer can certainly do a world of good. They can alleviate suffering, extend lives, and bring hope where once there was none. However, these same technologies, if misused or misdirected, could also do a great deal of harm. This weighty responsibility must shape our approach to biotech entrepreneurship. There's no room for cutting corners, for irresponsible risk-taking, or for misleading stakeholders about progress or potential. Every decision we make, every project we undertake, every experiment we run, is bound up with real-world stakes, with actual lives hanging in the balance.

The gravity of this predicament should not deter us from this important work, but rather inspire us to carry it out with the utmost integrity, diligence, and care. This is the essential ethic of the biotech entrepreneur.

Openness and Confidentiality: Talking About Your Idea

Entrepreneurship is an art that thrives on collaboration, feedback, and intellectual exchange. As such, the question of how open one initially should be about their business idea is an important consideration. A common instinct is to guard one's idea zealously, keeping it confidential for fear of being scooped or copied. However, I argue that this mindset is often counterproductive and can limit the potential of the idea.

Openly discussing your business concept reaps many benefits. Primarily, it invites valuable feedback and critique, allowing you to refine and strengthen your narrative. Every conversation provides an opportunity to see your idea from a new perspective, uncover overlooked aspects, and preempt potential challenges. Moreover, it enables you to gauge the market's response, test your idea's viability, and build relationships with potential collaborators, investors, or customers.

This openness, however, should not come at the cost of ignoring the importance of execution. Ideas, as we will explore in the next chapter, are a dime a dozen. It's the execution of these ideas that distinguishes successful entrepreneurs from the rest.

If your idea is easily replicable just by mentioning it, it suggests that its value proposition may not be strong enough, it lacks the adequate intellectual property protection, or that it does not carry a sufficient level of novelty or complexity. In essence, your idea should be such that it requires a specific team, with a specific set of skills and knowledge, to execute it effectively.

People Over Ideas: Investment Priorities

In the world of venture capital, there's a simple truth that is often overlooked: We invest in people, not in ideas. The allure of a brilliant idea can be intoxicating. It's often the first thing that captures the interest of an investor or stakeholder. However, an idea, no matter how novel or promising, remains intangible and dormant without the right people to breathe life into it. This is why seasoned investors often place a greater emphasis on the team behind an idea rather than the idea itself.

Execution is the process by which an idea is transformed from an abstract concept into a tangible product or service. It's the grueling journey that involves overcoming hurdles, navigating uncertainties, making critical decisions, and persistently moving forward despite setbacks.

A stellar team, characterized by their skills, tenacity, adaptability, and drive, can execute effectively, pivot when necessary, and turn even a mediocre idea into a successful venture. Conversely, a weak team could falter in the face of challenges, causing even the most promising ideas to fail.

At the end of the day, an idea is just the starting point. It's the team's execution of that idea that navigates the path to success. Thus, when considering investment priorities, it's essential to look beyond the spark of the idea and evaluate the people holding the torch — their experience, their strategy, their commitment, and their ability to execute. In the world of disruptive innovation, it's the people who make the difference, and that's where the smart money goes. Let's discuss this more deeply.

Rule #13

How Much Is an Idea Worth?

> *"I have been impressed with the urgency of doing. Knowing is not enough; we must apply. Being willing is not enough; we must do."*
>
> Leonardo da Vinci

How much is an idea worth? You might think that a bright idea, a spark that could change the world, is extremely valuable. But in the world of investing, this isn't necessarily true.

A lot of startup founders worry about the worth of their idea. I usually tell them that an idea by itself is worth nothing. Zero. Zilch. Nada. But, if you can turn that idea into a product or a service that people need or want, it could be worth billions.

Founders need to understand that the key isn't the idea itself, but how they make it real. Investors don't put their money into ideas; they invest in teams that can turn those ideas into reality. This might seem like an overstatement, and maybe it is a bit, but it highlights an important point.

Many people think that an entrepreneur's main asset is their idea or a scientific discovery that could solve a problem. But, as we'll explore in this chapter, investors might not value a bare-bones idea as much as the entrepreneur does. This could be surprising, but understanding the relationship between ideas and execution can shed light on what truly brings value to a startup.

Let's Dig Deeper

When we think of a startup, we usually picture a fresh idea that's going to shake up the industry and change how we do things. It's exciting to imagine a simple idea turning into a business worth billions of dollars. That's why a lot of people think that the value of a startup comes from how new and unique its idea is. However, this way of thinking can cause confusion because it implies that an idea, by itself, has value. But what we've learned from real-world experience is that an idea alone isn't worth anything.

You see, an idea is just the beginning, a sketch of what might be. It doesn't take into account real-world things like the market, what customers want, competitors, rules and regulations, and other important factors. It's only when an idea faces these realities that it starts to become something substantial. The real worth of an idea comes from making it happen, not just thinking about it. This is why investors care so much about how you plan to make your idea a reality.

It's also essential to remember that your idea needs to evolve over time. The startup ecosystem is dynamic and fast-paced, and the market and customer needs can change rapidly. Being able to adapt your idea and strategy based on feedback, changes in the market, or technological advancements is vital to maintaining relevance and achieving long-term success.

The journey from an idea to a successful business involves risk-taking. All startups encounter obstacles, be it technical difficulties, financial challenges, or market competition. A resilient team that can navigate these hurdles while staying focused on their vision is likely to succeed.

And the idea probably will need to be scalable. Investors are particularly interested in how an idea can grow and expand over time to create a significant return on investment. If your idea has the potential to scale, it can attract more investors and increase your chances of success.

Finally, the skills and strategy you bring to the table are critical. The different skills, experiences, and viewpoints of your team can make a big difference. You also need a strong and flexible plan that can handle the ups and downs of making your idea a reality. This is why investors like startups that can show they know how to execute. This could be through previous successes, early versions of their product, pilot projects, or any other proof that they can make their ideas happen. It gives investors confidence that the team has the skills, the grit, and the problem- solving ability to deal with the challenges that are sure to come up along the way.

In the end, it's a blend of a unique idea, robust execution plan, resilient team, adaptability, scalability, early validation, and a compelling pitch that makes a startup successful. These elements together give investors the confidence they need to back your venture. Investors don't just throw their money at cool concepts. They invest in the chance of those concepts actually working out. That's why how you make your idea happen is so important.

The Counterargument: Does Idea Value Really Equal Zero?

While the prior section proposed that an idea in isolation might be considered valueless, it's important to examine the other side of the coin. Ideas do play a critical role in the innovation process and can be instrumental in capturing initial interest.

An idea sets the direction for a startup. It provides the initial blueprint that influences strategic planning, operational structures, and the allocation of resources. It's the first point of reference, the starting point from which everything else flows. Therefore, one could argue that an idea holds intrinsic value as the compass guiding a startup's journey.

Moreover, an idea can serve as a unique selling proposition (USP). In a world inundated with products and services, a fresh, unique idea can capture attention and differentiate a startup from its competitors. It can attract early adopters and even create a new customer base that wasn't present before.

Also, it's worth considering that certain ideas are so incredibly transformative and disruptive that they can significantly change existing markets or even create entirely new ones. These are pivotal ideas, indeed. These ideas, coupled with exceptional execution, have led to the creation of billion-dollar businesses. Hence, such ideas could be argued to have inherent value.

The Value of Scientific Results as Ideas

Many startups in the biotech and deep-tech sectors are built around scientific results, not just abstract ideas. Think of these results as seeds, crucial starting points for a potential therapy or product. The question, then, becomes, what is the intrinsic value of these scientific results? To answer this, let's consider again the two sides of the coin.

Figure 17. Research Versus Innovation

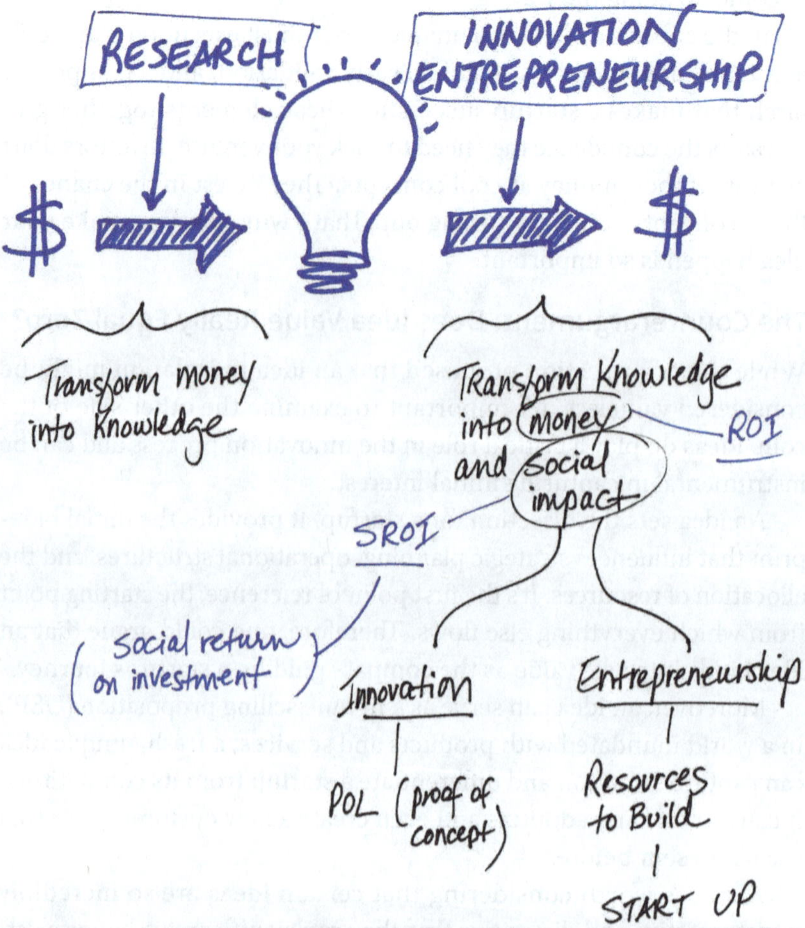

When asked about the distinction between research, innovation, and entrepreneurship, I typically respond that research is the process of converting money into ideas, while innovation and entrepreneurship involve translating these ideas back into money and creating a meaningful societal impact.

- **Research and Innovation:** Research, therefore, involves the transformation of financial resources into knowledge. In contrast, innovation and entrepreneurship focus on converting this newfound knowledge into financial gains — signifying return on investment — and substantial societal benefits, symbolizing social return on investment. Both elements are significant and often intertwined. In the realm of science-driven entrepreneurship, it is common to witness high social return on investment. This is particularly evident, for example, in the biotech sector. Each new therapy brought to market has the potential to address diseases that affect millions of people, creating a profound impact on the lives of these individuals.

- It's crucial to note, however, that while the primary goal may not be to create social impact, such impact often emerges as a byproduct of the mission to solve significant health problems.
- A subtle distinction between innovation and entrepreneurship lies in their objectives and focus. Innovation is centered around the development of a proof of concept, identifying issues, and establishing a framework to resolve them.
- Entrepreneurship, on the other hand, is more resource-oriented. It involves securing the necessary resources to build the solution, introducing it to the market, and converting that solution into a thriving startup. Innovation is the bridge between research and entrepreneurship. It involves taking the insights gleaned from research, developing a proof of concept, identifying the gaps and challenges, and crafting a potential framework for solutions.
- This process is inherently creative, requiring lateral thinking and the ability to see connections that others might miss. Entrepreneurship, then, is the vehicle that propels the journey forward. It takes the proof of concept provided by innovation, marshals the necessary resources, and focuses on introducing the solution into the market. Entrepreneurs transform these innovative ideas into practical, marketable products, and in the process, potentially build a thriving startup. They are the risk-takers who embrace uncertainty, viewing each challenge as an opportunity for growth and learning.
- **Return on Investment:** In the world of business and finance, return on investment (ROI) is a key metric used to measure the probability of gaining a return from an investment. It is a ratio that compares the gain or loss from an investment relative to its cost. A positive ROI indicates a profitable investment, whereas a negative ROI signifies a loss. While this metric is crucial in financial decision-making, it only paints a part of the picture in the context of science-driven entrepreneurship.
- **Social Return on Investment:** In contrast to ROI, social return on investment (SROI) quantifies the broader impact of an investment on society. Unlike traditional ROI, which primarily focuses on financial returns, SROI incorporates social, environmental, and economic costs and benefits into its analysis. It is a principle-based method for measuring extra-financial value, and it can play a vital role in strategic planning, performance management, and outcome reporting. In science-driven entrepreneurship, especially in biotech, SROI becomes profoundly significant as new therapies and innovations can potentially ameliorate the lives of millions of people.
- **High ROI and SROI:** But achieving a high ROI and SROI is a complex journey. It demands a harmonious blend of research, innovation, and entrepreneurship. Each plays a unique role in this expedition. Research fuels the voyage by providing the base of knowledge. It delves into the unknown, driven by curiosity and the pursuit of understanding.

The interplay of research, innovation, and entrepreneurship in the world of biotech forms a powerful triangle that can not only generate lucrative returns but also create transformative social impact. The primary goal may be to resolve significant health issues, but the ripple effect often results in broader societal benefits, enhancing the quality of life for many. This, in essence, is the magic and allure of science-driven entrepreneurship.

From one perspective, the value of scientific results is extraordinary. They are specific, often obtained after years of dedicated research and rigorous testing, and may indeed be enabling. Take, for instance, a groundbreaking scientific result that showcases the potential of a new gene therapy. The value of this result may be perceived as high because it signifies a significant leap forward in the scientific understanding of a particular disease. It paves the way for the development of an effective treatment, showing potential to dramatically improve patient outcomes.

Moreover, such scientific results can offer a competitive advantage in the crowded startup landscape, meaning they can be better than the results offered by other biotech companies. They can be protected via patents, ensuring a unique market position. This uniqueness, combined with the tangible progress toward a viable product, can make startups built around scientific results especially attractive to investors. We could claim the result has intrinsic value in itself.

However, as we discussed with ideas, scientific results are not the endgame but a starting point. A groundbreaking laboratory discovery is not a market-ready product. It must endure a winding road from the lab bench to the bedside, passing numerous hurdles along the way. It has to be translated into a practical application, which often requires further development and extensive testing. This process is time-consuming, resource-intensive, and fraught with uncertainty.

Some scientific results may look promising initially but fail to hold up under further scrutiny or larger scale testing. Furthermore, even the most promising scientific results need to navigate complex regulatory pathways before they can become commercially viable products.

Meeting regulatory requirements is a long, expensive, and uncertain process. And, of course, scientific results don't operate in a vacuum. They must be considered in the context of the current market, existing competition, and the evolving needs of patients and healthcare systems. If other companies are pursuing similar results, or if new technologies emerge, the value of the original results could be undermined.

So, as we discussed about raw ideas, the value of scientific results is also significantly influenced by the team's ability to create a startup and execute. They must not only understand the science but also have the business acumen to navigate the tricky terrain of product development and commercialization.

Rule #13: How Much Is an Idea Worth?

While scientific results provide a substantial starting point, their ultimate value is not inherent but heavily contingent upon their successful translation into a product or therapy. This process requires a stellar team, a robust strategy, and often, a healthy dose of patience and persistence. The key lesson for startups and investors alike is to not overestimate the value of raw scientific results without considering the challenges and requirements of the execution process.

Rule #14
Understand What Happens in the First Meeting with a Venture Capitalist

"Beauty is in the eye of the beholder."
Charles Bukowski

The initial encounter between ideas and capital serves multiple purposes. It provides a space for open dialogue between the entrepreneur and the venture capitalist, establishing the foundation for a potential relationship. It offers an opportunity for the entrepreneur to showcase their vision and the viability of their project, paving the way for future discussions. And crucially, it acts as a launchpad, thrusting the startup into the meticulous process of due diligence, which could potentially culminate in an investment.

While the structure of this initial meeting can vary, there are three focal points that invariably catch the venture capitalist's attention when considering a science-driven company: the team, the problem the company is aiming to solve, and the so-called "wow" factor. The team, with the CEO at the helm, must display a robust mix of skills, a shared vision, and a collective willingness to invest themselves wholly into the project. The problem the company proposes to solve should not just be substantial but immense — the kind that, if tackled successfully, can yield extraordinary returns. And finally, the "wow" factor: a scientifically grounded, data-rich proof of concept that separates the venture from the pack and signals its potential for disruptive innovation.

The Team

Investing in a startup goes far beyond merely funding a promising idea; it is, at its core, investing in a team of individuals who are committed to turning that idea into reality. Hence, the first component that a venture capitalist scrutinizes during the initial meeting is the strength and quality of your team.

At the helm of this team is the CEO, whose vision and communication skills often set the tone for the entire enterprise. A strong CEO articulates a clear, compelling vision for the future of the company and can effectively communicate this vision to a variety of audiences — from potential investors to team members. I've seen CEOs who could paint such a vivid picture of their company's future that you'd feel as if you were already there, even if the startup was still in its infancy. That's the power of compelling communication.

Venture capitalists also value a CEO and team with skin in the game, demonstrating a personal and financial commitment to the company's success. This level of commitment is a testament to their belief in the venture and their determination to see it succeed. Venture capitalists are more inclined to back a venture where the team has invested their own resources.

Another crucial factor is the complementarity of profiles among team members. A balanced mix of expertise across various domains — from technical and scientific knowledge to business and marketing acumen — can significantly enhance a startup's ability to navigate challenges and capitalize on opportunities.

Remember, a venture capitalist isn't just investing in an idea; they're investing in the people who will bring that idea to fruition. The strength of your team can be the key that unlocks potential investment opportunities.

That being said, keep in mind that a team isn't expected to be complete right from the start. In a startup's early stages, especially in specialized fields like biotech, it's typical to have key roles like the CEO and the chief scientific officer (CSO) filled early on. They carry the responsibility of driving the idea forward, seeking funding, and ensuring scientific accuracy and feasibility.

The CEO and CSO work together to lay the groundwork for the company, but as the company grows and evolves, so does the team. For

Figure 18. The First Meeting

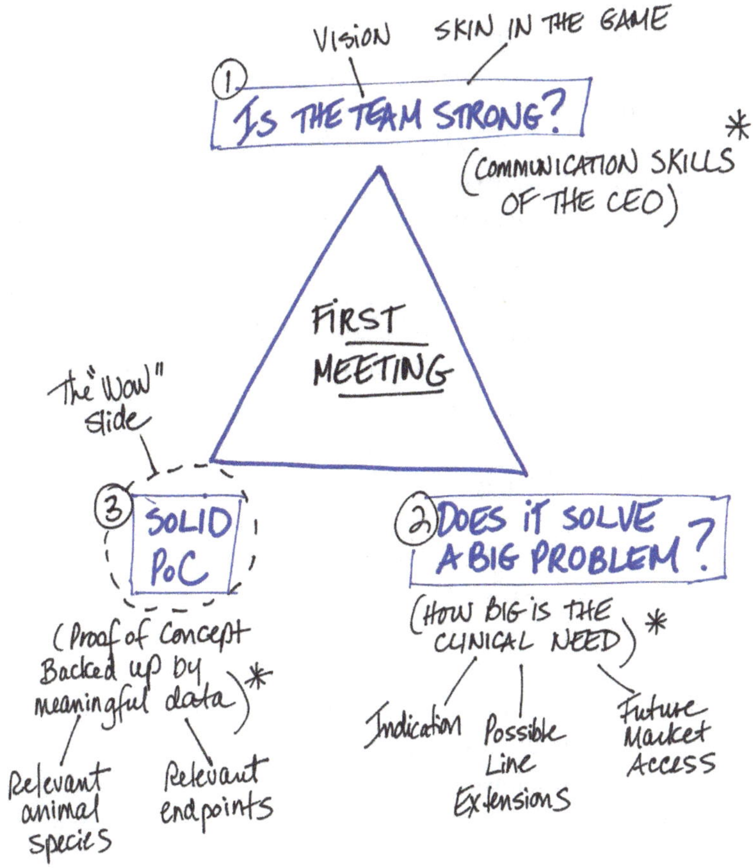

The first encounter with a venture capitalist (VC) is a high-stakes presentation where your every word, every slide, and even your demeanor are under scrutiny.

Preparation is key. Anticipate questions about the team, the problem your startup aims to solve, and, of course, the data-packed "wow" slide.

Understand that your task is to present your venture as a compelling opportunity for investment, one that balances potential risks and rewards. Remember, it's not just what you communicate, but also how you communicate it. Clarity and confidence are crucial. Whether you're discussing your team's dynamism or the scientific rigor behind your proof of concept, deliver your points with conviction. You're not just sharing facts; you're telling a story — a story of a problem that needs solving, a capable team ready for the challenge, and the groundbreaking science that makes it possible. As you approach that first meeting with a VC, do so with preparedness and self-assurance. Recognize that your objective is to pique curiosity and secure that all-important second meeting. Understand that a strong, cohesive team, a significant problem worth solving, and a compelling "wow" slide backed by scientific rigor are your most valuable assets.

instance, in a biotech company, a chief medical officer (CMO) might join the team a year before the first human trials. This addition brings essential medical expertise and leadership to the company as the team begins to navigate the complexities of clinical trials.

Further down the line, as the company transitions to a clinical-stage company, a chief financial officer (CFO) could join the team as well. Their role becomes increasingly important as the company grows, taking charge of financial planning, managing risks, record-keeping, and financial reporting.

For this first meeting, you need to be aware of how the startup should grow in the future and explain your plan. The evolution of the team structure over time needs to show flexibility and adaptability — two essential traits in the fast-paced startup world. It also needs to highlight the importance of each role within the team and at what stage their skills and expertise will be most needed.

In any case, these timelines and structures can vary greatly depending on the company. It's important to remember that there's no one-size-fits-all approach to building a startup team. Each startup is unique, and the team should be assembled with its unique needs and challenges in mind.

A final consideration: The CEO's role in a startup is crucial — they are the ones who set the vision, rally the team, and steer the company through the highs and lows of business. However, there is often debate surrounding who is best suited to occupy this role — the founder or a professional CEO.

Founders as CEOs hold a unique position. Being the original thinkers behind the startup idea, they have an intimate understanding of the business and its objectives. They have passion, drive, and a personal investment in the company's success. However, while these qualities are important, they are not always enough to scale a startup effectively.

The role of a CEO demands a diverse skill set, including strategic thinking, leadership, and business acumen, which not all founders have or have had the opportunity to develop. For instance, a biotech founder might have brilliant scientific insights but could lack the business savvy required to lead the company toward its clinical objectives.

As a result, startups often reach a stage in which bringing in a professional CEO becomes beneficial. These individuals come with proven experience, often having led other companies through similar growth phases. They can provide fresh perspectives, have established networks, and have a deep understanding of the business landscape. They are able to navigate complex negotiations, drive strategic partnerships, and make tough decisions that founders might shy away from due to emotional attachment.

However, the transition from a founder CEO to a professional CEO should be managed carefully. A founder's vision is deeply embedded in the company culture and abruptly changing leadership could destabilize the organization.

Sometimes the company will need an interim CEO who is not expected to steer the company long-term, but rather to guide it through specific challenges, often tied to growth and scaling. They bring stability during transitional periods and prepare the company for its next stage. The interim CEO can be an ideal solution when the startup isn't large enough or doesn't have enough funding to attract a high-profile, professional CEO.

In the end, whether a founder, professional, or interim CEO is best for a startup depends on several factors. It's crucial to consider the specific needs and stage of the startup, as well as the individual's skills and experience. For instance, in a biotech firm, a founder might transition into a role like the CSO, leveraging their scientific expertise while making way for a CEO with a stronger business background.

Ultimately, the decision lies in aligning the leadership structure with the startup's strategic objectives and the capabilities needed to meet these goals. The key is to recognize that leadership needs to evolve along with the company. After all, startups are about growth and adaptation, and their leadership should reflect that.

The Problem

A fundamental element that captures a venture capitalist's attention is the scale and significance of the problem your startup is aiming to solve. The bigger the problem, the larger the potential market, and subsequently, the higher the likelihood of profitability. This axiom holds true across industries and is particularly salient in high-risk, high-reward sectors such as biotech and deep tech.

Consider this: If your startup is tackling a sizable problem, it implies a substantial potential customer base eagerly awaiting a solution. This

Figure 19. How Big Is the Problem Is Not Its Market Size: The Special Case of Rare Diseases

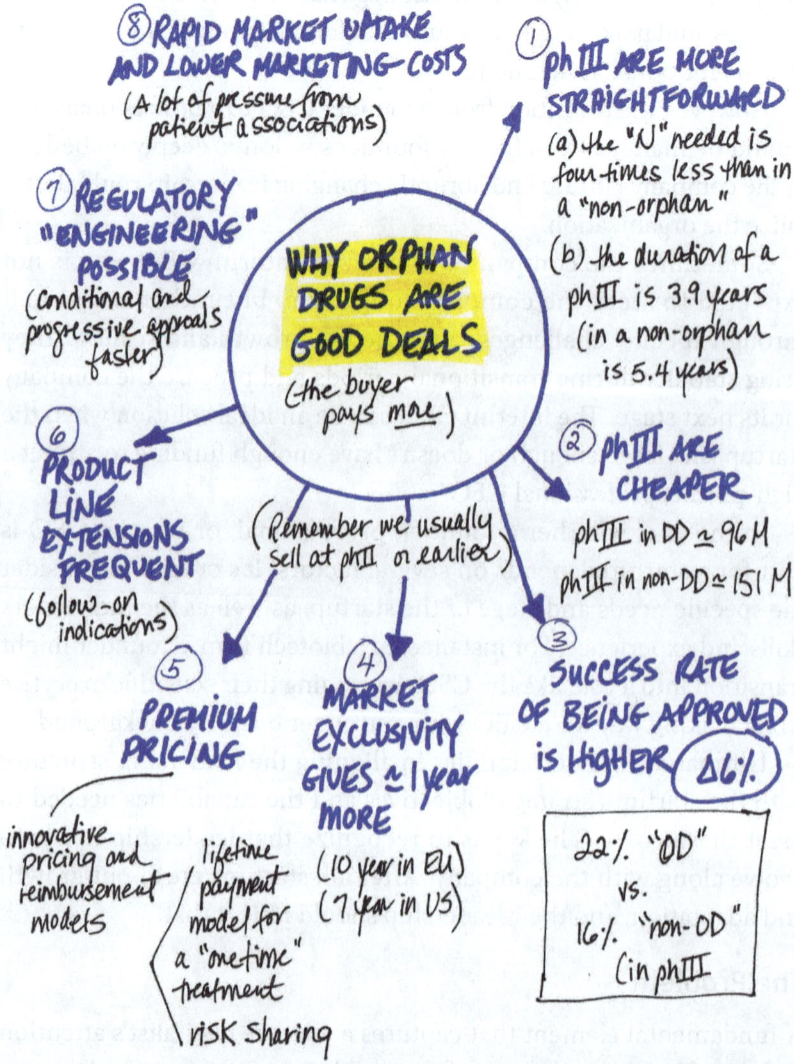

The allure of orphan drugs (drugs specifically intended to treat rare diseases) as viable investment opportunities is far from unfounded. From superior buyer incentives during liquidity events to efficient and cost-effective drug trials, orphan drugs present a unique proposition for investors seeking rewarding avenues within the biotech industry. This intrigue is not merely anecdotal; there are concrete reasons behind this appeal. Several distinct reasons are elucidating this trend.

- **Favorable Timing for Liquidity Events:** For investors in the rare disease therapy space, liquidity events often occur following phase 2 trials once proof of concept and human efficacy have been established. They might of course happen much earlier but the case is then even more valid. At this point, a pharma company typically acquires the therapy for further development. This approach accelerates the realization of investment returns, as the acquirer shoulders the task of conducting the phase 3 study.
- **Streamlined Phase 3 Trials:** Orphan drug studies are simpler and quicker to execute in phase 3 compared to non-orphan diseases. The required endpoint numbers are generally four times less, and the study duration is significantly shorter. This reduced complexity translates into cost and time efficiency, which is a definite plus for investors.
- **Lower Development Costs:** Phase 3 trials for orphan drugs cost, on average, $96 million — significantly less than the $151 million required for non-orphan diseases. This lower cost profile makes orphan drugs financially attractive for venture capitalists.
- **Higher Approval Rates:** Orphan diseases show a 22% approval rate, a notable 6% increase compared to the 16% seen in non-orphan diseases. This higher likelihood of approval enhances the investment prospect, providing a more secure route toward market success.
- **Market Exclusivity and Premium Pricing:** Orphan drugs often come with the benefit of market exclusivity, typically adding an extra year of patent protection. In addition, these drugs often command premium pricing or adopt innovative reimbursement models, allowing for higher revenue generation.
- **Potential for Product Line Extensions:** It's not uncommon for orphan drugs to find follow-on indications, thus expanding their market reach. By addressing multiple rare diseases that share similar biological issues, the drug's market potential can be significantly broadened.
- **Regulatory Advantages:** Conditional and generally faster approvals offer a clear advantage when developing orphan drugs. Regulatory engineering, as it is often called, expedites the process of bringing the drug to market, shortening the return-on-investment timeline.
- **Data Exclusivity:** In addition to patent protection, orphan drugs can also benefit from data exclusivity, which prevents generic drug manufacturers from using the originator's clinical trial data to support the marketing of a generic version of the drug for a certain period. This can extend the profitability of the orphan drug beyond the life of its patent.
- **Rapid Market Uptake and Lower Marketing Costs:** With patient advocacy groups often rallying behind orphan drugs, these treatments typically enjoy rapid market uptake and face lower marketing costs. This factor enhances the overall investment prospect, as it accelerates the path to profitability and mitigates a significant expense.
- **Focused Physician Networks:** In rare diseases, the pool of treating physicians is typically smaller and more focused. This makes it easier for pharmaceutical companies to communicate with them and educate them about the new therapy, thereby accelerating drug adoption.
- **Lower Competition:** Due to their rarity, orphan diseases often face less competition in the marketplace compared to more common diseases. Lower competition can mean better market penetration and higher market shares for the orphan drug.

can translate into considerable revenue, which can justify a high valuation and attract significant investment.

A casual investment mantra states, "If you want to make money, invest in a startup that solves a big problem. If you want to make an extraordinary amount of money, invest in a startup that tackles a really, really big problem." As simplistic as it might sound, it embodies a profound truth about the nature of business opportunities. The problem you solve is important.

In the realm of biotech, evaluating the scale of a problem delves into nuanced aspects such as the clinical need, the indication, future market access, and potential line extensions. Here, venture capitalists often question: How pressing is the clinical need? What is the indication that the solution targets? How can the product be accessed in the market in the future? Are there potential line extensions (more problems to solve) that could help increase the market and reduce risk?

Assessing the clinical need entails understanding the extent to which the current treatment landscape fails to address patient needs. The indication is the specific disease or condition that the solution targets, and each indication corresponds to a particular subset of patients. Predicting future market access involves considering regulatory pathways, pricing and reimbursement strategies, and potential barriers to adoption. Lastly, potential line extensions — opportunities to use the product to address additional indications — offer a means of diversifying risk and broadening the product's market potential.

However, it's important to note that the size of the problem isn't merely about the potential market size, but also about the severity and urgency of the problem at hand. Big here means "important." It's about the impact of not solving this problem. For instance, is the patient's life at risk? Will their quality of life be severely compromised? Are there no other alternatives available? These factors weigh heavily when considering the significance of the problem your startup is trying to solve.

In fact, a startup may find itself addressing what might seem like a niche or smaller market, such as a rare disease, but because the problem is critical and the need is urgent, niches are significant opportunities. This is often the case in biotech. If the problem is a life-threatening disease with no existing cure, then even if it's a rare disease affecting a smaller population, solving this problem could lead to significant returns. And because the problem is so crucial, the impact of a solution is substantial. Moreover, solving a niche problem can sometimes lead to broader applications. A solution for a rare disease might reveal insights or technologies that could be applicable to more common conditions. This has the potential to expand the market substantially.

In biotech, the problem's importance can even have regulatory implications. For example, therapies for severe or life-threatening conditions can sometimes access expedited regulatory pathways, which can reduce the time and cost of bringing the product to market. This brings us back to the importance of understanding the nuances of the problem. Understanding the size of the problem is not only about the size of the market but also about the gravity of the problem, the implications of not solving it, and the opportunities that could emerge from tackling it. It's not just about market size; it's about importance.

So, while it's essential to consider market size when looking for investment opportunities, the real value lies in the importance of the problem and its potential solutions. Solving critical problems, whether they impact large or small populations, can lead to extraordinary opportunities and contribute meaningfully to society.

The "Wow" Slide

This is such an important concept that we will devote Chapter 17 to it. The "wow" slide is the moment when you unveil the hard evidence that your startup's solution holds water, where you prove that you are not just all talk. This slide, central to your presentation, presents compelling proof of concept. It is your scientific tour de force, embodying the essence of your innovation and its potential to disrupt the status quo.

The "wow" slide is fundamentally grounded in science and brimming with data. It showcases the result of your extensive research, trials, and experiments, and effectively presents your findings in a clear and concise manner. Your job here is to make the complex accessible and the innovative undeniable, highlighting the significance of your proof of concept in a way that is as engaging as it is irrefutable.

As you create your "wow" slide, bear in mind that it will be subjected to intense scrutiny. You are presenting to savvy venture capitalists who will dissect every aspect of it. The data you provide should be robust, meticulously collected, and convincingly analyzed. The slide

Figure 20. Strategies to Solve Rare Diseases

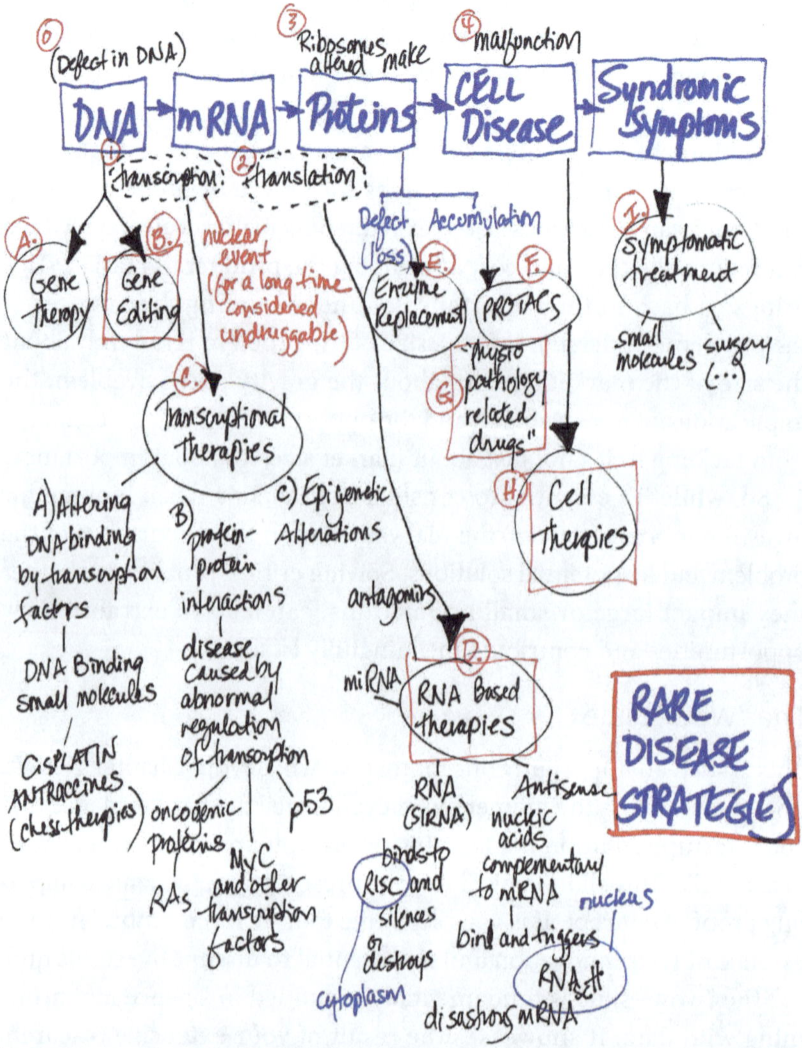

A "rare disease," as the term suggests, is a medical condition that affects a relatively small segment of the population. However, while the incidence of any one rare disease might be quite low, collectively, there are thousands of such diseases, affecting millions of people worldwide.

The precise definition of a rare disease can vary depending on the region or jurisdiction. For instance, in the United States, a disease is considered rare if it affects fewer than 200,000 people, according to the Orphan Drug Act of 1983. In contrast, the European Union defines a rare disease as one affecting no more than 1 in 2,000 individuals.

- These diseases often pose significant health challenges, partly because their rarity can make them difficult to diagnose and, in many cases, there may be a lack of effective treatments. The rarity of these diseases can also deter pharmaceutical companies from investing in research and development for these conditions, given the limited commercial potential.
- This brings us to the term "orphan disease," which is often used interchangeably with "rare disease." The concept of an "orphan disease" originally arose not merely from the rarity of the condition but from the fact that these diseases were often "orphaned" in terms of scientific and pharmaceutical interest. That is, they were neglected by the research community and the pharmaceutical industry because they affected too few individuals to attract substantial research funding or to provide a significant market for new medications.
- In response to this issue, governments introduced policies and incentives to encourage the development of "orphan drugs" — drugs specifically intended to treat orphan diseases. Such incentives may include tax breaks, subsidies, and market exclusivities, making the development of treatments for orphan diseases more financially viable and appealing to pharmaceutical companies.
- At the core of these disease is often a defect in the DNA that sets off a chain reaction of biological missteps, culminating in the disease symptoms we observe.
- Think of it as a game of "telephone," where the original message gets distorted as it passes from person to person. Similarly, a DNA defect causes an incorrect message, or messenger RNA, to be produced. This flawed messenger RNA then instructs the cell's protein factories, called ribosomes, to produce altered or faulty proteins. The result? Cellular dysfunction and the characteristic syndromic symptoms of the rare disease.
- Given this cascading chain of biological events, there are multiple points at which interventions can potentially correct or mitigate the disease process.
  - One approach is to intervene at the **DNA level**. This can involve strategies like gene therapy, which introduces a corrected gene into a patient's cells, or gene editing, which directly repairs the faulty gene.
  - Another strategy is to intervene at the **transcription** stage, where DNA is converted into messenger RNA. A suite of techniques fall under this category, including altering DNA binding by transcription factors, modulating protein-protein interactions, and modifying epigenetic alterations, among others.
  - Therapies can also target the **translation** stage, where messenger RNA is transformed into protein. RNA-based therapies like antisense oligonucleotides or microRNAs can correct or modulate this process, ensuring that the right proteins are produced.
  - In cases where the protein product is flawed or deficient, treatments can supplement or replace the faulty protein, as seen in enzyme **replacement** therapy. Alternatively, methods that destroy the accumulation of altered protein, using protein degraders, may be employed.
  - We can also intervene at the **cellular** level with cell therapies and immunotherapies, or through strategies that target the disease's symptomatic effects. These can involve small molecules, surgical interventions, or other treatments that help manage symptoms but do not address the underlying genetic problem, making this last method of addressing the disease the least desirable, as it only provides symptomatic relief without tackling the root cause.

should be capable of withstanding a rigorous examination and emerge even more persuasive. In short, your "wow" slide is your opportunity to shine, to present your startup's potential in the most compelling light. It is the moment when you demonstrate your commitment not only to innovation but also to scientific rigor and validity.

What Is the Goal of the First Meeting?

The first meeting with a venture capitalist is a chance to set the stage, to captivate with potential and promise. But remember: Securing an immediate investment isn't the objective of this initial encounter. Rather, this meeting is about stoking curiosity, inspiring further investigation, and ultimately, earning a second meeting.

So, what is the true goal of this initial engagement? To spark interest. To plant the seed of a compelling narrative that unfolds into a need to learn more. To present a case that warrants closer examination. Essentially, your goal is to engage the venture capitalist's interest sufficiently to instigate the process of due diligence — an intensive investigation into your startup's claims, potential, and viability.

Scientific due diligence is typically the first step in this process. Here, your "wow" slide, your data, your proof of concept are rigorously scrutinized. This step is about confirming the scientific validity of your proposition, validating your methodology, and verifying the relevance and reliability of your results. If your scientific foundations hold firm under this examination, then overall due diligence follows, scrutinizing science even more deeply , plus every other aspect of your business. So, when preparing for this first meeting, remember that your objective is to inspire a compelling need to know more.

What Goes Through Your Investor's Mind?

As the investor sits across from the entrepreneur during this initial meeting, a parallel story begins to unravel in their mind. The entrepreneur's pitch is not merely a proposal; it is a puzzle to be deconstructed and validated. Each claim made, each number quoted, each future projection presented, all of these must be verified.

The investor mentally goes through a list of key opinion leaders in their network. Who can be called upon to corroborate the presented facts? Who has the requisite knowledge and unbiased perspective to either confirm or challenge what the entrepreneur is saying? Networking, in this context, isn't just about connections; it's about building a trusted panel of experts who can provide reliable insights when needed.

Simultaneously, the investor begins to scrutinize the feasibility of the presented business model or scientific proposal. They start to connect the dots, comparing the proposal at hand with similar businesses or projects they've come across in the past. Which seasoned CEO, business development executive, or scientific expert would be the best fit for this venture? Who can take this idea and truly elevate it to its full potential?

Equally important is the process of identifying gaps — in the science, the business model, or the team. This is known as gap analysis and was covered in Chapter 10. The investor analyzes what experiments might be missing, what data needs to be collected, and what competencies are yet to be incorporated in the team. Are the endpoints this team is using the right ones?

This gap analysis is crucial to determine not just the immediate value of the proposal but also its future potential. The investor knows that while a successful investment might look like a fully formed enterprise at first glance, it is often a work in progress, an idea that needs the right people, the right resources, and the right timing to truly flourish.

While the entrepreneur might be focused on securing funding for this round alone, the investor's mind is already running the marathon, imagining the full equity story. They consider the current valuation of the startup and then project future valuations, visualizing how it might evolve over successive rounds of funding.

An important part of this exercise involves predicting who among their network of fellow co-investors might be willing to join in subsequent rounds. What would the ownership structure look like as new investors came onboard? How would that affect control dynamics within the company?

The investor knows that a prudent investment strategy doesn't stop at the here and now; it considers the future trajectory of the company, its financing needs, and the evolving landscape of ownership. It is this long-term, holistic vision that differentiates a savvy investor from the rest, enabling them to create a win-win scenario for themselves, their co-investors, and the entrepreneurs they back.

Figure 21. Are the Endpoints Clear Enough?

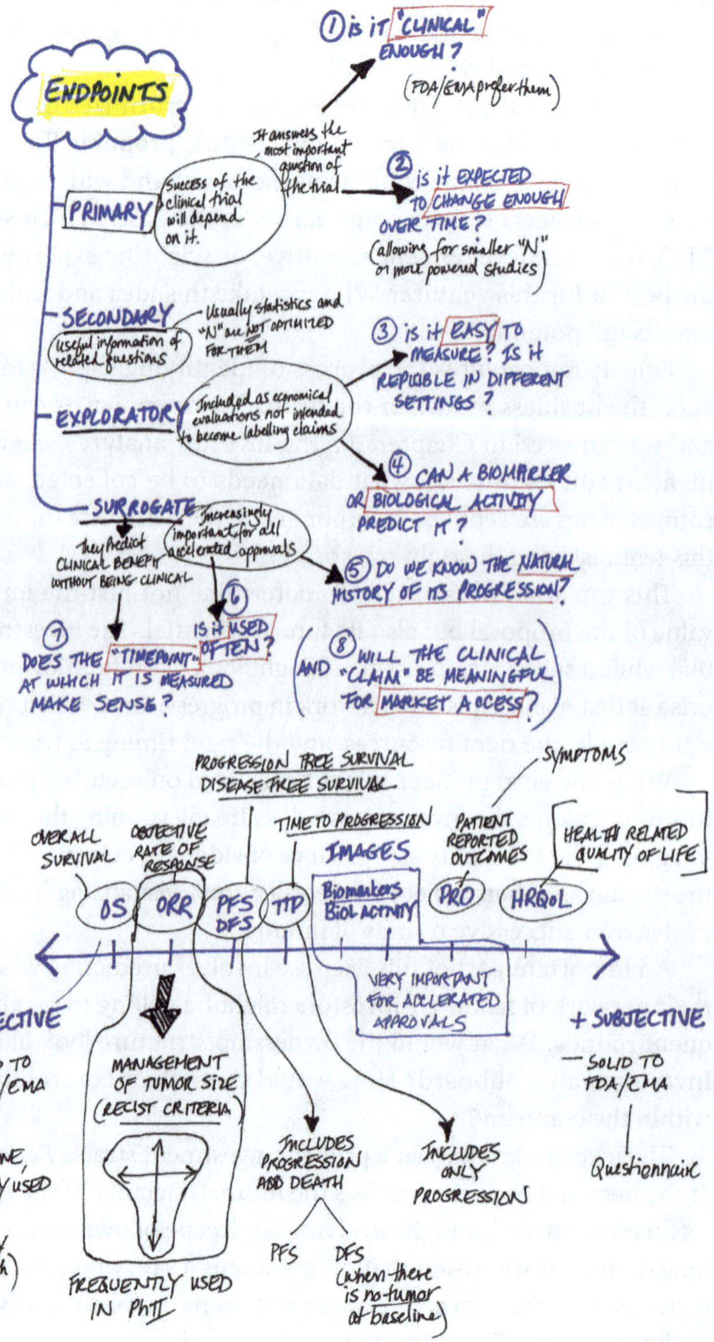

In the world of science-driven ventures, the "wow" slide often represents the crux of a company's investment pitch. What are you measuring matters.

- **What is an endpoint?** In the context of a research study, an endpoint refers to a pre-defined outcome or event that the study aims to measure. Endpoints are used to provide clear, objective criteria for measuring the efficacy, safety, or performance of the intervention or treatment being studied. Endpoints are generally divided into four categories:
  1. **Primary Endpoints:** These are the main outcomes that the study is designed to assess. The primary endpoint is used to determine the sample size for the study and is typically the most clinically relevant outcome. For example, in a study on a new cancer treatment, the primary endpoint could be overall survival.
  2. **Secondary Endpoints:** These are additional outcomes that the study measures and that provide additional information. They typically lack sufficient statistical power.
  3. **Exploratory Endpoints:** These are additional outcomes that are not the primary focus of the study but may provide useful information about the effects of the intervention or treatment. These endpoints can provide insights into the mechanism of action of a treatment, its effect on various biological markers, or its impact on subsets of participants.
  4. **Surrogate Endpoints:** Surrogate endpoints are biomarkers used as substitutes for a clinical endpoint of interest, such as mortality or morbidity. They are expected to predict clinical benefit based on epidemiologic, therapeutic, or other scientific evidence. They are increasingly important for accelerated approvals. For example, lowering of blood pressure is often used as a surrogate endpoint in clinical trials for stroke on the basis that lowering blood pressure has been shown to decrease the risk of stroke.
- **Key considerations** when selecting endpoints for a research study:
  - **Clinical relevance:** The Food and Drug Administration and the European Medicines Agency generally prefer endpoints that are tied as closely as possible to a direct patient benefit.
  - **Rate of change:** The faster an endpoint changes, the smaller the sample size required to detect this change, thereby enhancing the study's statistical power. Knowledge about the natural progression of the endpoint can provide a robust comparison.
  - **Ease of measurement:** An ideal endpoint is easy to measure and replicable across settings.
  - **Predictability by a biomarker:** It's beneficial if a surrogate endpoint can be directly linked and predicted by a biomarker of biological activity.
  - **Precedence:** It's often easier to persuade regulatory agencies about endpoints that have been widely used and are familiar to them.
  - **Timing of endpoint measurement:** The point at which an endpoint is measured can be as significant as what is being measured.
  - **Meaningfulness for market access:** The clinical claim derived from the endpoint should have substantial implications for market access.
- **In the field of oncology,** endpoints can range from highly objective (and thus more robust from a regulatory perspective) to more subjective. Examples include overall survival, objective rate of response, progression-free survival, disease-free survival, time to progression, biomarkers of biological activity (imaging), patient-reported outcomes, and health-related quality of life.

Alongside the entire equity story unfolding in the investor's mind, there's also the crafting of a compelling narrative that can be shared with their network of venture capital colleagues. Remember, venture capital investments are rarely solitary endeavors; they often involve syndication or co-investing where multiple investors come together to finance a startup. Thus, the investor starts to consider, from the very first meeting, how to frame the investment thesis in an interesting, bold, and convincing story. This narrative must highlight the unique selling propositions, potential for growth, and mitigation of risks associated with the startup.

An investor's ability to communicate a powerful narrative is crucial because it influences the willingness of other potential co-investors to contribute capital. The story must captivate, inspire, and convince these potential partners about the merit of the investment, the robustness of the business model, the potential market size, and the capability of the entrepreneurial team. Therefore, storytelling, in this context, becomes an invaluable tool for an investor, helping them to not only understand and shape their investment thesis but also to gather the needed support and resources from their network to make the venture a success. Ultimately, this weaving of facts, figures, and foresights into a compelling story forms a critical part of the venture capital investment process.

An investor is often concerned about the timing and chances of a cash-out event for a startup. Is there a chance of an accelerated pathway and hence, a potential for early exit? It's not just about "if" an exit will occur, but "when." The faster an exit happens, the sooner the investor sees a return on their money, making the startup more attractive. But quick exits aren't always doable or even the best move, as a startup might need more time to grow and reach its full value.

Because exits can happen at different times, smart investors develop backup plans — plan A for an early liquidity event and plan B for a later exit after more rounds of funding, like after a successful phase 2 trial in a biotech startup.

- **Plan A,** the early liquidity event, is ideal because it brings faster returns and frees up money for other investments. This could happen through a buyout by a bigger company, a merger with a similarly sized company, or even an early public offering, though this is less common for young startups.

- **Plan B** is about supporting the startup through more funding rounds until it reaches a more typical exit point. In the case of biotech, this might mean a sale after successful phase 2 clinical trials. The idea here is that a later cash-out event will be made up for by a higher startup value due to reduced risk and a proven concept.

In both plans, the investor's aim is to get the most return on their investment. By thinking about different scenarios and exit strategies, the investor can better predict future outcomes, equipping them to handle the investment journey, wherever it may lead.

An investor's mind might also be preoccupied with broader industry trends and geopolitical factors. How does this venture fit within the broader market context? Are there external market forces, legal changes, or potential policy shifts that could affect the venture's success? They may also contemplate the ethical implications of the investment. Will the investment align with their personal values or the values of the firms they represent? What might be the societal ramifications of the technology or business model being proposed?

Finally, an investor may ponder their individual contribution to the venture. What role do they anticipate playing as an investor? Will they be dynamically engaged in critical decision-making procedures? How much can they personally add to this project if they get a board seat?

Recognizing these expectations can guide investors to match their investments with their personal ambitions and abilities. After all, their role isn't just about providing funds, but could also encompass leveraging their knowledge, network, and experience to propel the venture forward. Each investment may require a different level of commitment, and identifying this requirement early on allows the investor to allocate their resources effectively, ensuring a fruitful partnership.

In essence, the investor's mind at this first meeting is a whirlwind of thoughts, connections, comparisons, and analyses. This complex mental landscape underscores the vital role that a broad and diverse network, a deep understanding of the field, and a keen analytical mind play in successful investment decision-making.

Ultimately, it is not about making a decision on the spot, but about setting in motion a series of actions that will lead to a well-informed, thoroughly validated, and strategically sound investment decision.

Figure 22. Is There a Chance of Accelerated Pathway?

Drug discovery and development is a lengthy and complex process that typically takes years, sometimes even decades, to complete. However, there are instances when this timeframe needs to be expedited, such as when dealing with serious or life-threatening diseases for which no effective treatment is available, or when a new treatment is significantly better than existing options.

- To accommodate these needs, regulatory agencies like the US Food and Drug Administration (FDA) and the European Medicines Agency (EMA) have implemented **accelerated pathways.** These pathways — Fast Track Designation, Breakthrough Therapy, Priority Review, and Accelerated Approval in the US, and similar pathways in Europe — are designed to expedite the development and review of drugs intended to treat serious conditions.
- **Fast Track designation** is intended to facilitate the development and expedite the review of drugs that treat serious conditions and fill an unmet medical need. Once a drug receives this designation, it has increased access to the FDA for the purpose of expediting the development and review process through more frequent meetings and written communication. In the EU, the equivalent pathway is referred to as the **PRIME** (PRIority MEdicines) scheme. Both pathways aim to enhance support for the development of medicines that target an unmet medical need, offering increased interaction and early dialogue with developers.
- **The Breakthrough Therapy** pathway, specific to the FDA, is for drugs that treat a serious condition where preliminary clinical evidence suggests it may demonstrate substantial improvement over existing therapies. This designation intends to expedite the development and review of such a drug, and involves more intensive FDA guidance on an efficient drug-development program. The EMA equivalent is again the PRIME scheme, where support is provided to optimize development plans and speed up evaluation so these medicines can reach patients earlier.
- **A Priority Review designation** by the FDA means the review time of a new drug is reduced. Standard review is typically 10 months from the date of submission, but a Priority Review should be completed in six months. This expedited review is for drugs that may offer significant improvements in the treatment or prevention of a disease. In the EU, this is termed "Accelerated Assessment," which aims to expedite the approval of drugs that are expected to be of major public health interest, particularly from the viewpoint of therapeutic innovation.
- **The Accelerated Approval** pathway of the FDA allows for earlier approval of a drug for a serious illness that fills an unmet medical need based on a surrogate endpoint. A surrogate endpoint is a marker that is thought to predict clinical benefit but is not itself a measure of clinical benefit. The use of surrogate endpoints can considerably shorten the time required prior to receiving approval. The EU has a similar concept known as Conditional Marketing Authorization (CMA), intended to reach patients with unmet medical needs faster.
- While the terminology may differ between regions, the aim of these accelerated pathways is consistent: to bring promising therapies to patients suffering from serious conditions more rapidly, without compromising the rigorous standards of safety and efficacy. The judicious use of these accelerated pathways can dramatically affect public health by facilitating quicker access to innovative and life-saving therapies.

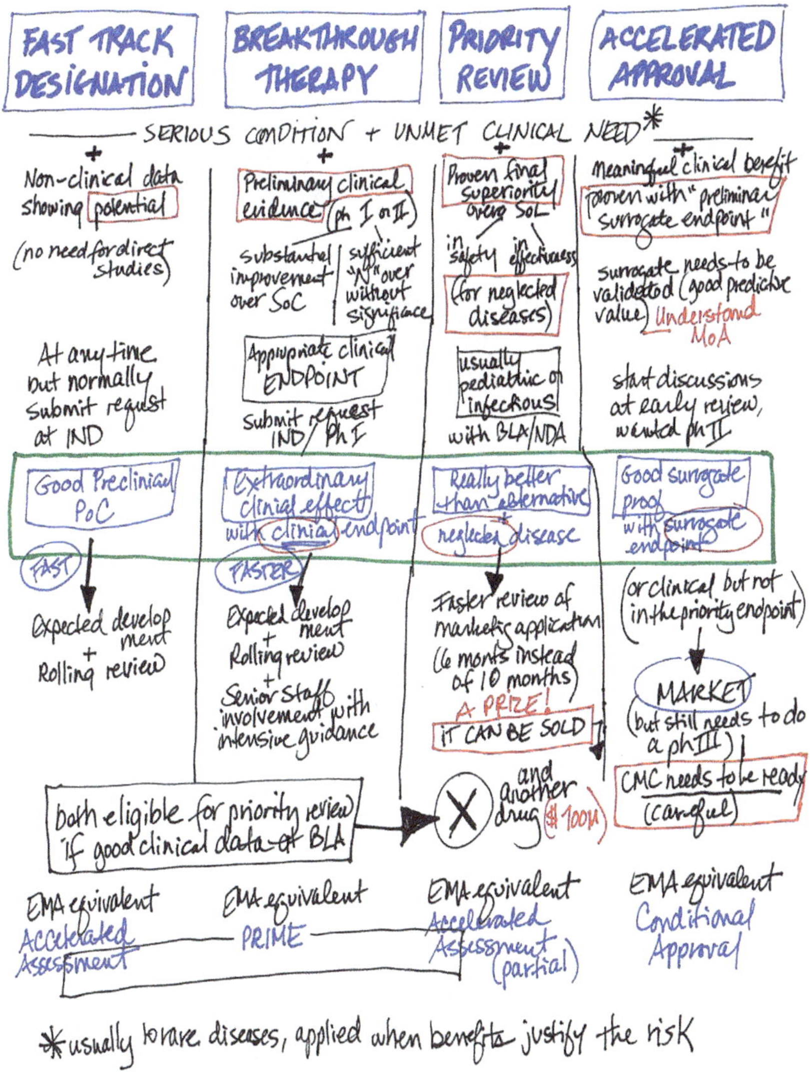
FAST TRACK DESIGNATION
BREAKTHROUGH THERAPY
PRIORITY REVIEW
ACCELERATED APPROVAL
SERIOUS CONDITION + UNMET CLINICAL NEED*
Non-clinical data showing potential
(no need for direct studies)
At any time but normally submit request at IND
Preliminary clinical evidence (ph I or II)
substantial improvement over SoC
sufficient "N" over without significance
Appropriate clinical ENDPOINT
Submit request IND/ Ph I
Proven final superiority over SoC
in safety
in effectiveness
(for neglected diseases)
usually pediatric or infectious
with BLA/NDA
Meaningful clinical benefit
proven with "preliminary surrogate endpoint"
surrogate needs to be validated (good predictive value)
Understand MoA
start discussions at early review, wanted ph II
Good Preclinical PoC
Extraordinary clinical effect with clinical endpoint
Really better than alternative + neglected disease
Good surrogate proof with surrogate endpoint
FAST
FASTER
Expected development + Rolling review
Expected development + Rolling review + Senior Staff involvement with intensive guidance
Faster review of marketing application (6 months instead of 10 months)
A PRIZE!
IT CAN BE SOLD
(or clinical but not in the priority endpoint)
MARKET (but still needs to do a ph III)
CMC needs to be ready (careful)
both eligible for priority review if good clinical data at BLA
and another drug ($100M)
EMA equivalent
Accelerated Assessment
EMA equivalent
PRIME
EMA equivalent
Accelerated Assessment (partial)
EMA equivalent
Conditional Approval
*usually to rare diseases, applied when benefits justify the risk

Figure 23. What Goes Through the Investor's Mind?

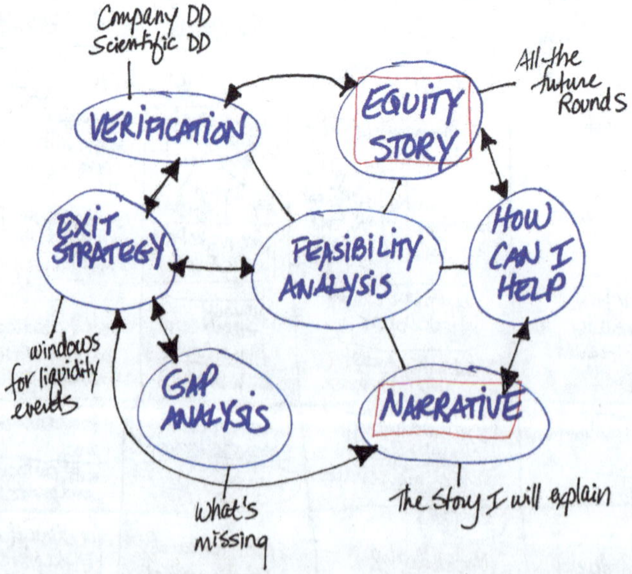

When an investor meets an entrepreneur for the first time, they are not merely hearing a pitch, but embarking on a comprehensive analysis of the venture at hand.

- **Verification:** The investor needs to validate the claims made by the entrepreneur. This involves the investor tapping into their own network of key opinion leaders who can provide unbiased perspectives and corroboration.
- **Feasibility Analysis:** The investor scrutinizes the viability of the business model or scientific proposal. This involves comparing the proposal with similar projects they have encountered and identifying suitable individuals who can elevate the venture to its full potential.
- **Gap Analysis:** The investor identifies gaps in the science, business model, or team. Understanding these gaps helps them assess not just the current value of the proposal but also its future potential.
- **Equity Story:** The investor considers the venture's current valuation and future valuations, predicting the venture's trajectory over successive funding rounds. They also contemplate who among their co-investors might participate in subsequent rounds and how the ownership structure will evolve.
- **Narrative Crafting:** Investors understand the power of a compelling narrative. They start framing the investment thesis in an engaging, bold, and convincing manner that will resonate with their network of venture capital colleagues.
- **Exit Strategy:** Investors need to gauge the potential for a liquidity event — how and when they can exit the investment profitably. This includes considering various scenarios and structuring contingency plans for both early and delayed liquidity events.
- **Role Assessment:** Investors assess the level of involvement expected from them in the venture. Understanding whether they are expected to be silent partners or actively engaged in strategic decisions helps them align their personal ambitions and capacities with the investment.

Rule #15

Types of Mistakes a Venture Capitalist Can Make

"Have no fear of perfection — you'll never reach it."
Salvador Dali

In the realm of emerging technologies, where the dichotomy of risk and reward often hangs in a delicate balance, being cognizant of potential missteps is as important as recognizing opportunities.

However, it's not just about understanding the nature of these mistakes, but also appreciating their origins and implications. This awareness extends beyond mere risk mitigation; it serves as a beacon that can guide entrepreneurs toward more astute decision-making, better alignment with investor expectations, and ultimately, greater chances of success.

A particularly intriguing facet of this journey is the concept of "calculated risks." These are risks that, while present, are recognized, understood, and accounted for in the venture's strategic plan. They represent a conscious choice by the entrepreneur and the investor to proceed with certain actions despite the inherent uncertainties, due to the potential of high returns. This calculated risk-taking forms the backbone of many successful ventures in the field of emerging technologies.

Mastering the art of calculated risk-taking while avoiding catastrophic errors is a skill that is honed over time. It requires a thorough understanding of the venture's landscape, an ability to foresee potential pitfalls, and the courage to make tough decisions when the path forward is fraught with uncertainty.

With the right mindset and tools, entrepreneurs can turn this challenging process into an exciting journey of discovery, growth, and eventual success. As we explore these potential errors, our aim is to provide a comprehensive guide that goes beyond risk aversion. It's about empowering entrepreneurs with the knowledge to make informed decisions, fostering an understanding of venture capital mindset, and providing a roadmap to navigate the tumultuous yet rewarding path of science-driven entrepreneurship.

Analyzing Errors in Investment Decisions: The 2x2 Matrix

To aid in our understanding and analysis of investment errors, we will employ a simple yet effective tool: a 2x2 matrix. This matrix provides a conceptual framework that captures the essence of the decision-making process in venture capital investing. It comprises two axes:

- **The Outcome Axis:** This axis represents the eventual reality of a company's fate in the future, which could end up as either a failure or a success. This outcome, though uncertain at the time of investment, will be revealed as time progresses and the company evolves.
- **The Decision Axis:** This axis embodies the investor's present action, which is to either invest in a particular company or to abstain from doing so. This decision is based on an assessment of the company's potential, drawn from current knowledge and the investor's judgment.

Four quadrants emerge from this matrix:

- **Investing in Success (IS):** The investor chooses to invest, and the company eventually succeeds. This is the desired outcome, representing a correct decision and leading to a profitable investment.
- **Investing in Failure (IF):** The investor chooses to invest, but the company eventually fails. This is an investment error, an unfortunate result where the investor incurs a loss.
- **Not Investing in Failure (NIF):** The investor chooses not to invest, and the company eventually fails. This is a correct decision, where the investor wisely avoided a loss.
- **Not Investing in Success (NIS):** The investor chooses not to invest, but the company eventually succeeds. This is an opportunity loss, a missed chance that could have led to profit.

Figure 24. Error Matrix

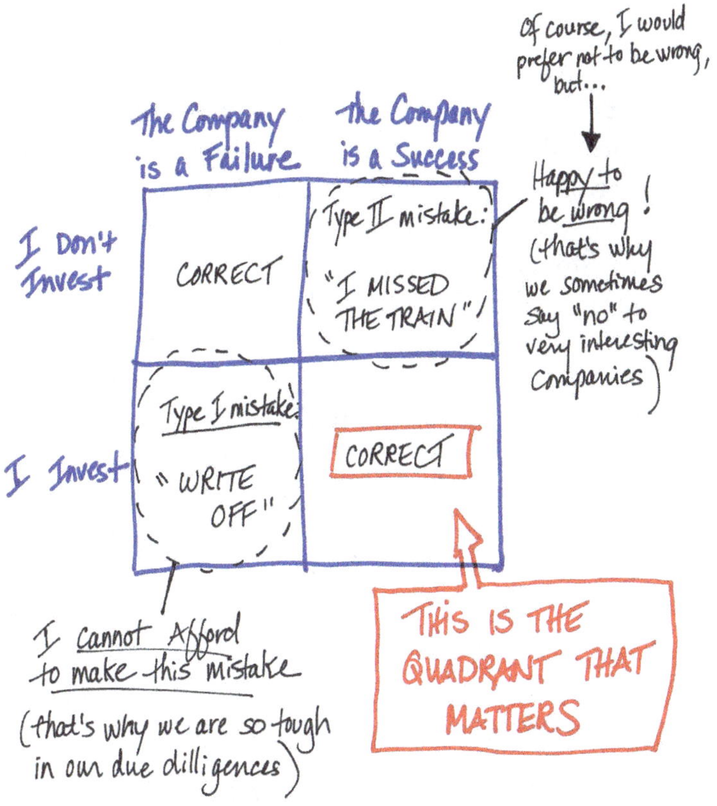

This figure represents a 2x2 matrix visualizing the possible outcomes of investment decisions in venture capital. The matrix's horizontal axis represents the real outcomes of the company — either a failure or a success. The vertical axis represents the investor's decision to invest or not to invest.

- On the flip side of errors is **the art of being right** — successfully identifying and investing in the companies that go on to realize their potential. This is the ultimate goal of every investor: to discern the diamond in the rough, the startup that, despite all odds and uncertainties, will make groundbreaking strides in its field.
- Being right involves a combination of smart analysis, thorough due diligence, and sometimes, a dash of intuition about what will belong to the future of society. It's about understanding the nuanced interplay between technological feasibility, market demand, and the startup's ability to execute effectively. Moreover, being right isn't simply about avoiding errors. It's about making strategic choices that maximize returns and contribute to a balanced, resilient portfolio capable of weathering the inevitable storms of the startup ecosystem.
- This matrix underscores the need for risk management, due diligence, and a forward-looking approach in venture capital investing. It also illustrates the dynamic nature of decision-making in this field, where not all mistakes are detrimental, and some might even signify a robust and flourishing innovation ecosystem.

At the outset, let's consider the two quadrants where the investor's decisions are perfectly aligned with the eventual fate of the company. The first is the scenario in which a company does not succeed, and the investor wisely chose not to invest. This scenario, depicted in the upper left quadrant of our matrix, signifies the right decision — no investment in failure (NIF). Similarly, the lower right quadrant represents a scenario where a company is successful and the investor, presciently, chose to invest, thus investing in success (IS). This too is a situation where the investor has made the right decision.

When an investor makes a correct decision to invest in a successful company (IS), they generate significant returns on their investment. On the other hand, the decision not to invest in a company that eventually fails (NIF) also has broader economic implications. By correctly identifying and avoiding potential failures, investors help to channel economic resources more efficiently. Capital that might have been tied up in unsuccessful ventures is instead available for more promising opportunities.

However, these two quadrants, while representing ideal scenarios, do not capture the complexity and potential pitfalls of investment decisions. It is in the other two quadrants that we find the mistakes and, consequently, the greatest opportunity for learning.

Understanding Type I Errors: False Positives

Venturing into the terrain of investment mistakes, we encounter the type I error, aptly classified as a "false positive." This type of error is represented in the lower left quadrant of our 2x2 matrix and manifests when an investor backs a company that ultimately fails — an investment in failure (IF). The crux of a type I error lies in the misjudgment of the company's potential, a misstep that leads to a financial loss and an expensive learning experience for the investor.

In a bid to circumvent such errors, venture capitalists undertake a rigorous due-diligence process. This involves undertaking a comprehensive analysis, conducting extensive market research, soliciting expert opinions, investigating the competition, and performing risk assessment, among other things. This process, while time-consuming and labor-intensive, is essential to make informed investment decisions and minimize the risk of landing in this error-laden quadrant.

The gravity of type I errors requires their minimization. This type of error is particularly damaging as it depletes financial resources and yields no return on investment. Therefore, it is paramount for investors to safeguard themselves by meticulously evaluating investment opportunities, maintaining a diverse portfolio, and continually refining their investment strategy based on past experiences and emerging industry trends.

Grasping Type II Errors: False Negatives

The next quadrant in our analysis of investment mistakes features type II errors, or "false negatives." These errors arise when an investor declines an opportunity to back a company that ultimately flourishes. Captured in the upper right quadrant of our 2x2 matrix, type II errors — not investing in success (NIS) — represent missed trains: opportunities that slipped through the investor's fingers, only to prove their worth later on.

While type II errors may initially seem unfortunate, they embody a somewhat positive aspect. A high occurrence of such mistakes is a testament to a rich, vibrant ecosystem brimming with promising and innovative ideas.

The frequency of these errors can, paradoxically, serve as a measure of the health and vitality of the entrepreneurial landscape. As such, investors may view these missed opportunities not solely as errors but as indicators of a thriving market teeming with potential.

Besides, let me share a secret with you: Many more trains will pass by. Every train is an investment opportunity, and the reality is that it's impossible and often unwise to hop onto every one of them. Instead, ensure that you optimize your strategy to minimize the occurrence of type I errors as much as possible.

So, a key factor in venture capital investing is the delicate art of portfolio balance. To mitigate risk and maximize returns, investors need to manage their portfolios judiciously. This often means making hard choices and passing on potentially profitable investments. While this might lead to an increased likelihood of type II errors, it is a necessary concession to maintain a balanced, diversified portfolio.

Understanding that this balance requires careful judgment and sometimes saying "no" to appealing projects is an integral part of successful venture capital investing.

The Uniqueness of Emerging Technologies and Innovation

The world of emerging technologies and innovations presents a distinct and challenging landscape when it comes to managing errors. The high levels of uncertainty and rapidly changing dynamics inherent in these sectors amplify the potential for both type I and type II errors.

For example, a promising technology today might fail to meet expectations due to unforeseen hurdles or rapid advancements in competing technologies. On the other hand, investors might overlook a breakthrough due to its novelty or perceived risk.

The unique characteristics of science-driven companies can amplify the complexity and uncertainty of investment decisions. These features bring their own challenges and considerations, which can influence the likelihood and impact of both type I and type II errors.

- **Technological Complexity and Unpredictability:** The science behind these companies is often cutting-edge and highly complex. Unforeseen technical issues can arise, causing promising projects to fail (leading to type I errors). Conversely, the complexity and novelty of the technology might lead to underestimation of its potential, leading to type II errors.
- **Long Development Cycles:** Science-driven companies, particularly in sectors like biotech or pharmaceuticals, often face long development cycles. The time lag from initial research to commercial product can span years, even decades, requiring a lot of capital. This prolonged timeline can increase the risk of both types of errors, as predictions made at the time of investment may be rendered inaccurate by changes in the market, technology, or regulatory landscape.
- **Regulatory Environment:** Many science-driven companies operate in heavily regulated industries. Regulatory decisions can significantly impact a company's success or failure. A negative regulatory decision can lead to a type I error if an investment has already been made, while an unexpected positive regulatory decision could trigger a type II error in cases where investors opted not to invest.
- **Market Access:** The acceptance and utilization of new biotech solutions by payers and regulators often present unpredictable challenges, especially when the solutions are highly innovative

or disruptive. Factors such as stringent regulatory requirements, complex pricing negotiations, or the necessity for extensive clinical evidence can slow down the process of market access, leading to type I errors. Conversely, if a drug or technology swiftly secures favorable reimbursement and regulatory approvals, this can lead to type II errors if an investor initially underestimated a company's potential for market access. Therefore, understanding the dynamics of market access, from the perspectives of regulators and payers, becomes a vital part of the evaluation process in biotech investing.

- **Competition and Timing:** The competitive landscape can drastically change during the time it takes for a science-driven company to develop its technology. An influx of competitors or advancements in alternative solutions can significantly influence a company's success or failure.

Balancing type I and type II errors in venture capital involves a meticulous investment process, grounded in thorough due diligence, diversification, and risk management.

- **Rigorous Due Diligence:** Obviously, one of the most effective ways to mitigate type I errors (investing in startups that fail) is to conduct rigorous due diligence. This includes an in-depth analysis of a startup's business model, market potential, competitive landscape, management team, and financials. Thorough due diligence can identify potential red flags or challenges that might lead to startup failure.
- **Portfolio Diversification:** Diversifying your investment portfolio across different sectors, stages, and regions can help manage both type I and type II errors. If some investments fail (type I errors), others might succeed, thus balancing out the losses. Moreover, by having a broad portfolio, you increase the chances of investing in a startup that becomes successful (thus reducing type II errors), even if you might miss some along the way.
- **Risk Management:** Implementing a robust risk management strategy can help. This involves making investment decisions based on your risk tolerance. For instance, if you have a high risk tolerance, you might be willing to accept a greater likelihood of type I errors, hoping that the successful investments will more

than make up for the failures. On the other hand, if you have a low risk tolerance, you might focus on minimizing type I errors, even if it means passing on some potentially successful startups and thus increasing the likelihood of type II errors.

- **Expertise and Network:** Leveraging industry expertise and your network can also help reduce both type I and type II errors. With a deep understanding of an industry, you're more likely to spot red flags that others might miss (reducing type I errors) and identify potential winners early (reducing type II errors). Your network can also provide valuable insights and information that can aid your investment decision-making process.
- **Post-Investment Management:** Lastly, active post-investment management can help mitigate type I errors. By closely monitoring your investments and providing strategic guidance to the companies you've backed, you can help them navigate challenges and increase their chances of success.

Alpha and Beta in Venture Capital

In the realm of statistical hypothesis testing, type I and type II errors hold significant implications, often intertwined with concepts of Alpha (**α**) and Beta (**β**). These concepts are frequently used as statistical benchmarks in investment decision-making processes, especially in venture capital where risk and uncertainty are inherent. Drawing the parallels between these statistical terms and investment errors can help illuminate how these concepts play out in real-world decision-making.

First, let's delve into what type I and type II errors mean in a statistical context. A type I error, also known as a false positive, occurs when a hypothesis is rejected when it is, in fact, true. The probability of committing a type I error is denoted by the Greek letter Alpha (**α**), also known as the level of significance. Lowering **α** reduces the chances of a type I error.

As we have already discussed, one common strategy to manage type I errors (investing in startups that fail) is portfolio diversification. By investing in a wide variety of companies across different sectors, stages, and regions, investors can mitigate the risk associated with any single investment. If some investments fail, others might succeed, thus balancing out the losses. This strategy can also help limit type II errors by ensuring a broad range of investment opportunities.

Conversely, a type II error, or a false negative, occurs when a hypothesis is not rejected when it is, in fact, false. The likelihood of a type II error is denoted by Beta (**β**). The statistical power of a test, defined as 1-**β**, is the probability that a hypothesis will be correctly rejected when it is false. Enhancing statistical power reduces the likelihood of a type II error. Building and leveraging industry expertise can reduce type II errors. Investors with a deep understanding of a specific industry are more likely to spot opportunities others might miss. This industry insight can help investors make informed investment decisions and identify potential winners early.

The relationship between **α** (type I error) and **β** (type II error) is often described as a trade-off. Minimizing type I errors could increase type II errors, and vice versa. As a venture capitalist, it's essential to manage this delicate balance. If you're overly cautious to avoid type I errors, you might miss out on potentially lucrative investments, thereby increasing type II errors. Conversely, if you're too aggressive in chasing every potential "unicorn," you could end up with a portfolio filled with type I errors.

A Few Final Concepts

Adding to this interesting interplay of type I and type II errors, one could consider the role of "false discovery rate" (FDR), the expected proportion of false positives among all discoveries. In the context of investing, this would equate to the expected proportion of unsuccessful startups in the portfolio of companies an investor has backed. The investor should aim to minimize the FDR to enhance the portfolio's overall success rate.

Moreover, let's delve as well into the concept of "opportunity cost," which is an integral part of the investment decision-making process. Opportunity cost represents the potential benefits an investor misses out on when choosing one alternative over another. In terms of type I and type II errors, every investment decision carries an opportunity cost. When an investor commits a type I error by backing a failing startup, the opportunity cost is the foregone investment in a potentially successful venture. Conversely, a type II error represents the missed opportunity of not investing in a startup that eventually succeeds.

Lastly, the concept of "risk tolerance" plays a pivotal role in determining the acceptable levels of type I and type II errors for an investor.

Risk tolerance is the degree of variability in investment returns that an investor is willing to withstand. It's highly individual and influenced by factors such as financial goals, investment horizon, and personal disposition. An investor with a high risk tolerance might accept a higher probability of type I errors, anticipating that the successful investments will compensate for the failures. Conversely, an investor with low risk tolerance might focus more on minimizing type I errors, even at the risk of increased type II errors.

Rule #16

Every Investment Is a Story

"There's always a story. It's all stories, really. The sun coming up every day is a story. Everything's got a story in it. Change the story, change the world."

Terry Pratchett

Every investment is a story, a narrative of progress and promise, ambition and anticipation. This is especially true in the world of leading-edge science-driven companies where success often hinges on the ability to tell a compelling tale. Unlike traditional business models that often generate quick returns, these ventures typically require significant time and funding before their pioneering products or solutions ever hit the market. In this field, the narrative woven around a venture is not a luxury, but a necessity.

It is important to understand that there's a longer game at play. Essentially, the narrative crafted today must be robust and convincing enough to be passed on and further elaborated by these initial investors to subsequent potential investors down the line.

Venture investments, particularly in the realm of biotechnology and other science-driven sectors, are often characterized by high capital requirements spread across various financing rounds. The capital-intensive nature of these ventures necessitates the continuous acquisition of new investors, each of whom requires persuasion and assurance of the venture's viability and promise. Hence, the original investor doesn't just need to be convinced about the investment's potential. They also need to become advocates for the venture, equipped with a compelling story that they can relay convincingly to others. Essentially, the initial investors play a crucial role as storytellers, carrying the investment narrative forward to subsequent rounds of financing.

This critical role of the initial investor highlights the utmost importance of crafting an engaging, persuasive, and robust narrative from the get-go. The investment story must be grounded in strong scientific rationale, showcasing a significant problem and a unique, viable solution. It should illuminate the competitive landscape and underline the venture's unique selling proposition. It must also resonate with future aspirations, highlighting the potential growth and long-term prospects of the venture.

The Importance of Story in Investment

The narrative of a leading-edge company is not just a marketing tool, it is an integral part of the venture itself. It acts as the blueprint of the journey that the company has embarked upon, illuminating the path from the initial idea to its potential realization. This narrative doesn't merely tell "what" the company does; it expresses "why" it does what it does and "how" it plans to accomplish its goals. It paints a picture of the problem at hand, articulates why it matters, and describes how the company's unique approach or technology provides an effective solution.

Importantly, a good story distinguishes a company from its competitors, carving out a niche that highlights its unique selling proposition. It underlines the novelty and the potential of the technology or science that the company employs, and positions it within the broader context of the field, reinforcing its relevance and promise.

As much as facts, figures, and data points are essential, investment decisions are also emotionally charged. No investor will ever make a decision because of a number: We need a story. A story stirs the imagination, inspires trust, and triggers an emotional connection. This is crucial, especially in the often-uncertain early stages of a venture, when the financial returns are yet to materialize, and it's the strength of the story that keeps investors engaged and committed. Several critical elements form the structure of a compelling investment story:

- **Problem Identification:** At the heart of every innovation lies a problem in dire need of a solution. The story of an investment should start with clearly identifying this problem. The issue at hand must be significant, relevant, and compelling enough to warrant the need for a solution. The problem's gravity provides a strong motivation for investors, inspiring them to contribute to a venture that aims to solve it.

- **Unique Solution:** Once the problem is established, the narrative should introduce the unique solution that the company brings to the table. This solution should be grounded in advanced scientific development and innovation, highlighting the company's unique capabilities and resources. The narrative should communicate how the proposed solution effectively addresses the identified problem and why it is better than existing solutions, if any.
- **High Activity in the Area:** A crucial part of the investment narrative involves shedding light on the level of activity in the particular industry or sector. This includes the number of financing deals that are taking place, the volume of these transactions, and, most importantly, the frequency and size of liquidity events, exits, or transactions with pharmaceutical companies or Initial Public Offerings (IPOs).

  High levels of activity often indicate a vibrant and growing market, one that holds substantial promise and potential for investors. Such activity also signifies the confidence of other investors in the sector, thereby offering some level of validation. It is important to explain the implications of these activities — for instance, large liquidity events signal profitable exit opportunities, and frequent deals might suggest a fast-paced, competitive environment. This element of the narrative helps investors understand the dynamism and potential profitability of the investment area.
- **People Behind the Idea — Scientific Stature:** When considering an investment in a science-driven venture, it's crucial to assess the scientific stature of the team and those backing the idea. The creator of the science's importance in the field, their academic credentials, and previous achievements can have a significant impact on the viability and potential of the venture. The publication of research associated with the venture in reputable scientific journals enhances credibility and provides validation from the scientific community.

Additionally, the participation of experienced independent directors on the board signals faith in the venture's potential, offering further reassurance to investors. Furthermore, endorsement from key opinion leaders, respected individuals in the field, implies that the venture's science is promising and worth investing in, thereby boosting investor confidence and enhancing the compelling nature of the investment narrative.

- **Future Potential of the Field or Technology:** A compelling story should resonate with the investors' aspirations for the future. Tying back to the "forest and the trees" concept, the narrative should demonstrate the investment's relevance to the future of the field, pointing out the trajectory it is expected to take.

  A compelling story should spark enthusiasm and create a sense of anticipation about the company's potential for growth and success. This aspect of the narrative contributes to the sustainability of investor engagement and commitment.

Thus, the importance of story in investment is twofold. On the one hand, it provides the necessary context and clarity that helps potential investors understand the vision and potential of a venture. On the other, it serves as an emotional anchor, providing a sense of purpose and direction that can inspire trust and commitment.

An Amazing Truth

The dynamic nature of cutting-edge fields such as biotech, synthetic biology, AI, or any leading-edge space for that matter, is what makes them so incredibly fascinating. It's also what makes them challenging, and to succeed in these fields, one needs to be adaptable and forward-thinking.

As I reflect on my journey, one fact stands out starkly: The field evolves with staggering rapidity. It is a testament to this that even the companies in which I once saw immense potential and that yielded great success, I might not choose to invest in today.

If these same companies, which once were great winners for us, were to approach us now, they might not make it through to a second meeting. This is not because these companies have lost their value, nor does it undermine their past achievements. Instead, it underscores the accelerated pace at which the landscape is evolving and, consequently, our ever-evolving benchmarks for investment potential.

Like natural evolution, it's survival of the fittest. Companies that were once fit for the investment environment may not meet the evolved standards of today's context. This constant flux underscores the need for investors and entrepreneurs to continually update their strategies rather than resting on past laurels.

Another angle I want you to consider here is the role of serendipity and randomness in venture success. As much as we'd like to believe that success is purely a function of strategic decision-making and superior judgment, the reality is often far from it.

Sometimes, it's about being in the right place at the right time, spotting an opportunity that others missed, or simply riding a wave of favorable market conditions. Recognizing this aspect can make us more humble and open to diverse investment opportunities.

We, as investors, evolve with the landscape. Our understanding deepens, our perspectives widen, and our strategies refine. We learn from every decision, every investment, every success, and every setback. We are not the same investors we were 20 years ago, or even a year ago. And that's exactly how it should be.

In essence, past success does not guarantee future success in this rapidly evolving field. Being open to change, crafting good stories to tell other investors along the way, staying curious, and continually learning — these are the traits that will allow us to navigate the shifting landscape of leading-edge spaces. We need to keep our fingers on the pulse of change, to anticipate the direction of evolution, and to adapt accordingly. This is our pathway to continued success in a world where the only constant is change.

Rule #17
Identify Your "Wow" Slide

"I paint my reality."
Frida Kahlo

The "wow" slide is no ordinary component of a pitch deck. It stands as a pivotal point in the narrative of the company, embodying the transformative potential of the venture.

My decision to invest in a company often hinges on one or two slides that capture the essence of why the company sparks my enthusiasm and curiosity. Typically, this is a slide rooted in science, presenting a compelling piece of evidence such as the extraordinary outcomes of an experiment, the significant improvement the company can contribute to a patient's condition, the extent to which we can alter the manifestation of a disease, or the encapsulation of the company's unique value proposition, among other things. It is here that the groundbreaking results of an experiment are unfolded in all their wonder.

In essence, the "wow" slide functions as a storytelling tool, translating the complex, multifaceted essence of a venture into a simple, compelling detail of the narrative that grips the audience and fuels their imagination.

The potency of the "wow" slide is not confined to its informational value. The slide, if crafted with precision and creativity, can wield a significant emotional and psychological impact on potential investors and stakeholders. It acts as a catalyst. The "wow" slide does not merely present a fact or argument; it stages a "What if we accomplish this?" moment that invites the audience to envision the future, the possibilities, and the impact of a company's success.

Crafting the "Wow" Slide

The "wow" slide stands as a testament to the potential, vision, and value proposition of a company. Its preparation calls for an in-depth understanding of the business and a knack for conveying complex ideas in a compelling, easily understandable format. So, how does one go about crafting an effective "wow" slide?

At the heart of an impactful "wow" slide lies robust, data-driven facts. This means that rather than making sweeping statements or building upon conjecture, the slide provides concrete, evidence-based insights that firmly establish the company's potential and the feasibility of its vision. It might include, for example, impressive experimental results, the considerable difference that a product or service can make to customers (a significant "delta"), or compelling evidence demonstrating a product's ability to reverse the phenotype of a disease.

The data used should be precise and backed by solid statistical treatment, offering a clear snapshot of the company's capabilities and future promise. The power of the "wow" slide rests on its factual integrity, where each claim is substantiated with substantial evidence, echoing Carl Sagan's sentiment that "extraordinary claims require extraordinary evidence."

Therefore, a pitfall to avoid when crafting a "wow" slide is a lack of precision or absence of compelling data to support a claim. Incomplete data, vague statements, or information that lacks context and explanation can significantly dilute the impact of the slide and might even cast doubt on the credibility of the company.

It's crucial, as well, that the aesthetics do not overshadow the core message. Personally, I prefer black over white, simple and no design, but all investors have different attitudes.

In any case, the "wow" slide needs to engage the audience, not just visually, but also intellectually and emotionally. It's the key slide that you would proudly share to illustrate the reasons behind your investment in the company, underlining the pride and belief you hold in its potential.

The Role of the "Wow" Slide in a Successful Pitch

As our understanding of science and technology deepens, we see an increasing number of startups venturing into complex fields such as biotechnology and synthetic biology. This increase in competition has led to a relative uniformity in proposals, with multiple companies offering similar solutions for the same problem.

In this environment, the "wow" slide takes on an even more critical role. It serves as the beacon that sets a company apart, differentiating its proposal from the rest. By articulating a unique selling proposition, a unique vision, or a unique result, the "wow" slide helps a company stand out amid the noise, be noticed, and be remembered.

For example, in my early investing days, more than 20 years ago, only a handful of groups were working on a solution for breast cancer. The proposals these groups presented were distinctly different from one another.

Fast forward to today, and we see an entirely different scenario. Today, hundreds of new companies are vying to solve the problem of breast cancer, often with scientifically sound proposals that bear striking similarities. The scientific nuances between these companies, in many cases, are not substantial enough to enable easy differentiation.

This context amplifies the importance of having a standout "wow" slide in a company's investment pitch. It becomes crucial to have that one slide that differentiates your proposal from those of the numerous other companies seeking to address the same problem. With an increasing number of companies working on similar solutions, differentiation becomes paramount. The "wow" slide thus takes on a vital role in helping companies stand out in the crowd.

The "wow" slide is often the moment where the investor starts leaning toward the possibility of investing in a company. It encapsulates the "eureka" moment, the "what if we accomplish this" moment that stimulates imagination and ignites interest. However, the "wow" slide isn't a magic bullet: Its power relies on the foundation built by preceding slides and the supportive evidence that follows. Nevertheless, it can serve as the critical push that tips the scales in favor of investment consideration.

Figure 25. A Solid Proof of Concept in Biotech

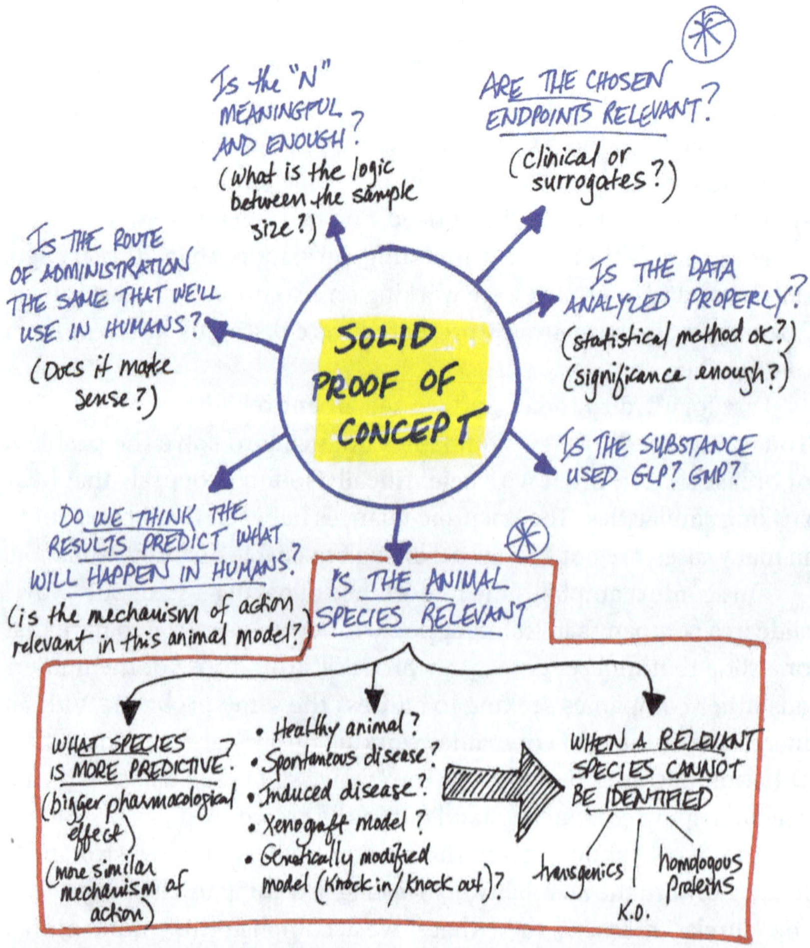

In the world of science-driven ventures, the "wow" slide often represents the crux of a company's investment pitch. Typically, this slide presents the proof of concept, the critical piece of data or insight that serves as evidence of the company's capabilities and the feasibility of its value proposition. As such, the importance of the proof of concept being "solid" or robust cannot be overemphasized. It must hold up to scrutiny from a scientific, statistical, and practical perspective.

- **Relevance of Chosen Endpoints:** These endpoints, whether clinical or surrogate, should be thoughtfully selected to sustain the venture's thesis. Surrogate endpoints, in particular, are often scrutinized, as they might not directly reflect a clinical outcome but rather anticipate it, such as the levels of a protein in blood or an image from magnetic resonance imaging. The relevance and credibility of these endpoints can significantly impact the perceived solidity of the proof of concept.

- **Correctness of Data Analysis:** This entails examining the statistical methods used and assessing the level of statistical significance achieved. Faulty statistical methods or insufficiently significant results can undermine the reliability of the presented proof of concept.
- **Quality of the Substance Used in the Research:** Questions around whether the substance is of good laboratory practice (GLP) or good manufacturing practice (GMP) quality, and whether its chemistry has been enhanced for specific properties like a longer half-life, can impact the perceived robustness of the proof of concept.
- **Relevance of the Animal Species Used:** Investors might seek to understand how predictive the chosen species is for the particular indication under study, whether the animal is healthy or immunosuppressed, whether the disease model is spontaneous or induced, etc. Further complexity is added when considering genetically modified models, such as knock-ins or knock-outs, and their relevance and predictability for human outcomes.
- **How Predictive the Experiment Is:** The predictability of the experiment's results for human outcomes forms another important consideration. Investors might question the relevance of the mechanism of action in the animal model and whether it accurately reflects what might happen in humans.
- **The Route of Administration:** The route used in the experiments, and whether it would be the same in humans, is another critical aspect.
- **The Logic Behind the Proof of Concept:** The logic behind the sample size, the presence of a control group, and whether the experiment's design allows for comparison against the standard of care plus the company's compound also weigh heavily in assessing the solidity of the proof of concept.
- **Regulatory Considerations:** Has the company taken into account potential regulatory issues that might impact the development and marketing of the product or service? An understanding of regulatory requirements is vital for any science-driven venture and can significantly contribute to the perceived robustness of the proof of concept.
- **Feasibility of Scaling:** Do the data presented indicate that the solution or product can be scaled in a cost-effective and efficient manner? Investors are often concerned about scalability since it impacts the venture's growth potential and profitability.
- **Ethical Considerations:** Especially in fields like biotechnology, ethical considerations play a crucial role. Has the company conducted its experiments ethically? This can involve considerations about the treatment of animals in testing or ensuring the solution doesn't exploit vulnerable populations.

Crafting a solid "wow" slide calls for consideration of various factors, ranging from the relevance of endpoints to the predictability of results and the robustness of experimental design.

Rule #18

Use the Right Pitch Structure

"It is coming so fast I can hardly get it down, and shakes me like a great black wind through the bones."

William Burroughs

One of your most vital tools is a clear and compelling pitch. This applies not only when you're pitching to potential investors but also in all your professional interactions. Whether you're aligning your team toward a common goal, seeking buy-in from colleagues, discussing your project with key opinion leaders, negotiating with providers, communicating with the media, or liaising with regulatory bodies, clarity and conviction in your communication are of utmost importance.

An effective pitch doesn't merely convey what you want to accomplish; it also inspires confidence, demonstrates your understanding of the landscape, and highlights your unique proposition. This pitch structure isn't restricted by time constraints — it can be effectively scaled to suit the situation. Whether you're working with a one-minute timespan or a two-hour meeting, you can adapt this structure to fit your needs.

On a lighter note, despite my career in the industry spanning over 25 years, I've yet to be pitched in an elevator. So, let's focus less on the concept of the "elevator pitch" and more on the art of crafting and delivering a compelling narrative, regardless of the setting.

When the Pitch Is About Science

Presenting a compelling pitch is a crucial skill in many professional arenas. However, when the subject matter revolves around science, the stakes are even higher. Not only does one have to persuade potential investors or stakeholders about the value of an idea, but also convincingly portray its scientific soundness.

A successful scientific pitch requires a delicate balance between detail and simplicity, precision and accessibility, caution and boldness. Despite the varying levels of scientific understanding among audiences, you should expect high scientific literacy when presenting your pitch, especially in investment circles.

Many potential investors, particularly those in biotech and similar fields, either have robust scientific knowledge themselves or have access to key opinion leaders and advisors to provide expert consultation. The scrutiny your pitch may undergo can be intense, with every claim dissected and every piece of data evaluated.

This scrutiny emphasizes the importance of maintaining utmost scientific rigor in your presentation. Your pitch should therefore uphold the standards of Science with a capital "S," able to withstand thorough examination and inspire confidence in its scientific soundness.

Depending on the setting and time available, some of these tips may apply:

- **The Imperative of Truth:** At the core of any scientific pitch must be the unwavering commitment to truth. Science values facts, evidence, and reality, and as such, any proposition must be firmly grounded in verifiable data. This necessitates extensive background research, thorough understanding of the scientific principles involved, and diligent fact-checking. Embellishment or fabrication of details can lead to loss of credibility and trust.
- **Scientific Relevance:** It's important not only that your science is sound, but also that it's relevant. The problem you aim to solve should be significant, and your proposed solution should have a clear impact on that problem. Ensure that you establish the importance of your work in a broader context.
- **Level of Detail:** Depending on your audience's scientific literacy, the level of detail you include in your pitch may need to be adjusted. While it's crucial to provide evidence supporting your claims, overly technical details may become a hindrance rather than a benefit. Be prepared to explain complex concepts in accessible ways, but also be ready to delve deeper if prompted.

- **Use of References:** Citing relevant, high-quality scientific references is a powerful way to demonstrate the validity of your proposition. It indicates that your ideas are not developed in isolation, but are built upon the existing body of scientific knowledge. References also show you are informed about the latest research in your field and that your idea aligns with current understanding. Also, transparency is paramount. This includes being open about your data collection and analysis methods, conflicts of interest, and any external funding received.
- **Incorporation of Graphs:** Visual representations, particularly graphs, are essential to convey complex scientific data. A well-designed graph can provide a snapshot of large volumes of data, reveal patterns and trends, and facilitate comparisons. However, these graphs must be accurate, easy to understand, and not manipulated to distort the truth.
- **Avoiding Overly Bold Statements:** While bold ideas are often celebrated in the world of entrepreneurship, science values caution and skepticism. Overly bold claims, especially without sufficient evidence, may raise doubts about your judgment and your understanding of the scientific method. It's important to make it clear that all scientific findings are provisional and are subject to revision in light of new evidence. This doesn't undermine your pitch, but rather strengthens it by demonstrating your scientific integrity.
- **Feasibility:** You should convincingly demonstrate the feasibility of your proposed idea. This includes having a realistic timeline, a capable team, the required resources, and a plan to navigate regulatory pathways if applicable.
- **Addressing Limitations and Risks:** Every scientific endeavor carries uncertainty, risks, and limitations. Addressing these upfront in your pitch not only demonstrates your thoroughness but also your readiness to tackle challenges. It shows potential investors that you've thought about potential pitfalls and have plans in place to mitigate them.
- **Clear Communication:** The ability to convey complex scientific ideas in a manner that is easily understandable to non-experts is a highly valued skill. Using clear, jargon-free language, illuminating

Figure 26. Structure of a Compelling Pitch

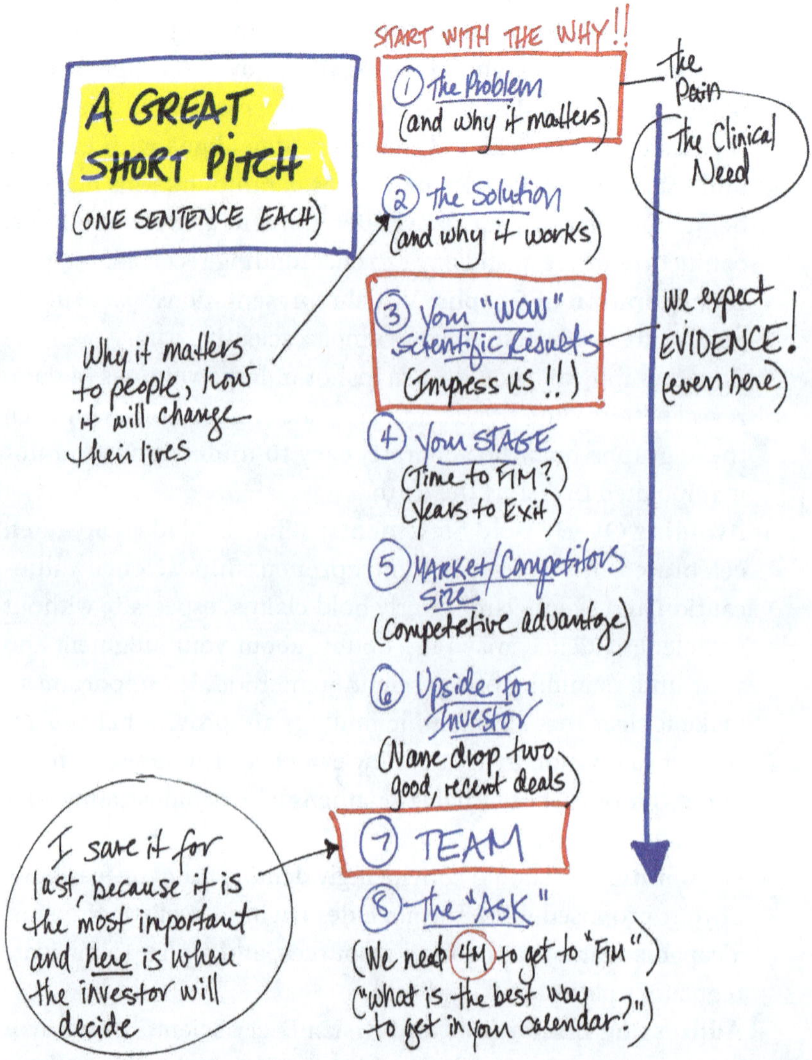

This figure depicts a pitch structure that, in my experience as a biotech investor who has heard thousands of pitches, I find particularly effective. Of course, this is one of numerous potential pitch structures, and different narratives may require different approaches.

Let's delve into each of the eight key components in detail.

- **The Problem:** Every captivating story begins by setting the scene. In the context of your pitch, this involves answering the "why" — why does the problem you're addressing matter? What is the significant "pain" you are striving to alleviate in the marketplace? Identifying and articulating the problem forms the cornerstone of your pitch, shaping the context in which your proposed solution will be presented.

- **The Solution and How It Works:** Having established the problem, you can now introduce your solution. Why does it matter to people? How is it going to change their lives? This is where you elucidate your innovative idea, explaining how it will effectively address the identified problem. Your audience needs to understand your offering and how it functions.
- **Your "Wow" Science:** This component is your chance to astound the audience with your unique scientific proposition or groundbreaking technological innovation. However, remember that your claims must be substantiated with compelling evidence — "wow" without validation may leave the audience skeptical.
- **Market Size and Competitive Landscape:** Delve into the market dynamics here. An overview of the market size and an analysis of key competitors are crucial. Don't forget to spotlight your unique selling proposition and articulate your competitive advantage, addressing the "why us" part of your pitch. Why is your company not just another player, but a game-changer?

As you can see, a compelling pitch is much like a novella — it unfolds with a rhythmic logic, weaving a tale that draws in the listener. It all begins with a pressing problem that sets the stage, swiftly followed by our hero, the ingenious solution. Of course, no story is complete without the thrilling "how" — the dazzling science that makes our solution possible. And then, the plot thickens as we enter the crowded marketplace, teeming with competitors. But fear not! For our hero stands tall, backed by our distinct advantages that make it not just another player, but the game-changer. The narrative threads of a good pitch aren't meant to just entertain — they're designed to weave a compelling vision that plants itself firmly in the investor's mind. Now we follow with:

- **Your Stage, Time to Market, and Years to Liquidity Event:** This segment provides the logistical and strategic details of your venture. Define your current stage, estimate the time to market, and offer potential timelines to liquidity events. This helps investors understand the realistic timeline they're looking at and sets appropriate expectations.
- **Potential Upside for Investors:** Investors, while interested in your story, ultimately want to know about potential returns. Demonstrate the potential upside of investing in your proposition. Using illustrative examples from recent deals in similar fields can lend credibility to your claim.
- **The Team:** The backbone of your venture is your team. Highlight each team member's expertise, skills, and unique contributions, painting a holistic picture of a capable, dynamic team poised to drive the venture to success.
- **The Ask:** Lastly, communicate clearly how much capital you're seeking and for what specific purposes this funding will be used. What milestones will the investment help the company achieve? Conclude by asking for a clear next step, usually a follow-up meeting to discuss the proposition in more detail.

This carries your audience logically from problem identification to your unique solution, through your offering's potential and logistics, and concludes with a clear "ask." It's an articulate, persuasive narrative, a story that has the potential to secure the investment you seek.

examples, and engaging narratives can help make your scientific pitch accessible and relatable to a broader audience.

- **Innovation and Novelty:** The field of science is driven by new ideas, fresh perspectives, and novel approaches. While your pitch should be rooted in existing scientific knowledge, also highlight the innovation in your proposition. What makes your idea stand out? How is it different from what's already out there?
- **Responsiveness to Questions:** In scientific discussions, questions are inevitable and a sign of audience engagement. Be prepared to handle questions with poise, clarity, and humility. If you don't know the answer, be honest and admit it rather than trying to bluff your way through. This will show your honesty and respect for scientific rigor.

In conclusion, a successful scientific pitch requires a commitment to truth, a thorough understanding of the subject matter, careful presentation of data, caution in making claims, acknowledgment of limitations, and clear communication.

Rule #19

The Anatomy of a Term Sheet in Science-Driven Companies

"Signing a term sheet is like getting engaged, and the full financing is the wedding."
Guy Kawasaki

If, after numerous meetings, potentially spanning months, the investor becomes convinced about the future prospects of your company, they will progress to the next stage. Eventually, they will send you a term sheet.

In the world of startups and venture capital, a term sheet plays a pivotal role in outlining the key terms and conditions of an investment. This pivotal document serves as the foundation upon which the intricate relationship between an investor and a startup is built. Its significance in the investment process is paramount as it maps out the contours of the proposed deal, laying the groundwork for future negotiations.

In essence, a term sheet is a non-binding agreement, a sketch of the investor's offer that stands contingent on the completion of a thorough due diligence process. It's akin to a roadmap outlining the potential journey both parties will embark upon together, yet neither is legally obligated to follow this course until the agreement is formalized. It provides the entrepreneur with a glimpse into the investor's vision for the partnership, including their expectations, proposed financial contribution, and the structure they envision for the partnership.

Understanding the anatomy of a term sheet, therefore, is of critical importance for entrepreneurs. It equips them with the knowledge required to navigate the complexities of venture capital negotiations, enabling them to protect their interests and ultimately secure a deal that aligns with their vision and objectives.

Term sheets, while universal in their use, can vary in their content and complexity, depending on the nature of the company and the sector in which it operates. A term sheet for a science-driven company, particularly one involved in cutting-edge research or technology, often encompasses more complex elements, including:

- **Intellectual property rights** are of significant concern in science-driven companies, given the crucial role of patents and proprietary technology in defining their competitive edge. As such, term sheets in this sector often include provisions related to the protection and licensing of these rights.
- **Regulatory milestones,** especially in industries like biotech and pharmaceuticals, are also vital. Investments can be tranched, or portioned-out, based on the achievement of these milestones, such as successfully completing clinical trial phases or obtaining regulatory approvals.
- Lastly, due to the specialized nature of the product or technology, **technical due diligence is typically more detailed**, requiring expert review. Hence, the term sheet may include provisions for further technical investigation and assessment. Let's review some of the most critical elements.

Valuation and Price per Share

Valuation is often considered the headline figure of a term sheet, and for good reason. The pre-money valuation defines how much the startup is worth before the investment, while the post-money valuation considers the startup's worth after the investment is made. These figures ultimately dictate the percentage ownership the investors will receive for their capital injection. While it's tempting to aim for the highest valuation possible, it's essential to strike a balance to avoid overvaluation, which can lead to issues in subsequent funding rounds (see Chapter 20 about the equity story).

Total Amount of Investment

Here, the investors indicate how much capital they are willing to inject into the company. In a cutting-edge science-driven company, the investment structure can be significantly nuanced. The total amount of investment detailed in the term sheet denotes the aggregate capital the investor is prepared to provide. However, given the specific challenges and high-risk nature inherent in these companies, this capital frequently is disbursed in portions, commonly known as "tranches."

The tranche-based disbursement structure is closely tied to the achievement of certain milestones. These milestones are predefined goals that the company agrees to meet. They may include a wide variety of objectives, such as securing regulatory approvals, completing a phase of research and development, or reaching some specific scientific results. In the context of science-driven companies, these milestones often are deeply technical and specific to the nature of the company's work.

The tranche-based investment provides investors with a degree of protection, ensuring that the company is progressing satisfactorily before additional funds are released. This approach can be advantageous for science-driven companies as well, as it provides them with a clear roadmap of expectations and the promise of continued financial support upon successful execution. It's also important to note that these milestones, as well as the amount and timing of tranches, are usually subject to negotiation between the company and the investors.

Board Composition

The makeup of the board of directors can significantly impact a company's strategic direction. This part of the term sheet outlines who will serve on the company's board of directors post-investment, who appoints board members, and how many boad members each party can appoint.

To maintain some control over the company's direction, venture capitalists often require board seats as a condition of their investment. It's crucial for entrepreneurs to carefully consider board composition and maintain a healthy balance of power.

In a cutting-edge science-driven company, the composition of the board can play a vital role in the direction and success of the company. With its profound responsibility of setting the company's strategic direction, the board is a crucial component in steering the company toward its goals.

Independent board members often play a key role in maintaining the balance of power on the board and ensuring the company stays on a steady course. These individuals bring an external perspective and unbiased judgment, adding diversity of thought and helping the company avoid potential conflicts of interest.

Science-driven companies often benefit substantially from their board members. These individuals, with their extensive technical knowledge, can provide valuable insights into the specific industry or scientific area the company operates in, contributing to more informed and effective decision-making.

It's common for the leadership structure to evolve as the company grows. Founders often serve as the initial CEOs of science-driven companies, leveraging their deep understanding of the technology and the vision that underlies the company's inception. However, as the company matures and expands, it may require different skill sets to navigate the new challenges and complexities that come with growth. In such cases, founders may step aside, making room for a more experienced CEO capable of steering the company through its next growth stage. The founder's ongoing involvement can take various forms, ranging from staying on the board, serving as chief scientific officer (CSO), or in some other strategic role.

Given the technical nature of science-driven companies, positions such as CSO and chief medical officer (CMO) are often integral to the board. The CSO, typically the founder or an expert in the company's specific field of science, provides crucial insights into the technical aspects of the company's work. The CMO, usually a seasoned medical professional, guides the company in medical matters, especially important in biotech companies dealing with patient-focused products or services.

Reserved Matters

In a term sheet, "reserved matters" refer to a predefined list of specific company decisions or actions that require the approval of the investors (maybe a special majority of them) or a specific class of shareholders. This provision protects the rights and interests of the investors by giving them a voice in major decisions that could significantly impact the company's direction or value.

The scope of reserved matters can vary significantly depending on the negotiation between the founders and the investors, but they generally encompass fundamental decisions that could alter the company's course. Such decisions may include:

- Changing the company's capital structure, such as issuing new shares.
- Amending the company's constitutional documents.
- Significantly changing the business plan or the nature of the business.
- Initiating large-scale expenditures, acquisitions, or disposals.
- Hiring or firing key executives or board members.
- Entering into significant debt.
- Selling the company or significant parts of its assets.

While this provision safeguards the investors, it's essential for the company founders to ensure that the scope of reserved matters does not stifle the company's ability to make timely decisions and remain agile. Hence, the definition of Reserved Matters often requires careful negotiation to strike a balance between investor protection and operational flexibility.

Conditions Precedent

"Conditions precedent" in a term sheet represents stipulations that must be fulfilled before the completion of the investment transaction. These conditions essentially serve as prerequisites, defining the obligations of the startup to ensure that the deal proceeds smoothly. If these conditions are not met, the proposed investor has the right to walk away from the deal.

In the context of a science-driven company, conditions precedent could be quite specific and varied, reflecting the unique risks and considerations of this industry. Here are a few examples:

- **IP Verification:** Ensuring that the startup holds valid intellectual property (IP) rights to the technology they're developing. This could involve the completion of patent applications or resolving any outstanding IP disputes.
- **Regulatory Approvals:** Companies may need to obtain regulatory approvals or meet certain milestones (such as successful completion of a phase in clinical trials) before investment proceeds.

- **Technical Validation:** This might involve independent third-party validation of the startup's technology or scientific claims. For example, reproducibility of experimental results could be a condition precedent in the biotech sector.
- **Key Personnel Appointments:** The appointment of key individuals, such as a CSO or CMO may also be required. These roles are crucial in science-driven companies as they guide the scientific and medical strategy of the startup.
- **Approval by Investment Committee:** This is a classical Condition Precedent that highlights the non-binding nature of the offer. It ensures that the investment has been vetted and approved by the investor's internal committee, a group typically composed of senior members of the investing firm who evaluate potential risks and rewards before giving the green light.

While a term sheet might be non-binding, it is a significant milestone in the investment process that signals a strong interest from the investor in proceeding with the transaction. It is essentially a statement of intent. The non-binding nature of a term sheet shouldn't be cause for concern; instead, it should motivate you to successfully navigate the due diligence process. This process can lead to the final, binding investment agreement that brings the funding into your company.

Remember, the term sheet is a starting point, a compass guiding the direction of the negotiations to come. Take it as a positive step and an opportunity to work diligently toward closing the deal.

Cap Table

The capitalization table, commonly known as the "cap table," is a crucial element of a term sheet that details the ownership structure of a company. The cap table is a detailed breakdown of the company's ownership structure, including current shareholders and their respective equity stakes.

This comprehensive document outlines current shareholders and their respective equity stakes, providing a clear view of who owns what, including the allocation of shares, options, and convertible securities. In science-driven companies, the cap table can be quite distinctive compared to more conventional startups. Here are some unique elements that may surface:

- **Institutional Ownership:** It's commonplace in science-driven companies, especially in the biotech or pharma sectors, to see institutions such as research institutes or universities on the cap table. These institutions often contribute fundamental research or patents that form the basis of the company's technology. In return, they may retain a stake in the company, often as part of a technology licensing agreement.
- **Scientific Founders:** Scientists who have played a key role in developing the technology or scientific insights that underpin the company might be listed as founders and, hence, have substantial equity stakes.
- **Equity for Collaborators:** Sometimes, a science-driven company will be involved in extensive collaboration with other research institutions, contract research organizations, or technology partners. These entities might hold equity as part of their compensation for services, especially in early-stage companies where cash resources are limited.
- **Option Pool for Future Hires:** Given the highly specialized nature of the talent required in science-driven companies, it's common to see an option pool set aside for future hires. This could include roles like CSO, CMO, or other specialist roles.
- **Investor Composition:** The cap table can also give an insight into the investor makeup of a science-driven company. Biotech-focused venture capital firms, strategic investors (like pharmaceutical companies), and government bodies that provide grants or funds may all hold equity.

Liquidation Preference

The liquidation preference determines the payout hierarchy in the event of a company's liquidation; essential it establishes who gets paid first when the company is sold or otherwise liquidated. This provision protects investors by prioritizing their stake over common shareholders, typically founders and employees, in case of a liquidation event such as a sale, bankruptcy, or shutdown.

In the context of a science-driven company, the liquidation preference takes on added importance due to the inherent risks associated with these types of ventures. These companies are typically engaged in high-risk, high-reward industries.

Given the lengthy product development timelines, regulatory hurdles, and the high capital requirements, the risk of company failure can be relatively high. For example, a liquidation preference for venture capital investors may be "1x participating." This means that in the event of a liquidation, the investor would first recoup their investment (hence "1x," or one times the original investment) before the remaining assets are distributed among all the shareholders, including the very same investors — usually called "a double dip."

Another variant is "multiple" liquidation preferences (e.g., 2x, or 3x), where investors are entitled to receive multiple times their original investment before all shareholders receive anything. While these terms can provide extra protection for investors, they also can significantly dilute the payouts for common shareholders in the event of a sale or liquidation. As such, the negotiation of liquidation preferences can be a crucial aspect of the investment discussions in a science-driven company.

As with any negotiation, achieving a balance that rewards investors for the risks they are taking, while also preserving the incentive for founders and employees, is key to a successful and fair outcome.

Dividend Rights

Dividend rights specifies the rights of shareholders to receive a portion of the company's profits. The term sheet typically includes a section stating something like this: "Holders of Series Preferred Shares (Class A) shall be entitled to receive cumulative dividends at the rate of 8% of the Series Preferred Purchase price per annum."

In this case, the term "cumulative dividends" signifies that dividends accrue over time. If for any reason dividends are not paid in a particular year, they accumulate and must be paid out in full before any dividends are distributed to other types of shares. The "rate of 8% of the Series Preferred Purchase price per annum" refers to the dividend yield, essentially the return on investment for the shareholders.

Pre-emptive Rights

Pre-emptive rights give current shareholders the first opportunity to buy new shares issued by the company. This is a right, but not an obligation, to purchase additional shares issued by the company before these shares are offered to external parties. The main purpose of pre-emptive rights is to allow current shareholders to maintain their proportional ownership in the company, thereby preventing dilution of their shares when new shares are issued.

In the context of science-driven companies, these rights are particularly significant due to the often-substantial capital requirements of these companies. As these companies progress, they might need to raise additional capital for further research and development, clinical trials, or scaling of operations. When this happens, companies generally issue additional shares. Shareholders then have the opportunity to purchase these new shares before others, ensuring they can maintain their percentage of ownership.

Tag-Along Rights

These rights allow shareholders to "tag along" if a majority shareholder decides to sell their stake in the company. In other words, if a major shareholder is selling their shares to a third party, the minority shareholder has the right to join the transaction and sell their shares under the same terms and conditions.

In the context of a science-driven company, tag-along rights can be an important safeguard for smaller investors or founders who may not hold the majority of the shares. These companies often involve a wide range of investors, from venture capital firms to individual angel investors, and even institutions or research institutes, each holding varying proportions of equity.

Drag-Along Rights

Drag-along rights allow majority shareholders to force minority shareholders to join in the sale of the company under the same terms and conditions. This is a crucial clause for investors, particularly in science-driven companies, as it provides a means of securing a clean exit.

When a potential buyer is interested in acquiring the company, having to negotiate with multiple shareholders can complicate and potentially derail the transaction. By enabling the majority shareholders to compel the minority shareholders to sell their stakes, the drag-along rights simplify the sale process and ensure a more streamlined exit.

Without drag-along rights, a minority shareholder could potentially hold out for better terms, slowing down the deal and reducing the majority shareholders' leverage. This clause ensures that all shareholders must participate in the sale, safeguarding the majority's investment.

Anti-dilution Provisions

Anti-dilution provisions are designed to safeguard the value of an investor's equity stake if the company issues additional shares at a lower price than the investor initially paid. Such a scenario might occur in a "down round," when a company raises more capital at a lower valuation due to circumstances such as market conditions, performance issues, or strategic pivots.

In the realm of science-driven companies, where the route to profitability can be longer and more complex than in other sectors, anti-dilution provisions carry substantial weight.

The path of these companies is often characterized by multiple funding rounds to support extensive R&D processes, clinical trials, regulatory approvals, and market penetration efforts. Each of these funding rounds carries the potential risk of dilution for existing shareholders.

There are two general types of anti-dilution provisions: full- ratchet and weighted average. The full-ratchet method gives the investor the right to have their investment reassessed at the new, lower price, thus preserving the percentage of their ownership. This method is highly protective of the investor but can be harsh on the company and the other shareholders, as it causes a significant increase in the dilution of their shares.

The weighted average method is less severe and more commonly used. It adjusts the conversion rate of the investor's preferred shares based on the size and price of the new issuance, leading to a less drastic dilution adjustment.

Employee Stock Option Plans

The Employee Stock Option Plan (ESOP) section details the proportion of equity that is set aside specifically for employee stock options. The ESOP is a crucial tool for attracting, retaining, and incentivizing high-quality talent, particularly in science-driven companies that operate in highly competitive fields where specialized expertise is a critical factor.

Incentives are a key driver of human behavior, and as such, they play a crucial role in business performance and success. They have the power to align the interests of the company's stakeholders, inspiring employees to contribute their best efforts toward the achievement of the organization's goals. Therefore, the phrase "people do respond to incentives" encapsulates a fundamental truth that applies not only in business but also in virtually every aspect of life.

In science-driven companies, the development and commercialization of innovative solutions often involve complex, high-stakes problems and long timelines. As a result, these organizations rely heavily on their talented scientists, engineers, and other professionals who have the necessary skills and dedication to navigate these challenges successfully.

To maintain a competitive edge, these companies must ensure that their compensation packages, including the ESOP, incentivize their employees to remain committed and motivated throughout the demanding journey of innovation.

An ESOP provides employees with a direct stake in the company's success, thereby cultivating a sense of ownership and investment in the company's future. It is also a form of non-cash compensation that can be particularly valuable in early-stage companies where cash resources may be constrained.

However, designing an ESOP requires careful consideration to balance the interests of the variety of stakeholders, including employees, founders, and investors. The allocation of options should take into account factors such as the employee's role, performance, potential, and tenure, as well as the company's strategic goals and the potential dilution of existing shareholders.

In addition, the ESOP terms and vesting schedule need to be crafted to ensure that they effectively serve their intended purpose of incentivizing long-term commitment and performance. The ESOP should be distributed with great care and strategic foresight. Once shares have been allocated through an ESOP, it's not easy to reclaim them; therefore, it's important to ensure that stock options are awarded to those employees who are integral to the company's growth and success, the individuals who significantly contribute to the value of the business and demonstrate long-term commitment.

Misallocation of ESOPs can dilute ownership and cause governance issues down the line. Hence, careful planning and strategic decision-making are crucial when setting up and distributing options through an ESOP. Remember, these shares represent a portion of your company's future, so ensure they're placed in the hands of those who will help shape that future positively.

Representations and Warranties

This section includes company statements regarding its current state and operations. These statements, known as reps and warranties, are assertions about the company's financial status, business operations, legality, and other pertinent details. The significance of reps and warranties cannot be overstated, particularly in the context of science-driven companies. This is due to the complex nature of these companies and the inherent risks associated with investing in them.

Intellectual property (IP) plays a crucial role in science-driven companies. Patents, copyrights, trade secrets, and other forms of IP are often the primary assets of these companies, and they form the basis for their competitive advantage and potential profitability. As a result, reps and warranties related to IP are of paramount importance. They may cover topics such as the ownership of IP, the status of patent applications, the existence of infringements or disputes, and the procedures in place to protect IP.

Moreover, given the regulatory scrutiny often associated with science-driven companies, especially those in industries like biotech or pharma, reps and warranties might also address compliance with laws and regulations, the status of necessary approvals or licenses, and the absence of pending or threatened legal actions.

By making these reps and warranties, the company provides investors with a clearer picture of its status and reduces the information asymmetry between the parties. However, it's important to note that any false or misleading reps or warranties can lead to serious legal consequences. Therefore, companies must ensure the accuracy of these statements and promptly disclose any material changes to the investors.

Expiration Date and Exclusivity

This section outlines the period during which the company agrees not to solicit or accept other offers. During the exclusivity period, the company agrees not to seek or entertain other investment offers. This phase allows the interested investor to complete the due diligence process without worrying about competitive bids, thereby providing a secure environment to evaluate the investment thoroughly. The exclusivity period is typically a few weeks to a few months, depending on the complexity of the deal and the due diligence required.

The expiration date, on the other hand, is the date on which the offer presented in the term sheet ceases to be valid if not formally accepted.

In the context of a science-driven company, these terms are particularly important due to the often complex nature of the company's technology or intellectual property. This complexity may require a more extended due-diligence process. Additionally, science-driven companies are often in high demand by investors due to their significant growth potential, making exclusivity a valuable privilege for investors.

Expected Date of Closing

This section indicates when the parties aim to finalize the transaction. It is just an approximation.

It's important to note that while this list covers most term sheet items, the specifics may vary based on the individual deal. It is vital that those involved in the transaction engage with legal counsel when reviewing and negotiating a term sheet.

The Translation of Term Sheet to Shareholders Agreement

A term sheet is just the beginning of the investment journey; it is the first step toward formalizing the investment relationship between the parties involved. Once both sides have agreed to the terms outlined in the term sheet, this understanding is converted into a more detailed and legally binding document: the shareholders' agreement and the investment agreement.

This formal agreement is an extension of the term sheet and provides a comprehensive structure to the relationship between the company and its investors, detailing the rights, responsibilities, and obligations of each party. However, unlike the term sheet, which is generally non-binding, the signed shareholders' agreement is legally enforceable, marking the official commencement of the investment.

Figure 27. Anatomy of a Term Sheet

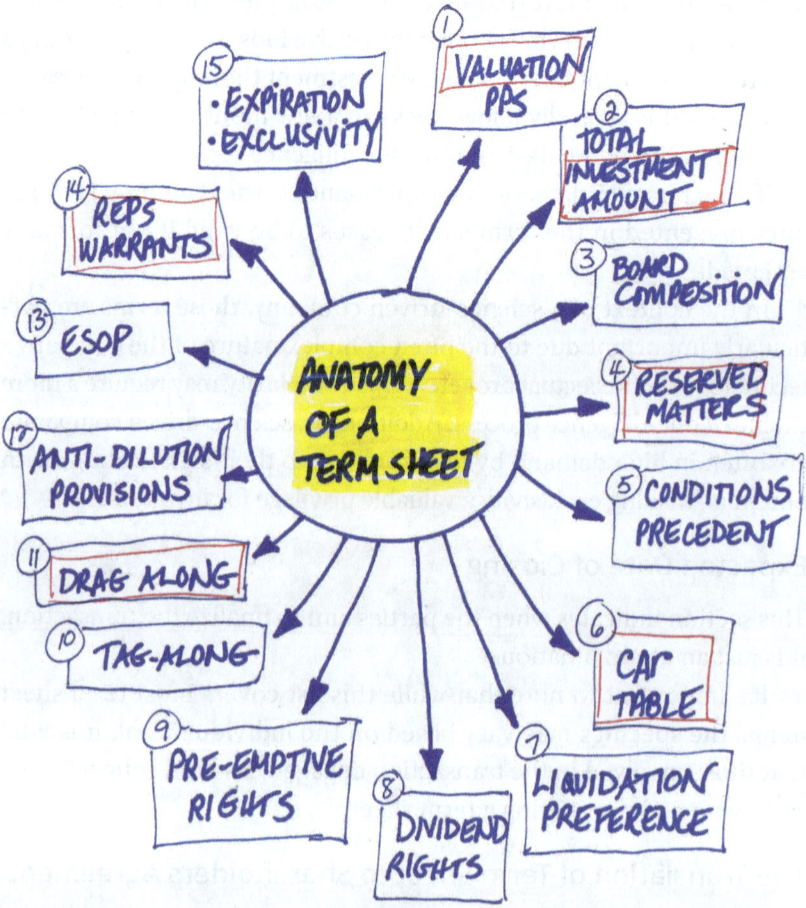

A term sheet is a vital document in the venture capital process, outlining the basic terms and conditions of an investment. While term sheets for standard companies are driven largely by financial and market considerations, science-driven companies, operating at the intersection of innovation, technology, and scientific discovery, necessitate unique considerations in their term sheets.

- **Valuation:** One of the key aspects in any term sheet is the valuation of the company. For standard companies, valuation is often straightforward, based on financial metrics like revenue, profit margins, and market share. In contrast, science-driven companies, particularly those in early stages, may not have any revenue or profits. Here, valuation is based on the potential of the scientific breakthrough, intellectual property, the experience of the team, and market potential.
- **Milestone-Based Financing:** Science-driven companies often face a more extended and uncertain development timeline, particularly if they are in the biotech or pharmaceutical sector. To manage this risk, investors may prefer milestone-based financing, where funds

are released as the company reaches specific development or regulatory milestones. This approach is less common in term sheets for standard companies, where funding is often upfront or based on business performance metrics.

- **Exit Strategy**: Exit strategies can be different for science-driven companies. Given the long development timelines and regulatory uncertainties, exits may take longer and be less predictable. Exits may come in the form of an acquisition by a larger pharmaceutical or technology company, or less commonly, an initial public offering (IPO). The term sheet may include clauses on preferred exit strategies and timelines.
- **Founder Vesting**: Given the critical importance of the scientific founders to the progress of the company, term sheets may include founder vesting schedules that are back-weighted, ensuring that founders are incentivized to stay with the company through critical periods of scientific development.
- **Regulatory and Compliance**: For science-driven companies, particularly those in sectors like biotechnology, healthcare, or environmental science, regulatory approval is a significant part of their journey. The term sheet may thus include provisions about regulatory compliance and how the company plans to achieve necessary approvals.
- **Research and Development Costs**: Science-driven companies often require significant capital for research and development (R&D), especially in the early stages. Term sheets may outline investor commitments toward R&D, highlighting the unique role of these costs in the company's growth. In standard companies, R&D expenses, while important, usually do not command the same level of emphasis.
- **Intellectual Property Rights**: Intellectual property is the lifeblood of science-driven companies. Their valuation largely depends on the uniqueness and potential applicability of their scientific discoveries or technologies. Hence, term sheets for science-driven companies often have comprehensive clauses addressing IP ownership, protection, and future development.
- **Partnerships and Collaboration:** For science-driven companies, especially in biotech and pharmaceuticals, collaborations and partnerships with academic institutions, research labs, or larger corporations play a crucial role. The term sheet may thus contain clauses regarding how these partnerships are to be managed and how the benefits are to be shared.

The anatomy of a term sheet for a science-driven company reflects the unique challenges and opportunities present in the commercialization of scientific discoveries. While it shares similarities with term sheets for standard companies, its emphasis on aspects like intellectual property, milestone-based financing, unique exit strategies, and regulatory compliance underscores the distinct path science-driven companies tread in their quest to transform scientific breakthroughs into marketable products or services. Understanding these nuances is vital for both entrepreneurs and investors to foster successful, mutually beneficial relationships.

This translation process is a meticulous one that requires the dedicated involvement of lawyers from both parties to ensure the document's accuracy and comprehensiveness. This agreement then sets the blueprint for the parties' conduct moving forward, providing both security and clarity.

The conversion from a term sheet to a shareholders' agreement signifies a commitment from all parties to proceed with the investment. It marks a transition from a broad preliminary understanding to a detailed and formalized agreement.

Role of Legal Assistance: Navigating the Legal Waters

In the complex landscape of venture capital investments, the importance of legal assistance cannot be overemphasized. Although this chapter provides a high-level discussion of the anatomy of a term sheet, it should not replace professional legal advice.

A proficient lawyer can illuminate the nuances of the language used in term sheets, decode the implications of various clauses, and assist in negotiating terms that best serve the interests of their client. This is particularly significant when considering science-driven companies, where intricate issues surrounding intellectual property, regulatory requirements, and highly technical aspects of the business model often intertwine with investment terms.

And Then... The Due-Diligence Process

The due-diligence process, a critical step in any business transaction, can initiate before but typically starts or continues more comprehensively after the presentation of a term sheet.

It is a rigorous investigation carried out by the potential investor to verify and validate the viability of the investment opportunity. This process serves as a risk management tool, aiming to uncover any potential issues or challenges that might impede the company's success.

At its core, due diligence is a two-way street. It requires active participation from both parties: the investor who conducts the investigation, and the company that provides the necessary information and facilitates the investigation process. It is in the best interest of both parties to be as transparent and thorough as possible during this process.

The scope of due diligence is wide-ranging and varies depending on the nature of the company and its industry. Typically, the process includes a detailed review of the company's financials, business model, management team, market and competition, legal and regulatory compliance, and, in the case of science-driven companies, intellectual property and technology validation.

Financial due diligence involves examining the company's financial records, projections, capital structure, and funding requirements. Business model due diligence aims to understand the company's revenue generation strategies or its regulatory plan moving forward, scalability, and sustainability. Assessing the management team involves evaluating their experience, competence, and commitment.

Market and competition due diligence includes understanding the size and growth potential of the market, the competitive landscape, and the company's unique value proposition. Legal and regulatory compliance due diligence ensures the company has complied with all relevant laws and regulations, has the necessary licenses and permits, and is not embroiled in any legal disputes.

Intellectual property due diligence, particularly critical for science-driven companies, seeks to validate the ownership, protection, and potential of the company's intellectual property.

Upon completion of the due-diligence process, the investor is equipped with a comprehensive understanding of the company, its potential risks, and its growth prospects. This information is crucial in informing the investor's final decision and executing the deal.

Rule #20

Pre-money Valuation Is Important, but Not as Important as the Equity Story

"You're going to pay a price for every bloody thing you do and everything you don't do. You don't get to choose to not pay a price. You get to choose which poison you're going to take. That's it."
Jordan B. Peterson

For first-time entrepreneurs, it's not uncommon to become somewhat obsessed with pre-money valuation. The fascination is understandable. After all, pre-money valuation is often perceived as a reflection of the company's worth even before it has fully proven itself in the market. It's a number that can spark excitement, instill confidence, or on the contrary, trigger a fair amount of stress and uncertainty.

Science-driven companies operate in a unique ecosystem that significantly affects how we should consider pre-money valuation. In industries such as biotech, medtech, cleantech, or any company heavily grounded in research and development (R&D), the growth trajectory tends to be more complex and the capital requirements more extensive.

These types of companies often need to pass through many stages of development, regulatory approval, and market adoption, all of which typically demand several rounds of financing and substantial capital. Given the heavy R&D focus, the period before reaching profitability can be longer than in other sectors, and the road to get there can be filled with significant scientific, technical, and market uncertainties.

This framework creates a sort of beautiful paradox. If a science-driven company performs well — makes significant scientific advances, clears regulatory hurdles, or demonstrates strong market potential — it likely will require even more money. Each significant milestone achieved often uncovers a new set of opportunities and challenges that require additional capital to address, such as the scaling of production, broadening of the product portfolio, or expansion into new markets.

Therefore, in the context of science-driven companies, it becomes even more crucial to look beyond pre-money valuation and focus on crafting a compelling equity story that makes sense over the long-term journey of the company. In such a scenario, the pre-money valuation of one isolated financing round could end up being a mere footnote in the grand narrative of the company.

Pre-money Versus Equity Story

In the simplest terms, pre-money valuation refers to the valuation of a company before it receives outside financing or the latest round of investment. It's the measure of a startup's worth before the injection of new capital. Founders and investors alike place significant importance on it because it serves as a key determining factor in the percentage of the company that the new investors will own. A higher pre-money valuation can mean retaining a larger slice of the ownership pie for the existing shareholders, including the founders.

Valuation is part science, part art, and is determined through a combination of methods: comparing similar companies in the market (comparables), estimating the potential future cash flows (discounted cash flow analysis), or in the case of early-stage companies, developing milestones achieved or the investment needed to reach the next set of milestones.

An equity story is essentially the narrative portraying how and why a company has grown in value until now and how it will continue to grow in value over time. To illustrate, let's consider a hypothetical scenario.

Suppose a company had a pre-money valuation of $5M at its inception. A group of investors then injects an additional $5M, making the post-money valuation after the round $10M. In this scenario, the entrepreneurs retain 50% control, while the investors hold the other 50%.

As time passes — let's say a year — the company makes progress and shows new results. Perhaps it successfully navigates all preclinical regulations and is now ready to initiate phase 1 clinical trials. This accomplishment enhances the company's value.

The company then seeks another round of investment. Now, the pre-money valuation won't be the same as the post-money valuation from the last round ($10M); instead, it might increase to $20M. This evolution represents the company's equity story to date.

However, if we consider a different scenario where the initial pre-money valuation was $20M (for the sake of argument), then after the first round of investment, the post-money valuation would be $25M. In order to achieve a 2x increase in value between the rounds, the new pre-money valuation would need to be $50M.

At this elevated valuation, it could become challenging for the company to raise new funds. Therefore, the valuation trajectory must be realistic and consistent throughout the company's development to attract continued investment. Caution is key as these valuation estimations need to make sense all along the journey.

So, it's important to understand the limitations of focusing too much on pre-money valuation. While a high pre-money valuation can minimize dilution for existing shareholders in the current round, it sets a high baseline for future growth and subsequent financing rounds. If the company doesn't live up to this high expectation, it could result in a "down round" later on, which could lead to a more significant dilution than what was initially avoided.

In the context of science-driven companies, it becomes even more crucial to look beyond pre-money valuation and focus on crafting a compelling equity story that makes sense over the long-term journey of the company. In such a scenario, the pre-money valuation of one isolated financing round needs to make sense in the context of future rounds of the company.

The Role of ESOP in Keeping Founders Aligned

Founders should remember that they have mechanisms, such as ESOPs (employee stock option plans), to compensate for some dilution effects in later rounds. This is particularly relevant in the science-driven

Figure 28. Equity Story

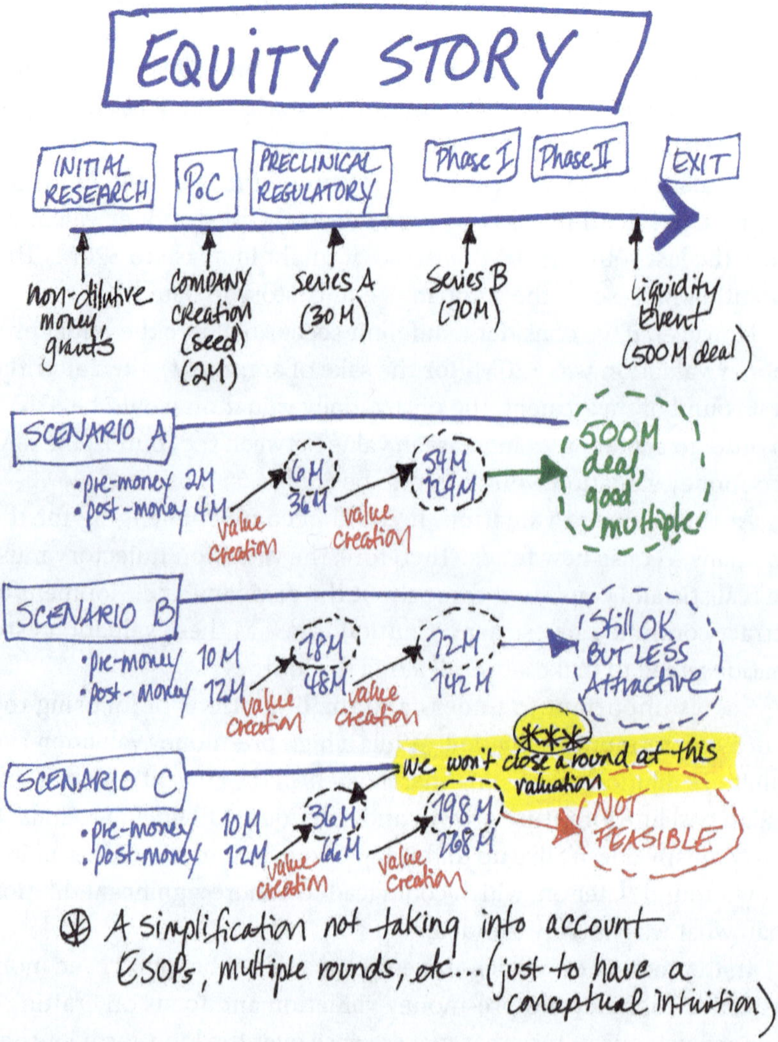

Here, we illustrate the concept of the "equity story" by providing a simplified scenario that should serve as a general guide for understanding the concept.

Let's break down the lifecycle of a hypothetical company and the financial steps it might take along the way. We're going to make some assumptions to better illustrate the concept:

1. A seed round is initiated, where an investor injects $2M into the company.
2. At some point, the company will need additional funding for preclinical regulatory studies and phase 1, which will be accomplished with a $30M Series A. After a successful phase 1, the company raises additional funds through a Series B to begin phase 2 studies.

In the biotech industry, the funding stages are somewhat similar to those in other sectors, but they have some unique aspects due to the longer development timelines, regulatory hurdles, and significant capital required for research and trials.

Pre-Seed: At the pre-seed stage in biotech, startups are typically in the concept or discovery phase. Founders may be university researchers or entrepreneurs with an innovative scientific idea. Funding is used for proof-of-concept experiments, initial research, and to establish that the science has commercial potential. Pre-seed funding might come from grants, university funds, angel investors specialized in biotech, or personal networks.

Seed: During the seed stage, a biotech startup is usually conducting preclinical studies. The funding supports further research and development, hiring a small team, and possibly early intellectual property filings. At this stage, the company needs to demonstrate that their concept can be developed into a viable product. Investors often include specialized angel investors, early-stage venture capital firms with a focus on life sciences, and sometimes strategic partners from the pharmaceutical industry.

Pre-Series A: Biotech startups may require a pre-Series A round due to the extended duration of the drug development process. This stage is crucial for reaching significant scientific milestones, such as successful animal model studies, and for preparing for the regulatory process, including IND (Investigational New Drug) applications. The funding also helps to set up the company structure and business strategy for clinical development.

Series A: By Series A, a biotech company is expected to have solid preclinical data and may be on the verge of early-stage clinical trials. This round is often quite large due to the high costs associated with clinical development. The funding is used to advance through Phase 1 and possibly Phase 2 clinical trials, further product development, and building a more significant business and operational team.

Series B: At the Series B stage, a biotech company has typically shown some clinical efficacy and is advancing through the later stages of clinical trials (Phase 2). The funding is crucial for completing these trials, which are more extensive and expensive, as well as for starting to think about commercialization strategies, manufacturing scale-up, and potential partnerships.

In biotech, the distinction between funding rounds can be quite fluid, and rounds may be larger and less frequent due to the sheer amount of capital required to develop and bring a new drug or medical device to market. Each stage also corresponds with significant scientific and regulatory milestones, which are critical in demonstrating the viability of the company's technology to investors.

3. The company is eventually sold.
   - **For the sake of consistency, the upvalues between rounds are arbitrarily set but are consistent throughout the different scenarios.** To fully understand the impact of different pre-money valuations and upvalues during the company's lifespan, let's examine three scenarios:

     Scenario A starts with a pre-money valuation of $2M. If we inject another $2M at the seed stage, the post-money valuation becomes $4M. As the company progresses through the proof of concept and initial preclinical regulatory stages, value is created, pushing the post-money valuation to $6M. This value becomes the pre-money valuation for the Series A round, and after injecting $30M, the post-money reaches $36M. Further value creation during phase 2 elevates the pre-money valuation to $54M for the Series B. After injecting $70M, the post-money valuation is now $124M. After that, we sell the company for $500M and it provides a reasonable multiple for founders and investors.

     Scenario B deviates from Scenario A with a higher initial pre-money valuation of $10M, resulting in a post-money valuation of $12M after the seed round. With a similar value increase as in Scenario A, the pre-money valuation at the Series A becomes $18M, and post-money valuation after injecting $30M becomes $48M. The question arises whether investors would find a Series B pre-money valuation of approximately $72M appealing or too expensive (probably too expensive). While this scenario might still be viable, it appears less attractive to investors.

Scenario C pushes things to the extreme with an incredibly high value increase between the initial two financing rounds. This increase leads to a pre-money valuation of $36M at the Series A, resulting in a post-money valuation of $66M after the round. Most investors would likely find this valuation too expensive. To successfully fundraise for a Series B, the company may need to negotiate a flat round or maybe even a down round, which could penalize founders (and any investors without an anti-dilution clause).

– **In summary, while a higher pre-money valuation may lead to the founders retaining a larger share of the company, it's crucial to maintain an equity story that aligns with the realistic expectations of all parties.** Pressing for unrealistically high valuations can result in difficulties securing future investments, necessitating flat rounds, or even down rounds, which could harm the company's long-term prospects.

DISCLAIMER: This illustration of the "equity story" is greatly simplified, and while it is useful as a conceptual tool, it's important to remember that the reality is often much more complex. Factors such as ESOPs, the impact of multiple investment rounds, market conditions, the state of the company's technology or product, and many other factors can significantly affect a company's valuation at each stage of its lifecycle. Also, the returns won't be the same for investors in the seed round versus investors in the Series B round.

In this example, we've made a series of assumptions to keep the focus on the primary variables of interest: pre-money valuation and the rate of value increase between rounds. However, in a real-world context, these figures would be influenced by a multitude of factors, including the success of the company's R&D efforts, the competitive landscape, regulatory considerations, and more.

Further, the "equity story" does not unfold in isolation. It is interwoven with the broader narrative of the company, including its strategic goals, operational milestones, and the evolving dynamics of its market. Therefore, while the concepts outlined here provide a foundation for understanding the "equity story," they are only a starting point. In the real world, each company's story will be unique, shaped by its individual circumstances, challenges, and opportunities.

ecosystem, where attracting and retaining top-tier scientific and management talent is critical to success. This applies not only to founders. The high-stakes, high-impact world of science-driven companies often demands a caliber of talent that is not easy to find. Individuals who have the right mix of scientific expertise, entrepreneurial spirit, and drive to navigate the challenges of this dynamic landscape are invaluable, and they often have many options when it comes to choosing where to invest their time and talents. This is where ESOPs can play a crucial role.

In the fiercely competitive talent market, offering a competitive salary may not be enough to attract and retain top-tier talent. Individuals drawn to science-driven companies often are looking for more than just a paycheck; they are seeking the opportunity to contribute to significant advancements in their field, and they want to share in the success of the enterprise. This is where ESOPs come into the picture.

ESOPs can be an effective tool for retaining talent. The typical vesting schedule of stock options encourages employees to stay with the company for a longer period, often three years or more. The promise of gaining full ownership of their stock options can deter key employees from leaving the company, thereby reducing turnover and helping maintain continuity in the team.

An ESOP is more than just an additional financial incentive; it is a symbol of trust and partnership. By offering stock options, a company is expressing its confidence in its team and its willingness to share in the risks and rewards of the venture. This can be an incredibly powerful motivator, especially for those who are drawn to the challenge and potential impact of working in science-driven companies.

For the prospective employee, ESOPs offer the potential for a significant financial return if the company is successful. They represent a stake in the company's future, a tangible link between their efforts and the company's success. This can be a significant factor in their decision-making process, often tipping the scales in favor of companies that offer generous stock options.

The Value of the Company in the Long Run

In conclusion, while pre-money valuation is an important part of the financing puzzle, it is not the only or even the most important piece.

In the world of science-driven companies, the emphasis should be on building a strong equity story, continuously validating it, and ensuring a sustainable and strategic financing path that will support the company's growth journey. Over-emphasizing pre-money valuation can also distract from other critical factors such as the company's long-term growth trajectory, its business model's scalability, market dynamics, and the potential exit strategies. These are the aspects that shape the company's journey and value in the long run, often having a more lasting impact than the starting valuation figure.

Rule #21

You Will Need a Different Kind of Board of Directors

"We're all mad here."

The Cheshire Cat in Lewis Carroll's Alice in Wonderland

The board of directors is a critical component in a company's organizational structure. The board is a collective body of individuals elected by shareholders (typically the new investors plus sometimes some key team and founders figures) to oversee the management and protect the shareholders' interests.

In a science-driven company, the role of the board extends beyond traditional business and financial oversight. The integration of scientific expertise within the boardroom not only brings a nuanced perspective to strategic decision-making but also holds paramount importance in driving innovation, managing scientific risk, and ensuring adherence to ethical standards in scientific pursuits.

The Role and Purpose of a Board of Directors

A board of directors plays a pivotal role in shaping the trajectory of a company. Its primary responsibilities revolve around corporate governance, strategic guidance, and oversight of management activities, ensuring the company's adherence to legal standards and ethical norms. In its capacity, the board approves budgets, establishes policies and procedures, elects the CEO, and makes significant decisions pertaining to mergers, acquisitions, and other large-scale business endeavors.

A company's board of directors is a critical component in guiding its strategic decision-making and value creation. The board is primarily composed of board directors who possess voting rights and hold the authority to make crucial decisions regarding the company's direction. However, the governance of a company doesn't rest solely in the hands of these voting board members.

Often, other non-board members, known as "guests," or sometimes more formally as "observers," also participate in board meetings. Although they do not have voting rights, their presence and contributions are highly valued. These individuals can include advisors, key executives, or representatives from significant stakeholders or investors. They offer unique perspectives, insights, or expertise that can greatly assist the board in making informed decisions. Their participation enhances the breadth and depth of the discussions, allowing for a more holistic evaluation of the scenarios the company faces. Consequently, even without a formal vote, these non-board participants play a critical role in shaping the company's strategy and driving its value creation.

In the context of a science-driven company, the board's role takes on an added layer of complexity. The rapid pace of scientific discovery and the intricacies of translating scientific knowledge into marketable products or services necessitate a board that understands the scientific underpinnings of the company's operations.

Here, the board aids in strategic planning by considering the business and scientific implications of their decisions. They are tasked with evaluating scientific risks, potential return on investments in research and development, and the impact of evolving scientific and technological landscapes on the company's competitive positioning. In this milieu, the board acts as a bridge between the scientific and business realms, ensuring decisions are balanced, risk-informed, and future-oriented.

Board Composition: Unique Aspects of a Science-Driven Company

A typical board of directors includes a diverse mix of individuals, each bringing a wealth of experience from their respective fields. This diversity ensures a comprehensive understanding of different aspects of business, from operations to science, from finance to business development. In biotech or science-driven companies, this mix may or may not include specialized roles such as the chief medical officer (CMO), chief science officer (CSO), and chief technology officer (CTO). Even without a formal seat, the CMO, CSO, and CTO may play critical roles within the board as guests.

- **Chief Medical Officer:** The CMO is an invaluable player in the biotech space, tasked with ensuring that medical perspectives, including patient care and safety, are prioritized in all decisions. They use their medical expertise to offer strategic direction in clinical development, focusing on the design and implementation of clinical trials, the evaluation of safety and efficacy data, and regulatory strategy for product approval. The CMO often serves as a key intermediary between the company and regulatory authorities, medical professionals, and the broader healthcare community. Their primary objective is to translate the company's scientific and technological endeavors into clinically meaningful advancements that improve patient outcomes.
- **Chief Scientific Officer:** The CSO is the lynchpin connecting the world of scientific research with the strategic aims of the company. They bring a comprehensive understanding of the scientific principles that underpin the company's products or services. Their key role is to evaluate the scientific merit of potential ventures and ensure that the company remains at the cutting edge of relevant scientific advancements. By fostering a strong research and development culture within the organization, the CSO ensures that the company is not just a participant in the scientific landscape but a key contributor and innovator. In biotech, this role may be assigned to one of the founders.
- **Chief Technology Officer:** The CTO's role is integral to the company's technological progression. They provide strategic leadership in understanding and navigating the technology landscape. As the technological landscape evolves rapidly, the CTO guides the board on technology adoption and helps address the technological challenges that the company may face. They ensure that the company's technology strategy aligns with its business objectives and that the company remains technologically competitive. In biotech, the CTO might be responsible for overseeing the

development and application of novel technological platforms, ensuring data security, or leading digital transformation efforts.

- **Independent Directors:** In a science-driven company, an independent director provides impartial and objective guidance to the organization. They are not directly involved in the day-to-day operations of the company, which affords them a unique perspective and allows them to focus on broader strategic and business development issues. An independent director's contribution is particularly vital in the context of a science-driven company, where the technical and scientific complexities of the business can potentially obscure the overall strategic direction.

  They are experts in the field of the company and with their external perspective they can scrutinize the company's scientific strategy in the context of market trends, financial sustainability, and long-term business goals. Moreover, their independent status allows them to effectively monitor the company's scientific integrity and ethical conduct. They help ensure that the science underlying the company's products or services is sound, transparent, and ethically conducted. In addition, they play a critical role in managing conflicts of interest and safeguarding shareholders' interests.
- **Chairperson:** The chairperson in a science-driven company is usually a seasoned professional with a robust network of contacts within the pharmaceutical industry, venture capital firms, and other relevant individuals and entities. Their extensive experience often includes participation in liquidity events, initial public offerings (IPOs), and successful exits from past ventures.

  The chairperson's breadth and depth of industry connections can be pivotal for the company. They can facilitate valuable introductions, forge strategic partnerships, and attract potential investors, all of which can significantly influence the company's growth trajectory. The chairperson's understanding of the intricacies of IPOs and mergers and acquisitions activity can also provide vital guidance as the company moves through various stages of its lifecycle, from initial funding rounds to potential exit scenarios.

Roles and Committees of the Board

A board of directors may include several committees, each responsible for a specific aspect of the company's governance. These may include an audit committee, and a compensation committee, among others. The audit committee ensures the company's financial reports are accurate and compliance standards are met, while the compensation committee sets the pay and benefits for company executives.

In science-driven companies, these committees may sometimes operate slightly differently; for example, the audit committee may need to scrutinize research and development expenditures more closely, or the compensation committee might have to deal with issues related to incentives and packages for key employees. This specialized structure ensures the board is equipped to guide the company in navigating the unique challenges of the science-driven industry.

Advice for First-Time Board Members in a Science-Driven Company

Stepping onto the board of a science-driven company for the first time can be a daunting experience. The decisions made at this level can significantly affect not only the company but also public health, patients, research directions, and even industry standards. Here are some key points of advice for first-time board members in such an environment:

- **Transparency and Proper Reporting:** Always maintain the highest level of transparency in your communications with the board. Accurate, thorough, and timely reporting is crucial in fostering an environment of trust and facilitates better decision-making. Understand the reporting procedures and follow them meticulously.
- **Value Addition from Your Vantage Point:** Each board member brings a unique perspective and set of skills to the table. Identify your strengths and look for opportunities where they can add the most value. Whether it's industry connections, scientific expertise, or strategic planning skills, leveraging your unique skills can significantly contribute to the board's effectiveness.
- **Strong Ethical Stance:** Serving on the board of a science-driven company requires a commitment to uphold strong ethical standards. Decisions made can have far-reaching implications,

Figure 29. How a Board of Directors Works

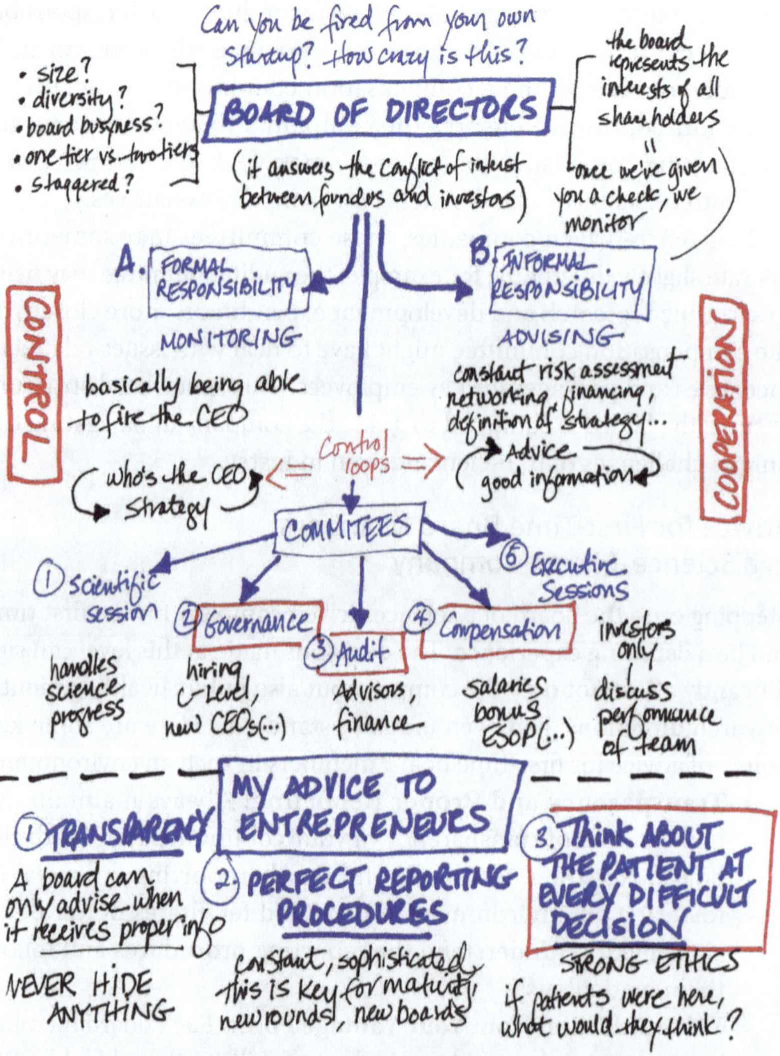

Founders are often thrown onto a board without much knowledge of how it works. Can I, as a founder, be fired from my own startup? What does the board do to help the company? What are the formal and informal roles of a board?

- It's important to understand that the board represents the interests of all shareholders, including new investors. Once you receive a check, they monitor your progress. The board addresses potential conflicts of interest between founders and investors. It has two separate roles: formal responsibilities and informal advising.

- The **formal responsibilities** for the most part involve monitoring and having the power to hire or fire a CEO. This is an ongoing cycle because the chosen CEO influences the company's strategy, and a different strategy may require a different CEO.
- The **informal responsibility** revolves around providing advice, constantly assessing risks, asking questions, networking, and defining the strategy.

• The board operates through a control loop. Board members provide advice, receive information, which leads to further advice, and the loop continues. Committees play a role in this process.
  - The Compensation/Governance Committee is responsible for hiring C-level executives, CEOs, and key team members, and deciding on ESOPs and incentives.
  - The Audit Committee focuses on auditing and finance, while the Compensation Committee handles salaries, bonuses, and employee stock option plans.

• Additionally, there may be **scientific sessions** for science-driven companies and executive sessions exclusive to investors to discuss team performance and future financial needs.

The role of an entrepreneur goes beyond just creating a novel product or service. Here are a few additional pointers that could benefit entrepreneurs navigating their interactions with the board of directors.

• **Transparency** is paramount in all your dealings with the board. The board's function is to guide and advise, and to do so effectively, they need to have accurate, comprehensive, and timely information. As an entrepreneur, it's your responsibility to ensure this. Hiding or distorting information can lead to misguided decisions that can ultimately harm the company. A culture of transparency fosters trust, facilitates effective problem-solving, and encourages constructive feedback.

• **Establishing robust, consistent, and sophisticated reporting** procedures is another critical step. It's not just about keeping the board informed, but also about tracking the company's progress, identifying potential issues, and making data-driven decisions. Good reporting procedures will also prove invaluable during future funding rounds, due diligence processes, and possible exit events. They offer investors a clear picture of the company's growth and potential, thereby increasing their confidence in your management.

• **Finally, when faced with tough decisions, never lose sight of the end customer**. Whether you're running a synthetic biology company focusing on patient outcomes or an artificial intelligence firm where user safety is paramount, make decisions with the customer's best interest at heart. Upholding this ethos speaks volumes about your company's integrity and commitment to creating true value. As I often tell young board members, when about to make a decision, imagine the customers were in the room. Ask yourself, "Would they approve of the decision I'm about to make?" Ensuring your actions align with the customers" needs and expectations will not only guide you towards ethical decisions but will also build trust and loyalty, both within the board and among your customers.

affecting not just the business, but public health and patients. When serving as a board member, always consider "what would the patient think if I make this decision?" Always keep the patient and the greater good in mind, adhere to the highest ethical standards, and never compromise your integrity.

In summary, as a board member in a science-driven company, your role is to contribute your unique skills and knowledge to the board, always with transparency and a strong ethical compass.

Rule #22

The Team!

"There is only one true aristocracy and that is the aristocracy of passionate souls!"
Tennessee Williams

The bedrock of every successful organization is its team. However, teams in science-driven companies are unique, operating under a distinct set of rules and constraints compared to companies in traditional business settings. The complexities of the science and technology sectors, the high-stakes environment of biotech startups, and the rigorous demands of research and development all contribute to the unique nature of such teams. As an investor I must say that it is an immense privilege to interact with these types of teams, as everybody is extremely savvy and intelligent, and they're usually the best of the best in their fields.

In this chapter, we will delve into the intricacies of these teams, exploring how they evolve, operate, and interact. We will discuss here topics ranging from leadership transitions to talent acquisition and employee turnover. Understanding these dynamics is vital, as these insights not only shape the way we lead and manage these teams but also guide how we can create an environment that fosters innovation, mitigates risk, and, ultimately, leads to groundbreaking scientific advancements.

This unique understanding also helps us appreciate the delicate interplay between scientific rigor, business acumen, and human factors that underlie the success of science-driven companies.

The Evolution of Leadership in Science-Driven Companies

In the lifecycle of science-driven companies, one of the most critical and often challenging transitions is that of leadership. This transformation typically sees a founder, often a scientist, step into the role of CEO at the founding of the company. However, as the business grows, the baton is often passed to a professional CEO better equipped to handle the demands of a growing organization.

- **Scientist-CEO to Professional CEO:** In the initial stages, a scientist-CEO brings invaluable insights and direction to the company, given their deep understanding of the core technology or scientific principles that the business is built upon. However, as the company matures and the operational complexities increase, a different skillset, often that of a professional CEO, becomes necessary. This individual, typically with experience in business strategy, finance, and operations, can navigate the company through growth, potential market changes, and increased competition.
- **Role of Founders Post-Transition:** Post-transition, founders often take up strategic roles within the company, such as chief scientific officer (CSO), chief medical officer (CMO), or board member. This shift allows them to continue contributing their deep scientific knowledge while leaving the day-to-day operations to the new CEO. Such a realignment of roles is crucial to maintain the scientific integrity of the company while embracing the necessary business acumen required for growth.

Be aware that the leadership transition in a science-driven company is a delicate process. It requires careful planning and execution to ensure that the organization continues to thrive while preserving its normal functioning.

Dealing with Scientific "Prima Donnas"

In science-driven companies, the prowess of the scientific team often determines the height of the company's achievement. Exceptional scientists who dominate their fields can be a tremendous asset. But, these extraordinary and high-achieving individuals, often termed "scientific prima donnas," can sometimes bring a unique set of challenges to the workplace dynamics.

The term "prima donna" is usually associated with individuals who have exceptional skills or knowledge but who sometimes can be perceived as difficult to work with due to their high standards. In the scientific world, a prima donna is often a scientist who has achieved significant acclaim in their field and whose contributions are pivotal to a project or the company. They might have specific ways of working or high expectations that can lead to friction within the team.

Working with a scientific prima donna requires a careful balance of managing egos, ensuring collaboration, and leveraging their expertise. It involves setting clear expectations, fostering a culture of mutual respect, and creating an environment that values individual contributions while promoting teamwork. It also means being patient and empathetic, understanding that these individuals are driven by their passion for science and their desire to make meaningful contributions.

Headhunters and Talent Acquisition

A unique blend of expertise and specialized knowledge is required in the realm of science-driven companies. These aren't areas where a general call for applications will necessarily attract the right talent. To locate the best talent in these highly specific fields, many companies turn to headhunters, recruitment specialists whose entire mission is finding the right fit for these demanding roles.

Whether it's a seasoned CEO, a savvy CFO, a geneticist with a specialty in oncology, a machine learning expert with a background in bioinformatics, or a CMO with experience in launching a specific type of drug, the roles to be filled are usually incredibly specific. Headhunters, with their extensive networks and industry know- how, are uniquely positioned to find and attract these rare profiles.

The headhunter's role goes beyond the simple act of locating potential candidates. They are also negotiators, persuaders, and even counselors, helping both parties navigate the process. From the first stage of identifying the exact requirements of a role, through the scouting process, to preliminary interviews and finally to salary negotiations, a headhunter acts as a bridge between the company and potential candidates.

The advantage of this is twofold. First, it provides the company access to a pool of talented individuals who would have otherwise

Figure 30. Things a CEO Needs to Oversee

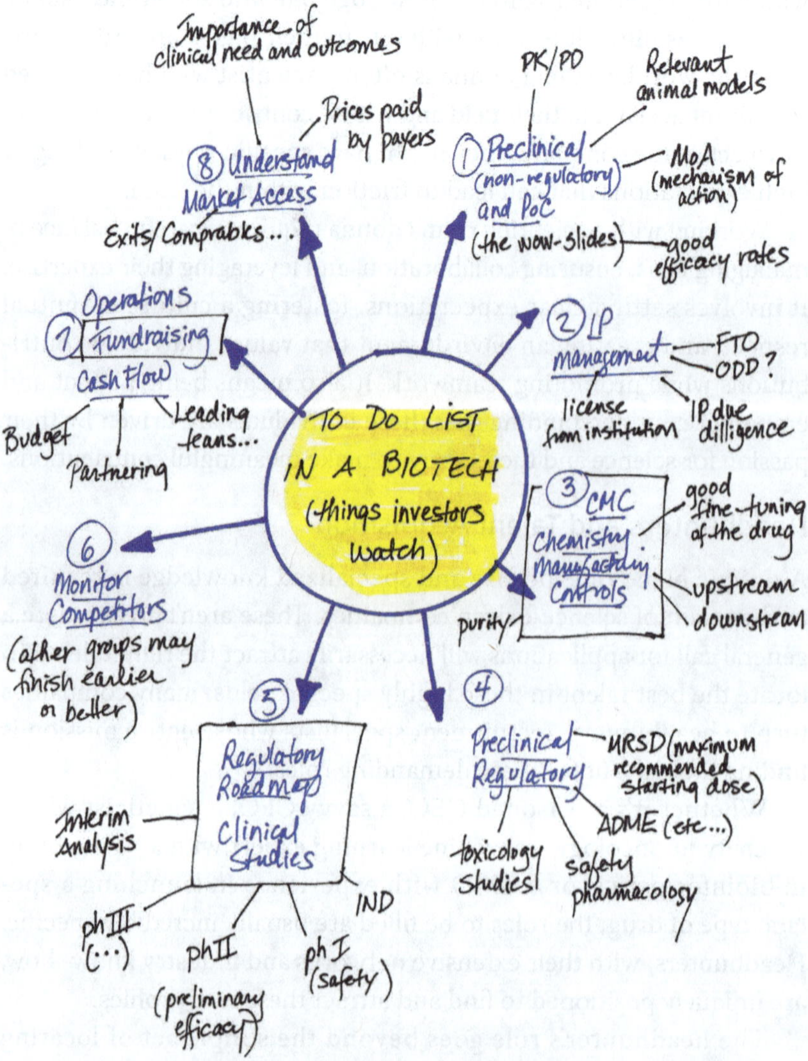

A CEO in a biotech company is akin to the conductor of an orchestra, responsible for overseeing and ensuring flawless execution of all internal operations while regularly reporting to the board of directors who set the strategic direction. The CEO's task list is extensive, and these are the very elements that investors monitor to gauge how they can best provide support.

- **Hire, manage, and supervise a competent team.** A company's success is deeply rooted in the collective efforts of its team members, and the CEO plays a pivotal role in bringing together a diverse group of individuals with the requisite skills and expertise. The CEO not only directs the hiring process but also sets the tone for the organizational culture, instilling values of integrity, collaboration, and innovation. Beyond hiring, the CEO continually manages and supervises the team, providing strategic guidance, nurturing professional development, and ensuring that each team member is motivated and aligned with the company's overarching goals.

- **Oversee preclinical, non-regulatory activities.** These activities include demonstrating the proof of concept in animal models and generating compelling scientific data such as pharmacokinetics/pharmacodynamics (PK/PD) data, data from relevant animal models, elucidation of mechanisms of action, and showcasing effective results.
- **Oversee the intellectual property (IP) strategy,** which involves licensing from the institution and conducting the company's own IP due diligence to assess the solidity of the IP. This process is typically carried out in collaboration with legal experts specializing in IP law.
- **Oversee chemistry, manufacturing, and controls (CMC).** This refers to the consistent and replicable production of the drug that will be used in trials, with strict control over its quality and purity.
- **Oversee preclinical regulatory activities.** These are studies mandated by regulatory authorities and include safety pharmacology, toxicology studies, and determining the maximum recommended starting dose.
- **Shape the regulatory roadmap.** This entails outlining the studies required, particularly clinical trials. The CEO needs to strategize on how the Investigational New Drug (IND) application will be filed, how the phase 1 safety trial and phase 2 preliminary efficacy trial will be conducted, including the number of patients, the number of centers, and whether an interim analysis will be necessary.
- **Monitor competition.** This is an essential task as competitors might complete their studies sooner or yield better results.
- **Oversee operations. This includes** tasks like fundraising, budgeting, cash flow management.
- **Foster partnerships and business development.** A CEO plays an instrumental role in fostering strategic partnerships and early business development. Through partnerships, the CEO helps expand the company's reach, introduce novel solutions, and gain competitive advantages in the market. This involves identifying potential collaborators, such as vendors, research institutions, or other businesses, whose offerings complement the company's products or services. The CEO oversees the negotiation of partnership agreements, ensuring they align with the company's strategic objectives.
- **Understand the market.** This includes understand future market access, recognize the clinical need and achieved outcomes, be aware of the prices paid by payers, and consider exits and comparables of transactions that have happened in the past with similar indications or technologies.
- **Report to the board of directors.** The board members bring their collective experience and diverse knowledge to provide strategic counsel, thus helping the CEO navigate complex business decisions and challenges. The board can provide connections to potential investors, clients, and strategic partners, which can be invaluable for a company in its nascent stages. They may also help mentor the CEO on leadership and governance issues, helping them develop the skills necessary to steer the company towards its goals. Furthermore, the board can assist in risk management, helping the CEO identify potential risks and devise strategies to mitigate them. The active involvement of the board in these early stages can significantly influence the trajectory and success of the company.

been inaccessible or unaware of the opportunity. Secondly, it allows the company to continue focusing on their core operations while the headhunter manages the time-consuming process of recruitment.

The importance of culture fit is another essential aspect that could be discussed in this context. While specialized knowledge and skills are paramount, a candidate's compatibility with the company's culture is also a critical consideration. The right culture fit can enhance employee satisfaction, performance, and retention. Headhunters, through their thorough understanding of both the candidate's and the company's values, can help ensure this alignment.

Similarly, the issue of diversity and inclusion in the recruitment process is becoming increasingly pertinent. Science-driven companies, like many sectors, are recognizing the importance of having diverse perspectives to foster innovation and drive better decision-making. Headhunters can play a significant role in attracting a diverse pool of talent and ensuring unbiased recruitment processes.

In essence, headhunters' unique blend of industry knowledge, extensive networks, and recruitment expertise can provide science-driven companies with a competitive edge in the constant quest for talent. They help build the teams that push the boundaries of science and technology, one recruit at a time.

The Role of ESOP in Aligning Goals

In an era when employee retention and engagement are critical for organizational success, employee stock option plans (ESOPs) are crucial as a strategy to motivate staff and align their interests with the growth of the company.

Traditionally, ESOPs have been viewed as a tool to attract and retain top talent in a highly competitive market. By offering employees a stake in the company, ESOPs can serve as a powerful motivator, encouraging individuals to contribute their best efforts to enhance the company's performance. But beyond the individual-level motivational effects, ESOPs can also serve as a strategic instrument to manage the dilution of shares in capital-intensive industries. In science-driven companies, where large financing rounds are often necessary, ESOPs can act as a buffer, maintaining the involvement and motivation of key team members while bringing in significant capital.

ESOPs can also foster a strong sense of ownership among employees. By giving employees a stake in the company's future, ESOPs transform them from mere workers to business owners. This shift in mindset can greatly benefit the company. When employees feel like owners, they are more likely to show increased commitment, greater effort, and better decision-making. They become more attuned to the company's needs and performance, contributing ideas, solutions, and strategies to enhance growth. This heightened involvement and engagement can, in turn, drive innovation and productivity.

In addition, ESOPs can also promote a culture of transparency and accountability. As shareholders, employees are more likely to demand transparency regarding the company's financial performance and strategic decisions.

The Prevalence of PhDs in Science-Driven Companies

In the landscape of science-driven companies, particularly in sectors such as technology, biotechnology, and artificial intelligence, one of the most noteworthy aspects is the prevalence of PhD holders as a strategic imperative.

First, it's important to understand the unique challenges and requirements of science-driven industries. The projects undertaken are usually complex, involving cutting-edge technology or innovative scientific concepts. Such projects demand an in-depth understanding of scientific principles and methodologies, beyond surface-level knowledge.

Here, PhDs, with their extensive research experience and specialized knowledge in their respective fields, fit naturally into the picture. They are trained to tackle complex problems, perform high-level research, and produce new knowledge — all of which are crucial in driving innovation in these companies.

Second, there's an inherent language and culture in the world of science that is best understood and navigated by those who have spent years within it. PhD holders in scientific disciplines, having been steeped in this environment through their years of research, bring a significant level of expertise to the table. They are adept at interpreting scientific literature, formulating research questions, conducting rigorous experiments, and making sense of the data. They bring a "science-first" mindset, which is essential in companies where science is not just a tool, but the very foundation of their products or services.

Furthermore, PhDs are instrumental in bridging the gap between science and business. They can translate the complex scientific jargon into terms that non-scientific stakeholders can understand. They are also better equipped to identify the commercial potential of scientific innovations, a skill that is key to the success of any science-driven company.

Finally, of course having a large number of PhDs is often seen as a mark of credibility and trust. Investors, clients, and collaborators often prefer companies that have a robust scientific team, as it is indicative of their commitment to scientific excellence and their capability to deliver high-quality, innovative solutions.

Managing Turnover: The CEO Exodus

Turnover, particularly at the top leadership C-level, can destabilize any company. However, within the context of science-driven companies, leadership turnover isn't just frequent but also somewhat inevitable. The reasons for this are multi-faceted, from the allure of new ventures to the innate curiosity that drives many scientists to explore and push boundaries.

Interestingly, a common pattern emerges in that a significant number of these C-level executives, especially those with a scientific background, leave to be promoted in CEO roles at other organizations. While it might initially seem disruptive, this so-called "CEO exodus" can be effectively managed and, in some ways, even harnessed for the benefit of the company.

One of the reasons for this high turnover rate lies in the very nature of individuals who are drawn to science-driven organizations. These are people who thrive on innovation, discovery, and the pursuit of the unknown. They are driven not just by the prospect of financial success but the potential to create something meaningful and impactful. Therefore, once they've helped build one successful venture, they often feel compelled to seek out new challenges, sometimes in the form of leading their own company.

To manage and mitigate the impact of such turnover, organizations must adopt a proactive approach. This begins with acknowledging the inevitability of turnover and building it into the company's strategic planning.

A robust succession plan for all top positions is critical to ensure a smooth transition when top executives decide to move on. This involves identifying potential leaders within the organization early and investing in their development. Additionally, creating a supportive environment that celebrates personal growth and exploration can turn a potential drawback into an advantage.

When an organization is known to foster leaders who go on to become successful CEOs elsewhere, it enhances its reputation, making it more attractive to ambitious, high-performing individuals.

Companies should also consider maintaining strong ties with their former executives. As CEOs of other science-driven companies, they are likely to continue operating within the same ecosystem. This presents opportunities for potential collaborations and partnerships, creating a mutually beneficial relationship.

Finally, the retention strategy should go beyond just monetary incentives. It should focus on providing a challenging and fulfilling work environment that can satisfy their intellectual curiosity and drive for impact.

Ensuring Confidentiality and Non-Competition

In the fast-paced, high-stakes world of science-driven companies, the preservation of confidentiality and the enforcement of non-competition clauses hold immense importance. As these companies often deal with proprietary and sensitive information, a breach of confidentiality can have severe implications, including loss of competitive advantage, legal implications, and damage to relationships with stakeholders. At the same time, non-competition clauses help ensure that key talent does not transition directly to a competitor, bringing their knowledge and experience to an industry rival.

Confidentiality in science-driven companies is of paramount importance due to the nature of their work. The development of breakthrough technologies, novel scientific methodologies, and proprietary algorithms demand the highest levels of security and discretion. Companies often spend years developing and refining their products, and the unauthorized release of this information can put all that effort at risk. Consequently, it's essential to establish strict confidentiality policies, backed by rigorous training and awareness programs to ensure that all employees understand the importance of maintaining confidentiality.

However, creating a culture of confidentiality goes beyond simply implementing rules and regulations. It involves nurturing an environment of trust where employees understand the gravity of their responsibilities and feel personally committed to safeguarding the company's sensitive information. Regular reminders, role-specific training, and a confidential reporting system can all contribute to establishing and maintaining this culture of confidentiality.

Simultaneously, non-competition clauses in employment contracts serve as a vital tool for protecting the company's interests when employees, particularly high-ranking executives and specialized scientists, decide to part ways with the company. These clauses prevent employees from working with direct competitors for a specified period after leaving the company, thereby safeguarding the company's trade secrets and competitive advantage.

Nevertheless, enforcing non-competition clauses can be a complex issue, with the legal validity of these clauses varying widely by jurisdiction. Therefore, it's essential to seek legal counsel when drafting these agreements to ensure they're enforceable and compliant with local labor laws. It's also crucial to strike a balance between protecting the company's interests and respecting the rights of employees to seek new employment opportunities.

Wrapping Up

Teams in science-driven companies operate in a uniquely challenging yet rewarding environment. Their composition, dynamics, and the rules of engagement differ vastly from those found in typical organizations. As such, understanding these nuances is crucial for the success of any venture operating in this innovative space.

In the rapidly evolving landscape of science and technology, understanding the unique intricacies of teams in this sector is not just beneficial — it's a necessity. This understanding helps create an environment where innovation thrives, individuals flourish, and the company prospers. The key lies in continuous learning, adaptation, and fostering a culture of mutual respect and shared purpose.

Rule #23

Hire the Right People

"Hire character. Train skill."
Peter Schutz

People — their potential, their competence, and their character — often constitute the defining factor in the success or failure of an investment. This reality underscores the significance of being an adept judge of character in the realm of investing and entrepreneurship. However, this is not a skill that can be acquired overnight. It requires patience, a keen eye for detail, and most importantly, experience.

The ability to discern the qualities, potential, and integrity of individuals, be it a CEO, an employee, or a co-investor, is a skill that grows sharper with time and practice. As an investor or entrepreneur, your ability to accurately assess people becomes one of your most powerful tools.

Consider this — a startup may have a revolutionary product and a seemingly solid business plan, but it is the team behind it that must execute the vision. They must adapt and steer the ship when challenges arise — and arise they will. Thus, the need to have the right employees in a startup cannot be overstated.

Similarly, as an investor, choosing the right co-investors is critical. A co-investor can bring more than just capital to the table; they also can bring invaluable experience, insight, and connections. The synergy between co-investors can enhance the potential success of an investment. Therefore, it's essential to assess not only the financial capabilities of co-investors but also their motivation and their strategic fit with the investment in question.

This chapter delves deeper into the importance of being a judge of character in the world of investing, providing insights and tools to hone this critical skill. We will explore concepts that will help you distinguish between authority and power, recognizing the importance of paranoia in leadership, identifying opportunities in discontent, and making effective hiring decisions.

Our journey will take us beyond financial reports and business strategies, into the heart of what makes businesses tick — its people.

The Duality of Power and Authority

Power and authority, two important concepts frequently used interchangeably yet fundamentally different, underpin our understanding of leadership. Power, often related to the position one holds, can compel or constrain others' actions. Authority, on the other hand, stems not from the ability to dictate, but from the respect and trust one earns from others. While power might secure obedience, it is authority that nurtures commitment, a critical distinction to comprehend as an investor or entrepreneur.

CEOs, by the virtue of their position, command power. However, the focus should not be on harnessing power but on cultivating authority, which involves leading by example and being freely chosen by others to lead. The most effective leaders are those whose authority is recognized and endorsed by their team members, not merely imposed upon them.

What, then, constitutes the essence of this authority? How does one cultivate it? Our answer lies within a framework from ancient Greece, the triad of *logos*, *ethos*, and *pathos*. These rhetorical modes of persuasion offer insights into the constituents of authority.

- ***Logos***, the appeal to logic, necessitates a rational and clear argument. An authoritative leader should be able to present logical solutions and display critical thinking skills.
- ***Ethos***, the appeal to ethics or credibility, requires the leader to be perceived as reliable and trustworthy, someone with integrity and good character.
- ***Pathos***, the appeal to emotion, underlines the need for a leader to connect on an emotional level, to understand, empathize, and inspire.

However, these three elements in isolation aren't enough. The strength of authority lies in the harmony of these three aspects. A leader who can combine a clear vision (*pathos*) with logical execution (*logos*), all underpinned by ethical conduct (*ethos*), stands a chance at earning true authority.

And so, the development of authority pivots on one's vision intensity, communication skills, logical acumen, and empathic capabilities. As we move forward, we will delve deeper into these attributes, exploring their roles and nuances in the context of effective leadership and the selection of the right individuals in a high-stakes investment environment.

The Value of Paranoid CEOs

The book *Only the Paranoid Survive* by Andrew S. Grove, holds a special place in my personal library. In the early stages of my journey, this book was more than just a guide; it was a beacon that illuminated the path ahead. Grove's wisdom served as a reminder of the ever-present threats in the volatile world of startups and investments. He emphasized the importance of maintaining a high level of alertness and the role of constructive paranoia in driving success.

Grove's philosophy resonated with me, underscoring the reality that only those who are constantly vigilant about potential challenges and proactive in addressing them are able to navigate the complexities of the market and make things happen. The CEO also needs to be 3 or 4 standard deviations above the mean in terms of resilience.

The book served as a stark wake-up call, molding my approach toward challenges and enhancing my ability to anticipate and mitigate risks.

A distinguishing trait among the most effective CEOs I've encountered in my career as an investor is a seemingly paradoxical one: paranoia. However, upon closer examination, it becomes clear that this isn't a pathological paranoia but rather a reflection of their intense commitment, their keen awareness of potential pitfalls, and their drive to continually safeguard their company's path forward.

When asked the question, "What keeps you up at night?" the CEOs I find most compelling don't respond with an unperturbed, "Nothing," nor do they singularly focus on a single concern like "fundraising." Instead, they enumerate a long list of worries.

They're concerned about a competitor's progress, about gaining regulatory approvals, about the solidity of their IP strategy, about the outcomes of ongoing experiments, and more, more, more.

This form of paranoia acts as a perpetual motivator, a constant reminder of what could go wrong and therefore needs attention. The paranoid CEO is vigilant, attentive to details, and prepared to confront problems before they escalate. This vigilance often enables them to anticipate and mitigate risks, significantly contributing to their company's resilience and longevity.

However, it is crucial to underscore the necessity of balance in this context. The same CEOs who can enumerate a litany of concerns are also the ones who exhibit a palpable sense of vision, enthusiasm, and intensity. These seemingly opposing forces aren't at odds with each other; rather, they work in concert. The vision serves as the guiding north star while the paranoia acts as a compass, pointing out the potential obstacles on the path to that star.

Thus, as an investor or entrepreneur, recognizing the value of paranoia and understanding its relationship with other crucial leadership traits can significantly impact your ability to select the right individuals, fostering a culture of innovation, vigilance, and resiliency within your organization.

Innovation from Dissatisfaction

Dissatisfaction and anger, often viewed as negative emotions, can actually be powerful indicators of opportunities for innovation. Understanding this correlation can help investors and entrepreneurs identify potential areas of breakthrough and improvement.

People generally express dissatisfaction or anger when their needs aren't being met or when existing solutions don't solve their problems. This dissatisfaction might stem from a range of issues: inefficient processes, substandard products, urgent clinical needs, inadequate services, or systemic failings. In such scenarios, the discontented individuals are highlighting areas ripe for innovation. They're essentially signaling that something isn't working, pointing to a gap that needs to be filled or a process that needs to be improved.

For instance, the disgruntled patient complaining about the inefficiency of something could be flagging an opportunity to develop a more intuitive and user-friendly solution. The frustrated patient upset about long waiting times might be highlighting the need for a more efficient appointment system or a digital health solution.

Therefore, developing an "eye" for spotting dissatisfaction can be a crucial skill for entrepreneurs and investors alike. By training yourself to pay attention to these signals, you can turn seemingly negative emotions into catalysts for innovation, transforming complaints and criticisms into opportunities to create value.

Discontentment and dissatisfaction often precede change. They remind us that the status quo isn't satisfactory and that there's a demand for better solutions. Recognizing this can help you stay ahead of the curve, anticipate shifts in consumer demands, and position your investments for success.

The Hiring Checklist: CPU, Hard Drive, and Printer

When it comes to selecting the right people for your team, having a reliable checklist or framework can greatly enhance your hiring process. To get to know people better, I've borrowed a simple analogy from the world of computers. I like to compare people's skills and abilities to three crucial parts of a computer: the CPU, the hard drive, and the printer.

- **CPU–Intellect:** The first attribute to consider is the individual's intellectual capacity. This includes how swiftly they connect ideas, how inventively they come up with fresh concepts, and how promptly they adapt to changing circumstances. This is the individual's processing power, similar to a computer's central processing unit (CPU). Just like a computer, a team member with a high-performing "CPU" can process information quickly and accurately, enabling them to make informed and intelligent decisions.
- **Hard Drive–Knowledge:** The second attribute is knowledge and memory. An employee's ability to remember and retrieve useful information can greatly contribute to the team's overall productivity and effectiveness. The capacity to absorb and recall information mirrors the hard drive of a computer. Those with a strong "hard drive" often exhibit a strong commitment to learning, demonstrating a broad base of knowledge and an ability to recall that information when it's most needed.

- **Printer–Communication Skills:** The third essential attribute is communication skills. Being able to clearly articulate thoughts, ideas, and strategies is just as crucial as having a sharp intellect and a good memory. This reflects the printer component of a computer. Just as a printer translates digital information into understandable output, strong communicators can convey complex ideas clearly and effectively, facilitating collaboration and understanding within the team.

While all three of these attributes are crucial, particular attention should be paid to communication skills. As an investor or a CEO, it's essential to ask: Does this person bring clarity?

Furthermore, beyond these core qualities, certain personality traits may also be desirable. For example, the degree of determination, the ability to get excited about the intricacies of science, a natural sense of curiosity, and even a degree of obsessiveness can be beneficial. In the highly competitive world of startups and biotech investment, these traits can often be the difference between moderate success and exceptional achievement. Obsessiveness, in particular, can demonstrate a level of commitment and focus that can drive progress and innovation.

Ultimately, the ability to judge character and identify these traits in potential hires can significantly impact the success of a company or an investment. The right people, with the right balance of intellect, memory, and communication skills, coupled with passion and obsessiveness, can truly make things happen.

Determination versus Expertise

A common debate arises when assessing founders: Should we prioritize determination, obsessiveness, and passion? Expertise? Or maybe intelligence? At first glance, the answer may seem obvious: Surely an expert in a given field will have the necessary knowledge to lead a company to success. However, a deeper look reveals that determination, particularly in the face of challenges, can be an equally valuable, if not more important, trait of a founder.

Obsessiveness, in this context, refers to an unwavering dedication to an idea, vision, or project. It's the sort of tenacity that keeps founders working late into the night, unwilling to rest until they've solved a problem. It's the relentless curiosity that drives them to explore every possible angle, relentlessly chasing their goals. It's the burning passion that keeps them going in the face of adversity, constantly pushing the boundaries of what is possible.

Expertise, on the other hand, is accumulated through years of study and experience. It's the intricate understanding of a field, the ability to navigate its nuances with confidence. Experts are undeniably valuable in any industry, bringing depth of knowledge, informed perspectives, and often, a network of connections.

Yet, in the volatile, uncertain landscape of startups and disruptive innovation, the static nature of expertise can sometimes be a limitation. The world is changing rapidly, and today's cutting-edge knowledge may be outdated tomorrow. This is where obsessiveness comes into play. An obsessive founder is continuously learning, adapting, and innovating, driven by a relentless desire to succeed.

Moreover, when it comes to mobilizing teams and driving projects forward, especially in science-driven, cutting-edge companies, drive and vision often outweigh expertise in importance. The ability to inspire others, to maintain morale and focus in the face of obstacles, is crucial. It's not enough to simply understand the science or technology at play; a successful founder must be able to rally their team and sustain momentum, even when the going gets tough.

Rule #24

Become a Chief Networking Officer

"Networking is about farming for new contacts, not hunting them...Proper networking isabout taking the time to cultivate relationships."

Ivan Misner

It is often said that "your network is your net worth," and this truism is arguably even more valid in the dynamic, rapidly evolving fields that characterize leading-edge investments. The relationships you build and maintain may unlock doors, expose opportunities, and provide invaluable insights that can significantly enhance your investment decisions.

The term "chief networking officer," although not typically found in traditional corporate hierarchies, is an apt descriptor for individuals who have mastered the art of networking. It encapsulates the skill set of individuals who strategically cultivate relationships, not only within their own organizations but also within broader industry circles. These individuals understand the importance of building, nurturing, and leveraging connections to facilitate information flow, access unique opportunities, and gain competitive advantage.

It's essential to understand that good networking isn't simply a skill; it's an inherent trait that develops and refines over time. Contrary to a common misconception, effective networking doesn't merely entail exchanging business cards at industry events or sending connection requests on LinkedIn. It involves taking genuine interest in others, actively listening, sharing knowledge, and making consistent efforts to nurture professional relationships.

Developing this trait requires practice, patience, and authenticity. In essence, the craft of networking resembles the growth of a tree. It begins as a small seed — an initial meeting or connection — and with care and attention, it can grow into a robust network. It's an ongoing process that requires nurturing and maintenance. As the tree grows, it also changes, adapting to seasons and weather conditions.

Similarly, your network will need to adapt and evolve, reflecting your changing professional interests, the dynamics of the industry, and shifts in the broader economic landscape.

Building a Network: A Long-Term Endeavor

The process of creating a valuable network is akin to constructing a magnificent edifice. It cannot be rushed; it requires patience, foresight, and consistent effort. Effective networking is not a sprint, but a marathon. It is about strategically building connections and relationships over time, with an understanding of the potential long-term benefits that they might bring.

One crucial aspect of building your network is maintaining an open attitude toward meeting others. Be open to introductions and engage in genuine conversations at industry events, seminars, workshops, or even informal gatherings. Be receptive to introductions and recommendations from existing connections. A proactive, open-minded approach can open doors to new opportunities and relationships.

The strategy to organically grow your network involves both breadth and depth. The breadth of your network pertains to having connections across different sectors, roles, and regions, which allows you to access a wide range of perspectives and opportunities. The depth of your network, on the other hand, speaks to the quality of your relationships — having a close-knit circle of trusted peers and mentors with whom you can collaborate, share insights and seek advice.

Networking is about smiles. Those who naturally gravitate toward effective networking often display qualities such as curiosity, respect for others, empathy, and sociability. It's less about the quantity of contacts one amasses and more about the quality of relationships one nurtures.

Individuals who have an innate curiosity, a keen interest in understanding others' experiences and perspectives, often excel at building networks. They actively seek out conversations and are genuinely interested in learning from others. This curiosity fuels their engagement in interactions, making the conversation mutually enjoyable and fostering a connection that goes beyond a mere exchange of business cards.

Similarly, individuals who harbor a deep-seated respect for others, irrespective of their status or role, are adept at networking. They value every interaction and treat everyone they meet with courtesy. This respect is evident in their interactions and creates an atmosphere of mutual trust and understanding, the bedrock of strong relationships.

Moreover, those who are able to empathize can connect on a deeper level. Empathy allows one to understand and share the feelings of others, a powerful tool in building long-lasting relationships. By demonstrating understanding and showing that they care, these individuals foster stronger connections.

While these traits might come naturally to some, they can be developed and improved by others. Reflecting upon and consciously working toward embodying these qualities can enhance one's networking capabilities significantly. After all, the most successful networks are built on strong, authentic relationships, and these traits are fundamental to establishing such connections.

Peer Network: A Goldmine of Future Opportunities

The value of a strong peer network is frequently underestimated, perhaps due to the immediate gratification often associated with connecting with established figures in one's field. However, peers are a veritable goldmine of future opportunities, and cultivating these relationships could prove invaluable in the long run.

To grasp this concept, one needs to view the networking landscape with an eye on the future. Today's peers are tomorrow's industry leaders. Your fellow graduates, colleagues, or even competitors are also on their own paths to success, honing their skills and carving out their niches. As they grow in their careers, they are likely to assume roles of increasing importance and influence.

Maintaining good relationships with peers today means building a robust network of future industry leaders.

This perspective shifts the networking focus from just seeking out established figures to valuing connections at one's own level.

It emphasizes treating everyone with respect, nurturing relationships over time, and growing alongside one's network. Therefore, the next time you attend a networking event or a professional gathering, remember that the person standing next to you might be the CEO, the innovator, or the influencer of tomorrow. Cherish these relationships, for they are the bedrock of your future network.

The Privilege of Intelligence: Leveraging Your Surroundings

Being part of the leading-edge investment field brings with it an exceptional advantage: the privilege of being surrounded by some of the most brilliant minds in their fields. These individuals, each excelling in their respective domains, form a reservoir of knowledge and insights that can significantly enrich one's learning journey and augment investment strategies.

It's important to acknowledge and appreciate this privilege. Being surrounded by intelligence is not a competitive threat but a collective resource. You are in an environment that is conducive to intellectual growth, where every conversation can offer new insights, and every interaction can lead to a new understanding of investment trends and opportunities.

How, then, can you best use this pool of intelligence? Actively seeking knowledge and insights from your network is crucial. This could involve asking thoughtful questions during conversations, requesting feedback on your investment strategies, or even organizing brainstorming sessions on investment trends. Such interactions not only facilitate learning but also strengthen your relationships within your network.

Promoting a culture of shared learning and mutual growth is another effective strategy. The principle is simple: As you learn from others, ensure they can learn from you as well. Share your insights, experiences, and expertise generously. Encourage open discussions and debates. A culture of shared learning not only enriches everyone's knowledge base but also fosters stronger, more collaborative relationships.

Furthermore, leveraging the knowledge of your network does not always require direct interactions. Even observing successful practices, understanding their decision-making processes, or analyzing their successful and failed investments can provide invaluable lessons.

In essence, being surrounded by intelligent individuals offers a remarkable opportunity to enhance your learning and improve your investment strategies. The key is to appreciate this privilege, actively seek learning opportunities, and promote a culture of shared knowledge and mutual growth.

As we look to the future, networking continues to evolve, shaped by technological advancements and changing societal norms. Emerging networking trends promise to influence investment strategies, and being aware of these trends is crucial for a forward-thinking investor.

One key trend is the rise of virtual networking. Enabled by digital technologies, virtual networking breaks down geographical barriers, enabling investors to connect with peers, experts, and potential collaborators worldwide. This brings a wider diversity of perspectives and opportunities. However, it also brings challenges, from building meaningful relationships in a virtual setting to navigating digital fatigue.

Conclusion: The Symbiotic Relationship of Networking and Investment Success

The relationship between successful networking and successful investments in the leading-edge field is symbiotic. The conversations you engage in, the relationships you foster, and the knowledge you acquire and share all have a direct influence on your investment strategies and their outcomes.

The importance of a robust network cannot be overstated. It offers access to a broad range of perspectives and insights, opens up opportunities for collaboration, and presents potential investment avenues. A good networker is not just someone who knows a lot of people, but someone who knows them well, understands their interests and perspectives, and fosters meaningful relationships with them.

Rule #25
On Negotiation Skills

"Standing on a street corner waiting for no one is power."
Gregory Corso

Negotiation is a ubiquitous aspect of our daily lives, present in everything from deciding what movie to watch with friends to reaching agreement in international peace talks. It's a dance that humans engage in continuously, consciously, and subconsciously. The art of negotiation is the art of life and living. It's the skill that enables us to navigate the myriad personal and professional situations we encounter daily.

Mastering negotiation is closely intertwined with mastering communication. The two are inseparable, like two sides of the same coin. Strong communication skills build trust, foster understanding, and create an environment conducive to effective negotiation. These skills allow us to express our interests clearly, understand others' perspectives, and craft solutions that address the needs of all parties.

In the world of the cutting-edge where the terrain of knowledge is constantly shifting, there are no formal strategic frameworks to fall back on. We're often charting new territory, creating our path as we go along. Here, negotiation morphs into an art of co-creating reality.

It requires not only a deep understanding of the scientific and technological aspects of the enterprise but also an appreciation of the broader societal and ethical implications. It demands a keen sense of timing, recognizing that the development of scientific breakthroughs often follows a nonlinear path. It also requires a willingness to embrace uncertainty and risk, knowing that today's leading-edge venture may be tomorrow's obsolete technology.

In such a dynamic landscape, successful negotiation hinges on the ability to navigate ambiguity, the capacity to foster collaboration among diverse stakeholders, and the adaptability to continually refine one's approach in the face of evolving knowledge and circumstances. Hence, in the pioneering fields of scientific and technological innovation, negotiation emerges as a vital skill, critical for shaping the future and delivering on the promise of breakthroughs that can transform our world.

When discussing negotiations in the field of cutting-edge technology or innovation, there are several high-importance topics you could consider. They're particularly relevant given the unique challenges these industries face, such as the rapid pace of change, high levels of uncertainty, and the often-significant potential impact on society:

1. **Intellectual Property (IP) Rights:** In cutting-edge fields, the negotiation of IP rights is crucial. This includes patents, copyrights, trademarks, and trade secrets. The ownership and usage of these rights can be a significant point of contention, especially when dealing with innovative technologies that have the potential to be highly profitable.
2. **Non-Disclosure Agreements (NDAs):** Negotiations in these fields often involve sensitive, proprietary, or confidential information. Therefore, the negotiation, crafting, and enforcement of NDAs are essential to protect the interests of all parties involved.
3. **Licensing Agreements:** When dealing with cutting-edge technology, negotiating licensing agreements can be complex but essential. This allows other entities to use the technology while protecting the owner's rights and interests.
4. **Collaboration and Partnership Agreements:** Partnerships are common in cutting-edge fields, as they often involve complex, interdisciplinary work. Crafting mutually beneficial collaboration agreements is, therefore, a vital topic.
5. **Future Innovation Clauses:** Given the fast-paced nature of technology, agreements may need to consider future developments. Clauses that cover future innovations, updates, or iterations of the technology can be important points of negotiation.
6. **Regulatory Compliance:** Cutting-edge fields are often subject to strict regulatory oversight, particularly if they involve health,

environmental, or privacy considerations. Negotiating with the regulatory authorities is very relevant.

7. **Equity and Investment Negotiations:** If the negotiation involves startup funding or partnership in a new venture, negotiating equity stakes and investment terms will be a crucial topic.
8. **Risk and Liability:** Innovative technologies often involve higher levels of risk due to their novel and untested nature. Negotiating the allocation of risk and liability, including the provision of warranties or indemnities, is a significant topic in these negotiations.

Each of these topics requires imagination and foresight. The landscape is rapidly evolving, and the negotiator must anticipate potential issues and incorporate flexibility into the agreements to allow for adjustments as needed. The role of this chapter is not to serve as a negotiation manual, but to show you some critical concepts that you should be aware of to understand how negotiation works. It is a preliminary approach to get you started in learning more about this field.

Introduction to Negotiation

Negotiation is an integral aspect of both our professional and personal lives. Essentially, our progress and success are often hinged on the decisions and actions of others with differing interests and perspectives. As an entrepreneur or an investor, your ability to reach beneficial agreements is crucial to the advancement of your initiative.

A common mistake that many entrepreneurs make is focusing too much on the tactical aspects of negotiation: Who should make the first offer? Should we disclose all the information upfront or keep some aspects secret? Is it wise to concede early or wait until later?

However, these tactical questions don't carry much weight without an understanding of negotiation as a process that extends beyond the actual discussion or "physical" negotiation. Being a proficient negotiator requires both knowledge and skills. While this chapter can equip you with the necessary knowledge, actual negotiating efficiency can only be honed through experience.

The most important thing to understand is that negotiation is a process aimed at problem-solving and value-creation. Every negotiation presents an opportunity to create value, thereby requiring creative thinking. Negotiators must realize that resolving the other party's issue is a pathway to solving their own. Thus, developing empathy — the ability to see things from another's perspective — is vital for negotiators. The following discussion introduces basic concepts for framing a negotiation and planning your negotiation strategy.

Types of Negotiations

There are two main types of negotiation: competitive and collaborative. In a competitive negotiation, one party wins at the expense of the other — a win-lose situation. Conversely, in a collaborative negotiation, both parties aim for a mutually beneficial outcome — a win-win situation. Understanding the nature of the negotiation at hand is important as it informs the strategy you will employ.

- **In a competitive negotiation,** the goal is to satisfy your own needs, even if that means damaging the short-term relationship with the other party. This might involve high aspirations, asserting your objectives, and leveraging your alternatives.
- **In a collaborative negotiation,** while you also want to achieve a good outcome, you understand that the best result can only be achieved by understanding and helping the other party. This approach prioritizes long-term relationships and aims to satisfy complementary needs in a mutually beneficial way. In such negotiations, it's crucial to generate options, display your power subtly, and avoid threatening the other party — all in a bid to find common ground.

BATNA

In the rapidly evolving realm of cutting-edge and science-driven companies, the concept of best alternative to a negotiated agreement (BATNA) holds significant utility. The negotiation process is a delicate dance of consensus, with an agreement arising only when both parties perceive it as superior to other potential outcomes. Hence, having a clear understanding of the possible alternatives is key to assessing our negotiation power and leveraging it effectively.

Fundamentally, BATNA, developed by Roger Fisher and William Ury of the Harvard Program on Negotiation. represents the course of action we would pursue in the absence of an agreement. It reminds us that at a certain juncture during negotiation, a decision must be made to either accept the agreement at hand or seek out more attractive alternatives. This decision point signals when it may be beneficial to cease negotiations.

It's important to underscore that BATNA isn't confined to financial or numerical aspects; it extends to a variety of other factors that may be particularly relevant in the context of science-driven and cutting-edge companies. These factors include the feasibility of implementing the agreement, the time pressures involved, the state of our relationships with the parties involved, our risk tolerance, and more. Each of these elements can influence our judgement of what is acceptable and what is not. Thus, the decision to "walk away from the table" should be made considering all these variables as a collective whole.

Identifying our BATNA and that of the other party involves both scientific and artistic prowess. The scientific aspect lies in meticulously analyzing all potential alternative agreements and determining the most favorable. On the other hand, the artistic aspect calls for imagination and creativity during negotiations, as we consider our alternatives and their relative worth. Here, such dexterity in negotiation can be a strategic advantage.

ZPA

The concept of the zone of possible agreement (ZPA) emerges once we've assessed both parties' BATNAs. These BATNAs demarcate a realm in which both parties can potentially reach an agreement that is beneficial for both.

Despite our thorough calculation of our own BATNA, the other party's BATNA remains a rough estimate at best, making it a challenge to form a precise picture of the ZPA. This underscores the importance of making every effort to gain a better understanding of how the other party views their alternatives, and how they might perceive ours.

Not only should the ZPA be estimated before the negotiation process, it also should be continuously evaluated during the process. This ongoing evaluation can sometimes prove frustrating, especially if both parties are overly cautious about sharing information regarding their needs and aspirations. In any negotiation, there's a familiar back-and-forth of offers and counteroffers which essentially serve as a means for both parties to evaluate the ZPA.

Yet, there are potential pitfalls to this approach. If both parties withhold too much information in their initial positions, the ZPA can remain obscured, making it difficult to identify opportunities to create value in the negotiation. This is particularly significant in science-driven and cutting-edge industries where innovative solutions and breakthrough agreements can hold substantial value.

Framing

Framing is one of my favorite concepts. Using it wisely can help negotiations end successfully. The manner in which we propose a solution to a problem — how we frame it — significantly affects the final result of the negotiation. The context of the negotiation, specifically the definition of the problem to be negotiated, can provide a notable advantage.

We can leverage it to shift the perspective of the party we're dealing with, focusing on articulating our demands. If the other party grasps the "why" behind our negotiation, aligning with our interests, it's simpler to shape their demands, even if the "why" isn't fully genuine.

Numerous studies have shown that the joy of "winning" is less intense than the sorrow of "losing." Consequently, the primary objective in negotiations is "not losing," with "winning" being secondary. Therefore, framing a decision in terms of potential losses to the other party can be more persuasive. As losses generally seem more significant than gains, people tend to adopt conservative strategies when presented with a problem framed in a positive manner and adopt riskier strategies when faced with a problem framed in a negative way.

Astute negotiators are aware of this dynamic and employ it to achieve their goals. For instance, Daniel Kahneman and Amos Tversky presented people with two scenarios around a disease outbreak expected to kill 600 people.:

- **Positive Framing Point A:** "Imagine that we are preparing for an infectious disease epidemic that is expected to kill 600 people. Two alternative strategies have been proposed to combat this epidemic: Alternative 1 will save 200 people. Alternative 2 has a 33% chance of saving no one and a 66% chance of saving everyone. What program would you support?"
- **Negative Framing Point B:** "Imagine that we are preparing for an infectious disease epidemic that is expected to kill 600 people.

> Two alternative strategies have been proposed to combat this epidemic: Alternative 1 will cause 400 deaths. Alternative 2 has a 33% chance that everyone will die and a 66% chance that everyone will be saved. What program would you support?"

The scenarios were identical, but the framing differed. As they reported in their January 1981 article in Science, "The Framing of Decisions and the Psychology of Choice," in scenario A, with a positive framing, 72% of doctors chose the fixed option Alternative 1, while only 28% chose the risky but potentially more beneficial option, Alternative 2.

However, in scenario B, with negative framing, 70% of doctors chose the risky Alternative 2, while 30% chose the conservative Alternative 1. Altering the framing from positive to negative drastically changed the perception of the problem, from saving lives to losing them.

Framing shouldn't always be cast in positive or negative terms. Occasionally, framing aims to distract the other party from what truly matters to us, or to focus on a positive aspect that benefits us.

For example, if we want the support of a crucial player in the value chain for a patented medical device, we could frame the negotiation by discussing the incredible benefits they would gain by supporting our company (potentially less effective), the wonderful impact on patients' lives along with profit-making (potentially more effective), or the recognition they would receive from the healthcare sector for their early support (potentially most effective).

Consider these strategies for successful planning or framing:

- Persistently emphasize the total value of our offer.
- Focus on making our adversary's potential concessions more appealing to them.
- Recognize that the other party may also be using framing techniques. In such cases, reposition the situation to regain control and demonstrate our awareness of their framing strategy.
- Recognize that preparing for the negotiation before sitting down at the table reduces our vulnerability to framing strategies.
- Understand that framing can break deadlocks. Often, negotiations stagnate because both parties perceive their offer as fair. Sometimes, reframing the problem or exploring alternative solutions can provide insight into each party's strategies.

Anchoring

Anchoring illustrates the significance of presenting (or withholding) the first offer in a negotiation. Skilled negotiators use an anchor to shape the other party's perceptions and expectations. Often, the initial offer dramatically alters the other party's assumptions about what we seek from the negotiation.

Consider this example. Suppose we are biomedical researchers trying to sell a patent to a biotechnology firm. The patent is highly innovative and too far away from reaching the market, so its value isn't immediately clear to the buyer.

In such a case, setting a high initial sale price as an anchor can be advantageous. If we assert a high value, the other party will undoubtedly counter, arguing for a lower value. However, we've already created a significant disruption in their strategy, as they now know our expectations are high.

Negotiations that start in this manner generally conclude with a better sales price than those where the other party defines their expectations first.

Why does this happen? Anchoring is a robust psychological phenomenon seen in many situations. When people try to predict the outcome of a negotiation, they often reference the initial value (the anchor) and adjust their expectations based on it. This approach helps them estimate the eventual value or desired agreement from the negotiation. Thus, the anchor can significantly alter the other party's expectations and meaningfully shift the zone of potential agreement (ZPA).

Anchors can be externally perceived (e.g., a previous agreement with other negotiators) or internally established by one of the negotiators through the first offer.

Assessing Sources of Power

Alongside understanding the needs and desires of both parties, it's crucial to evaluate our capacity to exert pressure on the other party — our sources of power — and to be aware of the sources of power working against us. These sources can vary significantly, but some noteworthy ones include:

- **Obstructive Power:** This relates to the ability of our audience to impede a potential agreement. Typically, there are two types of audiences: those who can accept or reject our demands, and those who cannot accept but can reject. Ideally, we want to avoid the latter group, as negotiating with them yields no benefits. The involvement of decision-makers is critical for successful negotiations.

- **Time Power:** The last mile is the most dangerous one. It is where value might be created or might disappear more quickly. Negotiations can be swiftly undermined during the final stages, especially when people are operating under pressure. Some people, while efficient in normal circumstances, struggle to perform optimally under stress. As the final stage approaches, we risk losing much of what we've achieved thus far. Thus, it's crucial to understand our productivity under pressure and aim to improve it.
- **Power of Alternatives:** Our BATNA, or the availability of appealing alternatives, can provide a significant source of negotiation power.
- **Personal Power:** This depends on a negotiator's prestige, their ability to communicate effectively, and their persuasiveness.
- **Representative Power:** This hinges on the prestige of the organization or institution that the negotiator represents. Representing a significant player in the healthcare value chain, for instance, carries more weight than representing a minor one with limited capacity to exert pressure.

Generating Options and Concessions

The most effective goal is to create value for both parties. Yet, many entrepreneurs quickly move from this creative stage to sealing the deal, without spending adequate time exploring options that could better satisfy both sides. It's crucial not to rush this stage or confuse it with finalizing the agreement. In this phase, the following elements are key:

- **Creativity:** Creativity plays a significant role in negotiation. It's vital to generate options and discover new ways to meet the needs of both parties. To do so, you should understand your opponents' reasoning, not just focus on your objectives. Using exploratory and hypothetical questions can help fuel creativity. However, beware of over-logic, as it can hamper your creative potential. You can foster creativity by:

- Preparing well and understanding the problem.
- Being a good listener.
- Regularly posing hypothetical questions.

Conversely, you can stifle creativity if you:

- Rely too heavily on assumptions.
- Stick rigidly to logic.
- Fear failure.
- Introduce too much tension into the negotiation.

- **Skillful Information Management:** Information should be revealed gradually, encouraging the other party to do the same. You must acquire all pertinent information, but only disclose what strengthens your position while concealing anything that could weaken it. For effective information management:
  - Always consider the impact of the information before sharing it.
  - Be prepared to discuss information in depth.
  - Conceal information that doesn't support your case.
  - Be mindful of how and when you provide information.
- **Concession Strategy and Timing:** Negotiations require making concessions. It's important to reflect on the timing and appropriateness of these concessions. Concessions should be made only when they've been earned by the other party. Making concessions without reason wastes an opportunity to sway the other party's position in your favor. A good concession strategy includes:
  - Never improvising concessions.
  - Making concessions only when there's something to gain in return.
  - Preparing a list of potential concessions analyzing what you'll get in return.
  - Ensuring concessions are proportional and don't appear arbitrary.
  - Understanding the value of each concession for both parties.
- **Setting High but Reasonable Expectations:** Generally, negotiators who ask for more tend to get more, as long as their expectations are reasonable. Bear in mind that it's easier to lower your expectations than to raise them once they're made public. The first offer, which should align with your negotiation style and the type of negotiation (collaborative or competitive), is rarely the final offer.

Negotiating "At the Table" and "Away From the Table"

So far, much of our strategy has been executed at the negotiation table, where we've built trust, positioned ourselves, crafted an appealing agreement, fostered creativity, and practiced active listening. However, it's equally important to be aware of what the other party might be planning "away from the table." Off the negotiation table, there are opportunities to bolster our position and chances of reaching an agreement, such as involving a third party or securing the support of a key player in the healthcare value chain.

Overcoming Roadblocks

Roadblocks can be daunting for all negotiators. Sometimes both parties understand the mutual benefits of an agreement but struggle to find a resolution that doesn't compromise their positions. Many negotiations fail when they hit a roadblock. To effectively navigate a roadblock:

- Remember that **negotiation isn't personal**; separate people from problems.
- Use various strategies to **defuse tension**, such as stepping away from the table for a breather or making a minor concession to foster trust.
- View the roadblock as an opportunity to **understand the problem better** and find ways to satisfy both parties.
- **Resist the urge to be competitive** in a collaborative negotiation or to unnecessarily flaunt your power.
- **Seek a new perspective** that emphasizes the benefits of an agreement.
- **Temporarily set aside the contentious issue** and explore value in other areas.
- **Consider objective criteria** that can present things in a different light.

Special Cases

Intellectual Property (IP) Rights

In the contemporary world, where innovation and creativity are the lifeblood of technological advancement and economic growth, the significance of intellectual property (IP) rights has reached unprecedented heights. Especially in cutting-edge fields, such as artificial intelligence, biotechnology, and deep tech, the role of IP rights in fostering innovation, protecting inventors, and facilitating market transactions is crucial.

Yet, negotiating these rights is no simple task — it often involves intricate considerations and potentially contentious discussions. The diverse nature of IP rights, which include patents, copyrights, trademarks, and trade secrets, adds complexity to the process of negotiation. Each type of IP right serves a distinct purpose and thus requires its unique negotiation strategy.

Patents, for instance, protect novel inventions for a specified period, granting the owner an exclusive right to use, manufacture, and sell the patented invention. A pivotal issue in patent negotiations often revolves around the terms of licensing. Who will be able to use the technology? Under what conditions? At what cost? Addressing these questions requires a delicate balance between safeguarding the patent owner's interests and allowing for the commercial exploitation and further development of the invention.

Similarly, copyright protects original works of authorship, such as software code, which is a significant component of many cutting-edge technologies. The negotiation of copyright licenses, especially in the context of open-source software, can be highly complex. Here, the goal is often to promote collaboration and innovation while protecting the author's rights and the integrity of the software.

Trade secrets, encompassing proprietary processes, algorithms, and business strategies, add another layer of complexity. Because they do not enjoy the same legal protection as patents or copyrights, the negotiation of non-disclosure agreements becomes critical to protect these secrets.

In each of these cases, the ownership and usage of IP rights can become significant points of contention. This is particularly true when dealing with innovative technologies that have high potential profitability. The owner of an IP right will naturally want to maximize its value and protect it from infringement. In contrast, those wishing to use the IP will look to minimize costs and maximize flexibility. Striking a mutually beneficial agreement requires skillful negotiation, a deep understanding of the technology and market, and a careful balancing of interests.

Moreover, in a rapidly evolving technological landscape, negotiators must anticipate potential future developments. IP agreements need to incorporate flexibility to allow for changes in the technology itself, shifts in market conditions, and alterations in the legal and regulatory environment.

Navigating IP rights in cutting-edge fields is a demanding but critical task. The negotiation of these rights shapes the innovation ecosystem, determines the commercialization of new technologies, and ultimately impacts societal progress. As such, it is a responsibility that demands careful consideration, thorough preparation, and, above all, a commitment to fostering a vibrant and fair culture of innovation.

Non-Disclosure Agreements

Non-disclosure agreements (NDAs), also known as confidentiality agreements, are instrumental legal tools used in business negotiations, particularly in industries at the forefront of technological innovation. These industries often grapple with sensitive, proprietary, or confidential information, making NDAs critical shields for protecting the interests of all parties involved. Understanding the nature, negotiation, crafting, and enforcement of NDAs is essential for maneuvering through the complex landscape of cutting-edge fields.

In essence, an NDA is a contract that establishes a confidential relationship between parties to protect any type of confidential and proprietary information or trade secrets. As such, NDAs are the gatekeepers of information in negotiations, setting the terms for what information can be disclosed, to whom, for what purpose, and for how long.

Negotiating NDAs requires a delicate balancing act. Parties must ensure that their interests are adequately protected without stifling the free exchange of information necessary for collaboration and innovation. During the negotiation process, clear communication about each party's needs and concerns can foster a mutual understanding and pave the way for an effective NDA.

Crafting a robust NDA involves tailoring the agreement to fit the unique circumstances of each negotiation. The definition of what constitutes confidential information must be clear and comprehensive, covering all potential types of sensitive information that may arise during discussions. Terms and conditions, such as the duration of the agreement and obligations upon termination, should be spelled out clearly. Penalties for breach of the NDA should also be outlined, providing a deterrent against the misuse of confidential information.

Furthermore, an NDA should account for potential future scenarios. For example, provisions might address the possibility of a party being legally compelled to disclose confidential information, such as by a court order. By anticipating and preparing for such situations, parties can avoid unpleasant surprises down the line.

Future Innovation Clauses

In the ever-evolving landscape of technology, the need to anticipate future developments when drawing up legal agreements has become paramount. Future innovation clauses are emerging as a crucial element in negotiations involving technology contracts. These clauses are particularly vital in agreements covering sectors at the cutting edge of technology, where developments and iterations can outpace the life of a contract. A successful negotiation should consider future innovations, updates, or iterations of the technology under discussion.

Future innovation clauses are essentially stipulations in a contract that deal with future changes to the product, service, or technology. These clauses can be quite varied, covering anything from minor updates and upgrades to significant technological leaps. They provide a legal framework to address and manage expected and unexpected changes in technology during the term of the agreement.

The negotiation of future innovation clauses requires a deep understanding of the technology involved and a clear vision of its potential trajectory. This can be a challenging task given the inherent uncertainty and rapid pace of technological advancements.

Parties must carefully consider and articulate their expectations and protections in relation to future innovations. In crafting these clauses, it's important to strike a balance between flexibility and certainty. The language should be specific enough to provide clear guidance and enforceability but also broad enough to accommodate unforeseen developments. Future innovation clauses might address issues such as ownership and rights to future iterations, revenue-sharing arrangements for future profits, responsibilities for ongoing maintenance and updates, and mechanisms for dispute resolution related to future innovations.

The enforcement of future innovation clauses can be complex, particularly in cases where the nature of the innovation was not anticipated at the time of the agreement. Enforcing these clauses requires careful interpretation of the contract language and, potentially, an understanding of the technological advancements involved. This can lead to complex legal disputes requiring expert testimony and intricate litigation strategies.

However, despite the complexities, future innovation clauses serve an essential purpose. They can protect parties from becoming disadvantaged as technology advances, ensure fair compensation for future developments, and provide a framework for ongoing collaboration. The introduction of these clauses signifies an understanding that technological development is a continuous process. It acknowledges that the products and services at the heart of the agreement will evolve over time and that this evolution should be contemplated as part of the contractual relationship.

Licensing Agreements

In the rapidly evolving sphere of groundbreaking technologies, negotiating licensing agreements is a vital yet intricate process. Licensing allows for the proliferation of technology, promoting innovation while ensuring that the rights and interests of the technology owner are safeguarded.

At their core, licensing agreements are legal contracts that grant another party permission to use, modify, or sell a product or technology owned by the licensor. The specific terms of the agreement define the scope of the license, including its duration, geographic region, exclusivity, and any applicable royalties or fees. By permitting other entities to leverage their technology, licensors can monetize their intellectual property (IP) and stimulate its adoption, all while retaining ownership rights.

Negotiating licensing agreements in cutting-edge fields is particularly complex due to several factors. First, the nature of the technology itself can be intricate and continually evolving. Defining the scope of the license can be a challenge when the technology is new, abstract, or subject to ongoing development and refinement. Detailed technical expertise is often required to ensure that the terms of the license accurately capture the specifics of the technology.

Second, valuing cutting-edge technology can be difficult. Establishing a fair royalty rate for a new and potentially disruptive technology is a sophisticated task, especially when there may be little precedent or market data to rely on. Negotiators must find a balance that fairly compensates the licensor without stifling the licensee's incentive to innovate or commercialize the technology.

Third, IP protection is of utmost importance in licensing negotiations. The agreement must clearly delineate the boundaries of the license to protect the licensor's IP rights. At the same time, it should ensure that the licensee has the necessary freedom to use the technology without fear of infringement.

Fourth, the rapid pace of technological development presents a unique challenge. Given that today's cutting-edge technology may be tomorrow's standard practice, licensing agreements often need to be forward-looking, encompassing potential future developments and iterations of the technology.

Finally, legal and regulatory considerations add another layer of complexity. The agreement must comply with relevant IP laws and regulations, which can vary significantly across different jurisdictions. Moreover, licensing agreements involving certain technologies may be subject to specific legal provisions or restrictions, such as data privacy or national security regulations.

Despite these challenges, successful negotiation of licensing agreements can yield significant benefits. For licensors, it can provide a revenue stream, enhance market reach, and foster innovation in their technology. For licensees, it offers the opportunity to leverage existing technologies as a foundation for further innovation and development.

Collaboration and Partnership Agreements: Emphasizing Early Business Development

Collaboration and partnership agreements hold a pivotal role in the realm of science-driven companies. The complexity and interdisciplinary nature of these fields often necessitate the pooling of resources, expertise, and effort. Therefore, the ability to negotiate and craft mutually beneficial partnership agreements becomes a vital topic. The sooner businesses venture into development deals, the better equipped they will be to tackle future challenges. This essay sheds light on the importance of early-stage business development and highlights the role of the chief business development officer (CBDO) in fostering these collaborative relationships.

First, let's examine the rationale for early-stage business development. In many respects, it's akin to sowing seeds for a bountiful harvest. The cutting-edge fields are characterized by rapid evolution and fierce competition. Companies that establish collaborations early on can share risks, combine resources, and jointly accelerate the pace of innovation. These partnerships can provide access to new technologies, markets, or expertise that may be otherwise inaccessible or too costly to develop internally.

The earlier a company initiates these strategic alliances, the more time it has to understand its partners, build solid relationships, and adapt to any unforeseen challenges. It also allows for the gradual alignment of objectives and the creation of shared visions — both crucial for long-term collaboration success. Additionally, early-stage partnerships provide an opportunity to establish a reputation as a collaborative partner, which can attract future alliances and create a virtuous cycle of growth and innovation.

Enter the role of the CBDO. A CBDO serves as a strategic architect, identifying and pursuing opportunities that align with the company's long-term goals. They oversee the negotiation and implementation of partnership agreements, ensuring they are structured to maximize mutual benefit and align with the company's strategic direction.

Here, a CBDO must possess a broad understanding of technology trends, market dynamics, and business models. They must also be adept at building relationships, persuading stakeholders, and negotiating agreements. It's a role that demands a unique blend of technical knowledge, strategic thinking, and interpersonal skills.

One of the CBDO's critical tasks is to assess potential partnerships for strategic fit. They must evaluate whether a potential alliance complements the company's core competencies, advances its strategic objectives, and offers a fair exchange of value. This involves not just assessing the partner's current capabilities, but also their future potential and the alignment of their strategic vision and values.

Once a partnership is established, the CBDO plays a crucial role in maintaining the relationship. They must ensure that communication is open and regular, that conflicts are promptly and effectively resolved,

Figure 31. On Negotiation

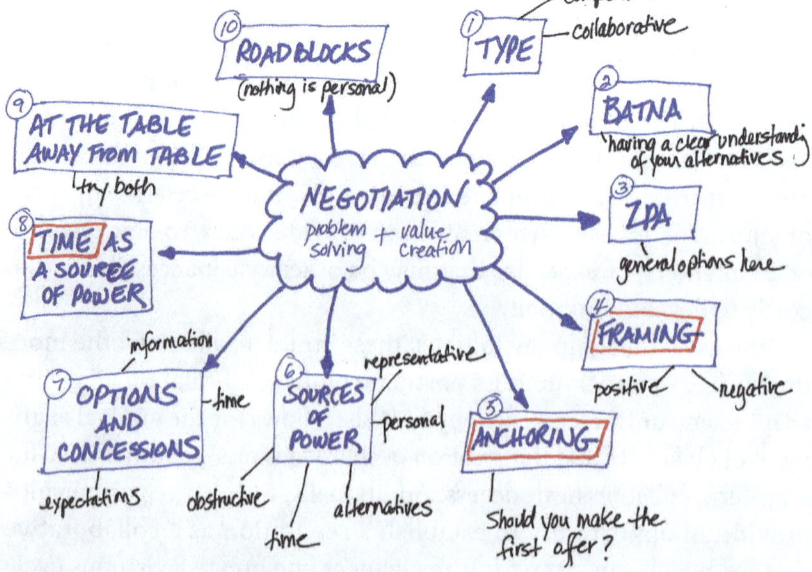

Negotiation, a ubiquitous activity in professional and personal realms, is a dynamic process wherein parties with differing interests attempt to reach a mutually beneficial agreement. Understanding and utilizing key negotiation concepts and strategies can often be the difference between a successful resolution and a disappointing stalemate.

- **First, it's essential to understand the two main types of negotiation: competitive and collaborative.** Competitive, or distributive, negotiation is a win-lose situation where one party's gain is another's loss. It's akin to dividing a fixed pie, where increasing your piece means reducing the other party's. On the other hand, collaborative, or integrative, negotiation is a win-win approach where parties seek to enlarge the pie through mutual cooperation, often by finding areas of common interest and creating shared value.
- **Best Alternative to a Negotiated Agreement (BATNA)** is a critical concept in negotiation. It represents a negotiator's alternative course of action if an agreement cannot be reached. Understanding one's BATNA enables negotiators to establish the threshold below which they would reject an offer, thereby providing leverage in the negotiation.
- **Zone of Possible Agreement (ZOPA)** represents the range of outcomes within which a negotiation is feasible, i.e., where the expectations of both parties overlap. It essentially frames the upper and lower boundaries of what each party is willing to accept, and a successful negotiation often falls within this zone.
- **Framing and anchoring** are pivotal psychological tactics in negotiation. Framing involves presenting information in a way that emphasizes certain aspects over others, thereby influencing perceptions and decisions. Anchoring, on the other hand, refers to the human tendency to rely heavily on the first piece of information (the "anchor") when making decisions. A negotiator can use an anchor to set the stage for negotiation, as subsequent discussions typically revolve around this initial reference point.

- **Power dynamics** significantly affect negotiation outcomes. Sources of power can stem from various factors, such as control over valuable resources, ability to apply or resist pressure, reputation, or expertise. Understanding and leveraging these power sources can provide an advantage in negotiations.
- **Generating options or crafting potential solutions to address parties' interests** is a creative aspect of negotiation. Instead of focusing solely on positions, negotiators should delve into underlying interests and devise multiple avenues to satisfy these, leading to higher satisfaction and potentially win-win outcomes.
- **Time** can also serve as a source of power in negotiation. The party with the least time pressure often has an upper hand, as they can afford to walk away or prolong the negotiation, potentially leading the other party to make concessions.
- **Despite best efforts, negotiators often face roadblocks**, such as impasses, hard-bargaining tactics, or miscommunication. To overcome these, negotiators should foster an open dialogue, seek third-party mediation when necessary, and strive to understand and address the root causes of these obstacles.
- In conclusion, negotiation is a complex yet essential skill, intertwined with various tactical and psychological components. Whether competitive or collaborative, successful negotiation hinges on comprehending and maneuvering around these elements to foster a mutually beneficial resolution. By employing the right strategies and understanding potential roadblocks, one can significantly enhance their negotiation capabilities.

and that the partnership continues to deliver value as circumstances change.

Wrapping Up

As we come to the close of this exploration into the complex dynamics of negotiation in biotech and cutting-edge fields, it is clear that the process is as nuanced as it is critical. Negotiation is not just about reaching a deal but about building relationships, fostering innovation, and establishing a foundation for long-term success.

In these rapidly advancing arenas, negotiations often go beyond the immediate transaction and involve considerations that can influence the trajectory of entire industries. They touch on issues of intellectual property rights, non-disclosure agreements, future innovation clauses, licensing agreements, and collaborations, each with its own set of complexities and implications.

Moreover, the significance of creativity and adaptability in these negotiations cannot be overstated. In fields where the pace of change is rapid and the future uncertain, the ability to think outside the box, imagine new possibilities, and adapt to changing circumstances is crucial.

Finally, remember that while negotiation involves compromise, it is not about winners and losers. A successful negotiation is one where all parties feel they have gained something of value, where relationships have been strengthened rather than strained, and where the stage has been set for future cooperation and mutual success.

Rule #26

On Communication Skills

"I sing the songs of experience like William Blake
I have no apologies to make."
Bob Dylan

Communication skills are not just about conveying your message effectively. They are also about the nature of your message, how you listen and respond. Scientists and science-driven entrepreneurs have a unique way of communicating that's based on evidence, precision, and logic. To communicate effectively, your task is to translate these complex scientific concepts into understandable language for non-scientific audiences. Stay accurate but use analogies, metaphors, and storytelling to make your message more relatable.

Credibility is crucial in entrepreneurship and especially in science-driven ventures. Always maintain truthfulness in your communications. Misrepresentations might provide a short-term gain but will always harm your reputation in the long run. The scientific community and knowledgeable investors value honesty and integrity, so ensure that your claims about your technology are always backed by data and evidence.

We all have biases, and they can influence how we communicate. You need to be aware of these biases, both intentional and unintentional. Intentional bias, such as overselling your technology, can harm your credibility. Unintentional bias, like cognitive bias, can lead to incorrect assumptions or overconfidence. Be aware of your own biases, question your assumptions, and be open to other perspectives.

Successful communication is not just about speaking; it's about listening too. Be open to hearing criticism and challenges to your ideas. This might come in the form of tough questions from investors or feedback from customers. Listen carefully, be responsive, and be open to changing your approach based on the feedback you receive. When you're faced with challenges, respond respectfully and thoughtfully.

Do not take criticism personally. Remember, these challenges often strengthen your business idea, strategy, or technology. Use evidence and logic in your answers and be open to having a dialogue. This will show that you're engaged, responsive, and willing to learn and adapt.

In conclusion, effective communication is a crucial skill for every entrepreneur, and for science-driven entrepreneurs in particular. It's not just about being able to explain your technology clearly, but also about conveying your passion, your vision, and your commitment to your venture. Practice active listening, manage your biases, and stay open to criticism and feedback. These are the skills that will help you succeed in the competitive world of deep-tech entrepreneurship.

Persuasion

We've all learned to express ourselves fluidly and attempt to influence others naturally. For healthcare professionals, whether it's participating in conferences, debating ideas with peers, writing scientific papers, or engaging in discussions with patients and their families, communication is woven into the fabric of our professional lives.

Occasionally, we encounter individuals who naturally command attention, compelling the undecided and swaying their opinions. So, is persuasion an art or a science? Numerous studies in psychology and behavior suggest that persuasion operates according to basic principles that can be taught, learned, and applied. Over the past few decades, behavioral researchers have conducted experiments that shed light on why people pay attention and are persuaded by what we say.

Communication principles are universal and apply equally across various situations. Whether we're explaining our entrepreneurial initiative to an investor, presenting at a conference, involved in a negotiation, or attempting to sway an audience of thousands or just one individual, the principles we'll explore in this chapter can enhance our communication and persuasion skills across all contexts.

As entrepreneurs, we'll need to draw on this knowledge when speaking with clients, suppliers, venture capitalists, or persuading those around us who aren't yet "on board." Indeed, generating creative ideas may come easily, but the real challenge lies in convincing others of their worth.

In many instances, entrepreneurs eagerly prepare their presentations, discuss the benefits of their ideas and companies, only to be ultimately rejected by decision-makers who don't seem to understand the real value behind those ideas. Why does this happen?

The issue often has as much to do with the way the idea is explained as with its intrinsic quality. We all like to think that others will judge us objectively based on our merits, but that is seldom the case. The reality is that as we begin to speak, they feel pressured to classify us into different categories. In some way, they stereotype us. Research suggests that as human beings, we categorize people in a few seconds. It becomes clear then, that in a conversation of, for example, 30 minutes, the audience will form a very firm value judgment about the communicator.

The fact is that those who listen to us do not have a formal, verifiable, or objective way to evaluate the quality of our project, but they are capable of judging us. The audience responds in a clear way using a series of rules and formal structures. Knowing this can help us be more effective in our presentations, conversations, and negotiations. We will learn how to structure our presentations and improve our interpersonal skills, analyzing the tools to develop a clear pitch, grab the audience's attention, and persuade them.

Our effectiveness in transmitting ideas depends on our capability to communicate the appropriate level of credibility (ethos), our ability to create a favorable emotional environment (pathos), and our capacity to generate convincing arguments (logos). These three points constitute the classic triad of rhetoric. To articulate a good communication strategy, we should focus on these three closely interrelated dimensions.

The ethos dimension will be defined by our credibility. The pathos dimension will be determined by our understanding of the psychology of emotions, both ours and the audience's. The logos dimension will be influenced by the force of our speech and the arguments we will use to gain approval or to change their way of thinking.

Let's delve into each of these three dimensions in more detail.

Ethos

Ethos pertains to the style and credibility of the communicator. It is the most important of the three dimensions and is also the hardest to shape in the minds of our audience. The audience's perception of us is based on our personal traits, our history, our achievements, the respect we command in our sector, and more. We must strive to align these perceptions with our interests because without credibility, our message will not be accepted by the audience.

Thus, we must try to build our credibility and maintain it throughout the conversation. If our audience is already familiar with us, and the subject we are addressing is one where we are particularly well-known and respected, we have little cause for concern. However, if our audience is unfamiliar with us, or the subject of the conversation isn't within our recognized area of expertise, we need to establish this credibility at some point during our discourse. It can be helpful to:

- Highlight past successes in the area we are discussing.
- Refer to the views of other respected experts that align with ours.

Later, when we examine the basic structure of any act of communication, we will identify the most suitable point in our "speech" to reinforce this first dimension of ethos. Apart from the audience's perception of our "excellence" as experts on the topic we are discussing, ethos also depends on displaying an image of integrity and sincerity that reflects our beliefs, principles, and values, and aligns with the opinions, attitudes, and behaviors we demonstrate at the outset of our communication.

Pathos

Pathos involves bringing the audience to the appropriate emotional state. This dimension concerns how to forge an emotional connection with our audience. Once our audience is in a suitable emotional state, they will be more receptive to our message. Hence, emotions are crucial for persuading our colleagues, our clients, our subordinates, our shareholders, and our financiers to collaborate with us.

We are drawn to effective communicators because they make us feel good. This process of engendering positive feelings is integral to successful communication. We persuade others by speaking their language and aligning our perspective with theirs. It's important to note that:

- The audience should be prepared to experience the **emotion** we wish to evoke.
- We need to select the **right kind of stimulation** to induce that emotion.
- The target of the emotion we want to provoke in the audience should be **appropriate for our message**. The emotional response should align with our objectives.

Without the sense of identification and trust that emotions foster, it's challenging to construct a positive impression in the minds of our audience. We must ensure that our face reflects our emotions as well as those of our audience

Logos

Logos relies on the inductive and deductive reasoning that we use to "construct" our narrative. Through logos, we create our "arguments" to win the audience's approval and thereby persuade them about our interests. When devising these arguments, the significant roles of three different aspects should be considered:

- **Invention.** We should discover or devise the arguments that support our premise. Arguments are formulated to bolster our ideas because ultimately, it's not the arguments that are critical (they merely play a supporting role), but the premise.
- **Structure.** This governs the flow of our arguments from beginning to end. A persuasive presentation should consist of five parts:
  - Introduction
  - Narration or elaboration of a fact
  - Proof
  - Refutation
  - Conclusion and call to action

  An orderly and clear structure that lucidly expounds the arguments and maintains coherence throughout the discourse is more successful in persuading our listeners. Similarly, the communication should use language that is appropriate for our audience. Speaking to a committee of doctors, where we can employ very precise scientific language, for instance, is different from addressing an audience of potential investors for our idea.

- **Style.** Style reflects the speaker's control over the balance of words and nonverbal forms of communication. Rhythm and body language are two vital elements of style that convey much about us. This style is seen in the formulas we use to underscore our discourse, such as repeating words or sentences, playing with words, using irony, employing paradoxes, and using questions and metaphors. Our style helps us paint a visual image of our message in the audience's mind.

Three Important Concepts

1. **Attention Grabber:** The first 15 seconds of any conversation, negotiation, or presentation are crucial for capturing our audience's attention. If we don't spark their curiosity and interest in our discussion, it's likely we will lose their attention and fail to foster an appropriate mindset. Given that we have much more to share with them, it is vital to grab their attention from the outset. The attention grabber must be short, relevant, and appealing.

   The most common elements to place the audience in a receptive state of mind before beginning with the central theme include:
   - A **personal anecdote** with a touch of humor.
   - An **impactful** quote.
   - A **rhetorical** question.

   This attention grabber creates a shared starting point for the speaker and the audience and projects an image of confidence and mutual understanding.
2. **Common Ground:** It is often helpful if the audience identifies with the speaker and considers them "on the same page." healthcare, we can achieve common ground by mentioning objectives we share with the audience so they feel aligned with us and trust us. Some of the most-used techniques to establish common ground are:
   - Appealing to **shared values.**
   - Showing that the speaker and the audience face the **same problem.**
   - Citing an **authority who is universally** accepted.

   When crafting our presentation, we must ensure that we incorporate common ground, thereby establishing a connection with our listeners.

3. **Closing Argument:** Beginning and ending a communication with a shared reference provides a sense of structure that reinforces the communication. For example, concluding presentations with a closing question that echoes the attention grabber, answering the rhetorical question, or repeating our initial one leads us to a perfect ending.

Basic Principles of Persuasion

Persuasion aims to appeal to deeply ingrained human needs. The six principles of persuasion that can help us influence those around us are:

1. **The Law of Reciprocity:** We tend to interact with people in the same manner they interact with us; therefore, we should give what we hope to receive. This is one of the fundamental pillars of persuasion.
2. **The Law of Social Convention:** Humans are social beings. We tend to gravitate toward the people around us and replicate what others have done before. Thus, understanding how they think, feel, and act. can make us highly persuasive. Persuasion can be remarkably effective when coming from "colleagues" or "equals." This is evident in the fact that the more venture capital firms that have engaged with you in the past, the more likely others will do so in the future.
3. **Law of Consistency:** To persuade effectively, we need people to feel not only attracted to us but also committed to us. Our chances of getting what we want increase considerably if we obtain a public or written promise from our audience. It's been demonstrated that once people commit in writing, they want to stay true to their promise. The implications are clear for entrepreneurs who aim to persuade those around them. If, for example, someone has promised to perform a task on our behalf, it is beneficial to ask that person to draft a summary of our conversation. With that summary, we enhance the likelihood that the person will fulfill the promise.
4. **The Law of Authority:** People trust experts. We must consistently demonstrate our level of expertise; we shouldn't assume it's self-evident. As healthcare professionals, we have a significant advantage in this regard because citizens and investors generally hold great respect for us. We need to recognize this source of

Figure 32. On Communication

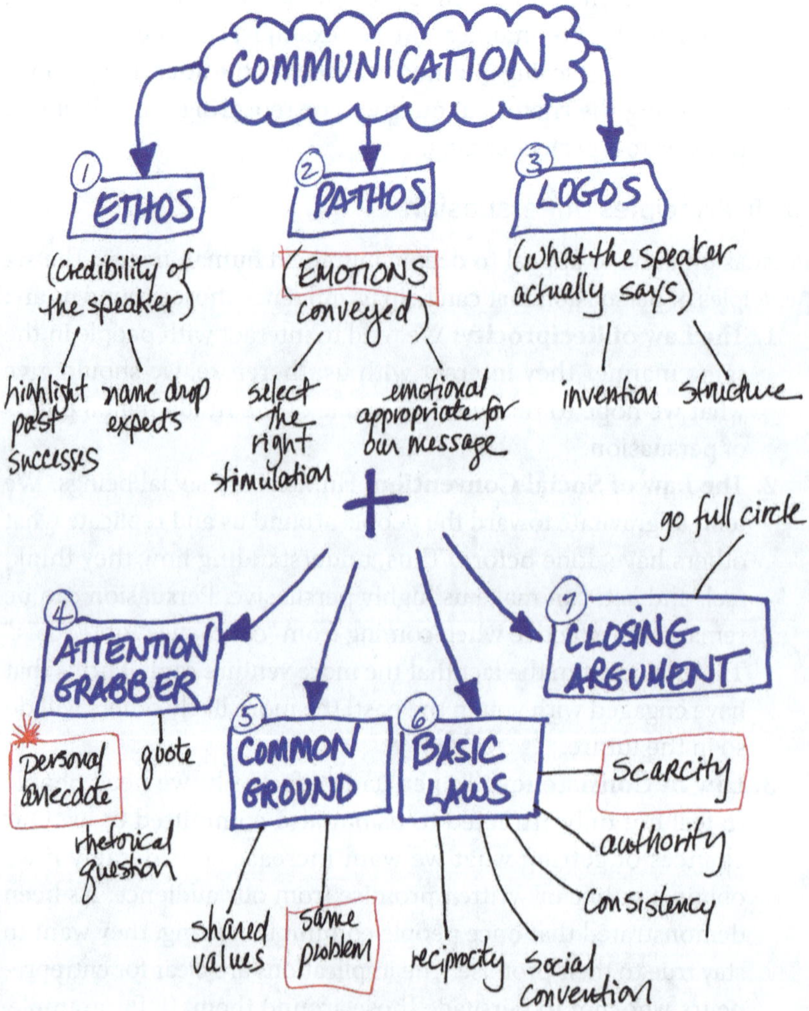

Effective communication is the cornerstone of human interaction, shaping personal relationships, business dealings, and political discourse. It extends beyond merely conveying messages and entails understanding and applying key principles like ethos, logos, and pathos; employing effective strategies such as attention grabbers and establishing common ground; and leveraging psychological principles for impact.

- **The modes of persuasion: ethos, logos, and pathos,** as proposed by Aristotle, serve as the bedrock of persuasive communication.

  - **Ethos**, representing credibility or ethical appeal, involves establishing the speaker's authority and trustworthiness on the subject matter. A speaker with strong ethos garners respect and is likely to be more persuasive.
  - **Logos** represents logical appeal, wherein arguments are presented with clarity, consistency, and supported by evidence, appealing to the audience's rationality.
  - **Pathos** refers to emotional appeal, which involves stirring emotions in the audience to persuade them. An effective communicator skillfully combines these modes to deliver compelling messages.
- **Attention grabbers** play a crucial role in piquing the audience's interest. These could range from intriguing statistics to provocative questions, relatable anecdotes, or compelling visuals. Intriguing statistics can be powerful attention grabbers, primarily when they defy common knowledge or challenge preconceived notions.

  A surprising fact can jolt the audience's attention into focus, as they will want to understand the why and how behind this statistic. Provocative questions also are useful tools for seizing attention. By asking a thought-provoking question, you invite the audience to engage with your topic mentally. You draw them into a conversation, even if it's just a silent conversation within their minds. Their curiosity about the answer or a desire to know if their answer matches yours keeps them engaged. Relatable anecdotes or stories can instantly create a connection with the audience. We are naturally inclined to listen to narratives, especially those we can see ourselves in or those that evoke emotions. Anecdotes can humanize a topic, making it more accessible and real to the audience. By immediately capturing the audience's attention, a communicator increases the likelihood of their message being heard and absorbed.
- **Establishing common ground** is a key strategy in communication, particularly in persuasive contexts. By identifying shared interests, beliefs, or experiences, the speaker creates a sense of camaraderie and understanding with the audience. This connection makes the audience more receptive to the speaker's arguments.
- **The closing argument** serves as the culmination of the speaker's message. It typically reiterates key points, reinforces the central argument, and often includes a call to action. A compelling closing argument leaves a lasting impression and can motivate the audience towards the desired action.
- In addition to these strategies, certain **psychology-related laws** play a vital role in communication. The **law of reciprocity**, for example, suggests that people tend to return a favor, which can be leveraged to elicit cooperation or concessions in negotiation. The **principle of consistency** suggests that individuals strive for coherence between their beliefs, attitudes, and actions. A speaker can leverage this by eliciting a small agreement or commitment, which increases the likelihood of subsequent larger commitments. The **law of authority** speaks to the influence exerted by perceived experts or authoritative figures. Hence, establishing one's authority or associating with authoritative sources can enhance persuasion. The **principle of scarcity** suggests that people assign more value to opportunities when they are less available. Communicators can highlight the uniqueness or time-bound nature of an opportunity to create urgency. Lastly, the **law of social convention** suggests that people are more likely to perform an action if they see others doing the same. Demonstrating social proof, such as endorsements or testimonials, can thus increase persuasion.

power and use it appropriately. Our authority is real and should be made more visible.

5. **The Law of Scarcity:** People want what they can't have. Numerous studies show that opportunities are perceived as more valuable when they're less accessible. Language emphasizing loss is much more effective in changing attitudes around us than language focusing on gains. For example, if we center our conversation on how our audience can "save" money, this approach will be less effective than demonstrating that they are going to "lose" the same amount. Those exposed to this key negative language are more likely to alter their attitude and align themselves with what we propose.
6. **The Law of Esteem:** People value those who value them. If we wish to be persuasive, we need to win over our audience as friends. Two factors are especially fundamental in fostering that esteem: similarity and flattery. Similarity makes people feel closer. A doctor speaking with another doctor unquestionably creates a communication realm that is intimate and favorable to mutual understanding. The same applies in the entrepreneurial realm. We can use these similarities to build relationships with employees, shareholders, financiers, and partners. Casual conversations we may have with them present an ideal opportunity to discover at least one common area of shared interest. The important thing is to establish this connection as soon as possible as it lays the foundation for good faith and trust in each subsequent encounter. The second factor, flattery, disarms and promotes interpersonal relationships. Intelligent use of flattery can foster a more favorable attitude for our interests in those who surround us.

Rule #27

On Leadership at the Cutting Edge: 25 Pearls of Management Wisdom

"All good work is done in defiance of management."
Bob Woodward

Leadership within the realms of science and technology is far from a pedestrian endeavor. It demands not only a keen understanding of technical nuances but also a deep appreciation of the human elements at play. As such, we will now seek to straddle both realms, studying interplay between human behavior, strategic foresight, and technological prowess.

We will delve into various facets of leadership, from the motivational power of incentives to the art of decision-making in a climate of ambiguity. We will use a blend of personal anecdotes, academic theories, and pragmatic insights to construct an introductory guide for leadership in the cutting-edge field.

Cultivating a deeper understanding of your own leadership style empowers you to steer your ship — regardless of the holes — toward the shores of success with unwavering resolve and informed competence.

Remember, as the field evolves, so must our leadership. I offer here 25 lessons I've learned over the past 20 years. Even if subjective and based on anecdotes, they've been invaluable to me, and I share them in the hope that they may be of some use to you as well.

1. People do respond to incentives.

The underpinning basis of modern economics, behavioral science, and management is that human beings respond to incentives. This concept not only is a staple in textbooks, it has profound implications in real-life scenarios as well, especially in the cutting-edge science and technology industries, where motivation, creativity, and productivity are crucial. Understanding how incentives work is a vital leadership tool in shaping behavior, driving performance, and influencing outcomes.

Incentives, at their core, are motivators that encourage individuals to perform certain actions. These can be tangible, such as monetary rewards or promotions, or intangible, like recognition, flexibility, or the opportunity to learn and grow. The premise is simple: When people stand to gain something of value by behaving in a particular way, they're more likely to do so.

In the context of a cutting-edge company, incentives can stimulate innovation, improve productivity, and enhance employee morale. Monetary rewards can act as powerful drivers, pushing individuals to strive for excellence and exceed their performance goals.

Employee stock ownership plans (ESOPs) are common in startups and tech companies to align the interests of the employees with the company's long-term success. However, leaders must also understand the value of non-monetary incentives. Recognition, for instance, satisfies the innate human need to be appreciated and can fuel a sense of belonging and motivation. Opportunities for learning and growth can attract and retain ambitious employees looking for personal development.

Moreover, incentives should be fair and transparent to foster a culture of trust and mutual respect. Leaders must ensure that the rewards are distributed based on merit and performance, avoiding any perceived favoritism or bias.

2. Trust is like a sheet of paper.

Trust, much like a pristine sheet of paper, is flawless and sturdy in its initial state. However, once it is wrinkled, no matter how much we try to smooth it over, it never goes back to its original state.

The metaphorical comparison here illustrates the fragility and value of trust, especially in industries as competitive and relentless as biotech investing. In this challenging field, as in many others, past victories or failures matter less than the reputation one builds along the way. What defines you is not the battles you've fought, the defeats you've suffered, or the scars you carry, but rather the trust you've earned from your colleagues, peers, partners, and investors.

Once lost, trust is hard to regain. A series of successful deals may be overshadowed by one failed promise or mismanaged situation. The damage caused by a breach of trust could result in long-lasting or even irreversible consequences.

Trust is not just about honesty or integrity; it is also about reliability and consistency. It's about making informed decisions, managing expectations, honoring commitments, and being transparent about what is possible and what is not. These principles hold especially true in the world of investing, where trust is often the most significant currency.

In the relentless world of venture capital investments, there are few second chances. The field is unforgiving and demands a high degree of competence, reliability, and above all, the ability to maintain the trust of all stakeholders involved. Without trust, no amount of talent or resources can ensure effective collaboration and long-term success.

Three key elements play a pivotal role in building and maintaining trust: transparency, truthfulness, and the avoidance of conflicts of interest.

- **Transparency** is the first essential component of trust. In an industry that deals with complex scientific concepts and vast amounts of capital, clear and open communication is vital. All stakeholders, whether they are team members, investors, or partners, need to have a clear understanding of the organization's goals, strategies, and progress. This involves sharing not just successes but also failures and setbacks. Transparency fosters a sense of shared responsibility and encourages an environment where challenges can be collectively addressed.
- **Truthfulness** is closely related to transparency but warrants separate consideration due to its profound impact on trust. Truthfulness is about being honest in all interactions, even when the truth is uncomfortable or inconvenient. It involves owning up to mistakes, admitting when one doesn't have all the answers, and being open about uncertainties or risks.

- **The avoidance of conflicts of interest** is critical as well. This involves ensuring that decisions and actions are taken in the best interest of the organization and its stakeholders rather than for personal gain. In the field of biotech investing, where leaders may be handling multiple portfolios or have diverse business interests, the potential for conflicts of interest can be high. Actively avoiding these, or managing them appropriately when they occur, is essential to maintain trust.

3. The leader is a seasoned captain.

The role of a leader, particularly in a dynamic and demanding field like biotech investing, is akin to that of a seasoned captain steering a vessel through turbulent waters. Every boat indeed has a hole, as Steve Jobs aptly put it. Every organization, project, or team has its unique challenges and weaknesses — the hole — that can potentially sink the boat. However, the leader's primary role is not necessarily to fix the hole but to navigate the vessel in the right direction and ensure it reaches the desired destination before water can flood in.

Leaders, much like experienced captains, must acknowledge the inherent vulnerabilities of their "boat" and be aware of the potential threats that could exacerbate them. They must have an unerring focus on the direction they want to steer their "boat" toward. The destination, the goal, the "right shore" to get to, is the north star that guides their decisions, actions, and strategies.

Time is the ocean that every boat is traversing, and it is as relentless as it is impartial. A good leader recognizes that time, much like water seeping through the hole, can exacerbate vulnerabilities and escalate problems if not managed wisely. Every decision, action, or delay has a time cost attached to it, and leaders must be judicious in how they manage this resource.

Importantly, leaders must also inspire confidence in their crew. When the team trusts their leader's judgment, they can focus on managing the "hole," i.e., the immediate challenges and tasks, while the leader focuses on the broader vision and direction.

In summary, the essence of leadership lies in the ability to steer the organization toward its goals while acknowledging and managing its vulnerabilities, maintaining a keen awareness of time, and inspiring confidence in the team. A leader's true role, therefore, is not just to manage or supervise but to chart a course and guide the "boat" unerringly toward its destination.

4. Or maybe not...

F. Scott Fitzgerald once said, "The test of a first-rate intelligence is the ability to hold two opposed ideas in mind at the same time and still retain the ability to function." This statement holds profound relevance for leaders in the realm of investing and managing science-driven companies.

As a CEO or investor, you are constantly faced with opposing ideas. Should we invest in this company or not? Do we go all-in on this technology, or do we diversify our interests? These binary questions can indeed be complex and overwhelming. However, a wise leader knows how to hold both possibilities in their mind simultaneously. They can see the potential upsides and downsides of both sides, carefully evaluating them before making an informed decision.

To illustrate this concept, let me share an anecdote from my previous life as a neurosurgeon.

I once had a mentor with whom I usually discussed complex brain tumor cases. After exploring different surgical approaches for every case, he would list all the reasons why we should use a particular surgical technique and seemed to settle on one path, saying, for example, "Yes, Luis, definitely, we should go under the temporal lobe...." Every time, the case he made for a specific approach was very clear and rational. But then, after a momentary pause, he usually added, "or maybe not..."

I got used to it. It is a perfect encapsulation of the mindset a first-rate leader should have. My mentor, a seasoned neurosurgeon, understood that clinging to one viewpoint might blind us to other valid options; therefore, he kept the debate alive, allowing room for uncertainty and further contemplation. Even though he appeared to make a decision, he didn't close the door on other possibilities.

This approach translates well into the world of leadership in science-driven companies. Leaders and investors should constantly challenge their own decisions, maintaining a mental debate. A decision might seem right in one moment, but as new information becomes available, it's crucial to reassess and adjust accordingly.

The capacity to hold opposing views, weigh them, and still function is a defining attribute of effective leaders.

Rapidly evolving industries require leaders with an agile mindset. They must avoid discarding options too quickly and continue pondering different possibilities. The complexities of the business world demand more than black-and-white thinking; they require an ability to navigate the gray areas with wisdom and discernment.

5. Create optionality and postpone decisions when possible.

Creating optionality and postponing decisions is a powerful leadership strategy, especially in the rapidly evolving world of cutting-edge science and technology. This approach not only preserves flexibility but also enables leaders to gather more information, reduce uncertainty, and make informed decisions.

Optionality, in its essence, refers to the state of having multiple pathways or choices available. It provides the freedom to adapt to new information or changes in circumstances.

In a business context, optionality could mean diversifying our pipeline, exploring different markets, maintaining a broad skill set among the team, or investing in various technologies. By creating a range of possible actions or alternatives, leaders ensure that their organization can pivot or change direction as needed.

In many cases, postponing decisions is a strategic move rather than an act of indecisiveness. In dynamic environments like science-driven companies, where the future is inherently uncertain, it may be prudent to wait for more information before making crucial decisions. With time, new data may emerge, circumstances may change, or previously unforeseen opportunities may arise, each of which could significantly influence the decision-making process.

Applying this strategy means considering different moods, contexts, and perspectives when evaluating an idea or decision. The same issue can look different when you're optimistic versus when you're pessimistic, when you're calm versus when you're stressed, or when you're satisfied versus when you're frustrated. These different perspectives can provide valuable insights, illuminating facets of the situation you may not have considered.

However, the strategy of postponing decisions needs to be applied judiciously. It is essential to distinguish between circumstances that call for swift action and those in which waiting might be beneficial. Additionally, the strategy should not lead to analysis paralysis, where the decision-making process is stalled indefinitely in the quest for more information. An effective leader recognizes when they have sufficient information to make an informed decision and acts accordingly.

Ultimately, the aim is not to avoid decisions but to make better ones. By preserving optionality and strategically delaying decisions, leaders can improve their chances of steering their organizations in the right direction, even in the face of uncertainty and rapid change.

6. FAA: Focus, Act Aggressively.

Bob Woodward, a renowned investigative journalist, coined the phrase "FAA: Focus, Act Aggressively," offering a potent insight into the mindset necessary for effective leadership. In the context of cutting-edge science companies, this concept takes on a unique flavor, balancing the rapid pace of scientific progress with the precision and caution that such work often demands.

"Focus" in this sense implies a deep, sustained concentration on the task at hand or the goal in sight. In a science-driven company, the goals can range from research and development breakthroughs, to product innovation, to conquering new markets. However, focus is not just about defining and aiming for a target. It is about eliminating distractions and not spreading resources too thinly across multiple projects. In a rapidly evolving landscape, staying focused can be challenging, but it is crucial for maintaining progress and ensuring the efficient use of resources.

"Act Aggressively" might initially seem out of place in a scientific context, where caution, precision, and thoroughness are prized. However, in Woodward's philosophy, it does not denote recklessness or unnecessary risk-taking. Instead, it suggests being proactive, taking the initiative, and not shying away from bold moves when they are called for. It implies a willingness to seize opportunities, drive hard toward objectives, and actively shape the future of the organization, rather than passively reacting to events.

In the world of cutting-edge science and technology, acting aggressively might mean investing in promising but unproven technologies, venturing into unexplored markets, or pushing the boundaries of what's scientifically possible. It's about being on the front foot, setting the pace, and not just keeping up with the competition, but striving to stay ahead.

Applying the FAA: Focus, Act Aggressively philosophy in a science-driven company requires a delicate balance. Leaders must maintain intense focus on their core objectives while also being prepared to act boldly and decisively. They must be grounded in the realities and demands of the scientific method, yet open to taking calculated risks to drive innovation. Striking this balance isn't easy, but when done right, it can be a powerful formula for success.

7. Most of what has happened up to this moment is essentially irrelevant; what truly matters is what you do next.

The most successful entrepreneurs understand and embrace a fundamental truth: Most of what has happened up to this moment is essentially irrelevant; what truly matters is what you do next. This forward-thinking mindset is both empowering and invigorating, pushing leaders and their teams to always strive for improvement, innovation, and progress.

Here, the landscape is ever-changing, and yesterday's breakthrough can quickly become today's standard practice. An entrepreneur's previous successes, while laudable, don't guarantee future results. The past, while useful for learning and drawing lessons, should not be used as a definitive roadmap for the future. Instead, it should be a guide, providing valuable insights and experiences to inform future actions and decisions.

Successful entrepreneurs focus on the future, continually asking what comes next. The future is an unwritten book, and the actions we take today shape its narrative. The best entrepreneurs know this, and they dedicate their efforts to writing a future that aligns with their vision and objectives. However, this doesn't mean disregarding the past entirely. Lessons can be learned, patterns can be discerned, and history can inform present decisions.

8. Past behavior is the best predictor of future behavior.

There's a certain level of validity to the claim that past behavior is the best predictor of future behavior, particularly when observing managerial and leadership roles. An individual's historical actions, responses, and decision-making processes can provide a significant insight into their future actions within similar contexts. This is, in part, because we are creatures of habit and often resort to established patterns of behavior in response to particular stimuli.

Nevertheless, we must tread lightly when extending this principle beyond the personal and into the realm of enterprise or scientific innovation. In a rapidly evolving field such as biotechnology, for instance, past behavior, or more specifically, past performance, might sometimes not be a reliable predictor of future results.

Disruptive technologies, shifting market trends, and unforeseen events, such as the global COVID-19 pandemic, can significantly deviate the course of progress from its historical trajectory. It is within these contexts that reliance on past behavior or performance can prove to be an inadequate strategy.

This is where Bayesian thinking comes into play (see Chapter 31 on Bayes theory). Named after Thomas Bayes, it offers a mathematical approach to probability inference. It is an effective method for updating the probabilities of hypotheses when given evidence. The essential idea is that our best prediction of future behavior is not solely the past behavior, but the past behavior as it is updated or modified by new evidence or data — the prior. We will dive deeper into the intricacies and applications of Bayesian thinking in Chapter 31.

9. A 10-0 victory is never in your best interest.

In the world of competitive sports, a 10-0 victory is often celebrated as a testament to a team's dominance and superiority. However, in the business world, such an approach could be counterproductive. Winning isn't merely about outperforming competitors; it's about creating sustainable success that benefits all stakeholders. Achieving this requires generosity, balance, and a focus on win-win situations rather than pursuing a win-lose strategy.

A lopsided victory, akin to a 10-0 score, may seem like a triumph in the short term, but it tends to create long-term issues. Overpowering other parties' can create resentment and tension that could manifest later, potentially leading to competitive backlash, negative publicity, or strained relationships. It can also create a false sense of invincibility, leading to complacency and neglect of potential threats or weaknesses.

Winning at the expense of others is not a sustainable strategy in the modern business landscape, where collaboration, partnerships, and mutual growth are increasingly important. A zero-sum game, where one's gain is another's loss, is less effective than a situation where all parties benefit — the essence of a win-win scenario.

Generosity, too, plays a crucial role in leadership. Generous leaders who share credit, opportunities, and resources foster a positive and supportive culture that drives both individual and organizational success. Generosity can also extend to competitors in the form of fair play and ethical conduct, which helps maintain a healthy, balanced industry ecosystem.

Balanced wins are also critical for preserving relationships with all stakeholders, including competitors, partners, customers, and employees. Relationships are the bedrock of long-term business success. Burning bridges for the sake of a big win today can lead to isolation and difficulty down the road.

Ultimately, a successful leader in a science-driven company knows the value of balanced victories. They understand that winning is not about crushing competitors but about fostering a thriving, collaborative ecosystem that propels everyone toward shared goals. This approach ensures sustained growth and success, where everyone feels like they're on the winning team.

10. Navigate ethics and ego.

Navigating the complexities of leadership in a science-driven industry requires confronting one's ego and the constant balancing act between vanity and the pursuit of an ethical legacy. The ego can be a driving force, propelling leaders to strive for excellence, seek recognition, and relish in the accomplishment of milestones. Yet, unchecked, it can become a vanity play, diverting from the core mission of benefiting society and leading to decisions made for self-glorification rather than for the greater good.

On the other hand, the pursuit of an ethical legacy requires making decisions not for immediate recognition or personal gain, but to leave a lasting, positive impact. This involves thinking constantly about the end users — i.e., the patients who depend on the healthcare solutions the company provides or those who bear the brunt of the consequences of the decisions made.

It's in boardrooms that this dichotomy between vanity and ethical legacy often comes into play. Decisions must be made collectively, with various stakeholders bringing their perspectives, biases, and interests to the table. A leader's role in such settings is to ensure the ethical path is taken, and that requires the ability to influence others, not through coercion, but by ethical persuasion and fostering an understanding of the wider implications of their decisions.

Difficult and uncomfortable conversations are inevitable when striving to align diverse perspectives with a common, ethical goal. Such conversations may involve challenging the status quo, questioning the motives behind certain proposals, or reminding everyone about the company's mission and the responsibility they hold toward patients and society.

It takes courage and straightforwardness to navigate these conversations, but they are essential for avoiding decisions swayed by personal vanity or short-term gains. Remember, challenges and opportunities are rarely solved in comfortable conversations.

Ultimately, as a leader, your focus should not be solely on making groundbreaking scientific strides or achieving impressive financial metrics, but on leaving an ethical legacy. It's about making decisions that stand up to scrutiny, uphold integrity, and ultimately benefit those who depend on your company's work.

11. This is not a popularity contest.

This is a reality we must embrace, especially in the high-speed, high-stakes world of cutting-edge biotech and deep tech. As leaders, entrepreneurs, or investors, we're not here to make decisions that make everyone happy. We're here to make choices that propel us toward our goal: breakthrough innovation.

Our decisions may make us unpopular. They might push us out of our comfort zones and those of others. They may stir the status quo, challenge existing norms, or even disrupt entire systems. But that's precisely what the cutting-edge industry is all about. It's not for the faint of heart. It requires a steadfast resolve, the ability to make hard choices, and the courage to stand by them.

In the world of biotech, for instance, this can mean cutting funding from a project that is lagging, or making changes in team structure or strategy that might not be well-received initially. These are not easy decisions, but they are necessary ones. Speed is paramount, and the industry is unforgiving of hesitations and mistakes.

This need for fast, sometimes hard decisions comes with a heavy responsibility. The industry is immensely capital-intensive, with vast amounts of money at stake. But, beyond the financial considerations, there's something even more vital on the line: potential patient benefits. Each decision we make can ripple out to affect countless lives. In every decision, we must remember the patients — the people who stand to benefit the most from our work.

It's not about pleasing everyone inside or outside the company; it's about doing what's necessary to create meaningful change. We're in the business of making an impact.

12. Embrace the art of optimistic paranoia.

To thrive, one must embody what may seem like a contradiction: optimistic paranoia. The term might sound paradoxical, but it encapsulates a fundamental truth about navigating this challenging field as a venture capitalist or an entrepreneur.

Optimism, in this context, is not mere rose-tinted positivity. It's a practical, forward-looking mindset that drives us to believe in possibilities and solutions, even in the face of daunting challenges. It's the belief that out of the crucible of rigorous research and trial, transformative technologies can and will emerge.

This optimism enables venture capitalists to take calculated risks, investing in ambitious startups that could potentially revolutionize the industry. It allows entrepreneurs to envision and create solutions that might seem impossible today. It's the propelling force that keeps us going.

On the other side of the spectrum is paranoia — not the debilitating, fear-induced kind, but a healthy, constructive paranoia. In an industry as dynamic and unpredictable as deep tech, complacency can be a silent killer. Rapid advancements mean that what's groundbreaking today might be obsolete tomorrow. Therefore, staying vigilant, always on our toes, is not just a survival tactic, it's a necessity.

Paranoia, in this sense, is about maintaining a 360-degree perspective, anticipating potential problems before they arise, and being ready to pivot and adapt swiftly when they do. It's about keeping a close eye on market trends, advances in technology, and competitive moves. It's about staying awake to the myriad elements that could go wrong, from technical glitches to market shifts, and having contingency plans in place.

13. Don't be the cavalry captain who can't ride a horse.

In an era dominated by technology and innovation, technical skills have become increasingly critical for success, and not just for those who are on the frontline of technological advancement. This sentiment particularly holds true for managers and investors operating in technical fields. The crux of this belief is that managerial success in these domains is not only a function of leadership skills, strategic acumen, or business savvy, but also hinges significantly on technical prowess.

The comparison to a cavalry captain unable to ride a horse is an apt one. In essence, how can one effectively lead a team of experts in a field that they themselves are not proficient in? Without a solid technical grounding, a manager in the biotech sector could be likened to a conductor attempting to lead an orchestra without understanding music — the result would be a cacophony of misdirected efforts rather than a symphony of seamless teamwork.

Technical expertise, for a manager in a technology-driven field, serves multiple key purposes. First, it engenders respect and credibility. A team led by a technically proficient manager is likely to have greater confidence in their leader's decisions. They are more inclined to trust a leader who can "walk the talk" and less likely to question their instructions or guidance.

Second, technical excellence enables managers to make better-informed decisions. They can engage in more nuanced discussions, understand the implications of technical challenges, and contribute meaningfully to problem-solving. This expertise can be crucial when making strategic decisions, as managers can better gauge the feasibility of technical projects, estimate timelines more accurately, and assess risks more effectively.

Third, technical proficiency allows managers to be more hands-on in their roles. This does not imply micromanagement — something I've been fighting against my whole life — but rather the ability to step in when required, provide valuable guidance, and understand the team's workload better.

Finally, managers with strong technical skills can bridge the gap between the technical team and other parts of the organization, effectively translating technical jargon into digestible information. This ability can lead to better communication, alignment, and cooperation across various departments.

In conclusion, technical excellence, especially at an early stage, is a non-negotiable quality for managers in the deep-tech industry. It is akin to the horse-riding skills of a cavalry captain: essential, not optional.

14. Verify even if your own mother loves you.

In the world of cutting-edge technology and high-stakes investment, success is often a product of balancing two seemingly divergent perspectives — the ability to see the "big picture" while simultaneously paying meticulous attention to detail.

The "big picture" perspective is all about understanding and navigating the broader landscape — recognizing industry trends, anticipating market shifts, and crafting strategies to steer one's organization through the ever-changing technology terrain. It involves asking questions like: "What is the market opportunity for this therapy?" "How does our technology stack against the competition?" "What is our long-term vision?" and "What strategic alliances can propel our growth?"

While this high-level view is crucial, it is equally imperative to be deeply rooted in the nitty-gritty of day-to-day operations.

Attention to detail, in this context, goes beyond ensuring that the "i"s are dotted and the "t"s crossed. It is about scrutinizing data, validating assumptions, questioning the status quo, and continually refining processes, systems, and solutions. It applies equally to young analysts, managing partners, CEOs — essentially, anyone operating at the leading edge of technology.

In this industry, one must be so committed to detail that they would even verify whether their own mother loves them, as humorously stated in Spanish: *"Hay que comprobar hasta si tu madre te quiere."*

Though it might sound excessive, this level of scrutiny underscores the gravity and significance of decisions made in the tech industry. Attention to detail is not about fostering a culture of distrust, but rather about cultivating an environment of vigilance and thoroughness. It reflects a commitment to excellence, a respect for the intricacies of the work at hand, and an understanding of the profound impact that seemingly minor details can have on outcomes.

15. Following the crowd in deep tech has its perils.

It's an often-unspoken rule in the venture capital world that following the crowd is a shortcut to mediocrity at best and disaster at worst. In a field where we are all two bad decisions away from total catastrophe, the worst thing one can do is invest in what everyone else is investing. Why? Let's delve into the intricacies of the deep technology investment landscape to unpack this.

First, remember that the world of biotech and deep tech is a world of innovation and disruption. By nature, it is characterized by bold ideas, ground-breaking technologies, and a future-oriented mindset. Investing in what everyone else is investing in contradicts this spirit. It suggests a preference for safety and consensus over innovation and disruption, which is the antithesis of what deep tech stands for.

Second, the "herd mentality" can often lead to inflated valuations and investment bubbles. When everyone is piling into the latest "hot" startup or technology, prices can quickly become disconnected from the underlying value. The dot-com bubble of the late '90s and the more recent blockchain hype are perfect examples of this phenomenon.

Third, if you're investing in what everyone else is investing in, it means you're not digging deep enough. Deep tech is a vast field with countless underexplored areas ripe for investment. By simply going with the flow, you're likely missing out on these untapped opportunities.

Also, it can hamper innovation, as companies end up chasing trends rather than creating them. They become followers, not leaders, and this leads to a slide toward mediocrity. It also risks diluting a company's uniqueness. If a company's strategy, products, or services are just echoes of others, it becomes just another name in the crowd. Finally, it can lead to complacency. Companies that follow the pack may not question current practices or spot new opportunities or threats.

So, what's the alternative? It's about going against the grain, daring to explore the less-trodden paths, and backing innovations that others may not yet comprehend. It's about maintaining a healthy skepticism of the popular, a relentless curiosity for the overlooked, and an unwavering faith in your convictions.

But going against the flow doesn't mean being contrary just for the sake of it. It requires a thoughtful strategy, backed by solid research, sound reasoning, and a clear vision, to know when and where to step away from the norm.

16. Internal drive is essential for success.

Internal drive, an inherent characteristic of ambition and determination, is often a crucial determinant of success in highly competitive fields like entrepreneurship and investment. This trait serves as an individual's internal compass, directing their actions toward the pursuit of their objectives, pushing them beyond mere professional competence into the realm of innovation and excellence.

The role of internal drive is powerfully illustrated by an urban legend centered around the consulting powerhouse, McKinsey & Company. As the story goes, a member of McKinsey's team would observe new candidates as they arrived for their interviews. If the meeting was on the second floor, the observer would note whether the candidate chose to wait for the elevator or opted to take the stairs. The candidates who demonstrated the highest level of enthusiasm, symbolized by sprinting up the stairs two at a time, were rated most favorably. This tale, though perhaps more allegory than fact, underscores the high value placed on evidence of self-motivation and drive as predictors of potential success.

For entrepreneurs and investors, cultivating this internal drive can be an essential strategy for success. Entrepreneurship requires an unflagging commitment to innovation and problem-solving, often in the face of substantial obstacles. An entrepreneur with a strong internal drive can maintain the energy, focus, and resilience necessary to navigate these challenges.

Similarly, successful investing is not merely a matter of financial acumen or industry knowledge; it requires a relentless pursuit of opportunities, a willingness to take calculated risks, and the determination to support portfolio companies, no matter the odds.

17. Delayed gratification is key.

Delayed gratification refers to the ability to resist the temptation for an immediate reward in preference for a later, often more substantial, benefit. This idea is highlighted in a well-known psychology experiment with children and candy. The kids are given a piece of candy and told they will get a second piece if they don't eat the first piece until the person running the experiment comes back. Some kids give into the temptation and eat the sweet right away, while others show patience, waiting for the bigger reward. A small group, about 1–2%, find a unique solution, licking the sweet without fully eating it, showing creativity in tackling the situation.

In the domains of investing and entrepreneurship, patience is an important skill. Investments, by nature, require patience and a forward-looking perspective. An investor must often wait for a long period before they see the fruits of their decisions, especially in innovative fields like biotechnology, where the time between the initial investment and eventual payoff can be extensive. Similarly, entrepreneurs must frequently invest significant time, effort, and resources upfront, without any immediate return, for a potentially greater payoff down the line.

In the candy experiment, the children who found a middle ground typify the creative problem solvers in the world of business. These individuals find unconventional solutions, navigating the space between immediate reward and delayed gratification, thereby optimizing outcomes. This ability to innovate and think out of the box is a highly valued trait in both entrepreneurship and investment.

The concept of delayed gratification also extends into the social realm. In my opinion, one of the best predictors of a kid's future success in life is the friends they have. If their friends want to go to Harvard, hold a PhD in astrophysics or any other bold ambition requiring high degrees of delayed gratification (hard study now, success later), the kid is more likely to adopt a similar mindset, contributing to future success. Therefore, understanding and practicing delayed gratification can serve as a strong predictor of success in both personal and professional life.

18. On Darwinism: Do not prolong the life of an underperforming venture.

Darwinism, originally a biological theory, can be applied as a conceptual framework in the business and innovation realm. It is based on the principle of survival of the fittest, which postulates that in any ecosystem — be it natural or business — only the entities best adapted to their environment will thrive, while others will be eliminated over time. This process of natural selection leads to the evolution of the ecosystem as a whole.

A significant element of business Darwinism involves the allocation of resources. Not all projects are destined to succeed. Governments and institutional funds often support projects that lack the potential for success, which can lead to inefficient resource allocation. Prolonging the life of underperforming projects with capital does not contribute to the growth and dynamism of the market; rather, it wastes resources that could have been invested in more promising initiatives.

This draws attention to the vital role of the market as a natural selector. Just as nature weeds out organisms unfit for survival, the market must identify and discard unsuccessful business projects, enabling resources to be funneled toward more promising ones.

This market-driven natural selection is what allows the most innovative and viable projects to thrive, driving overall market growth and evolution. Hence, embracing the principles of Darwinism in business — competition, adaptation, efficient resource allocation, and natural selection — can lead to a robust, dynamic, and innovative business ecosystem.

19. Overcome illusions.

The belief that one can fully control outcomes, predict results, or have total expertise can be misleading. The intricate and frequently changing landscape of scientific research and technological innovation requires humility, flexibility, and a mindset focused on continuous learning.

The "illusion of control" is when people overestimate their influence over events and results. This can be particularly risky in science-based companies where work involves complex scientific phenomena and market dynamics, often outside any single person's control. When experiments fail, or technological development hits unexpected roadblocks, or market trends shift suddenly, leaders in science-driven companies need to balance confidence and humility. They must be adaptable, open to feedback, and ready to change course when needed.

The "illusion of prediction" can be tempting in science-driven companies. The thrill of innovative research and the potential for disruptive technology may lead to the belief that future successes or technological progress can be guaranteed. However, reality is often more complex. Science can produce unexpected results, markets can change quickly, and innovative technologies can meet unforeseen hurdles. Maintaining a flexible mindset, reassessing plans regularly, and being ready to adjust based on new information or changes is vital.

The "illusion of competence" is the belief that one's skills or knowledge are always enough for any challenge. This can be dangerous in science-driven companies, where the fast-paced progression of knowledge and the cross-disciplinary nature of many problems necessitate constant learning and development. Regardless of how experienced or skilled, individuals and teams should keep a learning mindset, seek new knowledge and skills, and embrace different perspectives. Collaboration is key, as it brings together varied expertise to solve complex problems.

20. Plan for luck.

The role of luck is often underappreciated. Many entrepreneurs, investors, and innovators may believe that success is purely a product of hard work, strategic planning, and technical brilliance. While these elements are undeniably important, they exist within an ecosystem of variables, many of which are out of our control. It is this inherent unpredictability that ushers in the role of luck. Acknowledging this is not an admission of powerlessness, but rather an acceptance of reality that allows for more robust strategy development.

To effectively harness luck, we should strive to maintain a large "N" of initiatives, where "N" denotes the number of projects or investments. By diversifying what we do, we increase the chance that good luck will compensate for bad luck, thereby amplifying the impact of our skills, strategies, and decisions over time. In essence, it is a manifestation of the law of large numbers, a principle from probability theory that states that as the number of experiments increases, the actual ratio of outcomes will converge on the theoretical, or expected, ratio of outcomes.

This principle is illustrated vividly in the realm of venture capital. An investor may support a company that initially struggles, only to unexpectedly strike gold due to an unforeseen market shift or technological breakthrough — a stroke of good luck. Conversely, they may back a seemingly promising company that fails due to unpredictable challenges — a dose of bad luck. However, if the investor maintains a large and diverse portfolio of investments, over time, the successes and failures will balance each other out, revealing the investor's true ability to anticipate market trends, select promising companies, and manage investments effectively. Focus, however, is important as well, it is indeed a delicate balance.

21. Repeat what works.

The application of empirical learning principles is paramount for success. This is well-encapsulated in the phrase, "The fundamental algorithm of life — repeat what works. When something goes poorly, do less. When something goes well, do it much more." This simple yet powerful approach forms the backbone of iterative innovation, a concept that has proven to be effective across diverse scientific and technological disciplines.

When a strategy gives positive results, it's like a green light saying the approach is good, the problem was well-understood, and it's interacting effectively with the market or problem area. So, the next step is to use this strategy more often.

On the other hand, if the results are not good, it's a signal that the approach might not be right or perhaps the problem itself wasn't understood correctly. This is a sign that it's time to take a step back, learn from what's happened, and make necessary changes.

While this approach is a good starting point, it doesn't promise success. The world of science and business is complicated, and sometimes you need to use different strategies or consider different factors. Plus, it's important not to get complacent just because something works. Keep being creative and exploring new ideas.

22. No plan survives contact with the enemy.

As the saying goes, "No plan survives contact with the enemy." And in the words of renowned boxer Mike Tyson, "Everyone has a plan until they get punched in the face." These two adages highlight a fundamental aspect of dealing with high-risk and high-reward sectors:

the inevitability of disruption and the necessity for resilience and adaptability.

In the battlefield of business and innovation, the "enemy" represents external forces beyond our control — market changes, regulatory shifts, competitive maneuvers, technological disruptions, or even global events like pandemics. Just as a plan of attack in a boxing match is prone to crumble under an unexpected blow, business strategies in science-driven companies can falter when faced with unforeseen events. Tyson's quote drives this point home, reminding us of the importance of readiness to take a hit and adapt quickly.

This is not to discourage planning. Quite the opposite, careful and strategic planning is essential in navigating the scientific and technological landscape. However, the focus is on developing a flexible plan — one that acknowledges uncertainties and includes contingencies, rather than a rigid blueprint that may prove brittle in the face of change.

Embracing the "nothing is certain" mindset is about promoting agility and fostering a culture of continual adaptation. It means building the capacity to pivot, learning from the "punches," and reorienting strategies accordingly.

In essence, the science-driven company's journey is less about following a pre-established path and more about navigating through a dynamically changing landscape. It requires not only having a plan but also being prepared for that plan to evolve, shift, or even be discarded as the terrain of the market and the battlefield of innovation reveal new challenges and opportunities.

23. A majority of life's errors are caused by forgetting what one is really trying to do.

This observation is especially relevant for startups or companies operating in the life sciences. Here, the allure of new discoveries, the pressure of competition, the demand for short-term results, or even the promise of lucrative exits can divert attention from the main objective: helping patients.

If we focus on patients, return will always follow. Setting a "North Star" — a clear, overarching goal or vision — and keeping it front of mind, can serve as a constant reminder of what the company is truly striving for. The North Star acts as a guiding light in decision-making, a reference point against which to align strategies and objectives, and a rallying cry that fosters a shared sense of purpose across the organization.

To achieve something meaningful companies should constantly correct their course. Course correction can be difficult. It may involve tough decisions like pivoting the business model, reshaping the product pipeline, or even changing the leadership team. However, if such changes are in alignment with the North Star, they are not only necessary but also instrumental in driving the company toward its ultimate goal.

24. Embrace trade-offs over solutions.

In the realm of decision-making, understanding the concept of trade-offs is crucial. American economist Thomas Sowell suggested that "there are no perfect solutions, just trade-offs." This means that every decision we make has consequences, and we must be prepared to accept them.

Trade-offs are inherent in every aspect of our lives, from personal health to business strategies. For example, the trade-off for maintaining a healthy body may be giving up a favorite high-calorie food or dessert. Similarly, in business, launching a new product or deciding on a growth strategy involves trade-offs. We must weigh the potential outcomes and decide which consequences we're willing to accept.

The key to effective decision-making, therefore, lies in understanding and accepting the trade-offs involved. It's about being clear about the potential consequences of our actions and taking responsibility for them. This doesn't mean striving for a world without problems; instead, it's about accepting that problems are inevitable and focusing on how best to manage them.

In a rapidly changing world, where new technologies are constantly emerging, the ability to adapt and accept trade-offs is more important than ever. The skills you have today may not be relevant tomorrow. The challenge is not to seek idealized solutions with no negative consequences, but to accept the trade-offs and make decisions that align with your values and aspirations.

In conclusion, don't strive for perfection in solutions. Instead, embrace the concept of trade-offs, understand the consequences of your decisions, and make choices that align with your values and the person you aspire to be. Every action has positive and negative consequences, and the key to effective decision-making lies in understanding and accepting these trade-offs.

25. Understand impostor syndrome in disruptive innovation.

Impostor syndrome, characterized by feelings of self-doubt and perceived fraudulence despite evident success, is a common psychological hurdle in the realm of disruptive innovation and investment. This phenomenon often originates from high personal expectations, fear of failure, and the volatile nature of the innovation field.

In the roller-coaster world of disruptive innovation, the sentiment "we are the last thing that we did" often holds true. The rapid pace of change and the significant role of uncertainty and luck can lead to a constant swing between triumph and failure. This can amplify feelings of impostor syndrome, as individuals struggle to reconcile their successes and failures.

As an entrepreneur or an investor in this field, you must understand that your self-perception is constantly in flux due to the unpredictable nature of the innovation landscape. Neither your triumphs nor your setbacks define you entirely. They are simply reflections of the fluctuating nature of the field.

To navigate impostor syndrome, acknowledge the inherent difficulty of operating within the disruptive innovation field. Understand that feelings of inadequacy and self-doubt are common and do not reflect your actual competence or worth. Emotional resilience is key, as is a measured self-assessment. Your worth is not defined by your most recent successes or failures, but by the accumulation of skills, knowledge, and experiences you bring to the table.

Embrace the paradoxical concept that "feeling like an outsider is the essential feeling to belong to this science-driven field." In the realm of disruptive innovation, those who challenge the status quo and feel like outsiders often drive the most groundbreaking change. This unique perspective can serve as a powerful asset, enabling you to identify opportunities others might miss and think creatively about problem-solving.

So, managing impostor syndrome is a crucial aspect of navigating the dynamic landscape of disruptive innovation and investment. Embrace your perceived outsider status as a badge of honor — a sign that you are part of a select group of visionaries daring to operate on the cutting edge of innovation.

Remember, feelings of being an impostor are not a sign of personal inadequacy but rather a byproduct of playing the high-stakes, high-uncertainty game of disruptive innovation. Recognize self-doubt as a marker that you're pushing boundaries and driving transformative change. After all, in the world of disruptive innovation, being an "outsider" is often the greatest insider secret to success.

Bonus: A Personal Strategy Matrix

The personal strategy matrix is an effective strategic tool, conceptualized as a 2x2 grid. This matrix helps categorize and prioritize tasks and projects within an organization using two fundamental dimensions for evaluation: impact and effort.

The "impact" dimension is a measure of the potential effect a project can have on the organization. It could pertain to various parameters such as financial performance, scientific quality, or patient impact. A low impact suggests a minor effect on the organization; high impact implies a significant or transformative influence.

The "effort" dimension, on the other hand, gauges the amount of resources — like time, money, or personnel —required to execute a project. Low effort indicates a minimal resource requirement; high effort signifies a significant resource commitment. These two axes divide the matrix into four distinct quadrants:

- **High Impact, Low Effort (Quick wins):** This quadrant represents those tasks that deliver significant benefits with relatively little effort. These tasks are often minor adjustments or optimizations that can lead to notable improvements. Such initiatives not only deliver immediate value but also boost morale and instill a sense of progress within the team.
- **High Impact, High Effort (Long-term strategy):** This quadrant houses tasks that, while requiring a substantial resource commitment, promise high potential benefits. These projects often require complex planning and careful execution, and they

play a critical role in determining the long-term trajectory of the organization.

- **Low Impact, Low Effort (Invisible but necessary):** These are the tasks that might seem insignificant but are essential for the smooth operation of the organization. They require low effort and deliver low impact but are the bedrock that supports the daily functioning of the organization.
- **High Effort, Low Impact (Don't go there):** The fourth quadrant represents tasks that demand substantial resources but offer minimal strategic advantage. Wise leaders often avoid these tasks as the return on investment is poor, and the resources could be better utilized elsewhere.

Every task or initiative can be mapped onto one of these quadrants, allowing a visual representation of the effort-impact trade-off. This can guide decisions about project prioritization and resource allocation, providing a clear picture of where to focus for immediate results, what to plan for the long term, what to maintain, and what to postpone or abandon.

Adding a Risk Dimension

The personal strategy matrix, while inherently valuable, can be further enhanced by integrating an additional concept: risk assessment. This adds a third dimension to the analysis, considering not only impact and effort but also the potential risks associated with each project or task. Risk, in this context, might pertain to a variety of factors, such as the uncertainty of outcomes, the potential for unexpected complications or delays, regulatory hurdles, or market volatility. The impact of these risks can vary significantly, with some posing minor inconveniences and others having the potential to derail a project or even harm the organization.

Integrating risk assessment into the personal strategy matrix provides an even more robust framework for decision-making, allowing leaders to balance potential rewards against the investment of resources and exposure to risk. This nuanced understanding can inform strategic choices and facilitate more effective resource allocation and project prioritization.

Figure 33. Decision-Making Guidelines

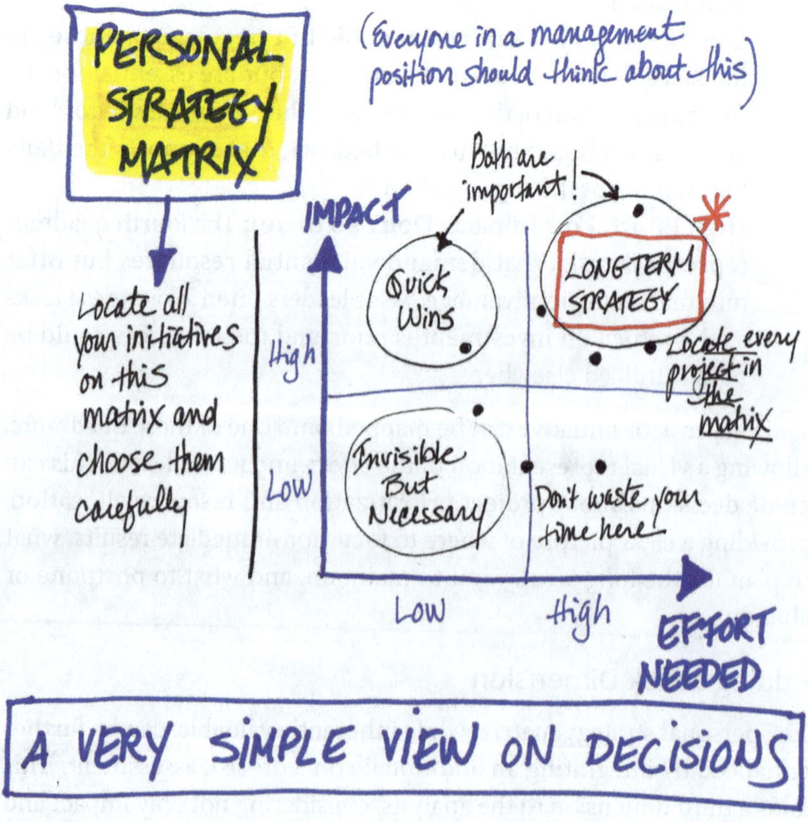

This figure illustrates the personal strategy matrix, a 2x2 grid that enables managers to categorize and prioritize projects based on their potential impact and the effort required to execute them.

- The top-left quadrant of the matrix lists projects that are "Quick Wins." These are characterized by a high impact and require minimal effort to accomplish. They usually offer immediate results and are a boon to any management strategy.
- The top-right quadrant is reserved for projects that form part of the "Long-Term Strategy." These initiatives, while being high in impact, also demand a high level of effort to accomplish. Their successful execution is crucial for the organization's sustained growth and future success.
- The bottom-left quadrant contains projects that are "Invisible but Necessary." These projects yield a low impact and require a low effort to maintain. While their contributions may not be readily apparent, their continued maintenance is crucial for the smooth functioning of the organization.
- Finally, the bottom-right quadrant consists of tasks that require a high amount of effort but yield a low impact. They are considered inefficient in terms of resource allocation, and managers are often advised to avoid or postpone these.

II

Mindset

Rule #28

Forecasting in Science: The Right Mindset

"I left the ending ambiguous, because that is the way life is."
Bernardo Bertolucci

Our goal with the next six chapters is to cultivate the right mindset to effectively forecast within the realm of science — to anticipate the future. To achieve this, we must progressively build an understanding of how trends evolve and get used to a specific "way of thinking." Each chapter will build upon the last, furnishing you with the right tools and mindset.

Our journey will begin with a discussion of game theory in emerging fields. Game theory provides valuable tools for modeling behavior. We'll explore real-world applications, like the prisoner's dilemma in investment decisions, zero-sum versus non-zero-sum games, and signaling games in due diligence, connecting these concepts with valuation, competition, and other relevant aspects of our industry.

Next, we'll dedicate an entire chapter to statistics, a domain crucial for understanding trends. We'll explore the concept of p-value, the normal distribution, sample size, type I and type II errors, sensitivity, and specificity, among other useful statistical tools applied to venture capital investing.

We will also delve into cause, effect, and regression, which will allow us to correlate variables to predict outcomes. To illustrate this, we'll analyze companies listed on the NASDAQ Biotech index, correlating their performance with factors like catalysts, the number of products in their pipelines, IPO dates, quality of the science, competitors, how cutting-edge their science is, their biological targets, etc. This will help us develop an intuition for using the present to anticipate the future.

Our journey will then lead us into Bayesian thinking and the Bayes theorem, mathematical tools born out of probability theory. The Bayes theorem will help us quantify uncertainty and revise our beliefs based on new information, a vital aspect in the world of investing where new information constantly surfaces.

Building on this momentum, we will delve into probabilistic thinking. We'll learn to understand events as probability distributions rather than discrete occurrences. We'll learn that predictions aren't binary, but exist within infinite shades of gray. We'll understand that a wrong outcome doesn't necessarily indicate a poor decision. We'll also explore the idea that investing resembles poker, a game of both luck and skill, rather than chess (pure skill) or roulette (pure luck). You'll see how useful all these concepts are.

Finally, we will get to the chapter on algorithmic thinking, which is arguably the most significant in this section. We'll learn how important programming languages are in our present world and how to code tools that enhance our future forecasting accuracy. Examples include predicting trends using IPOs, predicting NASDAQ Biotech index movements using deep neural networks, and using artificial intelligence and large language models to stay abreast of the rapidly evolving science-driven companies sector.

All this will help us keep pace with the field, which has accelerated to such an extent that it's become almost impossible to follow. We'll explore data summarization tools and even discuss training our own bot with domain-specific information to serve as an artificial intelligence analyst.

And finally, we'll focus on visual thinking, emphasizing how diagrams and schematics can enhance our understanding of the present.

This book, in many ways, serves as a visual thinking toolbox. Once we're done, we'll be well-equipped to analyze deal flow and more discerning in selecting companies for investment. In essence, we'll be prepared to differentiate the companies that will shape the future of medicine from those that won't.

When we get to the end of the section, this carefully woven chain of concepts will provide a robust mental framework for forecasting the future of science-driven companies and distinguishing potential frontrunners in the industry.

Forecasting in Science

The leading-edge industries are inherently forward-looking, characterized by their focus on pushing the boundaries of human knowledge and capabilities, thereby requiring a keen eye toward the future. Scientific progress, unlike many other fields, does not adhere to a linear path. It is marked by moments of steady advancement punctuated by breakthroughs, paradigm shifts, and even unexpected dead ends.

Companies and investors need to anticipate technological advancements, changes in regulations, and shifting market demand. Accurate forecasting can help us identify promising therapeutic areas, understand the impact of new fields, and assess the potential of new drug candidates.

Much of scientific progress is built upon a foundation of gradual, iterative improvements. Researchers incrementally build on existing knowledge, refining theories, honing methodologies, and progressively pushing the boundaries of understanding. These steady advancements often form the backbone of scientific fields, providing a reliable, if slow, trajectory of progress.

However, scientific progress is not solely defined by steady advancements. Every so often, breakthrough discoveries disrupt the steady march of progress, propelling a field forward in leaps and bounds. These breakthroughs often arrive unexpectedly, borne out of novel insights or innovative technologies. They can redefine what is considered possible and rapidly shift the direction of a scientific field. Examples range from the discovery of DNA's double helix structure to the development of CRISPR-Cas9 gene editing.

Join me on this exciting journey as we explore the right mindset.

Figure 34. A Different Way of Thinking

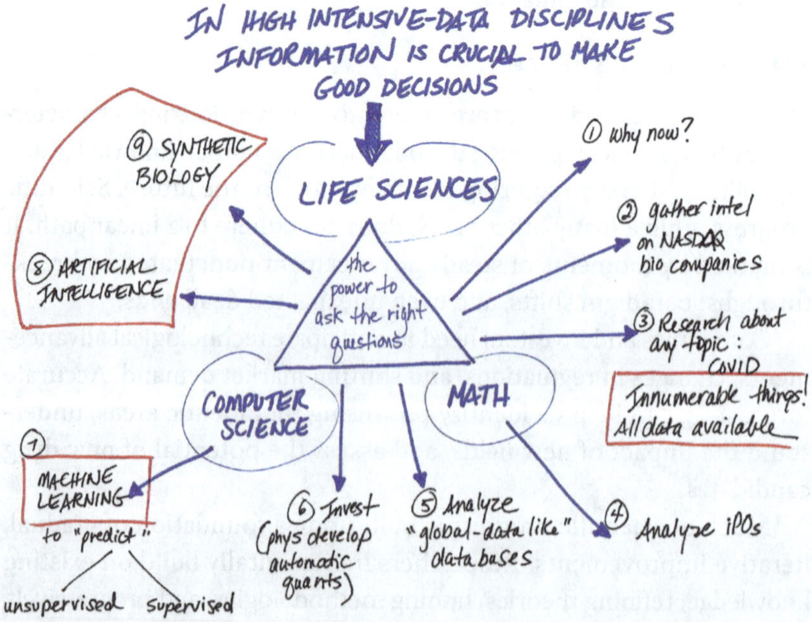

Math, computer science, and life sciences are coming together like never before, creating amazing changes in health and biotechnology. This mix is helping us understand more about living things and is changing how we use data to predict the future.

- **Understanding math and computer science is key to predicting what's going to happen in deep tech.** It's especially important for investors because this knowledge helps them see where these fields might go in the future. Especially in the context of venture capital, knowing how to interpret mergers and acquisitions deals, public market dynamics, and data from listed companies is crucial. As investors channel their resources into enterprises today, they are simultaneously paving the path for these firms to potentially go public or be acquired tomorrow. Therefore, this understanding is necessary to plan the best investment strategies.
- In fields like life sciences and technology that use substantial data, it's important to be able to understand and interpret the data to make good decisions. **The key is asking the right questions**, and this ability comes from a blend of life sciences, math, and computer science.
- When we talk about math here, we're talking about everything from statistics to theories like Bayes' theorem. Computer science includes areas like data science, machine learning, and artificial intelligence. These tools help us make sense of all the data we have today. Math helps us **understand patterns and relationships**, and this understanding can lead to big discoveries and advancements. We can use these patterns not just to learn new things, but also to make **predictions**. For example, we can use patterns in how diseases spread to predict future outbreaks. We can also use patterns in people's behavior to predict future market trends. Finally, math and computer science are also crucial for **dealing with uncertainty**.

Techniques like probability theory and statistics can help us manage the unknown, which is important for making predictions in many scientific fields.

- In the high-intensity data disciplines of life sciences and deep tech, the ability to **synthesize and interpret data** is fundamental to effective decision-making. The crux of this process lies in our ability to ask the right questions — questions that guide us to insights, facilitate innovation, and project the trajectories of future trends. This approach, which rests at the intersection of life sciences, mathematics, and computer science, forms the foundation of our current discussion. With so much information available today, we can research a wide variety of topics. With the right math and computer skills, we can analyze things like the performance of companies when they first go public and devise strategies for maximum value capture for our firms. We can even create automated tools for investing in the stock market.
- **These methodologies equip us to derive meaning from the abundant data** we grapple with in the 21st century. Mathematics universal language and analytical tools provide the framework for deciphering the order and structure underlying various phenomena. In scientific fields, the application of mathematical principles allows us to identify, classify, and interpret patterns and relationships within complex datasets, driving significant discoveries and advancements.
- One of the biggest impacts of math and computer science on medicine is the development of **artificial intelligence and machine learning.** These technologies are already changing healthcare in a big way, from early disease detection to the design of new treatments. They help us spot trends and find patterns in data. This is especially important in fields like synthetic biology, where we're starting to treat the code in cells like something we can change and adapt to our needs.
- One might wonder how this knowledge helps predict the future of medical domains like oncology, gene therapy, or synthetic biology. The answer lies in the power of data analysis and predictive modeling. These mathematical and computational tools enable us to identify current areas of interest and anticipate market trends. By harnessing this capacity, we can visualize and strategically prepare for future transformations in medicine. In the end, not everyone has to become a math or computer science expert. But understanding these fields is becoming more and more important for predicting and shaping the future in science and technology. Whether you're a scientist, a businessperson, or an investor, **this mix of skills could be the key to understanding and predicting the future**.

Rule #29

Game Theory in Emerging Fields

"The colour of truth is grey."
André Gide

I've always been fascinated by game theory, largely because it provides an elegant and insightful framework to understand and anticipate human behavior. It's intriguing to observe how individuals, each guided by their own interests, interact within a defined system to produce outcomes that can be cooperative, competitive, or somewhere in between.

Game theory has proven invaluable to my understanding of early-stage investments. It helps me grapple with the intricate dynamics that arise when multiple investment funds vie for the best opportunities, yet simultaneously there is a need for mutual collaboration. It illuminates the challenges and strategies involved in negotiations where information asymmetry is a key factor — where each party, armed with their unique set of knowledge, navigates the negotiation landscape to their advantage.

However, while game theory offers predictive tools, it is by no means an infallible prophecy of individual behavior. People often surprise us, for they are more than just "players" in a game — they are complex, irrational, and capable of growth. Therefore, while game theory provides a powerful abstract framework, it's crucial to remember that it's just that: a simplification of the real world.

Because I cannot fully elaborate on this topic in just one chapter, I present here a brief introduction. You should consider going deeper to fully grasp the potential of game theory in helping you understand what's going on around you.

The Concept

Game theory, woven from the threads of mathematics, economics, and social science, takes us into the labyrinth of strategic interaction. The landscape of cutting-edge fields is often characterized by a constant tug-of-war between collaboration and competition. Companies are locked in a race to outdo one another, yet they also rely on each other's progress to validate the field and stimulate market interest.

Game theory concepts such as the "prisoner's dilemma" provide an analytical framework for understanding these intricate dynamics. For instance, two firms might mutually benefit from sharing research findings, but the fear of giving away a competitive advantage might prevent cooperation.

Understanding these strategic interdependencies can also inform a company's positioning in the marketplace. For example, the concept of "first-mover advantage" suggests that the firm that is the first to introduce a new technology may gain significant advantages. On the other hand, the "second-mover advantage" theory argues that later entrants can learn from the mistakes of the pioneers and avoid them. The decision about whether to rush to market or wait and learn from others is an example of strategic decision-making illuminated by game theory.

Game theory also can shed light on scenarios where information is unevenly distributed — a common occurrence in cutting-edge fields where some companies may operate in "stealth mode," hiding their developments until the last moment. In these scenarios, the game theory concept of "signaling" can be crucial. A company might strategically release information to signal its strength, progress, or strategic direction, indirectly affecting the behavior of its competitors.

Yet, the art of applying game theory isn't about converting the vibrant world of entrepreneurship into a sterile mathematical model. Instead, it's about distilling insights from these models and using them to illuminate our understanding, enrich our strategy, and inform our decisions.

Overview and Basic Tools

Game theory, a branch of mathematical economics, has been a key component of strategic decision-making for over a century. Its roots can be traced back to 1838 when Antoine Augustin Cournot, a French mathematician, introduced the concept of strategic interaction in his research on duopoly markets.

The modern framework of game theory came into existence in the early 20th century with the groundbreaking work of John von Neumann and Oskar Morgenstern. Published in their book *Theory of Games and Economic Behavior* in 1944, this new approach to strategic decision-making revolutionized fields ranging from economics to political science, and from biology to computer science.

The foundational concept of game theory is the "game," a scenario involving multiple players who make decisions strategically, taking into consideration the likely actions of the other players. These games can be cooperative or non-cooperative, depending on whether binding agreements between players are possible or not.

In non-cooperative games, each player is assumed to act in their own best interest. The concept of "Nash Equilibrium," introduced by American mathematician John Nash, is a cornerstone of non-cooperative games. A Nash Equilibrium is a set of strategies, one for each player, such that no player can unilaterally improve their outcome by changing their strategy, given the strategies of the others.

Cooperative games, on the other hand, focus on how groups of players can coordinate their actions for mutual benefit. Key concepts in cooperative games include "coalitions," "the core," and "the Shapley value," which deal with group formation and equitable distribution of payoffs.

In addition to cooperative and non-cooperative games, game theory also involves "zero-sum" and "non-zero-sum" games. In zero-sum games, the gains of one player directly correspond to the losses of the other player(s). Non-zero-sum games, however, allow for the possibility of mutual gain or mutual loss.

Game theory further differentiates games into "simultaneous" and "sequential" games. In simultaneous games, all players make their decisions at the same time without knowledge of the others' decisions.

In contrast, in sequential games, players make decisions in a specific order; later players may have knowledge of earlier decisions.

In conclusion, game theory, with its focus on strategic decision-making and its rich array of concepts, has been a powerful tool

Figure 35. Game Theory Basic Tools

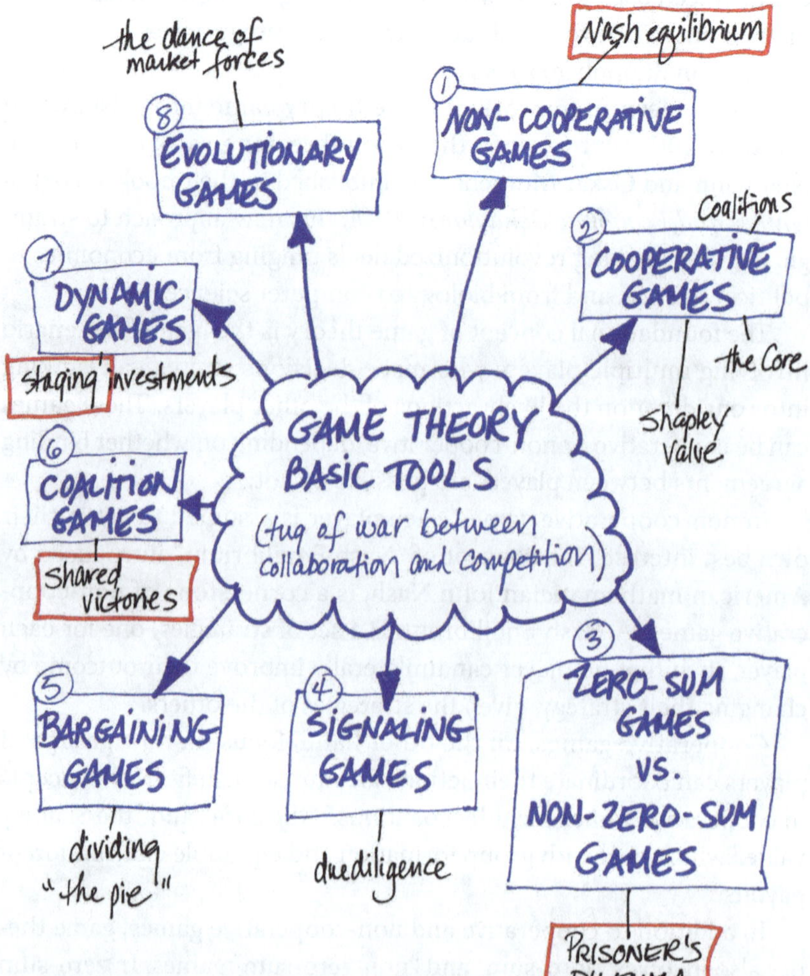

Game theory centers on "games," scenarios where multiple players make strategic decisions, considering others' likely actions. Games can be cooperative or non-cooperative, and they can be zero-sum or non-zero-sum. They can also be simultaneous or sequential, depending on the players' decision-making timing and knowledge of others' decisions.

- **The "prisoner's dilemma"** highlights the conflict between individual and collective rationality, showing how mutual cooperation can lead to beneficial outcomes. In the context of venture capitalism, it underscores the importance of trust and cooperation for successful investment strategies.

Rule #29: Game Theory in Emerging Fields

- **The Nash Equilibrium**, named after Nobel laureate John Nash, is a state of a game in which no player can improve their own outcome by unilaterally changing their strategy while the other players keep theirs constant. In other words, it's a situation where every player's strategy is optimal given what their competitors are doing. Understanding Nash Equilibrium allows investors to anticipate the decisions of other players in the market, which is crucial in competitive investment scenarios. However, it's important to note that reaching a Nash Equilibrium doesn't necessarily mean that the outcome is the best collective one; it simply means no investor could unilaterally change their strategy to better their outcome. This awareness could encourage investors to explore cooperative strategies or negotiate agreements to achieve more beneficial mutual outcomes.
- **"Zero-sum" and "non-zero-sum" games** are critical concepts in shaping investment strategies. Zero-sum games, where one player's gain equals another's loss, apply to competitive scenarios such as financial market trading. However, non-zero-sum games depict scenarios where total gains and losses aren't fixed at zero, often seen in early-stage investing, where cooperation can yield substantial mutual returns.

  These concepts help investors navigate the investment landscape more effectively, aligning their strategies with their risk tolerance and investment philosophy.
- "**Signaling games"** offer a powerful lens to examine the due diligence process in early-stage investing. Entrepreneurs, as informed players, send signals about their startups' potential through various channels. Investors, as uninformed players, interpret these signals to assess potential and evaluate risk. However, investors must be aware of potential pitfalls like "adverse selection," where entrepreneurs might overstate their startup's potential, and "moral hazard," where entrepreneurs take excessive risks knowing that investors bear the costs.
- "**Bargaining games"** provide a perspective to understand startup investment negotiations, especially those involving valuation. Both the investor and entrepreneur need to agree on a valuation, reflecting the company's worth, a negotiation process that mirrors the strategic dynamics of bargaining games. Influencing this outcome are factors like each player's bargaining power, their best alternatives, and their time preferences.
- Syndicated investments, common in early-stage investing, resemble **"coalition games,"** where players form coalitions to achieve a common goal and share the payoff. These investment syndicates allow investors to pool resources, share risks, and invest in startups that might be too costly for a single investor. The challenge lies in agreeing on the distribution of the eventual returns among syndicate members.
- **"Evolutionary Game Theory,"** which views strategies as evolving entities competing for survival, offers a dynamic perspective on investment decision-making. As certain investment strategies yield high returns, they attract more investors. However, market saturation or emerging trends may necessitate strategy adaptation. This continuous cycle of adjustment mirrors biological evolution, making it particularly evident in sector-specialized venture capital funds.
- Venture capital investing is a complex, staged process that can be likened to **"dynamic games."** Investors release funding in rounds, calibrating their investment based on the startup's performance and progress. Each funding round presents entrepreneurs an opportunity to prove their venture's worth, opening the door for further funding. This strategy allows both investors and entrepreneurs to manage their resources effectively, balance risks, and consider the potential impacts of their performance on future negotiations. The presence of potential investors can also influence the game dynamics, affecting the negotiation and competition strategies.

in advancing our understanding of complex interactive situations. From economics to biology, from politics to artificial intelligence, its influence is pervasive and profound, offering insights and strategies that guide decision-making in a complex world.

The Prisoner's Dilemma and Investment Decisions

The realm of investment decisions is filled with complexities and intricacies that require both mathematical precision and strategic foresight. One of the most profound theoretical frameworks that offers insights into this sphere is game theory, and within it, the concept of the "prisoner's dilemma." The application of this concept to investment scenarios can elucidate the often-subtle interplay between cooperation and competition that investors face.

The prisoner's dilemma is a model of a situation in which two individuals could benefit from cooperating but are inclined to act in their self-interest, resulting in a less optimal outcome for both. In the classic setup, two prisoners, unable to communicate with each other, must independently decide whether to betray the other or remain silent. The dilemma lies in the fact that while mutual cooperation yields a better collective outcome, individual incentives push toward betrayal, leading to a worse outcome for both.

Translating this to the investment landscape, consider two venture capitalists, Investor A and Investor B, evaluating a promising early-stage startup. They both recognize the potential of the startup, but the required funding exceeds the amount that either is willing to risk individually. In this scenario, the optimal outcome would be for both investors to cooperate, sharing the funding responsibility and, in turn, the potential rewards.

However, complications arise when we consider the individual incentives. For instance, suppose Investor A suspects that Investor B might provide the full funding, thus shouldering all the risk. In this case, Investor A may be tempted to withhold their investment, hoping to invest later, once the startup has proven its viability, and trying to keep the pre-money as close to the present one as possible — a move analogous to the betrayal in the prisoner's dilemma. Similarly, Investor B might reason along the same lines.

If both investors act on these suspicions and withhold their investments, the startup may fail to secure the necessary funding, leading to a "lose-lose" situation, much like the prisoner's dilemma's sub-optimal outcome.

Consequently, understanding the dynamics of the prisoner's dilemma can offer investors valuable insights. It underlines the importance of trust, communication, and sometimes even formal cooperation agreements in mitigating the risks of such dilemmas. Moreover, it highlights the fact that while individual rationality tends toward competition, collective rationality often leans toward cooperation.

Zero-Sum versus Non-Zero-Sum Games

Game theory introduces a variety of conceptual frameworks to understand and predict outcomes. Two of these frameworks are zero-sum and non-zero-sum games, each of which can be invaluable in developing investment strategies.

A zero-sum game is a situation in which one player's gain is precisely offset by another's loss. In other words, the sum of the total gains and losses remains zero. This dynamic is often found in competitive scenarios, such as trading in financial markets, where one trader's profit is another trader's loss.

In contrast, non-zero-sum games depict scenarios in which the total of gains and losses can be more or less than zero. These games often represent situations where cooperation between players can lead to mutual gains or where competition can result in collective losses.

Applying these concepts to investment scenarios can profoundly influence investment strategy. For example, when investing in a public company, the scenario can often resemble a zero-sum game, especially in the short term. If an investor buys shares at a low price and sells at a high price, someone else is on the other side of that transaction, buying high after selling low. However, early-stage investing, such as venture capital or angel investing, often more closely resembles non-zero-sum games.

The creation of a successful company can generate significant value, leading to substantial returns for all investors involved, thereby creating a "win-win" situation. This kind of investing requires collaboration, trust, and shared long-term vision among investors and founders alike.

Choosing to view an investment scenario as either a zero-sum or non-zero-sum game will greatly influence an investor's strategy. A zero-sum perspective might lead to a more competitive strategy, focusing on gaining an advantage over other investors. However, a non-zero-sum perspective encourages a more cooperative strategy, seeking mutual benefit with other stakeholders.

While the decision to treat an investment scenario as a zero-sum or non-zero-sum game largely depends on the specific circumstances, understanding these concepts allows investors to better evaluate their strategic options. By recognizing the potential for both competition and cooperation, investors can navigate the investment landscape more effectively, making decisions that align with their risk tolerance, investment philosophy, and the specific dynamics of the situation at hand.

Signaling Games and Due Diligence: Decrypting the Dance of Investment

Signaling games offer a powerful lens through which we can observe the due diligence process. Just like the players in a signaling game, the key participants in the investment process, namely the entrepreneurs and the investors, grapple with the nuanced interplay of information, making strategic decisions based on what they know and what they deduce.

Signaling games revolve around asymmetric information — a situation where one player has access to private information, while others do not. In this context, the player with more information sends a signal that other players must interpret.

The world of early-stage investing mirrors this model quite accurately. The entrepreneur, akin to the informed player in a signaling game, has deep and detailed knowledge about their startup — its technology, potential, risks, and competitive landscape. This proprietary knowledge forms the basis of the company's prospects and its potential for returns. On the other side, investors, like uninformed players in the signaling game, must decipher this potential from the observable signals that the entrepreneur sends. These signals can come in various forms: the entrepreneur's pitch, their science package, the team's credentials, existing prototypes or products, financial forecasts, and more.

In this complex signaling game, the due-diligence process takes center stage. Due diligence is a critical phase during which investors validate the signals sent by the entrepreneur. They probe all aspects of the startup — scientifical, financial, legal, and market- oriented — to verify claims, assess potential, and evaluate risk.

It's crucial to note, however, that signaling games also warn about potential pitfalls such as "adverse selection" and "moral hazard." Adverse selection occurs when the entrepreneur's incentives are misaligned with revealing the truth. For instance, an entrepreneur might overstate the startup's potential to secure funding. Moral hazard, on the other hand, refers to situations where one party takes excessive risks because the costs fall upon another party. For example, an entrepreneur could take risky decisions after securing funding, knowing that the downside is primarily borne by the investors.

Bargaining Games and Valuation: The Strategic Dance of Startup Investments

The process of investing in a startup is a nuanced negotiation, closely resembling a chess game. In this game, one of the most critical decisions revolves around company valuation. Drawing upon game theory, we can view this negotiation as a complex bargaining game — a strategic dance between the entrepreneur and the investor, each maneuvering to achieve their desired outcome.

In a bargaining game, players negotiate to divide a certain value (or "pie") among themselves. Each player has their own beliefs about what constitutes a fair division. This scenario perfectly encapsulates the valuation negotiation during startup investment. The "pie" in this case is the company's worth, and the entrepreneur and the investor must agree on how to slice it — i.e., decide the amount of equity the investor will receive for their investment.

The first step in this dance is for the entrepreneur or the investor to propose a valuation, usually based on factors like the startup's science, market potential, competition, and financial projections. The counter party then evaluates this proposal, considering not just the factors mentioned, but also the risk-return profile of the investment, comparable valuations in the market, and their fund's investment strategy.

Game theory suggests that several key factors can influence the outcome of this negotiation. These include each player's bargaining power, their alternative options (also known as their BATNA — best alternative to a negotiated agreement), and their time preferences (whether they are more concerned with immediate or future gains).

For instance, an entrepreneur with a unique breakthrough technology and interest from multiple investors might have high bargaining power and can command a higher valuation. On the other hand, an investor with numerous attractive investment opportunities might be less inclined to agree to a high valuation.

In conclusion, approaching valuation negotiation as a bargaining game offers profound insights into the strategic dynamics of startup investments. Game theory doesn't just elucidate the negotiation process; it also equips entrepreneurs and investors with the strategic tools to navigate this process effectively and reach a valuation that accurately reflects the startup's potential for value creation.

Coalition Games and Syndicated Investments: The Art of Shared Victory in Startup Funding

Venture investment often operates under the adage "no investor is an island." Just as startups thrive on collaboration, investors too often benefit from a collective approach, especially in the realm of early-stage investing. The formation of a coalition or syndicate of investors to jointly fund a startup is an increasingly common practice. This scenario presents an intriguing framework for the application of game theory — specifically, coalition games.

In a coalition game, players can form groups, or coalitions, that work together to achieve a common goal. The fundamental question is how to distribute the "payoff" or benefits among the coalition members. Similarly, in a syndicated investment, investors come together to fund a startup, and the eventual returns from the investment need to be distributed among the investors.

Coalition or syndicated investments can have several benefits. They allow investors to pool resources, share risks, and invest in startups that might be too costly for a single investor. Additionally, different investors can bring unique strengths to the table, such as industry expertise, networks, and experience, enriching the overall value of the investment.

However, syndicated investments also present challenges. The members of the syndicate need to agree on how to distribute the investment's returns, which is where game theory comes into play. Several solution concepts in game theory can provide insights into this problem. For instance, the concept of the "Shapley value" could provide one approach to fair distribution. It suggests that each member's share should reflect their marginal contribution to the coalition, i.e., the additional value the coalition gains by including them. In the context of syndicated investments, this could be interpreted in several ways. It might reflect the amount of capital an investor contributes, the unique expertise or networks they bring, or even the credibility they lend to the startup.

Evolutionary Game Theory and Market Trends: Adapting Investment Strategies to the Dance of Market Forces

Evolutionary game theory departs from classical game theory's assumptions of perfect rationality and fixed strategies. Instead, it borrows from biology's playbook, modeling the players' strategies as evolving populations. The "fittest" strategies — those that yield the highest payoffs — are more likely to proliferate over time.

Applying this framework to early-stage investing, we can envision different investment strategies as "species" in an economic ecosystem. Each investor chooses a strategy based on their evaluation of its "fitness," influenced by factors such as the potential return on investment, risk level, alignment with their expertise, and current market trends.

For example, consider a market trend like the rise of artificial intelligence (AI) startups. Initially, only a few forward-thinking investors may venture into this unproven territory. However, if these early investors achieve substantial returns, more investors may begin to adopt this strategy, leading to a proliferation of AI-focused investment.

Yet, as with biological evolution, the process doesn't stop there. The increase in investment in AI startups might lead to market saturation, increased competition, and lower returns, reducing the strategy's fitness. At the same time, new trends may emerge, creating fresh opportunities and prompting investors to adapt their strategies once again. This continual cycle of adaptation reflects the dynamic nature of evolutionary game theory. Sectorial specialized venture capital funds follow these cycles and rules.

Furthermore, evolutionary game theory offers valuable insights into how collective behavior can shape market trends. Just as a population of organisms can influence its environment, a population of investors adopting a particular strategy can shape the investment landscape. This perspective can help investors anticipate market shifts and adapt their strategies proactively.

Dynamic Games and the Staging of Venture Capital Investments

Venture capital investing is akin to a complex dance, performed over an extended period. This dance sees venture capitalists (VCs) and entrepreneurs move together through the stages of business growth, with funding released in a series of choreographed steps. These steps, or stages, reflect the progress of the company and its evolving needs. Game theory, especially its branch that deals with dynamic games, provides a fascinating framework for understanding this staging of venture capital investments.

Dynamic games are those in which the players make decisions at various points in time, and the decisions of one player can influence the future choices of other players. In the context of venture capital, the dance between the investor and entrepreneur can be viewed as a dynamic game.

The staging of investments, where funding gets released in rounds as the venture progresses, embodies this temporal aspect. Investors use this staging strategy to mitigate the inherent risks of early-stage investing.

Startups are ventures into the unknown, and their future is often uncertain. By providing funding in stages, investors can calibrate their investment to the startup's actual performance and progress, rather than committing large sums upfront based on speculative projections. Likewise, for entrepreneurs, each funding round is an opportunity to prove their venture's worth. Success in meeting the agreed-upon milestones can open the door to further funding and demonstrate to the investor (and the wider market) the viability and potential of their venture.

However, this game involves strategic decision-making for both parties. For investors, the question is how to structure the staging to balance risk mitigation with the need to provide enough funding for the venture to succeed. Timing is key; investing too little too early may stifle growth, while investing too much too soon might expose the investor to undue risk.

Entrepreneurs, on the other hand, need to consider how to meet the milestones while managing the resources at their disposal. They must also think about how their performance in earlier stages might impact their negotiating power in later funding rounds.

Furthermore, both parties should consider the potential payoffs of their decisions, as well as the strategies of other players. For instance, the presence of other potential investors might influence the dynamics of the game. An entrepreneur with multiple funding options might have greater leverage, while an investor may need to consider the strategies of competing investors.

Game Theory in Practice: A Real-Life Biotech Investment Dilemma

The principles of game theory apply to a vast array of real-life situations. One example that brings these principles into sharp relief was when a portfolio company we invested in found itself in a complex strategic decision-making situation. This story provides an illustrative example of game theory's utility and demonstrates the powerful insights it can offer in practical scenarios.

The portfolio company had received a non-binding acquisition offer from a pharma company, subject to the completion of scientific due diligence that could take three to six months. Simultaneously, the company was running low on funds and needed to secure financing to continue its operations and progress toward patient treatment. Funding had been secured from a syndicate of other VCs that was contingent on the company continuing its development trajectory without interruption.

The dilemma here was multifaceted. Should the company cease development and wait for the acquisition offer, which may or may not materialize? If the company ran out of money during the waiting period, it would lose leverage to negotiate an optimal acquisition price. Moreover, stopping development for a few months could lead to lost ground against competitors and potentially make the company irrelevant if the competition reached the marketplace first. There was also an ethical dimension to the problem: the delay could postpone a potential treatment for patients.

But on the value creation side, if the pharma acquired the company, this would mean a significantly higher return for our fund than the alternative, which was continue development and sell at a later stage with all the risk involved in this type of company.

In terms of game theory, this scenario resembles a combination of non-cooperative and cooperative games. From a non-cooperative perspective, each player in this game — the portfolio company, the potential acquirer, and the fund — acts in their best interest. The portfolio company wants to maximize its value and ensure its survival, the potential acquirer wants to minimize risk and costs, and the fund aims for the highest return possible.

Looking for a Nash Equilibrium in this scenario is challenging. If the portfolio company decides to wait for the acquisition offer (the strategy), it might end up with zero if the offer falls through. If the company decides to continue development with the new funding (another strategy), it may fail to materialize the potential higher returns from the acquisition. Zero- sum aspects also exist in this scenario. If the potential acquirer decides not to proceed with the acquisition after the due diligence, the portfolio company and the fund lose the time and opportunity cost, while the potential acquirer saves the acquisition cost.

Finally, in terms of sequential games, the decisions of the portfolio company (to wait or continue development) and the potential acquirer (to proceed with the acquisition or not) are not made simultaneously. The portfolio company's decision will influence the potential acquirer's decision and vice versa.

In conclusion, this real-life biotech investment scenario is a perfect illustration of how game theory principles can be applied to complex strategic decision-making situations. The dilemma faced by the portfolio company and the fund was multi-dimensional, with various game theory aspects coming into play, including non-cooperative and cooperative games, zero-sum games, and sequential games. The ultimate decision always depends on the specific circumstances and values of the players involved. However, having a game-theoretical understanding of the situation can undoubtedly enhance their decision-making process.

After careful deliberation, we decided to proceed with the syndicate and secure the funding round. This decision was rooted in several strategic considerations that arose from our game-theoretical analysis.

First, our bargaining power in the acquisition negotiations with the pharma company was heavily reliant on our financial standing. With limited funds in the bank, our leverage was weak. Securing the syndicate funding round would strengthen our financial footing and, consequently, our bargaining position in any acquisition discussions, present or future.

Second, our investment thesis revolved around the notion that a robust syndicate could lead to a higher valuation for the company down the line. This belief was grounded in the assumption that with more resources and time, the company could progress further in its operations and patient service, increasing its intrinsic value and, by extension, its attractiveness to potential acquirers.

We also factored in the possibility of involving a banker to help us attract bids from multiple pharmas. This move could stimulate a competitive bidding environment, which would likely drive the acquisition price upwards.

Moreover, from an ethical perspective, we believed that securing the syndicate funding was the best course of action. Our guiding principle has always been to keep the patient at the heart of our decisions. The continuation of development and progress toward patient treatment was more in line with this ethos than a potential halt in operations.

Venture capital often involves risky decisions, but it is important to avoid "win or lose" scenarios where the outcomes are binary and extreme. Instead, we aim for "win-win" situations where we can achieve our objectives without compromising other essential aspects. This decision meant we won, no matter the outcome. In retrospect, our game-theoretical analysis of the situation provided crucial insights that helped guide our decision-making process.

Rule #30
You Don't Want to Lie with Statistics

"For darkness restores what light cannot repair."
Joseph Brodsky

I will introduce you now to key statistical concepts that play a crucial role in our rapidly advancing, data-driven world. I'm not trying to transform you into a statistician; rather, I hope to provide you with a basic understanding of several important concepts that can help you understand statistical analyses and connect the dots.

In the next two chapters, we are going to cover basic concepts including the concept of *p* value, the normal distribution, the concept of sample size ("N"), type I and type II errors, sensibility and specificity, the ROC curve, and some other concepts useful for studying Nasdaq-listed companies at the stock market. Plus, we will explore Bayes' theorem and how it comes into play in the world of venture capital.

It might seem a bit much at first, but trust me, when we reach the rest of the chapters in this section, these concepts will start to click together and make sense. The goal here is not to teach you what to do or how to do it, but to show you examples and inspire you to dig deeper and familiarize yourself with this way of thinking.

Unfortunately, even if I keep the explanation simple, statistics can be a bit complex to fully understand without some solid math and stats knowledge. If you're serious about something like running a science-driven company or making smart investments, getting to know these tools can be helpful. So, this is just a start — if you're curious, there's a lot more to explore and learn.

One of my all-time favorite books is *How to Lie with Statistics* by Darrell Huff. Always within arm's reach, this insightful read continually reminds me of the importance of interpreting numbers correctly. It unveils the dual nature of statistics: they can shed light on truths, but they can also be twisted or misinterpreted to endorse misleading claims. This highlights the need to grasp statistical concepts well, not just to guard against deceit, but also to harness the power of statistics for successful investments.

A key mindset in the realms of entrepreneurship and investing is probabilistic thinking. Instead of viewing the world in terms of absolute outcomes, we consider a range of probabilities when we make decisions. This approach acknowledges the inherent uncertainty in predicting the future and allows for a more adaptable and nuanced decision-making process. We will delve deeper into this concept in a later chapter, enhancing our statistical toolkit and setting the stage for more comprehensive discussions.

Understanding Statistical Significance: Unraveling the *p* Value

In scientific studies, a common question is: Did we see a real difference, or did this happen just by chance? To answer this, scientists use special tests to see if their results are statistically significant. Let's unpack the concept of statistical significance, focusing specifically on a term called the "*p* value" that often gets misunderstood.

Imagine you're throwing a dice. You expect that, over time, all numbers would appear about the same number of times. This expectation is similar to what we call the null hypothesis (H0) in statistics. It's our starting point or assumption that there's no special pattern in our measurements.

Suppose we're studying a protein in the body. We'd take lots of separate measurements of this protein, imagining that it's expressed at a typical level. This would help us construct a "null distribution." This is like creating a model that shows us all the possible measurements we could get if the protein were behaving in a regular way. With this model or null distribution, we can then calculate how likely it is to see a certain level of this protein if it's being produced at a normal rate. If our observed measurement falls outside what's expected from this model,

Figure 36. What Is *p*?

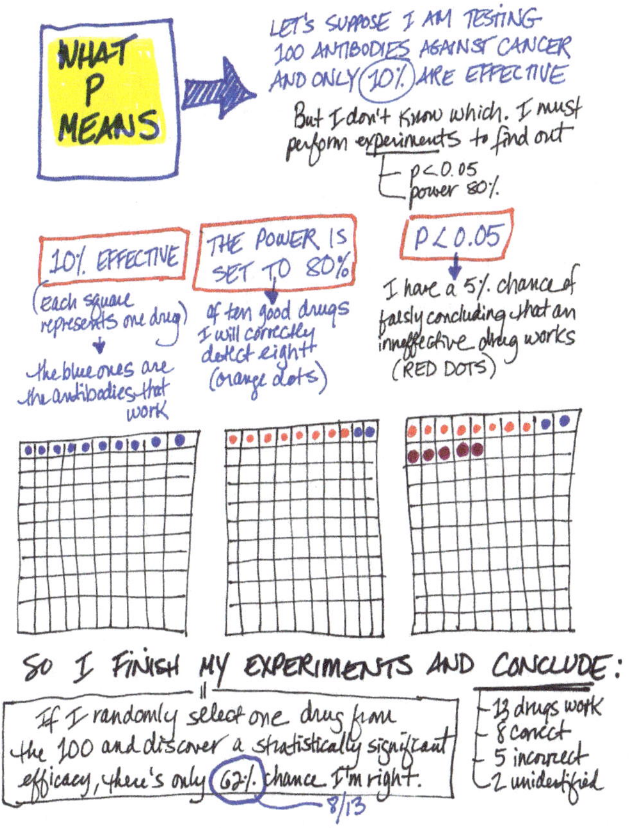

- To better **understand the concept of *p* values**, let's consider an example where we test 100 antibodies for their effectiveness against cancer, with only 10% of them actually being effective. Since we don't know which antibodies are effective, we conduct experiments to determine their efficacy. In this illustration, each drug is represented by a square, and the blue squares represent the antibodies that work.
- To ensure reliable results, we set a significance level (*p* value) lower than 0.05 and a statistical power of 80%. With these parameters, we expect to correctly detect 8 out of the 10 effective drugs, represented by the orange dots. However, there is a 5% chance of falsely concluding that an ineffective drug works, represented by the red dots.
- After conducting the experiments, we reach our conclusions. If we randomly select one drug from the 100 and discover a statistically significant efficacy, there is only a 62% chance that our conclusion is correct. This translates to 8 out of 13 cases, as depicted in the graph. Therefore, we can confidently say that 13 drugs are effective, with 8 being correctly identified, 5 being falsely identified, and 2 remaining unidentified.
- In conclusion, the example demonstrates the limitations and nuances of interpreting *p* values in statistical analysis. The *p* value alone does not provide definitive proof of effectiveness or ineffectiveness. Instead, it serves as a statistical measure that requires careful consideration of factors such as statistical power and the underlying prevalence of the effect being studied.

we might say our results are statistically significant. This is where the *p* value comes in, but we'll dig deeper into that a bit later.

The *p* value is a key component in statistics. It measures the odds of seeing a result as extreme as, or even more so than, the one we observed, provided our starting assumption, or null hypothesis, is accurate.

However, the *p* value isn't an indicator of whether our starting assumption is correct. This misunderstanding, often called the "prosecutor's fallacy," can lead us to the wrong conclusions. Instead, a small *p* value (e.g., $p = 0.05$) suggests the difference we observed is less likely to have happened just by chance, assuming our null hypothesis is true. It supports an alternate hypothesis that the data sample we're looking at is different from our expected reference value.

In a medical setting, for example, the *p* value helps determine if a result is statistically significant, meaning it's unlikely to have occurred by chance. However, it doesn't tell us if the result is biologically significant or important in the real world. To understand the practical importance of a result, we need to look at the size of the effect, the specific context, and relevant scientific knowledge.

To calculate our null distribution or expected outcomes, we make educated guesses. For the sake of simplicity, we often assume a normal distribution. We also estimate the range of this distribution by measuring the protein expression multiple times. These steps allow us to construct what's known as the sampling distribution of means and calculate the *p* value based on the observed difference between the sample mean and the reference value.

In real-life scenarios, especially when our sample size is small, the sampling distribution of means might not be exactly normal. To account for this, we use something called the *t* distribution, a method introduced by William Gosset. This *t* distribution considers the skewed distribution of sample variances, and we use a *t* statistic to compare our results to this distribution to accurately gauge statistical significance.

In conclusion, the *p* value helps researchers understand how likely it is that their findings occurred by chance. But it's important to view these statistical findings in light of the specific research field, taking into account the effect size and relevant scientific knowledge. By understanding statistical significance, you'll be better equipped to critically examine and interpret research findings.

Another View on *p*

The pervasive issue of misinterpreting statistical significance has led scientists to make flawed conclusions and create conflicts between studies where none exist. This problem arises from categorizing results into "statistically significant" and "statistically non-significant" groups, which falsely suggests that these categories are fundamentally different. As a result, researchers may wrongly conclude "no difference" or "no association" based solely on a p-value threshold or the inclusion of zero within a confidence interval. Such errors waste research efforts and misinform policy decisions.

This issue is widespread, with surveys indicating that statistically non-significant results are often misinterpreted as indicating "no difference" or "no effect." To address this problem, there have been calls to abandon the concept of statistical significance altogether. This does not mean disregarding *p* values or confidence intervals, but rather reframing their interpretation. Confidence intervals can be renamed as "compatibility intervals" to emphasize that all values within the interval are reasonably compatible with the data, given the statistical assumptions. Singling out one particular value, such as the null value, within the interval as "shown" is illogical.

To avoid the pitfalls of statistical significance, researchers should embrace uncertainty, discuss the practical implications of all values within the interval, and avoid overconfident claims. The default threshold of 95% for computing intervals should be recognized as arbitrary, and alternative levels justified based on the specific application.

Humility is crucial, as compatibility assessments depend on the correctness of statistical assumptions, which are inherently uncertain. Ultimately, decisions should be based on factors beyond statistical measures, such as background evidence, study design, data quality, and understanding of underlying mechanisms.

Retiring statistical significance requires a shift in methods sections and data tabulation, with an emphasis on estimates, uncertainty, and reasoned interpretation. It involves abandoning significance tests, reporting *p* values with sensible precision, and decoupling decisions from statistical thresholds. Ongoing vigilance is necessary to prevent new statistical abuses.

Although retiring statistical significance is not a cure-all, it will help counter overconfident claims, unwarranted declarations of "no difference," and the misuse of statistical measures. The scientific community must prioritize monitoring the literature for statistical abuses, as it is time for statistical significance to go.

The Base Rate Fallacy

The base rate fallacy emerges when we focus too much on specific information and ignore general information. This fallacy can lead us to make inaccurate judgments about people based on our initial impressions of them. For example, we might assume that all researchers in synthetic biology are hardworking and cocky because that was our initial impression of someone we met who is a researcher in synthetic biology. It can also affect our financial decisions, such as when we react too strongly to small changes in our investments and make hasty decisions that may not be wise.

This fallacy can have bigger consequences when it comes to important decisions such as those in the field of medicine. If doctors ignore general information about how common a certain condition is and focus only on specific symptoms, they might misdiagnose the condition and consequently not provide the best care for their patients.

There are different theories about why the base rate fallacy happens. One theory suggests that we ignore general information because we think it's not relevant to our judgment. Another theory is called the "representativeness heuristic," which means we judge the probability of something based on how similar it is to our idea of what it should be like. This can make us overlook the base rate information.

To avoid falling into this fallacy, we need to pay more attention to general information and not rely too much on specific details. We should also be aware that past behaviors or appearances may not always predict future outcomes. It's important to consider both general and specific information when making decisions.

Psychologists Daniel Kahneman and Amos Tversky studied this fallacy. They demonstrated that people often overlook base rate information and focus on individual characteristics instead. Another psychologist, Maya Bar-Hillel, suggested that people ignore base rates because they consider them less relevant compared to specific information.

Understanding the base rate fallacy can help us make better decisions and have a clearer understanding of the world around us. It's important to be aware of this fallacy and avoid it by considering both general and specific information when making judgments.

Avoiding Errors: Type I and Type II

In the realm of statistics, two types of errors frequently occur: type I and type II errors.

- **Type I error,** also known as a false positive, happens when we reject a true null hypothesis. It's akin to a false alarm. For instance, if an investor invests in a company based on particular data and later it turns out to be a failure, they've made a type I error.
- **Type II error,** also referred to as a false negative, occurs when we accept a false null hypothesis. This is equivalent to a miss. An example of a type II error in investing might be failing to identify a company as a good investment based on the data at hand, only to find out later that it indeed became successful.

The consequences of these errors can be significant, particularly in decision-making contexts such as investments. Misclassification can lead to missed opportunities or ill-advised risks.

Investing in disruptive innovation and emerging technologies is full of uncertainty, making it a breeding ground for type I and type II errors. For instance, an investor might incorrectly predict the future success of a company (type I error), or they might overlook a potential unicorn among a pool of startups (type II error). The concept of type I and type II errors can provide valuable insights for investors, particularly in terms of understanding the risks associated with decision-making under uncertainty. Recognizing that both types of errors can occur, and understanding the conditions under which they are more likely, is key to navigating the precarious world of innovative investments. Reducing the occurrence of these errors in investment decision-making necessitates a careful and methodical approach to data analysis and risk management.

- **For type I errors,** ensuring rigorous and extensive due diligence before rejecting potential investments can be crucial. A robust risk-assessment framework, taking into account both quantitative and qualitative factors, can mitigate the risk of prematurely dismissing a potentially successful venture.

Figure 37. The Base Rate Fallacy

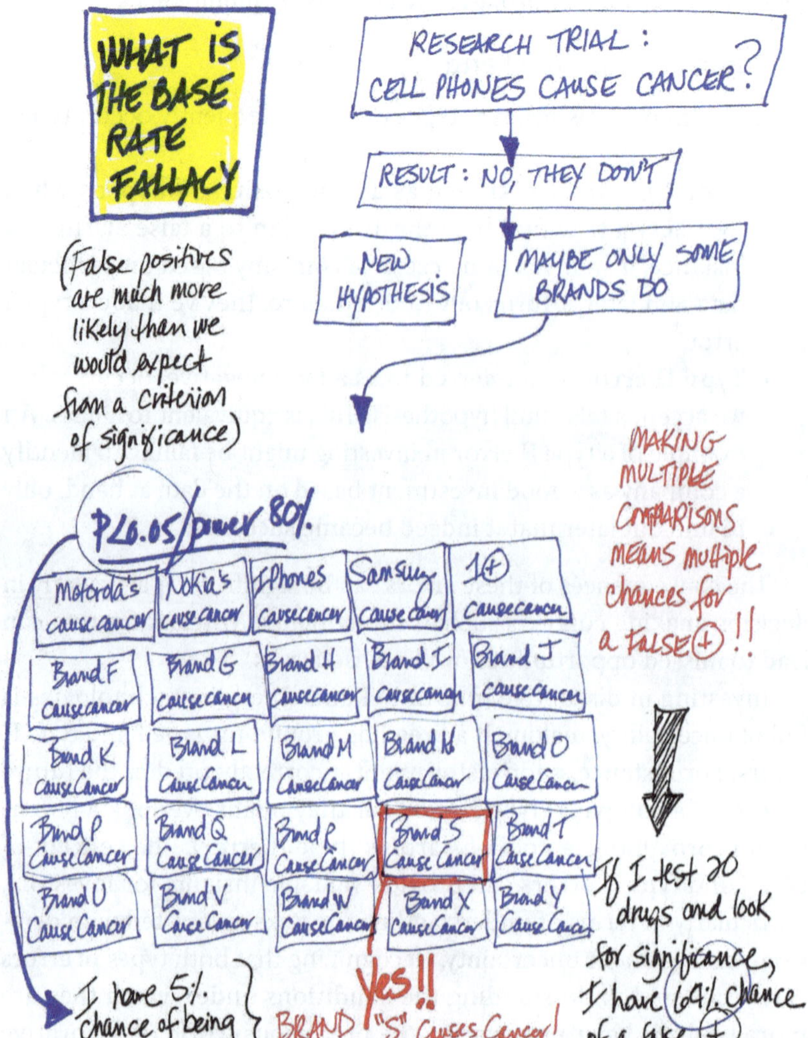

- The base rate fallacy reminds us that false positives are more likely than we might anticipate based on a significance threshold. To illustrate this concept, let's consider the example of investigating whether cell phones cause cancer. Suppose we conduct a research trial and conclude that cell phones, in general, do not cause cancer. However, if we delve deeper into the data and introduce a new hypothesis, such as the possibility that only certain brands of cell phones are linked to cancer, we face a potential challenge.
- Using a significance level of less than 0.05 and a power of 80%, we conduct 20 separate trials, each focusing on a different brand like Motorola, Nokia, iPhone, and so on. With multiple

comparisons, there is a higher likelihood that one of these 20 trials will, by chance alone, show a false positive association between a specific brand and cancer.

- Considering the 5% chance of making a type I error (false positive), we should expect one of the 20 trials to yield a false positive result. Consequently, we might incorrectly conclude that a particular brand of cell phone causes cancer. In essence, when conducting multiple comparisons, the increased number of chances for a false positive becomes evident. For instance, if we test 20 drugs and assess their significance, there is a 64% chance of encountering a false positive.
- This demonstrates the importance of accounting for the base rate fallacy. It highlights the need for researchers to consider the potential for false positives and employ appropriate statistical measures to address this issue.

Figure 38. Type I and Type II Errors

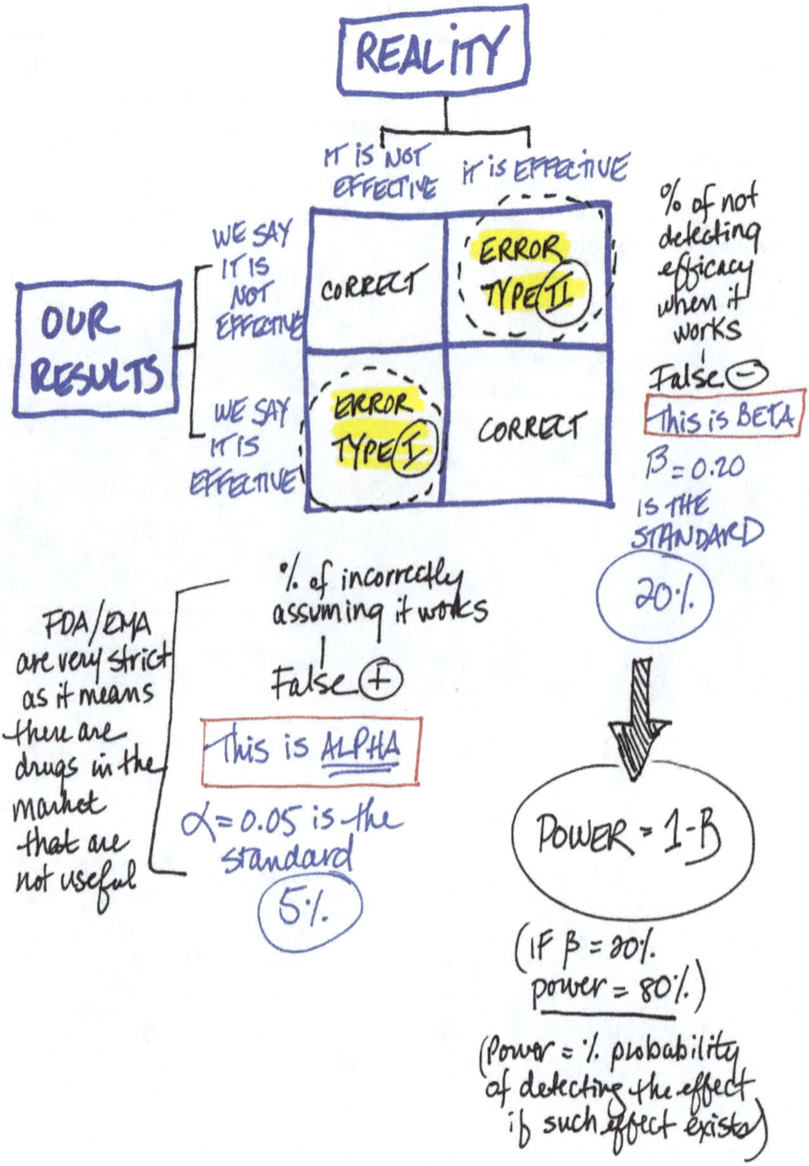

- Let's visualize the relationship between reality and study outcomes using a 2x2 matrix. On the x-axis, we have the reality of a therapy's effectiveness, with one end representing the therapy being ineffective and the other end representing the therapy being effective. The y-axis represents the conclusions drawn from a study (what we found).
- There are **two quadrants in which our conclusions align with reality**, representing correct assessments. When we correctly identify an ineffective therapy as not effective or correctly

identify an effective therapy as effective, we are accurate. These correspond to the top left and bottom right corners of the matrix.

- However, **there are two scenarios in which we make mistakes**. The first is **type I error**, also known as false positives, which occurs when we conclude that the therapy is effective despite it being ineffective in reality. This error typically is denoted by alpha, with a common standard of alpha-0.05 in scientific research. Alpha represents the percentage of times we mistakenly assume effectiveness.
- The second error is **type II error**, or false negatives, which happens when we fail to detect the effectiveness of a therapy that is actually effective. In this case, we incorrectly conclude that the therapy is not effective. Beta is used to represent the percentage of times we fail to detect efficacy when it actually exists. Power, on the other hand, is defined as 1 minus beta. If beta is 20%, then the power would be 80%, which is a commonly used standard in our calculations.
- It's important to note that regulatory bodies like the FDA and EMEA have stringent criteria for accepting clinical trials. They typically adhere to an alpha of 0.05 as the market standard. However, this means that 5% of drugs in the market may be deemed ineffective.

- **For type II errors,** maintaining an open and forward-thinking mindset is beneficial. Recognizing that data available at the point of investment is merely a snapshot and not the full picture can help investors remain open to opportunities that may not immediately appear promising. Regular re-evaluation of past decisions can also help identify patterns or biases that lead to type II errors.

Ultimately, a blend of critical thinking, diligent research, and continual learning can go a long way in minimizing these statistical errors in the challenging domain of investment decision-making.

The Power of N: Sample Sizes and Their Implications

In statistics, "N" refers to the sample size, or the number of observations or data points in a study or a dataset. The sample size plays a pivotal role in determining the reliability and validity of the results of a study. If the sample size is too small, the study might not have enough power to detect an effect even if one truly exists. This can lead to a higher probability of making a type II error, where we falsely conclude that there is no effect when, in reality, there is.

The sample size not only influences the reliability of study results but also impacts the margin of error and the statistical significance of a study. The margin of error essentially captures the uncertainty in an estimate and is inversely proportional to the square root of the sample size. This means that as the sample size increases, the margin of error decreases, resulting in more precise estimates.

In terms of statistical significance, a larger sample size can often provide the statistical power needed to detect an effect if it truly exists. This is why, when comparing two groups or investigating a potential correlation, larger sample sizes can provide more robust evidence to support a hypothesis.

Calculating Optimal Sample Sizes for Specific Scenarios

Calculating an optimal sample size for a specific scenario takes into account several factors, including the desired level of confidence (often set at 95%), the margin of error one is willing to accept (often set at 5%), and the population size (if known).

A simplified method to estimate the sample size for a scenario involving a large population (e.g., over 20,000) and a binary outcome (e.g., yes/no or success/failure) is as follows:

- Decide on the confidence level, Z — for a 95% confidence level, Z is 1.96.
- Choose your expected proportion, P — this is a best guess of the outcome proportion, often set at 0.5 if unknown.
- Set your desired margin of error, E — this might be set at 0.05 for a 5% margin.
- Then plug these values into the following formula:

n = (Z^2 * P * (1-P)) / E^2

This formula gives you the sample size needed to estimate the true population proportion with the desired level of confidence and margin of error.

However, it's important to note that the reality of sample size determination can be more complex and often requires consideration of additional factors, particularly for studies involving multiple groups or predictors. Hence, it's often wise to seek professional statistical advice or use dedicated sample size calculation software for more complex study designs.

Sensitivity and Specificity: Navigating Trade-offs

Sensitivity and specificity are statistical measures used in binary classification problems to assess the performance of a model. They are particularly important in fields like medical testing, machine learning, and yes, investment strategies.

Sensitivity, also known as the true positive rate, measures the proportion of actual positives that are correctly identified as such. For example, if you have a model that predicts whether a company will succeed, sensitivity would measure the proportion of companies that did succeed and were correctly predicted by the model to do so.

Specificity, on the other hand, is the true negative rate. It measures the proportion of actual negatives that are correctly identified as such. Continuing with the same example, specificity would measure the proportion of companies that in fact did not succeed and were correctly predicted by the model to fail.

Figures 39-40. How to Quickly Approximate N

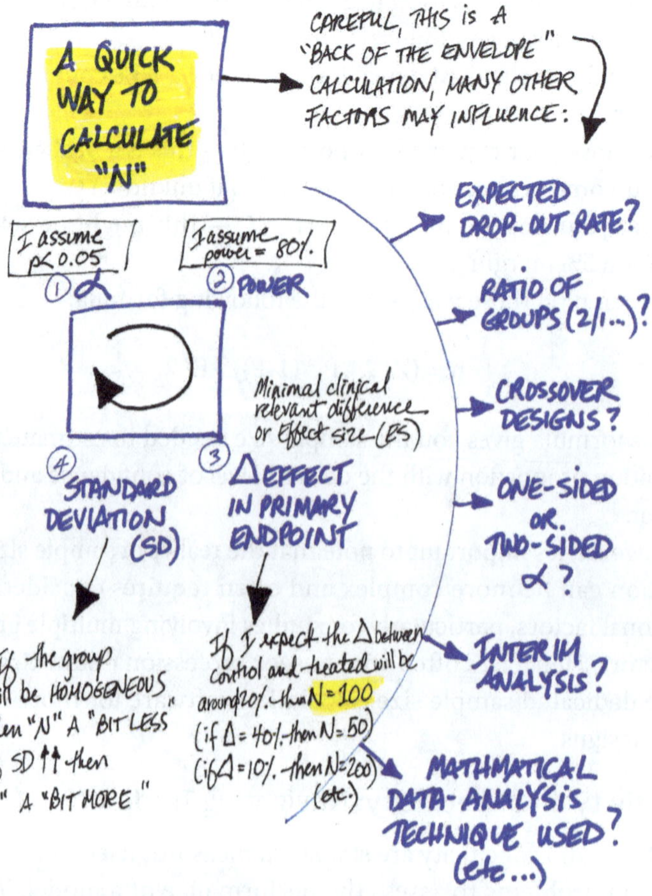

Here, I provide a simplified approach for estimating the sample size (N) required for a clinical trial. However, I must emphasize that this is a rough estimation, and it's crucial to consider various other factors that may influence the actual sample size determination.

- Please keep in mind that these calculations are based on the assumption that the desired **significance level (*p*)** is less than 0.05 and the desired **power** is set at 80%.
- To begin, we need to consider the **effect size (delta)** in the primary endpoint, which represents the expected difference between the untreated control group and the treated group. As a rule of thumb, if we anticipate a 20% delta, the estimated sample size (N) would be around 100. Doubling the delta to 40% would halve the required sample size to approximately 50. Conversely, if the delta is halved to 10%, the sample size would need to be doubled. This relationship follows a linear pattern, but it's important to note that this is a rough estimation and not an exact calculation.

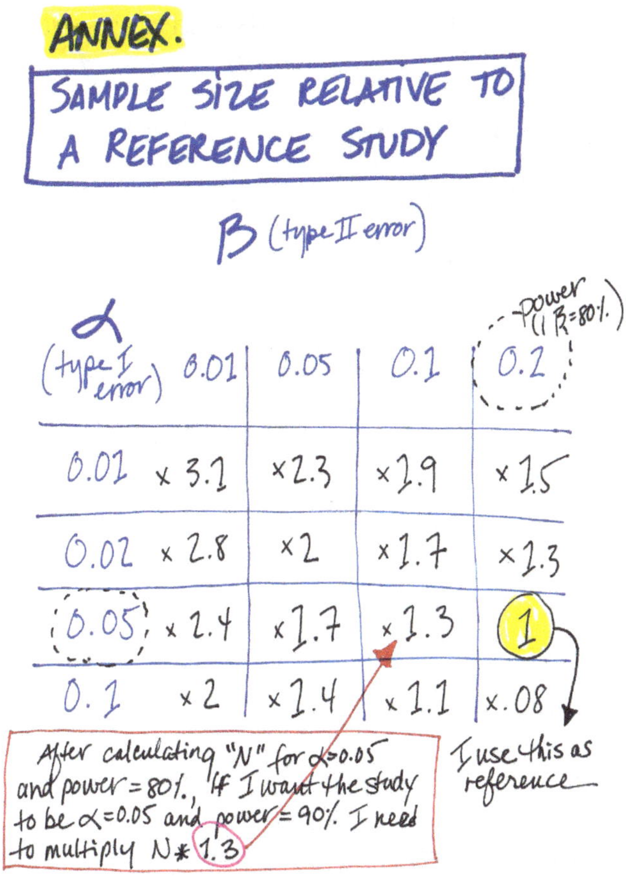

- Another factor to consider is the **homogeneity or heterogeneity of the study** group. If the group is more homogeneous, meaning the patients are very similar, the required sample size might be slightly reduced. Conversely, if the group is more heterogeneous, resulting in a higher standard deviation, a larger sample size may be necessary. This is also taken into account as part of the rough estimation process.
- It's crucial to recognize that there are **additional factors** that can influence the sample size determination. Some of these factors include the expected dropout rate, the ratio of participants between the treated and control groups, the use of crossover designs, whether the analysis is one-sided or two-sided, the inclusion of interim analysis that may consume a portion of the significance level (alpha), and the specific mathematical data analysis technique employed, among others.
- In summary, while the estimation of sample size is more complex than this simplified approach suggests, the intention is to provide a **quick rule of thumb** for initial calculations. However, it is essential to conduct a more comprehensive and rigorous analysis considering all relevant factors to arrive at an accurate sample size determination.
- The right figure is another quick back of the envelope calculation I use when I need to change the alpha or the power of the study quickly with a **conversion factor**. Once you get used to it, it comes as second nature thinking.

Figure 41. Understanding Sensitivity and Specificity

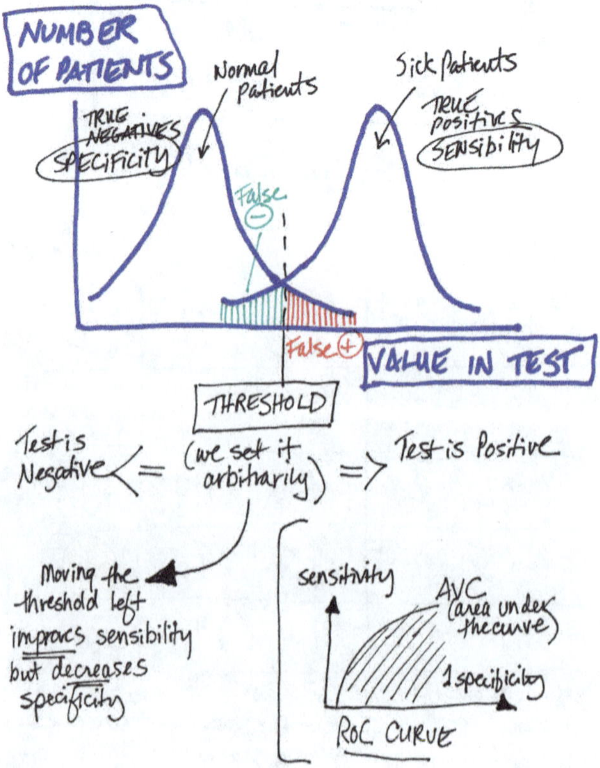

Understanding sensitivity and specificity is crucial for comprehending science and research.

- Let's consider a scenario where we have a group of normal patients and a group of sick patients. We aim to detect a specific biomarker in their blood that can distinguish whether a patient belongs to the normal distribution or the sick distribution.
- To illustrate this, we can plot the biomarker measurements on the x-axis and the number of individuals on the y-axis. We set a threshold, which is arbitrarily determined, to classify individuals. Above the threshold, individuals are considered sick patients; below the threshold, individuals are considered normal patients.
- By setting the threshold, we can identify two important outcomes. To the right of the threshold, we find true positives, which represent the correctly identified sick patients (sensitivity). However, we also have false positives (orange) in this region, which are individuals mistakenly classified as sick. To the left of the threshold, we find true negatives, representing correctly identified normal patients (specificity). However, there are also false negatives, which are patients incorrectly classified as normal.
- **Adjusting the threshold position can influence sensitivity and specificity.** Moving the threshold to the left improves sensitivity but decreases specificity, while moving it to the right has the opposite effect. It's a trade-off between correctly identifying sick patients and correctly identifying normal patients.

Together, sensitivity and specificity provide a comprehensive picture of a model's performance, each focusing on a different aspect of the model's predictive capabilities.

In an ideal world, we would want a model with both high sensitivity and high specificity, meaning it accurately identifies both positives and negatives. However, in reality, there is often a trade-off between the two. Increasing sensitivity might lead to a decrease in specificity, and vice versa. This is because raising the threshold for a positive classification might result in fewer false positives (increasing specificity), but at the cost of more false negatives (decreasing sensitivity).

This trade-off is highly relevant in investment strategies. For instance, an investor might use a model to decide whether or not to invest in a company. A model with high sensitivity might recommend investing in most companies that end up doing well, but it might also recommend some that do not, leading to losses. On the other hand, a model with high specificity might avoid most bad investments, but it could also pass on some good ones.

The choice between sensitivity and specificity depends largely on the investor's risk tolerance. A risk-averse investor might prefer a model with higher specificity to avoid potential losses, while a risk-seeking investor might prioritize sensitivity to capture potential high returns.

Understanding the concepts of sensitivity and specificity, and the inherent trade-offs, can greatly improve the accuracy of investment decision-making. By recognizing that no model is perfect and each will have its strengths and weaknesses, investors can better interpret model predictions and align them with their individual risk profiles. This knowledge also encourages the use of multiple models or approaches to decision-making, which can provide a more balanced view and account for the different strengths of each model. Furthermore, awareness of these concepts can guide the ongoing refinement of investment models.

By evaluating the sensitivity and specificity of a model, investors can identify areas where the model may need improvement and make informed adjustments to better meet their investment goals and risk tolerance.

The ROC Curve: Unraveling Sensitivity and Specificity

Whether you're in the world of medical therapies, machine learning, or investing, the Receiver Operating Characteristic (ROC) curve plays a pivotal role in decision-making. The ROC curve is a graphical representation that helps us understand the performance of a classification model or diagnostic test. Let's break down how it relates to two fundamental concepts: sensitivity and specificity.

Picture a graph where the x-axis represents "1-Specificity," and the y-axis represents "Sensitivity." The ROC curve is plotted on this graph, showcasing the trade-off between sensitivity and specificity for various decision thresholds. The curve illustrates how sensitivity and specificity interact as the criteria for a positive test result change.

For a perfect test, the ROC curve would go straight up the y-axis and then along the top of the plot. This would mean that our test can identify all true positives without any false positives, which is the ideal scenario. Most tests, however, aren't perfect, and the curve will bow downward and towards the right.

But why is this important? Because in real-world scenarios, we often need to balance sensitivity and specificity. As we discussed, if we want a test that catches every single positive case (high sensitivity), we might have to accept more false positives (lower specificity). Similarly, if we want to be absolutely sure when we say a case is positive (high specificity), we might miss out on some actual positive cases (lower sensitivity).

A common way to summarize the overall accuracy of the test is by calculating the area under the ROC curve, often abbreviated as AUC-ROC. A model with an AUC-ROC score close to 1 is considered excellent, while a score near 0.5 (the AUC-ROC of a random guess) is seen as poor.

In conclusion, the ROC curve is a valuable tool, helping us understand the balance between sensitivity and specificity. It allows us to visually assess the performance of a test or model across all possible thresholds, guiding us in choosing the best one. While it might seem like a complex idea, once broken down, it becomes a simple yet powerful concept that can help in making informed decisions.

The Normal Distribution: A Key Tool in Science and Investing

One concept that pops up almost everywhere in the world of science and investing is the idea of "normal distribution." Often visualized as a bell-shaped curve, normal distribution has played an instrumental role in our understanding of natural and financial phenomena alike.

But what exactly is normal distribution? Imagine you measured the heights of all the adults in your town. Most people would likely be around the same height, with fewer people being very tall or very short. If you were to plot everyone's height on a chart, you'd end up with a graph that looks like a bell. This, essentially, is a normal distribution. The "bell curve" is characterized by its symmetry, with the highest point in the middle representing the average (mean), and the sides (tails) showing less frequent, extreme values. The shape of the bell shows how data are distributed around the mean, with most data points clustering near the average and fewer as you move away.

In the realm of science, this concept is crucial. For example, in psychology, the normal distribution is used to understand and interpret results from intelligence tests, with most scores hovering around the average and fewer at the extremes. In meteorology, it helps predict weather patterns, understanding variations around an average temperature. In the world of investing, normal distribution is just as invaluable. It can be used to model the behavior of stock returns and market indexes. For example, if you look at the average return of a particular stock over a certain period, most days will likely have a return close to the average, with fewer days seeing extreme gains or losses. This helps investors estimate the likelihood of different outcomes, informing their risk management strategies.

However, as helpful as the normal distribution is, it's essential to recognize its limitations. In the real world, data doesn't always neatly fit a normal distribution. For instance, stock market returns can sometimes exhibit "fat tails," meaning extreme events occur more often than predicted by the bell curve. As we saw in the 2008 financial crisis, these rare events can have significant impacts.

The normal distribution, while a powerful tool, should not be seen as a perfect representation of all data or phenomena. It's one piece of the puzzle in understanding complex systems in science and investing.

Figure 42. A Look at the Stock Market Right Distributions

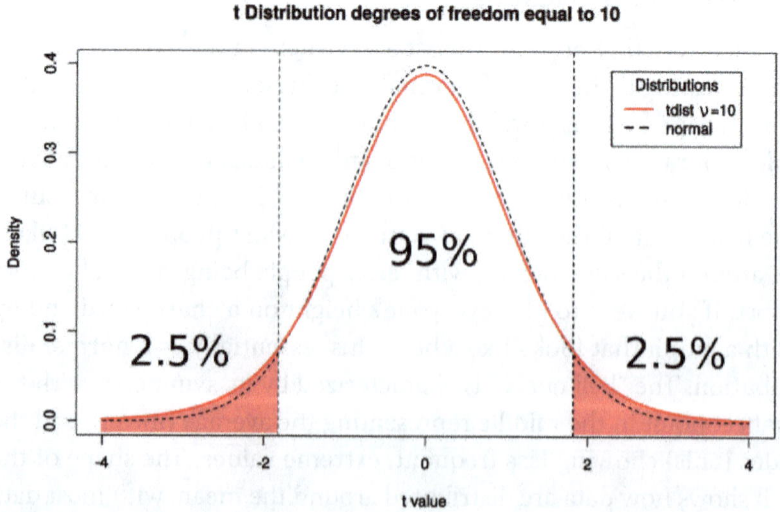

The stock market is a complex ecosystem that is influenced by countless variables. Predicting its movement can sometimes feel like trying to predict the weather. Yet, we often rely on certain mathematical models, or "distributions," to understand and anticipate market behavior.

- To make sense of these patterns, we often begin with a simple mathematical model known as the "normal distribution" or "bell curve." Now, if stock returns were normally distributed, most of the daily changes would be small, with bigger changes being rare, creating a similar curve. However, while the normal distribution is a useful starting point, it doesn't quite capture the reality of the stock market. The real-world stock market often shows "fat tails" and "skewness," which the normal distribution fails to represent.
- **Fat tails** refers to more frequent extreme events than would be expected under a normal distribution. In stock market terms, this means large changes or "shocks" to the market are more common than the bell curve model would suggest. For example, the global financial crisis of 2008 was such an extreme event.
- **Skewness** is when one tail of the distribution is longer or fatter than the other. This means the market tends to move more dramatically in one direction than the other. Negative skewness, for example, suggests that while most days might see small gains, there are occasional dramatic falls.
- Given these factors, some experts believe that the **Student's T-distribution** better represents the stock market. The Student's T-distribution has fatter tails than the normal distribution, which accounts for the greater likelihood of significant market shifts.
- The **Cauchy distribution and the Levy distribution** are other distributions that have been used. While no single distribution perfectly fits the stock market, understanding these models can provide investors with useful frameworks. It's essential to remember, however, that while these distributions can guide us, they are simplifications of a highly complex reality.

It's vital to consider other statistical models and empirical data when making predictions or decisions.

Understanding Confidence Intervals

Imagine you and your colleagues decide to measure the average height of partners in venture capital funds. You pick 30 partners randomly and find that the average height is 172 cm. Now, here's the question: Can you be entirely sure that the average height of "all" partners in VC funds is exactly 172 cm? Well, you can't, right? That's because you didn't measure every single partner, only 30 of them.

This is where the important concept of confidence intervals comes in, which is a way of dealing with this type of uncertainty. You see, in the real world, whether it's about measuring partners' heights or evaluating a biotech startup's success, we usually can't check every single detail. Instead, we gather a sample — a smaller group that represents the larger one — and make our best estimates based on that.

So, back to our height example. Instead of saying the average height is 172 cm, we can use a confidence interval to say something like: "We are 95% confident that the average height of all partners is between 168 and 178 cm." This gives us a range and reflects how sure we are about our estimate.

But where do confidence intervals come from? Well, it involves a little bit of complex math. Confidence intervals are calculated using the data from the sample (like the average and standard deviation), the size of the sample, and the level of confidence we want. The level of confidence tells us how sure we want to be about our estimate. The most common level is 95%, but it could also be 90%, 99%, or any other percentage below 100.

The fascinating part about confidence intervals is that they show us the uncertainty in our estimates, but in a useful way. It's like saying, "We may not know the exact answer, but we have a pretty good idea where it lies." And in the uncertain world of investing, having a pretty good idea is often more than enough to make a decision.

Let's look at the math behind calculating a confidence interval. To start, let's clarify that a confidence interval gives a range of values that likely contains an unknown population parameter, like the average (mean) value of something. To calculate confidence intervals, we use data from a smaller group (sample) that we've measured or surveyed. We need three things to calculate a confidence interval:

1. **Sample Mean (M):** This is the average value of our sample data. To find it, you simply add up all the values and divide by the number of values.
2. **Sample Standard Deviation (SD):** This measures how spread out your data is around the mean. Calculating this involves a bit more math. First, subtract the mean from each data point, square the result, then take the average of these squares, and finally, take the square root of that average.
3. **Sample Size (N):** This is simply the number of data points you have.

The confidence interval is calculated as follows:

$$M \pm (Z * SD/\sqrt{n})$$

The '±" means that we add and subtract the value from the mean to get the range of the interval. The "Z" is a value from the Z-table (also known as the standard normal table), which depends on the confidence level we want. For a 95% confidence level, Z is approximately 1.96.

Let's put these ideas into practice with an example. We randomly select 10 kids and measure their heights in cm: 160, 155, 163, 158, 161, 154, 162, 159, 157, 160.

First, we calculate the sample mean (M), by adding up all the heights and dividing by 10 (the number of heights). The mean comes out to be 158.9 cm.

Next, we calculate the sample standard deviation (SD). After some math (you might want to use a calculator or spreadsheet for this), we get about 3.11 cm.

Then, we apply the formula for the confidence interval:

$$158.9 \pm (1.96 * 3.11/\sqrt{10}) = 158.9 \pm 1.93$$

So, we are 95% confident that the average height of all kids is between 156.97 cm and 160.83 cm.

In essence, confidence intervals are like casting a net in the ocean of uncertainty. We might not know exactly where the fish (our unknown population parameter) is, but with this net (the interval), we have a pretty good chance of catching it.

Remember, investing in science-driven companies involves taking calculated risks. Venture capitalists must consider many factors, including scientific data, the company's team, the potential market, and more. The magic of confidence intervals is that they help investors quantify uncertainty, making the unknown a little less scary. So, confidence intervals may sound like a tough concept at first, but once you break it down, it's just another tool that helps us make sense of the uncertain world.

Regression Analysis

Imagine you're playing your favorite video game, and you noticed that the more time you spend practicing, the higher your score tends to be. You start wondering: If I play for two more hours each day, how much could my score improve? This is a perfect situation to use regression analysis, a statistical tool that helps us understand relationships between variables.

Regression analysis is a way of predicting how one thing (like your game score) changes when another thing (like the time spent practicing) changes. The thing we want to predict is called the dependent variable (because it depends on something else), and the thing that causes the change is the independent variable. In our video game example, the score is the dependent variable, and the time spent practicing is the independent variable.

Now, let's take this concept to the world of science-driven companies. Suppose a tech company is making a fitness app. The app collects data like steps walked, calories consumed, hours of sleep, and so on. The number of steps walked per day might be a good predictor for calories burned. To verify this, we can use regression analysis.

Here's how it works. First, we would plot all the data on a graph, with the number of steps walked indicated on the horizontal axis (independent variable) and calories burned indicated on the vertical axis (dependent variable). Each person using the app would be represented by a point on this graph. What we would likely see is a cloud of points.

The magic of regression analysis is that it can find the best straight line that fits this cloud of points — the "line of best fit" or "regression line." This line represents the average relationship between steps walked and calories burned. So, if someone tells us they walk 10,000 steps a day, we can use this line to predict approximately how many calories they might burn.

But here's an important point: Regression analysis shows only a general trend. It doesn't mean every point falls exactly on the line. In real life, lots of factors can influence the calories burned (like a person's metabolism, or how fast they walk), not just steps. That's why it's crucial to remember that the relationship described by regression analysis is an average, not a precise prediction for each individual case.

When it comes to venture capital investing, understanding these relationships between variables can be incredibly useful. It can help investors evaluate the potential of a product or predict a company's growth. It can show how changes in one aspect of the business (like increasing marketing spending) might affect another aspect (like sales).

Let's dive into the math behind regression analysis. At its heart, regression analysis is about finding the line of best fit through your data. If you've ever played connect the dots, you might remember that not all dots line up perfectly, but you can still draw a line that seems to fit the overall trend of the dots. That's the idea here.

Suppose we're interested in understanding the relationship between the number of hours studied each week (independent variable) and the final exam score (dependent variable). To keep it simple, let's say we collected data from five of your friends:

- Alice studied for 2 hours and scored 60.
- Bob studied for 3 hours and scored 70.
- Charlie studied for 4 hours and scored 80.
- Dana studied for 5 hours and scored 90.
- Ethan studied for 6 hours and scored 100.

If you plot these data points on a graph, with hours studied on the horizontal (x) axis and the exam score on the vertical (y) axis, you'll see a rough upward trend: the more hours studied, the higher the exam score.

The line of best fit represents this trend. In statistics, this line is often called the "regression line," and it's defined by an equation: $y = a + bx$, where "y" is the dependent variable (exam score), "x" is the independent variable (hours studied), "b" is the slope of the line, and

Figure 43. Regression Analysis

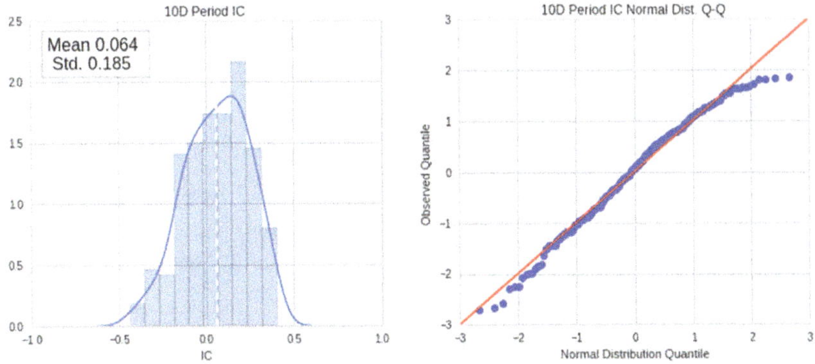

Regression, Correlation, and Their Roles in Scientific Inquiry: An Exploration of Cause, Effect, and Complexity

- Regression and correlation are fundamental statistical techniques that serve as the bedrock of empirical scientific research. They enable us to scrutinize patterns, relationships, and trends among variables, providing insights that help drive evidence-based decisions. Yet, as powerful as these tools are, they require careful use and understanding, particularly when navigating the complexities of cause-effect relationships and single- vs. multiple-variable analysis.
- At the most basic level, correlation measures the degree to which two variables move in relation to each other. For example, a positive correlation between exercise and life expectancy would imply that as one's exercise levels increase, so does their life expectancy. However, correlation doesn't establish causation — it simply suggests a relationship. This brings us to a critical point: the cause-effect problem. Correlation can be misleading when it comes to discerning cause-effect relationships because it can't distinguish between causal influence and mere association. This conundrum is vividly demonstrated in the case of "spurious correlations," where two variables appear to be related but are actually influenced by a third, unseen factor.
- Regression analysis, on the other hand, provides a more sophisticated toolset for understanding these relationships. In its simplest form, single-variable (or simple) regression models the relationship between a single predictor variable and a dependent variable. It draws a line of best fit through the data points, providing a mathematical relationship that can be used for prediction.
- However, the world is seldom simple. More often than not, a dependent variable's behavior is influenced by more than one predictor. Enter multiple regression, an extension of simple regression, that models the relationship between two or more predictors and a response variable by fitting a linear equation to observed data. By considering multiple variables, we gain a more holistic understanding of the system we're studying. Multiple regression allows us to hold all other variables constant while investigating the effect of a particular independent variable, making it a valuable tool for teasing out cause-effect relationships among many interacting variables. This has profound implications in diverse scientific disciplines, from public health (where researchers might explore the interplay between genetic factors, lifestyle choices, and disease outcomes) to environmental science (where scientists may study the collective impact of various factors on climate change).

"a" is the y-intercept (the point where the line crosses the y-axis). The slope b shows how much y changes for each unit increase in x, and the y-intercept a shows the value of y when x equals zero. In our case, b represents how much the exam score changes for each additional hour studied, and a is the score when no hours are spent studying.

To find the values of a and b, we use formulas that involve the means (averages) of x and y, and how much each x and y deviate from their respective means. The equation of the line of best fit in a simple linear regression is y = a + bx. Here, a is the y-intercept, and b is the slope of the line. The slope b represents the average change in our dependent variable "y" for a one unit increase in our independent variable x. The y-intercept a represents the estimated value of y when x equals zero.

The formulas to calculate a and b are derived from the principles of least squares, which says the best fit line is the one where the sum of the squared distances of each data point from the line is the smallest.

- **Calculating b (the slope):**

  $$b = [\ \Sigma(xi - X)(yi - Y)\ ] \ /\ [\ \Sigma(xi - X)^2\ ]$$

  Here, xi and yi are the individual sample points indexed with i, X and Y are the means (averages) of x and y, and Σ symbolizes the sum of the data points from i=1 to n (n being the total number of points). The expression (xi - X) is called the deviation of xi from the mean, and similarly for (yi - Y). So "b" is essentially the sum of the product of x and y deviations divided by the sum of squared x deviations.

- **Calculating a (the y-intercept):**

  $$a = Y - bX$$

  Once b is known, a can be calculated by subtracting the product of b and the mean of x from the mean of y.

If you apply these formulas to our data, you'll find that the line of best fit is y = 10 + 15x. This means for each additional hour studied, the exam score increases by 15 points. And if no hours are spent studying (x=0), the score would be 10.

This is a very simplified explanation; actual regression analysis can be much more complex, especially with more variables or when the relationship isn't a straight line. But the core idea is the same: finding the best way to represent the relationship between variables. And remember, it's all about spotting trends, not making exact predictions. So, regression analysis is like a superpower that can help you see connections between things.

Whether you're trying to improve your video game skills, predicting calories burned from walking, or deciding which startup to invest in, regression analysis gives you a clearer view of what to expect when something changes. Just remember: While it's a powerful tool, it doesn't predict the future perfectly — it just gives a statistics-informed best guess!

A Special Case of Regression: Deep Neural Networks

Deep neural networks offer a way to learn regression analysis (the capacity to predict the future) from the data itself.

First, let's set the stage. Imagine you're playing a game in which you have to predict how many points a player will score in a basketball game. You're given information like the player's height, age, shooting percentage, and how many hours they practiced that week.

In a traditional regression analysis approach, you might look at each piece of information separately and figure out how each one affects the number of points scored. Maybe taller players score more points, or players who practice more score more points. By using the regression formula to figure out how much each factor affects the score, you can make a prediction for any player.

Now, let's switch gears and imagine a deep neural network (DNN). A DNN is like having an incredibly smart team of colleagues who work together to make a prediction. Instead of looking at each piece of information separately, your friends (the "neurons" in the network) pass the information between themselves, each adding a bit of their own insight. They start from the raw data (height, age, shooting percentage, practice time), and by working together, they extract complex patterns that are hard to spot if you just look at each piece of information separately.

How does this work? Each neuron in the network receives some data, does a small calculation on it (like adding them together or

Figure 44. Finding Trends in Nasdaq-Listed Biotech Companies: Part 1

4																		
5										less 1q=4 / less 2q=3 / less 1	one=1 2-4=2	YES=1 NO=0		NOW+MEDIUM			1-5 TR	ALL Z
6	XC	NT	P				COMPANY NAME	MARKET CAP	FUTURE	CATALYSTS	PIPELINE	IPO	IPL	WOW SLIDE (resul	INDICATION	EASY PRO	LEADING EDGE	BIOLOG TARG
7	1	1		872	514	PIRS	Pieris Pharmaceuticals	0.22	5	11	6	0		56%	-50%	6%	5	
8	1	0		644	458	BNGO	Bionano Genomics	2.12	3	6	3	0		40%	50%	90%	5	
9	1	1		1082	510	ORPH	Orphazyme	0.26	6	10	4	1	1	0%	0%	0%	2	
10	1	1		114	256	GERN	Geron Corporation	0.58	4	7	3	0		8%	-50%	-42%	4	
11	1	1		400	389	ASXC	Asensus surgical	0.75	2	4	2	0		56%	50%	106%	4	
12	1	1		580	81	ITRM	Iterum Therapeutics	0.36	3	5	2	0		88%	50%	138%	4	
13	1	1		701	85	VXRT	Vaxart	0.95	5	8	3	0		40%	-50%	-10%	4	
14	1	1		385	427	NBRV	NaBriVa TX	0.47	4	9	5	0		-100%	-100%	-200%	4	
15	1	1		715	390	TNXP	Tonix Pharma	0.40	4	9	5	0		72%	50%	122%	0	
16	1	1		26	532	CTXR	Citius Pharma	0.50	2	6	4	0		100%	100%	200%	4	
17	1	1		542	87	CLVS	Clovis Oncology	0.62	3	8	5	0		-8%	-50%	-58%	3	
18	1	0		462	144	VTRS	Viatris	17.24	2	2		1	1	0%	0%	0%	5	
19	1	0		672	185	GILD	Gilead	83.54	5	11	6	0		72%	50%	122%	4	
20	1	1		573	446	APRE	Aprea Tx	0.10	5	10	5	0		-40%	-50%	-90%	4	
21	1	0		877	6	IOVA	Iovance	3.79	3	7	4	0		-88%	-100%	-188%	5	
22	1	1		710	557	BTX	Brooklyn ImmunoTx	0.68	10	13	3	1	1	0%	0%	0%	0	
23	1	0		877	622	PRPO	Precipio	0.09	2	4	2	0		100%	100%	200%	4	
24	1	1		801	22	INO	Inovio	1.78	4	8	4	0		-40%	-50%	-90%	4	
25	1	0		455	416	RGLS	Regulus Tx	0.07	10	14	4	0		-72%	-50%	-122%	4	
26	1	1		753	559	TXMD	Therapeutics MD	0.47	2	4	2	0		-40%	-50%	-90%	4	
27	1	1		408	394	AGEN	Agenus	1.17	5	11	6	0		56%	50%	106%	5	
28	1	1		111	530	IBIO	Ibio	0.33	4	8	4	0		-40%	-50%	-90%	0	
29	1	1		684	340	SEEL	Seelos Tx	0.24	4	8	4	0		-8%	50%	42%	5	
30	1	1		621	275	XERS	Xeris Pharma	0.27	2	5	3	0		-48%	-50%	-98%	4	
31	1	1		737	264	VSTM	Verastem	0.82	4	9	5	0		100%	100%	200%	4	
32	1	1		159	463	COCP	Cocrystal Pharma	0.13	5	10	5	0		-48%	-50%	-98%	4	
33	1	1		418	355	PDSB	PDS Biotech Corp	0.26	5	10	5	0		100%	100%	200%	5	
34	1	1		1068	482	GRAY	Graybug Vision	0.11	3	6	3	1	1	0%	0%	0%	3	
35	1	1		758	501	MNKD	Mannkind Corporation	1.06	2	4	2	0		24%	25%	49%	5	
36	1	1		75	421	ARPO	Aerpio Pharmaceuticals	0.09	5	10	5	0		56%	50%	106%	3	
37	1	1	1	674	135	VTGN	Vistagen Tx	0.41	4	7	3	0		100%	100%	200%	5	
38	1	1		66	237	ENDP	Endo Internatilonal	1.22	3	8	5	0		-80%	-100%	-180%	4	
39	1	1		174	434	NMTR	Nine Meters Bio	0.34	4	8	4	0		24%	50%	74%	5	
40	1	1		490	609	PROG	Progenity	0.18	3	6	3	1		-56%	-50%	-106%	3	
41	1	1		875	571	CCXI	Chemocentrix	0.94	5	10	5	0		-88%	-100%	-188%	4	
42	1	0		754	42	BCRX	Biocryst	2.82	3	7	4	0		100%	100%	200%	5	
43	1	1		444	305	ANVS	Annovis Bio	0.65	5	10	5	0		100%	100%	200%	4	
44	1	0		877	392	SLRX	Salarius Pharma	0.05	5	8	3	0		-56%	-50%	-106%	0	
45	1	0		704	183	BIIB	Biogen	58.48	4	9	5	0		100%	100%	200%	4	
46	1	0		737	429	ELOX	Senesco	0.10	5	9	4	0		-64%	-50%	-114%	4	
47	1	1	3	307	76	CRIS	Curis	0.69	4	8	4	0		24%	50%	74%	5	
48	1	1		732	320	GNMK	Genmark Diagnostics	1.76	4	8	4	0		100%	100%	200%	0	
49	1	1		782	8	CNST	Constellation Pharmaceuticals	1.62	5	8	3	0		56%	-50%	6%	3	
50	1	0		877	207	AMRS	Amyris	4.68	3	5	2	0		72%	50%	122%	5	
51	1	0		847	519	MITO	Stealth Bio	0.09	5	8	3	0		8%	-50%	-42%	4	
52	1	1		797	255	SPPI	Spectrum Pharmaceuticals	0.69	3	7	4	0		40%	-50%	-10%	5	
53	1	0		877	401	RSLS	Reshape Lifesciences	0.02	2	4	2	0		-24%	50%	26%	0	
54	1	1		210	9	IMGN	Immunogen	1.34	5	9	4	0		-40%	-50%	-90%	4	
55	1	0		709	49	FOLD	Amicus Therapeutics	2.64	5	10	5	0		-40%	-50%	-90%	4	
56	1	1		699	101	PLX	Protalix Biotherapeutics	0.09	4	6	2	0		-88%	-100%	-188%	4	
57	1	1		492	443	AVXL	Anavex Life Sciences	1.55	4	9	5	0		100%	100%	200%	4	
58	1	1		771	67	AMRN	Amarin Corporation	1.96	3	4	1	0		-40%	-50%	-90%	4	
59	1	1		671	376	XXII	22ND century	0.68	4	7	3	0		80%	100%	180%	0	
60	1	1		802	188	GLTO	Galecto	0.13	4	7	3	1	1	0%	0%	0%	4	

- Venture capitalists should **understand the behavior of listed companies**. After all, the companies we invest in today could be sold or become public tomorrow. Staying abreast of trends in our eventual market is vital. This awareness helps us identify current areas of interest and anticipate the market's evolution and the future of sectors like oncology, gene therapy, synthetic biology, and, broadly speaking, medicine.

3	ZS	SA		*			0,5 PALE, 1 GREEN, +1 IF		all the green in HM						HF SENT	WE SENT
L	STORY	Q	SA	WS*	CLINICAL NEED TO	PHENOTYPE REVERSI	BIG PROBLE	LP HIGHL IG	CLINICAL NEED	AVG ABOVE COMPETITI	SEVERITY	Cash	PROBLEMS/ PLUSES	SCORE SCIEN	HOUDINI	LP RANK
1	1	2.75	3.00	4.67	2.75									98.00	0.00	179.67
1	1	2.89	3.00	3.75	2.89				1					54.00	3.00	172.50
1	0	3.00	3.00	2.67	0.00									112.00	25.00	75.67
1	1	3.61	2.00	4.50	3.61	-60	0.5		1	0	1			64.00	15.50	142.00
1	1	2.55	3.00	3.50	2.55									36.00	0.00	166.00
2	1	2.64	3.00	4.75	2.64	50	0		3	2	2	21	caida 17%	46.00	9.00	199.50
1	0	3.00	3.00	3.00	0.00	60	0		3	0	1	39		74.00	9.00	133.00
1	1	2.85	3.00	4.17	2.85				1					80.00	3.00	94.67
0	0	3.00	3.00	5.00	0.00									80.00	0.00	116.00
0	1	4.96	4.00	4.00	4.96		1		1					52.00	28.00	198.00
1	1	2.58	3.00	4.67	2.58	50	0		2	-1	0	8		70.00	6.00	133.67
2	1	4.27	3.50	5.00	4.27	100	1		20	0				40.00	110.00	175.00
2	1	2.70	4.00	4.25	2.70	33	0		4	0	2	50		98.00	12.00	196.50
1	1	2.90	3.00	4.67	2.90	17			0.5					90.00	1.50	129.67
0	0	2.62	4.00	4.25	0.00	45	0.5	1	9	-1	2	49	Son TILs	62.00	139.50	98.50
0	0	3.00	1.00	3.00	0.00									144.00	25.00	40.00
0	0	3.62	2.00	4.00	0.00									36.00	0.00	158.00
1	0	2.56	4.00	4.00	0.00	60	0		3	0	0	95		72.00	9.00	113.00
0	1	4.83	3.00	3.86	4.83		2		4.5					132.00	63.50	100.57
2	1	1.32	3.50	4.80	1.32				1					36.00	3.00	141.00
1	1	2.77	3.00	3.57	2.77									98.00	0.00	178.71
-1	1	3.57	3.00	5.00	3.57									72.00	0.00	75.00
1	0	2.83	3.00	4.43	0.00									72.00	0.00	135.29
0	1	2.53	3.00	4.00	2.53	-60	0.5	1	1	0	1			44.00	115.50	114.00
3	0	3.00	3.00	5.00	0.00	67	1.5	1.5	6	0	1			80.00	205.50	193.00
1	1	3.39	4.67	4.60	3.39		1							90.00	25.00	141.67
2	1	1.16	4.00	4.27	1.16					-2				90.00	0.00	222.73
1	1	1.09	3.00	4.00	1.09									74.00	25.00	131.00
0	0	2.61	2.00	4.50	0.00				1					36.00	3.00	137.00
1	1	3.54	3.00	3.67	3.54		1		1					90.00	28.00	155.67
1	1	1.11	3.00	3.88	1.11	100	2.5	1	9	-1	0	121		64.00	189.50	203.75
0	1	3.92	4.00	4.08	3.92	-100	0		0	-2	1	50		70.00	0.00	108.83
1	1	3.00	3.00	4.40	3.00				3					72.00	9.00	171.00
3	1	3.00	3.00	3.20	3.00				1					74.00	3.00	105.00
-1	0	1.01	3.00	3.63	0.00	18			1.5					90.00	4.50	65.25
1	1	2.56	3.00	5.00	2.56	50	1	1	4	-2	0	27		62.00	137.00	215.00
0	0	2.53	3.00	4.50	0.00		0			-3		50		90.00	0.00	173.00
0	0	2.78	3.00	4.80	0,00									74.00	0.00	50.00
1	1	2.61	3.00	4.67	2.61	39	0		11	0	1	50		80.00	33.00	199.67
0	1	2.58	4.00	4.75	2.58									82.00	0.00	123.50
1	1	2.58	3.00	4.60	2.58	50	2.5	1	3	-3	1	94	big bet 2	72.00	171.50	173.00
0	0	3.00	3.00	4.33	0.00		1							72.00	25.00	123.33
1	0	3.00	4.00	4.75	0.00	45	0		10	-1	1	43		74.00	30.00	156.50
3	0	3.00	3.50	4.75	0.00	44	0.5		5	-3	0	50		46.00	27.50	193.50
0	1	1.17	3.00	4.00	1.17									74.00	0.00	142.00
2	1	1.19	3.00	4.33	1.19	40	0.5		3	0	2			62.00	21.50	183.33
0	0	2.66	3.00	4.33	0.00									36.00	0.00	61.33
1	1	3.00	3.00	4.60	3.00	50	0.5		1	-1	1	20		82.00	15.50	129.00
1	1	2.61	4.00	4.44	2.61	43	0		9	-1	2	32		90.00	27.00	137.38
0	0	2.52	3.00	4.80	0.00	50	1		1	-1	1	57	old bet	56.00	28.00	82.00
0	1	2.58	3.00	5.00	2.58				1					80.00	3.00	198.00
1	1	1.28	3.00	4.75	1.28	35	0		6	0	0	1		38.00	18.00	130.50
1	1	1.21	3.00	4.00	1.21									64.00	0.00	135.00
1	0	3.00	3.00	4.50	0.00	100	0.5		4	-1	2	50		84.00	49.50	128.00

- For this purpose, I maintain a **database of NASDAQ-listed biotech companies**. Note that the grading and the names have been randomized to avoid expressing any specific opinion. The database includes various parameters about each company such as the presence of imminent catalysts, the number of drugs in its pipeline, the date of its IPO, the impressiveness of its pitch (the "wow" factor), the feasibility of proving its proposed medical indication, the cutting-edge nature of its approach, the strength of its target biology's rationale, its clinical need, and its potential to achieve phenotype reversion, among many others. I adjust these grades as new information about each company comes in, with the goal of anticipating the direction of the company's stock market movement. I use about 50 parameters and follow about 1,000 companies, providing a robust dataset for detecting major trends. I use regression to find relationships between these parameters to predict a company's future value (see next quick note).

Figure 45. Finding Trends in Nasdaq-Listed Biotech Companies: Part 2

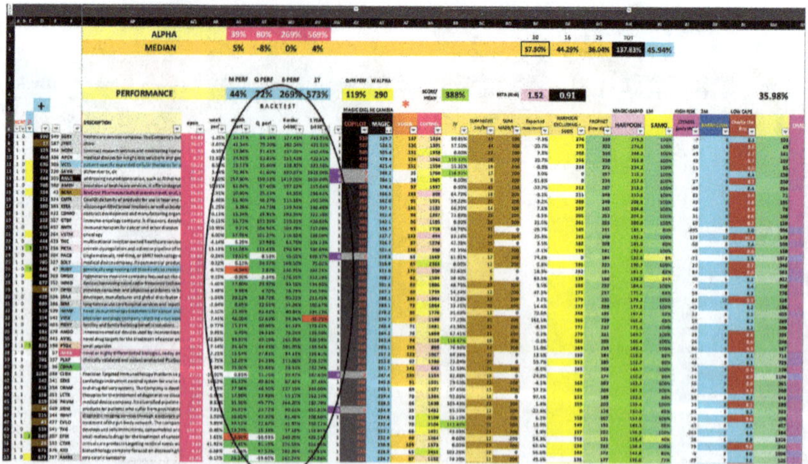

- Companies are evaluated and ordered based on a composite score derived from various parameters indicating their value. As depicted in the corresponding upper figure, certain ranking methodologies showcase a potent capability for identifying high-performing entities. This is demonstrated by the significant presence of green (indicating superior performance) in the one month, quarter, six months, and yearly assessments. Conversely, there's a notable prevalence of red (indicating inferior performance) in the lower-ranked positions, as illustrated in the subsequent figure. Although the method is not perfect, with some underperformers slipping through and some top performers missed, the goal is to maximize the detection of true positive signals, even at the cost of missing some companies that perform well (see my discussion on sensibility versus specificity in the text.

- An important note is that the performance metrics used for scoring are forward-tested, not backtested, making them more reliable as they are based on real, not historical, data. As with any predictive models, the real-life results do not perform as well as in backtesting scenarios, but they nevertheless provide a strong indication of value creation potential in NASDAQ-listed biotech companies.
- Multiple regression analysis is a statistical technique used to predict the value of a dependent variable based on the values of two or more independent variables. In the context of listed companies, the dependent variable might be a company's stock price, while independent variables can be various parameters such as the presence of imminent catalysts, the number of drugs in a pipeline, the date of an IPO, and other factors that potentially influence stock price.
- Even if the math involved is not complex, you'll need to use some math and that is outside of the scope of this book. The steps to perform multiple regression analysis in Excel are summarized here:
  - **Prepare the Data:** Assemble your data within Excel, with each row representing an observation (company), and each column representing a variable. Ensure that the dependent variable (the one you wish to predict) and the independent variables (the ones you believe influence the dependent variable) are all included.
  - **Insert the Data Analysis ToolPak:** Excel doesn't inherently come with regression capabilities. You'll need to install a Data Analysis ToolPak add-in.
  - **Run the Regression:** Input the range of cells that contain your dependent variable under "Input Y Range" and your independent variables under "Input X Range." Check the "Labels" box if your first row contains labels. Select the output range if you want the result in the same worksheet or a new one.
  - **Interpret the Results:** After clicking "OK," Excel will provide an output table. The "Multiple R" is the correlation coefficient and gives a measure of the quality of the prediction. "R Square" is the coefficient of determination, representing the percentage of the dependent variable variation that a linear model explains. The "Significance F" gives the total overall significance of the regression model. The individual coefficients for each independent variable give their respective weightage in the model.
- This process provides a numerical model that predicts the behavior of listed companies based on the independent variables. However, be cautious to ensure that the assumptions of multiple regression (linearity, independence, homoscedasticity, and normality) are met and that the model makes sense in the real-world context.
- Always remember that while Excel is a powerful tool for running multiple regressions, it is ultimately the analyst's understanding of the business landscape, intuition, and critical thinking that make the prediction robust and useful. The outputs of the regression model are not definitive predictions but rather tools for informing decision-making processes.
- In conclusion, the utilization of multiple regression in Excel can provide insightful predictive models for the behavior of listed companies. By understanding and correctly implementing this technique, one can take a data-driven approach to make more accurate predictions and thus more informed investment decisions.

multiplying them), and then passes the result to the next neuron. These calculations are tiny and simple, but when you have a whole team of people (the "deep" in deep neural network refers to having many layers), they can extract complex patterns from the data.

For example, instead of just noting that taller players score more points, a deep neural network might discover that taller players who also practice a lot score an especially high number of points. These complex patterns are hard to capture with traditional regression analysis.

A key part of training a deep neural network is adjusting how much each colleague (neuron) listens to the others. This is like the weights in a regression analysis — just like in regression, the DNN learns the optimal way to combine the input information to make accurate predictions.

How does this work in practice?

- **First,** it's important to remember that a DNN is made up of layers of nodes or "neurons." These neurons are arranged in a sequence from the input layer (where we feed in our data), through one or more hidden layers, to the output layer (which gives us our final prediction). Let's take a simplified scenario where we're trying to predict the basketball points scored (as in the previous example) based on two features: hours practiced and height.
- **Step 1: Feeding the data:** The first step is to input the data. Let's say one player practiced for 5 hours and is 6 feet tall. These numbers go into the first layer of the DNN, the input layer.
- **Step 2: Weighted sum:** Each connection between the neurons has a weight, which the network will learn during the training process. At the beginning, the weights are random. Each neuron in the hidden layer takes the inputs, multiplies them by their weights, and adds them up. Let's say the weights are 0.1 for practice hours and 0.2 for height. The weighted sum for the first neuron in the hidden layer would be:

$$(5 \text{ hours} * 0.1) + (6 \text{ feet} * 0.2) = 1.7$$

- **Step 3: Activation function:** Next, this sum goes through what's called an activation function. The activation function introduces non-linearity into our network. This helps the DNN model complex patterns. A common activation function is the ReLU (Rectified Linear Unit) function, which is simply: if the input is less than 0, output 0. If the input is greater than 0, output the input. Our weighted sum is 1.7, which is greater than 0, so the output of our first neuron after the activation function is 1.7.

- **Step 4: Repeat for each layer:** This process repeats for every neuron in the hidden layer. Each neuron has different weights, so they might output different values for the same input. The process repeats for the next layer, using the outputs of the first hidden layer as inputs. Finally, when we reach the output layer, we might use a different activation function suitable for the type of problem we're solving (for example, a sigmoid function for a binary classification problem).
- **Step 5: Training the network:** Once the network has outputted its prediction, we can compare this prediction to the true value and measure the error using a loss function. The goal of training is to adjust the weights in the network to minimize this error. This is done using a method called backpropagation, which involves calculus and can be a bit complex. But in essence, it calculates the gradient, or the slope of the error function, and adjusts the weights slightly in the direction that most decreases the error. This entire process repeats with many different basketball players' data, iteratively updating the weights to reduce the error, until the model is good at predicting the points scored.

And that, in a nutshell, is the math behind a deep neural network! Despite the complexity, the core concept is straightforward: it's about determining the right weights on the connections between neurons, which is learned from the data through a process of gradually reducing the prediction error.

For a science-driven company, using a deep neural network can be a powerful tool. Let's say a biotech company is trying to predict how well a patient will respond to a treatment based on their genetic information. This is a complex problem with a lot of data. A DNN can capture the complex relationships in the data, possibly leading to more accurate predictions than traditional regression analysis. For a venture capitalist, understanding how a company uses DNNs can help evaluate its potential. If a company can show that its DNN-based method provides more accurate predictions than traditional methods,

Figure 46. Deep Neural Networks

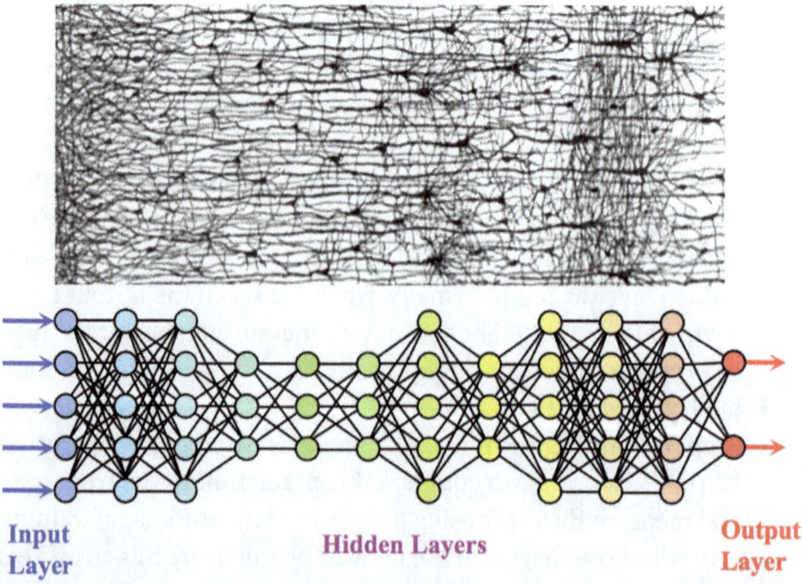

Deep neural networks (DNNs) and the human brain have often been compared, given that DNNs are fundamentally inspired by our understanding of biological neural networks. Recently, the success of language learning models (LLMs), a type of DNN, in understanding and generating language, has further emphasized the correlation between these artificial constructs and human cognition.

- A deep neural network functions by applying a series of mathematical transformations to input data, enabling the network to "learn" and extract patterns from the data. It does so via an architecture that is organized into a series of layers. Each layer is composed of multiple nodes or "neurons," which are simple processing units. Each layer's output is passed to the subsequent layer, thus forming a network.
- DNNs are called "deep" because they contain more than one hidden layer between the input and output layers. The first layer, known as the input layer, receives the raw data, while the last layer, the output layer, produces the final output. Between these two, there are one or more hidden layers, where the actual computation is done.
- In a process analogous to synaptic strengthening in the human brain, every node in each layer of the network is associated with a weight. These weights adjust as the network learns from data, forming the backbone of the network's learning process.
- Each node multiplies the received input with its associated weight to produce a value, which is then passed through a non-linear function known as an activation function. The result is passed on to the next layer.
- The "learning" in a deep neural network occurs during a process known as backpropagation, an algorithm for adjusting the weights of the network. During this process, the network compares its final output to the actual output. The difference between the two, known as the error, is then propagated back through the network, adjusting the weights of the nodes as

it goes. This process is repeated multiple times, with the network adjusting its weights each time to minimize the error. The rate at which weights are adjusted is governed by a parameter known as the "learning rate."

- However, learning is not always straightforward. Overfitting, where a model learns the training data too well and performs poorly on unseen data, is a common issue. Techniques such as dropout, where randomly selected neurons are ignored during training, and regularization, which adds a penalty to the loss function, are recommended to prevent overfitting.
- Deep neural networks are powerful tools capable of learning complex patterns and relationships. However, one downside is that they are often seen as "black boxes," as it can be hard to interpret what is happening within the network. Ongoing research focuses on improving the interpretability of these models, making it easier for humans to understand why a network made a specific prediction.
- One of the striking similarities between DNNs and the human brain is their ability to learn from experience. In the human brain, neurons are connected by synapses, and learning occurs when these synaptic connections strengthen or weaken over time. Similarly, in DNNs, artificial neurons, or nodes, adjust their connections or weights based on the learning from input data. This process, known as backpropagation in DNNs, mirrors the brain's ability to learn and adapt over time.
- Moreover, DNNs and the human brain process information hierarchically. In the human brain, simple sensory data is processed in lower-level neurons and then passed to higher-level neurons for more complex processing, forming a hierarchy of understanding. Similarly, in DNNs, raw input data is transformed through multiple layers of computation, with each layer extracting more abstract, high-level features, enabling complex pattern recognition.
- The recent successes of LLMs like GPT-3 from OpenAI serve as a testament to this hierarchical process. These models, trained on extensive text corpus, are capable of understanding the structural patterns in language and predicting the next word in a sentence. This is analogous to how the human brain processes language, understanding context, grammar, and semantic relationships to anticipate what comes next in a sentence.
- However, significant differences set DNNs apart from the human brain. One primary distinction is their structure. While DNNs are organized in uniform layers with each node connected to every other node in adjacent layers, the human brain consists of a diverse array of neuron types arranged in a complex, non-uniform architecture.
- The similarities offer valuable insights into developing more efficient and effective neural networks, while the differences remind us of the uniqueness and complexity of human cognition. As our understanding of both domains deepens, we may continue to draw inspiration from one to enhance the other, propelling us further into the era of artificial intelligence.

it might suggest the company has a competitive edge and could be a good investment.

So, in the end, while a deep neural network might seem more like a game of pass-the-message than a traditional statistical technique, it's a powerful tool for making sense of complex data. And just like regression analysis, it's all about figuring out the best way to combine information to make accurate predictions.

Meta Analysis

Imagine you and your colleagues are trying to decide the best ice cream flavor. There are tons of flavors out there, but you're all curious about which one is the most popular. You decide to find out by checking out online ice cream flavor reviews from several websites. Each website has its own rating for different flavors based on people's votes or reviews. This is a lot like individual studies in scientific research — each study collects and analyzes its own data.

Now, you could pick one website and go with whatever flavor is most popular there. But what if that website has a lot of mint chocolate chip lovers and another website has more fans of vanilla? If you look at only one website, you're not getting the whole picture. So you decide to combine the flavor ratings from all the websites. This way, you're taking into account more people's opinions and getting a more reliable answer. This is similar to what a meta-analysis does. It combines the results of many studies to get a clearer overall picture.

This technique is very important in the context of science and medicine. Let's say multiple research labs around the world are conducting independent studies on a new vaccine for a particular disease. Each study might involve a different number of patients, be conducted at a different location, and might even have slightly different methods. All these factors could influence the results.

Instead of simply picking one study and using its findings, a meta-analysis takes all these studies, standardizes the results to account for differences in study design, and combines them. This allows researchers to obtain a more reliable estimate of the vaccine's effectiveness.

For science-driven companies, using meta-analysis can be a powerful tool to make informed decisions. Just like the ice cream flavor example, a meta-analysis is a way to combine information from multiple sources to get a more comprehensive and reliable understanding. Whether it's picking the most popular ice cream flavor or deciding where to invest millions of dollars, it's always a good idea to consider as much good-quality information as you can. And that's where a meta-analysis shines.

The Indispensable Role of Statistics in Investment Decision-Making

Investing relies heavily on the ability to make sound decisions based on data. At its core, statistics provides the fundamental tools for understanding, interpreting, and making sense of these data. Whether it's interpreting a company's science package, understanding market trends, or evaluating the performance of an investment strategy, a strong grounding in statistical concepts is vital for any investor. This understanding allows investors to scrutinize data more critically, make more informed decisions, and ultimately, to increase the probability of their investments being successful.

However, statistical illiteracy can lead to a number of pitfalls. Misinterpretation of data can result in misguided decisions, and a lack of understanding can leave an investor vulnerable to manipulation, whether intentional or not.

For example, concepts like the base rate fallacy and the misinterpretation of p-values can lead to flawed conclusions if not properly understood. Further, the misuse of statistics can present a skewed narrative, which may result in an investor making decisions based on incorrect or incomplete information.

Moreover, an inability to understand the subtleties and nuances of statistical data can lead to overconfidence in the face of uncertainty. Investments are inherently risky, and a failure to appreciate the uncertainty involved can result in an underestimation of risk.

So, the complexities of investment decisions, particularly at the leading edge, demand the application of probabilistic thinking and statistical savvy. Embracing this mindset does not guarantee success, but it does provide a framework for better understanding the risks and potential rewards inherent in investment decisions. It's not about predicting the future with certainty — it's about understanding the probabilities and making informed decisions that align with one's investment goals and risk tolerance. The role of statistics in investment decision-making is, therefore, not just important, but truly indispensable.

Further Considerations: Other Important Statistical Concepts

Beyond the statistical principles discussed thus far, additional concepts play a significant role in understanding and interpreting data.

First, there's the issue of correlation versus causation. Just because two variables move together does not necessarily mean that one causes the other. Yet, this misinterpretation is a common error, and being aware of it help avoid reaching erroneous conclusions.

Second, there's the concept of regression to the mean, which posits that after an extreme event, the next event is likely to be less extreme, reverting back toward the average. This phenomenon can often be observed in investment scenarios, such as stock performance, and is important to understanding how markets behave over time.

The relevance of these concepts in investment decision-making cannot be overstated. A solid understanding of the difference between correlation and causation can save an investor from making misguided decisions based on unrelated or coincidental market trends. Understanding regression to the mean can provide perspective during times of exceptional performance, either good or bad, and prevent overreactions based on short-term results.

While this chapter has provided a foundational understanding of some key statistical concepts, continued learning and application of these principles are encouraged. By deepening your understanding of correlation versus causation, regression to the mean, normal distribution, and other statistical concepts, you can further refine your investment strategies and potentially improve outcomes. Remember, effective investment is not just about understanding the market — it's also about understanding the numbers behind the market.

Rule #31
On Bayesian Thinking

"We must be free not because we claim freedom, but because we practice it."
William Faulkner

Bayes' theorem is a powerful mathematical formula used for calculating conditional probabilities. Put simply, it provides a way to update our beliefs about an event happening based on new evidence. The theorem was named after the Reverend Thomas Bayes, who first provided an equation that allows new evidence to update beliefs in his "An Essay towards solving a Problem in the Doctrine of Chances" (1763). It's a practical tool that helps us navigate through the uncertainty of our world.

In today's data-driven world, Bayes' theorem plays a crucial role across many scientific fields. It forms the bedrock of several modern technologies and is instrumental in numerous areas including machine learning, artificial intelligence, statistical inference, and medical testing. It provides a mathematical framework for understanding how to update our beliefs when presented with new data, making it invaluable in decision-making processes, especially in areas that involve high uncertainty and complex systems.

Let's consider an example to develop an intuition. One morning, you wake up feeling unwell, but you don't know why. You decide to see your doctor, who also isn't sure what's causing your discomfort. To find out, to the doctor runs many tests. After a week, you get your results: You've tested positive for a rare, harmful disease that affects only 0.1%

of people. Naturally, you ask the doctor, "Are you certain I have this disease?" The doctor tells you the test is very accurate — it correctly identifies 99% of people with the disease, and only wrongly identifies 1% of people without the disease.

You might think there's a 99% chance you have the disease because the test is 99% accurate. But that's not right! Bayes' theorem helps us find out how likely something is to be true based on a test result. We start with our first guess of how likely we thought the disease was before the test (this is called the "prior"). We then use the test's accuracy to adjust this guess. This gives us our new best guess (or "posterior"). In this case, the prior is 0.1%, the chance of having the disease in the general population. If we use Bayes' theorem with these numbers, we find that after testing positive, you actually have only a 9% chance of having the disease, which is much less than 99%.

Bayes' theorem isn't magic — it's just good math. Imagine a group of 1,000 people. Only one person in this group is expected to have the disease, and the test will likely find them. But the test will also wrongly identify 10 healthy people as having the disease. So, if you test positive, you're now in a group of 11 people, only one of whom has the disease. This means there's a 1 in 11, or 9%, chance you're the one with the disease.

This way of thinking wasn't seen as revolutionary when Bayes first came up with it. In fact, he didn't think it was worth publishing. His friend Richard Price found it in Bayes' papers after he died. Bayes had used this thinking in a thought experiment about guessing where a ball was on a table based on where other balls landed.

Bayes' theorem isn't just for one-time use, it's for updating our guesses as we get more evidence. If you took a second test and it was also positive, you would use the 9% as your new prior. Then, using Bayes' theorem again, you would find that there's now a 91% chance you have the disease.

The Concept of Probability

At its core, probability is a measure of uncertainty. It quantifies the likelihood of an event or outcome occurring among a set of possible outcomes. Probabilities are typically expressed as a number between 0 and 1 (inclusive), or alternatively, as a percentage between 0 and 100%.

Figure 47. Understanding Bayesian Reasoning

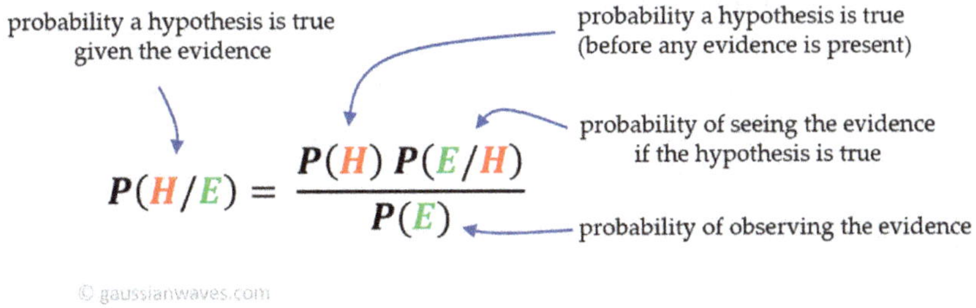

Bayesian reasoning is a powerful methodology that finds application across a broad spectrum of life domains.

Anytime we aim to make accurate predictions or judgments, the process of Bayesian reasoning has the potential to guide our decision-making process, providing a solid framework to assess the likelihood of various outcomes.

At its core, Bayesian reasoning advocates a thoughtful approach to decision-making. It urges us not to rush to judgments or conclusions without carefully considering our existing knowledge (the prior) and any new information or evidence that becomes available (the likelihood). By doing so, it safeguards against hasty, potentially ill-informed decisions, helping us avoid the pitfalls of reactive thinking. Instead, it promotes proactive, data-driven decisions, leveraging both our prior knowledge and new evidence.

Concurrently, Bayesian reasoning also cautions against ignoring signals in the data. Even subtle signs can be instrumental in shaping our beliefs and judgments. This aspect is particularly crucial in domains such as scientific research or financial analysis, where ignoring seemingly minor data points can lead to significant errors or missed opportunities. Hence, the methodology fosters a culture of vigilance and comprehensive examination, where every piece of data is taken into account before drawing a conclusion.

Despite its merits, Bayesian reasoning isn't universally applied. In some instances, the pursuit of fairness and justice or the prevention of harmful cycles may take precedence over rigorous statistical predictive power. For example, in hiring practices or college admissions, using certain types of Bayesian reasoning (such as using demographic data to make decisions) might lead to perpetuating societal inequities. In these situations, Bayesian reasoning is intentionally limited to prevent discriminatory outcomes, even though it might statistically "optimize" the decision-making process.

Similarly, in criminal justice, while a Bayesian approach might indicate a higher likelihood of a certain demographic committing a crime based on past data, acting on this information could contribute to a self-perpetuating cycle of profiling and discrimination. Consequently, there's a conscious effort to distance decision-making from purely Bayesian reasoning in such contexts to uphold fairness and avoid prejudiced decisions.

A probability of 0 signifies an impossible event, while a probability of 1 represents a certain or guaranteed event.

Consider a simple scenario where you flip a fair coin. It has two possible outcomes: heads or tails. As the coin is fair, it doesn't favor either side, so both outcomes have an equal chance of occurring. This means the probability of getting heads (or tails) is 0.5, or 50%. In essence, if you were to flip the coin many times, you'd expect about half the flips to result in heads and the other half to result in tails.

To further illustrate the concept of probability, let's consider another simple scenario: predicting the weather. If a weather forecast tells you there's a 70% chance of rain tomorrow, it means that, given the current data and weather patterns, it is estimated that it will rain on 70 out of 100 similar days. It doesn't guarantee rain tomorrow, but it indicates that rain is more likely than not.

Or, consider a lottery draw. If you buy a ticket in a lottery with 1,000,000 tickets sold, and only one ticket will be drawn as the winner, the probability of your ticket being the winner is 1 in 1,000,000, or 0.000001. This is an example of a very low probability event — although it's not impossible, it's extremely unlikely.

Now that we have a basic understanding of probability, let's move on to a more specific concept: conditional probability. This is where things get a bit more interesting, and where Bayes' theorem starts to come into the picture.

Unlike simple probabilities, conditional probabilities consider the likelihood of an event given that another event has already occurred. This is important because in many situations, the probability of an event can change if we have additional information about other related events. This additional layer of complexity takes us a step closer to understanding Bayes' theorem, a tool that expertly navigates the intricacies of conditional probability to improve decision-making in a variety of scientific fields.

Introduction to Conditional Probability

In everyday life, the outcome of certain events often depends on the outcomes of other events. This is where the concept of conditional probability comes into play. Conditional probability is the probability of an event occurring given that another event has already occurred. It is represented mathematically as P(A|B), which reads as "the probability of event A occurring, given that event B has occurred."

Consider a deck of 52 playing cards, which consists of four suits: hearts, diamonds, clubs, and spades. Each suit has 13 cards: 9 numbered cards and 4 face cards (Jack, Queen, King, and Ace). Suppose you draw one card from the deck. The probability of drawing a heart is 13/52 (or 1/4). Now, let's say that you've drawn a card and you know it's a face card. Given this new information, what's the probability it's a heart? There are 4 face cards in hearts and 16 in the entire deck, so the conditional probability is 4/16 (or 1/4).

Despite the additional condition, in this case, the probability hasn't changed. However, that's not always the case in other scenarios.

In the realm of conditional probability, two particularly important concepts are false positives and false negatives, which often come up in the context of diagnostic tests. These terms relate to the accuracy of tests and their potential to produce incorrect results.

A false positive occurs when a test incorrectly indicates the presence of a condition when it is not actually there. For instance, imagine you take a test for a rare disease that you do not have, and the test comes back positive. This is a false positive — the test result (a positive) is false (you do not have the disease). Conversely, a false negative occurs when a test wrongly indicates the absence of a condition when it is indeed present. Using the same scenario, suppose you have the rare disease, but the test result comes back negative. This is a false negative — the negative test result is false (you do have the disease).

The rates of false positives and negatives play crucial roles in the calculation and interpretation of conditional probabilities and, as we will see, in the application of Bayes' theorem as well.

The Basics of Bayes' Theorem

Bayes' theorem is a principle in probability theory that describes how to update our beliefs about a hypothesis when given new evidence. In other words, it allows us to refine our predictions about the likelihood of an event, taking into account both what we already know and new information that comes in. The formula for Bayes' theorem is typically written as:

$$P(A|B) = [P(B|A) * P(A)] / P(B)$$

This might look a bit intimidating, but don't worry, we will break this down using straightforward terms. Let's start with the term P(A|B), which is the probability of event A occurring, given that event B has occurred. This is what we're trying to calculate, and it's often called the "posterior" probability.

On the right side of the equation, we have three terms: P(B|A), P(A), and P(B).

- **P(B|A)** is the probability of event B occurring, given that event A has occurred. This is often referred to as the "likelihood."
- **P(A)** is the probability of event A occurring. This is known as the "prior" probability because it's what we believe about the event before we have any specific information about event B.
- **P(B)** is the probability of event B occurring, also known as the "marginal likelihood."

Now let's illustrate Bayes' theorem using a modified version of our previous real-world example, but now plugging the formula. Imagine you've taken a test for a rare disease. The test is said to be 99% accurate — meaning that if you have the disease, there's a 99% chance the test will be positive, and if you don't have the disease, there's a 99% chance the test will be negative. But the disease is rare and only affects 1 in 1,000 people.

You take the test and get a positive result. How likely is it that you actually have the disease? As we already discussed, it's not as simple as saying there's a 99% chance, as one might initially think. In this case, event A is having the disease, and event B is testing positive.

The prior probability P(A), the probability that you have the disease before considering the test result, is 1 in 1,000, or 0.001.

The likelihood P(B|A), the chance of testing positive if you have the disease, is the accuracy of the test, or 0.99.

The marginal likelihood P(B), the overall probability of testing positive (regardless of whether you have the disease or not), is a bit tricky to calculate, but essentially it combines the chance of a true positive (having the disease and testing positive) with the chance of a false positive (not having the disease but testing positive).

Plugging these numbers into Bayes' theorem, we can calculate the posterior probability, P(A|B), which tells us the probability of having the disease given that we've tested positive. The result might surprise you — despite the test's high accuracy, the likelihood of having the disease even after testing positive is much lower than 99%, due to the disease's rarity. This demonstrates the power and nuance of Bayes' theorem.

Let's calculate it using the values provided:

- **The prior probability P(A),** the probability of having the disease before considering the test result, is 1 in 1,000, or 0.001.
- **The likelihood P(B|A)**, the probability of testing positive given that you have the disease, is 0.99.
- The false positive rate is 0.01 and the probability of not having the disease is 0.999. So, **the marginal likelihood P(B),** the overall probability of testing positive, is (0.99 * 0.001) + (0.01 * 0.999).

Using these figures, we plug them into Bayes' theorem to calculate the posterior probability P(A|B):

$$P(A|B) = [P(B|A) * P(A)] / P(B) = [0.99 * 0.001] / [(0.99 * 0.001) + (0.01 * 0.999)]$$

$$P(A|B) = 0.00099 / (0.00099 + 0.00999) = 0.00099 / 0.01098$$

$$P(A|B) \approx 0.09 \text{ or } 9\%$$

So, despite the test's 99% accuracy, there's only about a 9% chance that you actually have the disease if you test positive, due to the rarity of the disease. This demonstrates the critical importance of considering prior probabilities (in this case, the base rate of the disease) when interpreting test results.

The Importance of Bayes' Theorem in Decision-Making

Bayes' theorem isn't just a mathematical curiosity; it's a practical tool for decision-making. In any situation where we need to make a decision based on uncertain information, Bayes' theorem provides a formalized way of incorporating new evidence into our existing beliefs. By using this theorem, we can calculate the probability of various outcomes and make more informed decisions.

Think of a medical doctor deciding on a treatment plan for a patient. She has some initial belief about what disease the patient might have, based on their symptoms. As she collects more information

— blood tests, X-rays, MRI scans — she updates her beliefs about the most likely diagnosis, and thus the best treatment plan. This process of updating beliefs in response to new evidence is at the heart of Bayesian decision-making.

In a Bayesian framework, our beliefs are not static. Instead, they are constantly updated as we gather more evidence. When we first encounter a problem, we have some prior belief about what the solution might be. As we gather evidence, we adjust that belief, becoming more certain or uncertain depending on what the evidence suggests.

This ability to revise our beliefs in light of new evidence is one of the key advantages of Bayesian thinking. The fact that we can update our beliefs means that our understanding of the world can continually improve. As we gather more data, our predictions become more accurate. This is fundamentally different from a more traditional, or "frequentist," approach to statistics, where probabilities are fixed and do not change with new information.

Bayes' Theorem in Cutting-Edge Fields

In the rapidly advancing realms of machine learning and artificial intelligence, Bayes' theorem plays an indispensable role. It provides a mathematical framework for computers to make educated guesses or predictions. This theorem enables computers to update their predictions as they process new data. The use of Bayesian inference in machine learning allows these systems to adapt and learn from their experiences. This capability is fundamental to the operations of recommendation systems like those used by Amazon, predictive typing like Google's auto-complete, and more sophisticated applications like self-driving drones.

In the field of medical diagnosis, Bayesian inference has a profound impact. It enables physicians and researchers to quantify uncertainty and revise beliefs based on new information such as test results, thereby aiding in the diagnosis and treatment of diseases. In clinical trials, Bayesian statistics can even be used to modify the trial design as results accumulate, allowing for potential improvements in efficiency.

As an example here, the influence of Bayes' theorem is illustrated by its application in genetic testing. For example, in the case of breast cancer, the BRCA1 and BRCA2 genetic tests indicate a woman's risk of developing breast or ovarian cancer. However, a positive test result doesn't necessarily mean cancer is certain. Doctors use Bayesian methods to interpret the test result, incorporating prior knowledge about the patient's family history and age to assess the actual risk.

In climate science, Bayes' theorem is applied in interpreting the complex climate models used to predict future conditions. It provides a rigorous methodology for incorporating new data, like temperature or CO_2 concentrations, and updating predictions accordingly. This is crucial for the assessment of climate change scenarios and the subsequent policymaking decisions.

Artificial intelligence is another field greatly shaped by Bayes' theorem. In robotics, Bayesian methods have been pivotal in advancing perception and cognition in robots. For example, in self-driving cars, the vehicle uses Bayesian inference to interpret sensor data and predict potential obstacles in its path, thereby determining the safest route.

Thus, Bayes' theorem has had a pivotal role in the progression of various cutting-edge fields, underscoring its value and versatility in a world that increasingly relies on data-driven decision-making.

Closing Thoughts

The journey of understanding Bayes' theorem doesn't end here. It's a complex subject that intertwines math and philosophy, demanding a healthy degree of curiosity and persistence to explore. I encourage you to continue delving deeper into this fascinating theorem. As you grow more familiar with it, you'll begin to notice its applications everywhere. In this increasingly data-driven world, the ability to think like a Bayesian might be one of the most essential skills one can cultivate. After all, life, much like Bayesian inference, is about learning from experience and continually updating our understanding in light of new information.

Rule #32
On Probabilistic Thinking

"I do everything I think possible or acceptable to escape from this trap."
Jacques Derrida

In our preceding discussions, we ventured into the world of statistics, understanding its language and using it to comprehend and analyze the wealth of information around us. We explored concepts like statistical significance, correlation and causation, and false positives and negatives. Next, we plunged into the Bayesian theorem, which allowed us to better understand the nature of prediction and uncertainty.

With its unique approach to probability, the Bayesian theorem provided us with a way to update our beliefs and make better predictions about the future based on new evidence. It presented us with a systematic way of incorporating our prior knowledge and experience into our current understanding of a situation or problem. These statistical tools help us dissect the information we encounter in our lives, particularly in the dynamic world of cutting-edge science and technology.

As we transition from these necessary foundational topics, we now arrive at an important chapter — the realm of probabilistic thinking. This methodology is a logical progression from our discussions on statistics and Bayesian inference. Probabilistic thinking is more than just understanding odds or crunching numbers; it's about honing a mindset that accepts uncertainty as a part of life rather than a nuisance to be avoided.

When we think probabilistically, we accept that our knowledge of the world is limited and that our predictions and decisions must reflect this reality. We don't just think in terms of "yes" and "no," but rather in degrees of certainty. This mindset can be particularly powerful in areas where we're dealing with high levels of uncertainty and ambiguity, such as the cutting-edge technology landscape.

Embracing probabilistic thinking doesn't mean abandoning the pursuit of certainty or precision. Instead, it's about refining our approach to uncertainty, treating it as an inherent feature of reality that can be navigated effectively. In this chapter, we will unpack this concept further, exploring how we can harness the power of probabilistic thinking in the fast-paced, ever-evolving domain of scientific research and our quest to predict the future to make sound investments.

Understanding Events as Probability Distributions

As we move deeper into the world of probabilistic thinking, a key concept we need to embrace is understanding events not as single, fixed outcomes, but as probability distributions. To put it in simpler terms, instead of viewing the future as a single point that will inevitably occur, we should instead imagine it as a range of possible outcomes, each with its own probability of occurrence.

This kind of thinking is a departure from our instinctive approach to the world. We often seek definiteness and certainty; we crave clear, unambiguous answers. But in many cases, especially when dealing with the future, such definitive outcomes are a rarity, if not entirely nonexistent. When making decisions about the future, we're often dealing with complex systems where variables interact in intricate and often unpredictable ways. Consequently, instead of one "correct" answer, we are faced with a whole spectrum of possibilities.

This paradigm shift is essential when we apply it to the realm of investing, particularly within the venture capital and startup ecosystems. In this space, certainty is virtually nonexistent and complexity is the order of the day. When you invest in a startup, you aren't buying into a guaranteed outcome; rather, you're purchasing a slice of a probability distribution.

A startup's future isn't a fixed point; it's a broad array of possible outcomes. These can range from bankruptcy to modest success, all the way up to becoming the next industry titan. As an investor, you're essentially placing a bet on this distribution, hoping that the startup will fall on the more successful side of the spectrum.

This means that as an investor, you're not just investing in companies — you're investing in probability distributions. Each investment is a wager on a complex interplay of factors, including the team's competence, the product's viability, market trends, competition, and countless others. These factors create a distribution of potential outcomes, each with its own likelihood.

Understanding this is crucial to making wise investment decisions. It shifts the focus from trying to predict a single outcome to understanding and managing a range of possibilities. This approach helps in mitigating risks, optimizing returns, and cultivating a more resilient investment strategy that can weather the storm of uncertainty that is inherent in the venture capital landscape.

Embracing this probabilistic mindset is a key step toward navigating the exciting yet unpredictable seas of scientific research and technological innovation. It's a tool that allows us to dance with uncertainty, rather than trying to wrestle it into submission.

Do Casinos Lose Money?

On the surface, this question might seem puzzling. Casinos, in fact, are masters of probabilistic thinking. Their business model isn't based on predicting a single outcome, but on understanding the distribution of possible outcomes and using this knowledge to their advantage. They leverage the law of large numbers — a principle in probability theory that states that as a sample size grows, its mean gets closer to the average of the whole population. That means they don't need to put a stop loss just in case they lose, they know for sure they will never lose, as long as they let statistics work for a reasonable amount of time.

In practical terms, this means that while a single game of roulette or a hand of blackjack might result in a loss for the casino, over thousands or millions of games, the odds average out in the casino's favor. They might lose some battles, but they're guaranteed to win the war.

This is where science comes into play. Probabilistic thinking is essentially science-driven thinking; it's grounded in solid, empirical principles and uses statistical tools to analyze and make sense of the world. Having a "statistics mind" means not being swayed by anecdotal evidence or individual outcomes, but instead focusing on the broader trends and patterns.

So, what can venture capitalists and forecasters learn from casinos? A great deal, it turns out. Just like casinos, successful forecasters and investors aren't those who always predict the correct outcome. Instead, they're the ones who understand the range of potential outcomes and make their decisions accordingly. They don't treat the future as a single, inevitable event but as a spectrum of possibilities. They don't consider a single bet as a win-or-lose scenario but as one play in a long series of games. They don't see decisions as right or wrong but as better or worse in light of the available evidence and the inherent probabilities.

In essence, they embrace the unpredictability of the future and, instead of attempting to assert control over it, learn to navigate it. They understand that the future is not a single point but a distribution of possibilities, and they place their bets accordingly. They know that they might lose some hands, but if their strategy is sound, they will win in the long run.

This probabilistic, science-driven thinking is the hallmark of successful gamblers, forecasters, and venture capitalists. It allows them to remain grounded in the face of uncertainty and to make sound decisions based on a deep understanding of probabilities and trends.

The Bayesian Path to Less Wrongness

With incomplete information, decision-makers must chart a path through complex terrain where nothing is black and white. It is in this shadowy world of half-lit truths and obscured facts where the concept of "less wrongness" comes into play. Being "less wrong" doesn't necessarily imply being right; rather, it signifies that our understanding of the world is continually evolving, that our knowledge is constantly being updated and refined, bringing us closer and closer to the truth, but never quite arriving there.

It's a powerful reminder of the tentative and transient nature of knowledge, especially in the world of emerging technologies and startups where today's breakthrough can be tomorrow's obsolete idea.

At the heart of this concept of "less wrongness" is, again, Bayesian thinking, a method of statistical inference that provides a formalism for updating our beliefs in the light of new evidence.

Consider an initial hypothesis. A venture capitalist might estimate that a particular startup has a 70% chance of success. As new information becomes available — perhaps a competitor releases a similar product, or there's a significant market downturn — the Bayesian method allows for the initial hypothesis to be updated. Instead of clinging doggedly to the initial belief, the Bayesian thinker acknowledges the new evidence and recalibrates the probabilities accordingly. This shift in perspective doesn't mean that the original prediction was wrong, but that it's become "more wrong" in light of new information.

With each new piece of data, the Bayesian method nudges us closer to a more accurate understanding of the world. It's an ongoing journey, a constant learning process that keeps our assumptions fluid and our minds open to new information. In the context of startup investing, this means that successful venture capitalists don't stand still; they maintain a flexible outlook, ready to adjust their sails when the wind changes.

The Bayesian path to less wrongness, then, is not a straight line but a meandering journey, always striving toward better understanding and greater accuracy, one updated hypothesis at a time.

Probabilistic Thinking in Action: Poker as an Example

Poker is more than a game of chance; it's a cerebral contest that requires a deep understanding of probabilities, human psychology, and strategic decision-making. At its core, poker is a testament to the power of probabilistic thinking, a vibrant real-world example of how statistical insight can turn the tide in one's favor.

Unlike games of pure chance like roulette, where the outcome is determined solely by luck, poker is a game of skill where players can influence the outcome based on their understanding of the game's dynamics, the tendencies of their opponents, and the statistical likelihood of certain events. The poker player, akin to the venture capitalist, doesn't merely gamble on luck; they make calculated decisions based on incomplete information, using their understanding of probabilities to guide their actions.

Investing is poker, not roulette. Investing, like poker, involves making decisions under uncertainty, but with potential rewards worth the risk. In both situations, the players — whether they're at the poker table or in the world of venture capital — need to assess their hand, weigh the potential outcomes, and make decisions accordingly.

Interestingly, a study of online poker players revealed that 52% of them have at least a bachelor's degree — about twice the rate in the

U.S. population as a whole and four times the rate among those who purchase lottery tickets. This points to a more educated, deliberative group of people who understand and apply principles of probabilistic thinking, not only to poker but potentially to other aspects of life and work, such as investing.

Poker players' decision-making process also reflects a nuanced grasp of probabilities. A seasoned poker player doesn't just consider the strength of their current hand; they also factor in how the hand could potentially evolve in subsequent rounds of betting, the strategies of their opponents, and the size of the pot. In short, they look at the bigger picture, a holistic view that is a hallmark of probabilistic thinking.

This is a vital lesson for venture capitalists. Like poker players, investors must consider not only the current state of a startup but also its potential evolution in the market, the strategies of competitors, and the overall state of the sector. In short, successful investing, like successful poker, demands a mastery of probabilistic thinking.

The Market as a Game of Blackjack

Delving further into the realm of card analogies, the startup ecosystem and venture capital investment bear intriguing parallels to the game of blackjack. While the objective in blackjack is to get as close to 21 without going over, in venture capital, it's about making the right investments that yield the maximum return without overexposing oneself to risk.

Like each card dealt in a game of blackjack, every company in the startup ecosystem contributes to changing odds. Each new startup, exit, investment, or write-off shifts the landscape, altering the prospects and potential outcomes for investors. This dynamic nature requires a constant reassessment of probabilities, demanding an adaptability and vigilance that is characteristic of Blackjack players.

In blackjack, a player's decisions are influenced by the cards that have been dealt and those likely to come. Similarly, investors need to be aware of market trends, new investments, and other factors affecting the startup ecosystem. In essence, they need to have a pulse on the ever-evolving market to make informed decisions.

Venture capitalists, like proficient blackjack players, don't merely react to the game's immediate circumstances. Instead, they strategize based on the entire deck's composition and the cards likely to appear next. They understand the importance of discerning patterns, predicting future trends, and making calculated bets. It's not just about the hand you're dealt, but how you play it, keeping in mind the wider context of the game.

Understanding Uncertainty in Experimental Results

In the dynamic landscape of venture capital, particularly within the realm of deep- tech and science-driven companies, one essential skill is the interpretation of scientific data from early-stage research. This task often requires a nuanced understanding of uncertainty and variance in experimental results.

Scientific experiments, by their very nature, are fraught with uncertainty. This uncertainty arises from a number of sources: intrinsic variability in the system being studied, measurement error, and the inherent randomness of many natural processes. As a venture capitalist, understanding and quantifying this uncertainty is paramount when evaluating the potential and risks associated with an innovative technology or a scientific breakthrough.

When examining scientific data, it's essential to assess the methodology used to obtain the results. Is the experimental design sound? Is the sample size sufficiently large to yield reliable results? Were controls implemented to mitigate confounding variables? Answering these questions can provide valuable insight into the reliability of the findings and the level of confidence one can place in them.

Another key consideration is the statistical analysis of the data. A firm grasp of statistical concepts such as confidence intervals, standard deviations, and p values is necessary to interpret the results correctly. A low p value, for instance, indicates that the observed result is unlikely to have occurred by chance, which strengthens confidence in the finding. On the other hand, wide confidence intervals or large standard deviations signify a high degree of uncertainty.

Moreover, understanding the concept of variance is vital when evaluating experimental results. Variance reflects the dispersion or spread of data points around the mean. High variance implies a wide spread, meaning the data points are quite different from each other. Conversely, low variance indicates that the data points are relatively similar. High variance in experimental results could signify potential issues with the consistency or reproducibility of the results, which are crucial factors to consider when investing in a science-driven company.

In the context of venture capitalism, understanding the uncertainty in experimental results can greatly inform investment decisions. It provides a means to assess the risk associated with an investment and can serve as a guide when choosing between potential investments with varying degrees of uncertainty.

In conclusion, evaluating uncertainty and variance in scientific data is a critical aspect of venture capital within the cutting-edge technology sector. This understanding can not only aid in risk assessment but also enable venture capitalists to make informed and strategic decisions.

The Statistical Mind: Embracing Approximation

Embarking on the path of probabilistic thinking fosters a unique transformation — our minds begin to operate like statistical processors. This shift is a testament to the ability of our brains to adapt to the demand for increasingly complex decision-making methodologies.

With a continually evolving startup ecosystem and venture capital industry, probabilistic thinking and a statistical mindset have become necessary tools for survival.

Problem-solving in the complex world of startups and venture capital is rarely a straightforward process. Instead, it often requires approximation, a strategy inherent to the statistical mind. Exact solutions are not always possible or practical due to the complexity and uncertainty of the business environment. Hence, the statistical mind seeks to grasp the core elements of a problem and make educated guesses or estimations. It is a constant balancing act between precision and pragmatism, where finding an approximately correct answer often holds more value than striving for perfect accuracy.

This brings us to a fascinating quote, "There are lies, there are terrible lies, and then there are statistics." This saying underscores the power and peril of statistical data. On one hand, statistics offer valuable insights, guiding our decisions and actions in the complex world of investing. On the other, they can be manipulated or misinterpreted, leading us astray.

In essence, having a statistical mind means embracing approximation, understanding the power and limitations of statistics, and using this knowledge to make informed, probabilistic decisions. It means separating the outcome from the quality of the decision. Sometimes the outcome will be bad, but we'll know the decision was still the right one. It's about wielding the double-edged sword of statistics with discernment and integrity, extracting its benefits while being wary of its pitfalls.

The Wrong-Side-of-Maybe Fallacy

The "wrong-side-of-maybe" fallacy presents a notable challenge in our understanding of probabilistic thinking. This fallacy occurs when we misinterpret a probability prediction based on the outcome of a single event.

Suppose a meteorologist forecasts a 70% chance of rain, and it doesn't rain. Many would hastily conclude that the forecast was incorrect. However, this conclusion stems from the wrong-side-of-maybe fallacy. It overlooks the implicit 30% prediction of it not raining. The only way to accurately assess the meteorologist's prediction would be to replicate the same conditions hundreds of times, a task virtually impossible in real life. If it didn't rain 30% of the time in these repetitions, the meteorologist would have been exactly right.

The implications of the wrong-side-of-maybe fallacy on decision-making are profound. It highlights how easily we can misinterpret probability and be misled by outcomes. It encourages a more nuanced understanding of probability, reminding us that a low-probability event is unlikely but not impossible.

In the venture capital world, this fallacy is particularly pertinent. A startup might fail despite being assigned a high probability of success, or succeed despite being deemed unlikely. Misjudging these situations based on a single outcome can lead to incorrect conclusions about our decision-making capabilities and the effectiveness of our predictive models.

Understanding and accounting for the wrong-side-of-maybe fallacy can refine our perception of probabilities and enhance our decision-making process in this complex and uncertain field.

Relevant Statistical Principles

To fully engage with probabilistic thinking, it's crucial to understand

and incorporate several key statistical principles. Among these are Laplace's Law, the Copernican Principle, and the application of Bayes' theorem using real-world priors.

- **Laplace's Law:** Also known as the rule of succession, Laplace's Law is a principle of inductive reasoning that provides a prediction for the probability of an event based on the number of times it has occurred in the past. In essence, it suggests that the probability of an event happening in the future is equal to the number of times it has happened in the past, divided by the total number of opportunities it had to happen.

  While this rule is simplistic and may not always provide a precise prediction, it serves as a good starting point in situations where you have limited data. When evaluating a startup or new technology, it can help approximate the likelihood of success based on historical trends.
- **Copernican Principle:** The Copernican Principle, or the principle of mediocrity, posits that we should assume we are not special or unique unless there is evidence to the contrary. This principle can be employed to manage the biases that tend to creep into our decision-making process. For instance, when evaluating a new investment opportunity, it may be tempting to believe that this opportunity is "special" or "unique" compared to others.

  The Copernican Principle reminds us to challenge this notion and to consider that it may be just as likely to succeed or fail as any other, unless there's clear evidence suggesting otherwise.
- **Bayes Reasoning Plus Real-World Priors:** The integration of Bayesian reasoning with real-world prior probabilities allows for a dynamic and responsive probabilistic framework. Bayesian reasoning, as we've already discussed, involves updating our beliefs based on new evidence. Real-world priors refer to our initial beliefs about the likelihood of an event occurring, grounded in empirical evidence and experience.

  By combining these two, we can establish a robust decision-making tool. For example, when deciding to invest in a startup, we can start with our prior belief about the likelihood of success for startups in that industry (our real-world prior), and then update this belief as we gather more information about the specific startup in question (applying Bayesian reasoning).

Each of these principles complements the other, providing a holistic approach to understanding and applying probabilistic thinking in the venture capital and startup ecosystem. By understanding and applying these principles, we can make more informed and balanced decisions, acknowledging the inherent uncertainties in this complex and evolving field.

Game Theory and Nash Equilibrium in the Cutting-Edge Field

Let's revisit here the practical applications of what we saw in the previous chapter. Venture capital, particularly when dealing with the cutting-edge industry, often involves complex strategic interactions among various players, which can include entrepreneurs, investors, competitors, regulators, and even the broader public. Here is where game theory and Nash Equilibrium become incredibly useful tools for navigating this intricate landscape.

- **Game Theory:** This field of mathematics deals with the study of strategies for dealing with competitive situations where the outcome of a participant's choices depends critically on the actions of other participants.

  Game theory has found wide applications in economics and is particularly relevant in the startup ecosystem where multiple actors are constantly strategizing and responding to one another's moves. In the cutting-edge field, game theory can help investors understand the competitive dynamics between startups and their rivals, assess the potential strategies and counter-strategies, and anticipate possible outcomes.

  For instance, when deciding whether to invest in a particular startup, an investor might want to consider how the startup's competitors might respond if the startup were to receive significant funding and scale rapidly. Game theory can provide a framework to analyze such competitive dynamics and make strategic decisions.
- **Nash Equilibrium:** Named after John Nash, this concept is a fundamental principle in game theory that describes a state of a game where no player can gain any advantage by unilaterally changing their strategy, assuming the other players keep their

> strategies unchanged. In the context of the cutting-edge industry, the Nash Equilibrium can be seen as a metaphorical "stable state" where each company in a competitive space is executing a strategy that is optimal given the strategies of its competitors. No company has an incentive to change its strategy unilaterally because doing so would put them in a less favorable position.
>
> Understanding this concept can help investors and entrepreneurs anticipate market dynamics and craft strategies that consider not just their actions, but also the potential reactions of other market players.

These tools are not meant to predict exact outcomes, as the real world of cutting-edge technology and venture capital is more complex and dynamic than any game model can fully capture. However, they provide useful frameworks for thinking about strategic interactions and potential outcomes.

The Role of Predictive Modeling in Decision-Making

In a world filled with data, the ability to create effective predictive models has become a crucial skill for venture capitalists, particularly when dealing with cutting-edge technology companies. With the sheer volume of data available from myriad sources — startups' performance metrics, market trends, scientific advancements, competitive landscape, and much more — venture capitalists can utilize statistical models and machine learning algorithms to parse this data and make well-informed predictions about potential outcomes. This will be further explored in the next chapter.

Predictive modeling in venture capital involves creating mathematical models that can predict an unknown event or future value based on known inputs. For instance, an algorithm could be developed to predict the success probability of a startup based on variables like the experience of the founding team, the uniqueness of the technology, the size of the market, and the current competition. This type of algorithm would use historical data to establish relationships between these factors and the startup's eventual success or failure.

Machine learning and artificial intelligence take predictive modelling a step further. Instead of relying on predetermined equations or algorithms, they use computational methods to "learn" from data.

Over time, as more data are fed into the model, it can adapt its predictions to better reflect the observed outcomes, continuously refining and improving its accuracy. This can be particularly useful when dealing with complex datasets with many variables or when the relationships between variables are non- linear or involve complex interactions.

Conclusion: Investing Is Poker, Not Chess nor Roulette

By now, it should be clear that the practice of venture capital — much like life itself — is more akin to a game of poker than a game of chess. While chess is deterministic and solely depends on the player's skill, and roulette only depends on the player's luck, poker, like life, involves both skill and luck. Chess pieces don't have concealed information; poker players have to play their cards close to their chest. Chess is about perfect knowledge and flawless execution; poker, on the other hand, is about making optimal decisions under uncertainty, about being right just often enough within the laws of probability.

This idea rings true in the world of venture capital, particularly in the cutting-edge field. Venture capitalists don't have perfect information about how a startup or a technology will perform in the future. They don't know what turns the market will take or what regulatory changes may arise. Instead, they must make the best decision possible based on the available information, the trends they can discern, and the risk they're willing to bear.

The beauty of embracing probabilistic thinking lies in its capacity to soothe the sting of bad outcomes. Recognizing that an unfortunate outcome doesn't necessarily denote a poor strategy — that it could simply be a manifestation of the inherent uncertainty — allows us to learn, adjust, and move forward without being paralyzed by past failures. A single card dealt, a single move made, a single company's performance does not define the entirety of our decision-making prowess.

In the end, life, like poker, isn't about being right all the time. It's about making decisions that are probabilistically favorable, continually learning, updating our knowledge, and enhancing our intuition. It's about becoming "less wrong" over time and understanding that each decision we make is an opportunity to learn, refine, and improve our game.

Rule #33
On Algorithmic Thinking

"Step by step, one goes very far."
J.R.R. Tolkien

Let's take it up a notch. Programming, once exclusive to computer scientists and engineers, has become essential for venture capitalists and decision-makers. It's like a superpower, allowing us to interpret and manipulate data to our advantage.

Today's world is data-driven. Every internet click, swipe, and interaction produces information that, when processed, offers potent insights. For venture capitalists and science-driven companies, these insights could mean backing a unicorn or missing an opportunity. However, the massive amount of data produced daily requires an algorithmic approach.

This chapter ties together statistics, Bayes' theorem, and probabilistic thinking with programming. In a way, programming naturally extends these topics. It packages statistical analysis principles, Bayes' theorem's conditional probabilities, and probabilistic thinking's foresight into algorithms, providing systematic procedures for problem-solving and decision-making.

In the sections ahead, we'll see how coding can help us understand complex data, encourage algorithmic thinking, and why these skills are vital in today's tech-driven world. We'll use real-world cases to show how combining knowledge of probabilistic decision making with practical coding skills can be transformative. Instead of a step- by-step guide, I'll use examples to get you excited to learn more independently. While I can't share my personal investment tools for understandable reasons, I'll certainly tell you how I've used them to create useful tools over time. As we progress, you'll see how statistics, Bayes' theorem, probabilistic thinking, and programming merge to form a powerful decision-making toolkit. Let's dive in and start shaping a smart investing mindset.

Programming as an Extension of the Mind

Programming is much more than a technical skill — it's a new way of approaching problems and thinking about the world. When you code, you're fundamentally restructuring your mind to think algorithmically. You learn to break down complex problems into manageable parts, to approach challenges step by step, and to create elegant solutions through logical reasoning.

The process of coding encourages an understanding of the problem's core and a clear definition of the desired outcome. Each line of code represents a building block, each function an abstract representation of a process, and the resulting program, a synthesized solution. This approach of problem decomposition, process abstraction, and solution synthesis extends far beyond the realm of software development — it's applicable to any complex problem-solving scenario.

In the world of cutting-edge science, two fields are particularly impactful: deep learning and data science. Deep learning, a subset of machine learning, uses neural networks with many layers (hence, "deep") to model and understand complex patterns. These deep neural networks are designed and refined through programming, requiring a keen understanding of both the problem at hand and the relevant mathematical principles. Data science, on the other hand, utilizes a combination of statistical methods, machine learning techniques, and programming to derive insights from data.

The beauty of programming is that it offers a form of intellectual leverage — it's like having an extension of your mind that tirelessly works for you, even while you sleep. Once you've written and run a program, it can process data, generate insights, or even make decisions on your behalf. And it can do so at scale, providing insights from datasets far larger than any human could manually process. It's as though you've multiplied your cognitive capabilities, augmenting your natural intelligence with the speed and scalability of digital computation.

This "background thinking" capability is incredibly beneficial in fields characterized by vast amounts of data and complex, multifaceted problems. With the power of programming, you can set your digital extension to work, retire for the evening, and wake up to new insights, fresh perspectives, or potential solutions. It's not an exaggeration to say that this ability to extend your mind through programming is one of the most potent advantages you can possess in the data-driven world of today.

The Importance of Coding Skills

You might find my approach unconventional, but I believe it will soon be mainstream. In our fast-paced 21st-century world, coding is becoming an essential skill, especially with the rise of large language models (LLMs). It's not just for computer scientists or software engineers, but for everyone, including investors.

Particularly in deep-tech and science-driven companies, coding is priceless. At its core, coding is about problem-solving. It requires structuring thoughts into an algorithm that solves a problem or completes a task. Coding trains you to think logically, breaking down problems into manageable parts and structuring them into a clear solution.

Algorithmic thinking isn't just about creating code — it's about structured thought processes. It's about logical sequencing, conditional reasoning, and understanding that different problems require different solutions. This cognitive structure lends itself well to the decision-making process, especially in the investing world.

One could argue that coding has become the new literacy. Just as writing allows you to organize your thoughts and convey your ideas to others, coding enables you to articulate your problem-solving process and create implementable solutions.

But unlike traditional literacy, the language of coding is continually evolving. New programming languages emerge, old ones get updated, and coding paradigms shift as technology advances. Furthermore, coding is easier thanks to artificial intelligence large language models such as ChatGPT.

This rapid pace of change might seem daunting, but it's actually an opportunity. The ability to code doesn't just enable you to create software — it changes your mindset, enhances your problem-solving abilities, and equips you to navigate a world increasingly driven by data and technology. It might seem like a significant investment of time and effort, but the returns in terms of skills acquired, problems solved, and opportunities opened are immeasurable.

In this chapter, we will delve into some personal examples that illustrate how coding can prove to be a potent tool in navigating the complex world of technology and venture capital. These case studies serve as testimonials to the transformative power of coding and its real-world implications.

Case Study 1: Predicting Trends in IPOs

One of the significant advantages of coding is its ability to analyze large datasets and uncover patterns and trends that would be impossible for a human to discern manually. This is particularly handy in the world of finance and venture capital, where making informed decisions is crucial.

Take, for example, the initial public offerings (IPOs) in the stock market. IPOs can be a chaotic time, filled with speculation, anticipation, and often, a great deal of volatility. Predicting how these IPOs will perform, and which sectors will be affected, is crucial for venture capitalists and investors.

I built a tool using Python, a high-level programming language prized for its simplicity and power, that could analyze the performance of IPOs in their first 15 days of trading. I consider this period as a gauge of the market's enthusiasm for a particular sector or technology. After these initial days, the performance of the company is largely driven by its leadership, its technology, and other specific factors.

Through coding, I was able to monitor the performance of various IPOs, categorize them based on their industry, technology, or other factors, and animate their performance over time. This gave me a dynamic, visual representation of how the market reacted to these companies, which sectors generated the most excitement, and where potential investment opportunities might lie.

Such an endeavor would be almost impossible to accomplish manually, given the sheer volume of data and the need for real-time analysis. However, with coding, I could automate the process, analyze the data, and draw insightful conclusions with relative ease.

Figure 48. A Simple Data Request

```
# (1)
import yfinance as yf
import matplotlib.pyplot as plt
import pandas as pd

# Get the stock data for Moderna for the last year
moderna = yf.Ticker("MRNA").history(period="2y")

moderna
```

Date	Open	High	Low	Close	Volume	Dividends	Stock Splits
2021-03-15	136.770004	143.850006	135.009995	143.660004	7321700	0	0
2021-03-16	148.500000	157.750000	145.839996	156.020004	16991600	0	0
2021-03-17	150.250000	152.082993	143.250000	147.550003	12884900	0	0
2021-03-18	144.449997	147.610001	140.860001	141.460007	7135800	0	0
2021-03-19	143.059998	145.179993	138.529999	143.740005	6933700	0	0
...	...	...	...	...	...	...	...
2023-03-07	143.779999	145.740005	139.679993	141.050003	2777700	0	0
2023-03-08	140.320007	142.529999	140.320007	142.080002	2193800	0	0
2023-03-09	142.039993	144.029999	136.516006	137.360001	3092600	0	0
2023-03-10	137.059998	141.550003	135.591995	138.289993	3885600	0	0
2023-03-13	138.490005	148.940002	138.059998	147.899994	5676700	0	0

503 rows × 7 columns

```
# Plot the close prices
plt.figure(figsize=(20, 6)) # (2) × fixed afterwards
plt.plot(moderna['Close'])
plt.xlabel('Time')
plt.ylabel('Close Price')
plt.title('Price Action for Moderna')
plt.show()
```

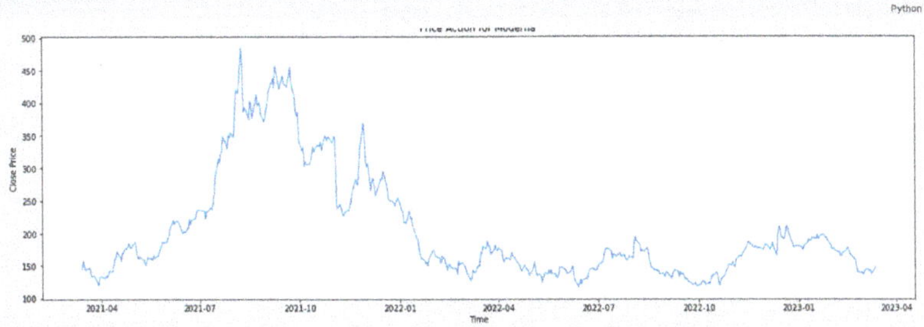


```
# Add new column 'opportunity' with True or False
moderna["opportunity"] = (moderna["Close"] - moderna["Close"].shift(1))/moderna["Close"].shift(1) < -0.15
moderna
```

With the advent of Python libraries like yfinance, downloading and visualizing stock performance data has become more straightforward than ever.

- You can replace "MRNA" with the ticker symbol of the stock you're interested in. Also, ensure that your start and end dates cover the period you want to investigate.
- The above commands will create a line graph of Apple's closing price over the two-year period.
- This is a very basic example, but the possibilities are vast. With a few more lines of code, you could calculate and plot moving averages, generate trading signals, compute technical indicators, detect trends, train neural networks to predict stock behavior and so much more.

Figure 49. IPO Trends

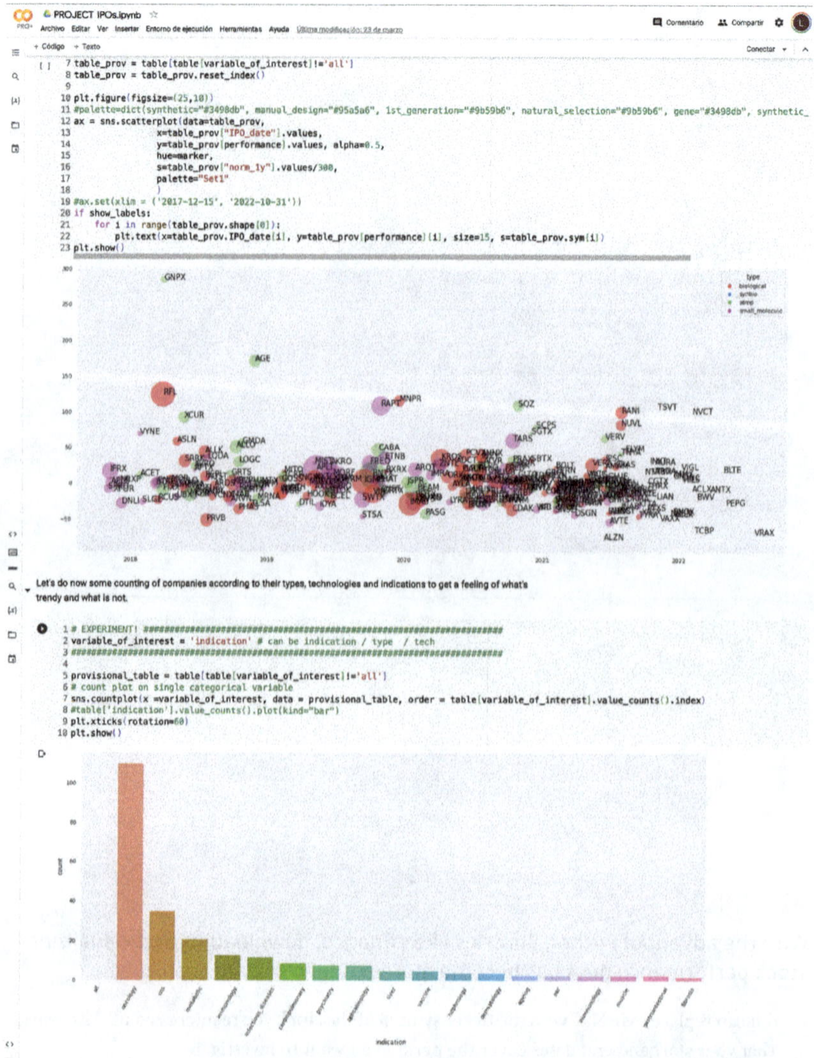

In today's digital age, where immense volumes of data are at our fingertips, the capacity to mine, analyze, and interpret this data is paramount. This is especially true in the world of investment and financial decision-making, where every bit of information can translate into potential gains or losses. So, let's create a tool to analyze the trends in initial public offerings (IPOs), which can hint at emerging popular technologies.

- With the advancement of programming, we can harness this information in more ways than ever before. A compelling illustration of this lies in analyzing the performance of biotech companies listed on the NASDAQ, specifically during their initial public offerings (IPOs).

- Why focus on the IPOs? The answer lies in their potential to signal market trends. Over the years, I've developed a system that uses these data to detect trends in a consistent and reliable manner. My analysis suggests that a stock's performance in the weeks following its IPO can be a strong indicator of the market's reaction to a particular sector, technology, or disease area the company is working in.
- Of course, the performance of a stock a few weeks after an IPO may be influenced by myriad factors. However, at the time of its market debut, the company's performance gives us a unique insight into how quickly the market reacts to that specific sector. This rapid reaction can be a crucial factor in identifying emerging trends.
- Imagine having a tool that continuously analyzes the performance of the latest IPOs in the biotech space, categorizing them by technology, therapeutic indication, or any other parameter you consider relevant. Such a tool could then compare the performances of these companies to identify and visualize trends.
- Consider the following example: Let's say we have data from companies operating in four different categories: small molecules, biologicals, advanced therapies, and synthetic biology. We represent time on the x-axis and the performance on the y-axis, with the total market cap represented as a diameter. By doing so, we can visualize how these companies move week-by-week.
- Suddenly, we notice several oncology companies in the advanced therapy space ascending the graph, their circles ballooning. This signals that cell therapy in a particular oncological indication is gaining traction, becoming increasingly popular. This detection of the trend could provide an early signal before it becomes apparent to a broader audience.
- In summary, the ability to efficiently retrieve and process large amounts of data provides us with a significant advantage in today's information-driven world. With this approach, the performance of stocks around the time of their IPOs becomes more than just numbers on a page; it becomes a valuable tool to understand market reactions and trends, giving us insights that could potentially guide more informed investment decisions.
- The case of biotech IPOs exemplifies the transformative power of combining programming skills with an in-depth understanding of the sector. This blend of data science and market know-how could well be the next frontier in investment strategy.

Case Study 2: Quant to Predict with Deep Learning the Direction of Value in the Nasdaq Biotech

Deep learning, a subset of machine learning, offers a potent set of tools for making predictions in complex domains. It becomes even more powerful when combined with the insights offered by Quantitative Finance. I used this potent combination to predict the direction of value in the Nasdaq Biotech index.

For those unacquainted, quantitative finance or "quant" involves using mathematical models and large datasets to make predictions about financial markets. I decided to apply this approach to the Nasdaq Biotech index, a performance benchmark for companies listed on the Nasdaq stock exchange that are classified as either biotechnology or pharmaceuticals.

Initially, I started this project for fun — a way to delve deeper into the world of quants. However, as the accuracy of my predictions improved, it turned into an interesting challenge. What began as an amateur exploration of quantitative finance and deep learning turned into a tool for making strategic investment decisions. At the heart of this tool was a deep learning model, trained to analyze patterns in the Nasdaq Biotech index and predict future trends.

In the vast and complex financial markets, the quest to accurately predict the future performance of specific companies is often an exercise in futility. Myriad factors are at play, including global economic indicators, specific industry trends, regulatory environments, and individual company performance, making prediction an overwhelmingly intricate task. In my perspective, however, there's another approach that could provide a slight statistical edge: focusing on the behavior of the people who make up the market.

Market movements are, in essence, a reflection of the aggregate decisions of countless individuals. Investors, both retail and institutional, bring their emotions, biases, perceptions, and predictions to the table. These human elements, when aggregated, can often form predictable patterns. Rather than trying to decipher the future trajectories of specific companies, a more effective strategy might be to predict what these "people" will do.

Consider this example: When news breaks about a revolutionary technological breakthrough by a company, it's natural for people to react. Some might feel excitement and invest heavily, anticipating a massive surge in the company's stock price. Others might become wary, considering the inherent risks in the technology's adoption and potential regulatory hurdles.

As these individual actions aggregate, we can observe market movements — a surge in the company's stock price due to increased buying, followed by a potential correction as more cautious investors step in. These patterns, driven by human emotion and reaction, can be more predictable than the company's actual future performance.

And more importantly, we don't need to predict the future perfectly. We just need a slight statistical advantage. Given the volume of transactions in the financial markets, even a slight edge can, over time, result in significant gains, thanks to the law of large numbers. As we explored a few chapters ago, this law suggests that as the number of trials (in our case, transactions or investments) increases, the actual outcome will converge to the expected outcome.

Let's imagine that our strategy of predicting human behavior in the stock market gives us a slight edge, say a 55% chance of making a profitable trade. In a single transaction, this advantage might not make a noticeable difference. But when you make hundreds, thousands, or even millions of trades, that 55% advantage starts to significantly impact the overall performance.

In essence, my perspective is that we should shift our focus from attempting to predict the inherently unpredictable — specific company performances — to something slightly more within our grasp: human behavior. And though this strategy doesn't guarantee success and requires nuanced understanding and analysis, it might give us that slight statistical edge that, leveraged effectively, can lead to substantial gains in the long run. This viewpoint might not be mainstream, but as any investor in the fast-paced, ever-evolving world of finance will tell you — sometimes, the unconventional path makes all the difference. And that's what quant hedge funds do.

Case Study 3: Automating Information Gathering and Report Generation

In the information age, staying up-to-date with the latest research and trends can be a Herculean task, especially in fast-paced fields

Figure 50. Can the Stock Market Be Predicted?

```python
print(f'------------------------------------------ DRAWDOWNS DURING THE BACKTEST PERIOD (top five drawdown periods) ------------------------------------------')
qs.plots.drawdown(intel, figsize=(15.95, 5))
qs.plots.drawdowns_periods(intel, figsize=(15.95, 5))

print(' ')
print(' ')
print(' ')
```

[18] Python

```
REPORT FOR ALPHA FACTOR:        (db['DPO_20']) * (db['prediction'])

The best measure of return is not capital, because it depends greatly on the timing of the first big return. We can estimate better the potential of an
alpha factor by adding all the log returns (percent_no_compund) and even better, substracting the greatest outliers, that is, the max log return and the
min log return (percentage_no_compound_no_outliers):
Percent_no_compound:                    -1.13
Percentage_no_compound_no_outliers:     -1.17

My personal surrogates of efficiency for alpha factors are three: (1) LPS_Return: shows the percent_no_compound divided by the maximum drawdown (a measure
of risk/reward), (2) LPS_Quality: Same as (1) but adjusted for the number of trades, as a restrictive alpha factor will achieve less return if it trades not
too often, and (3) LPS_Optimus: A sophisticated combination of (1) and (2) with a threshold that when not met gives a measurement of zero (meaning I dont
accept the alpha factor in my tradeable quants).
LPS_Return:          -1.19
LPS_Quality:         -0.41
LPS_Optimus:         0.00
CAPITAL:             85.44

Mean (Alpha_factor):   -0.0020        Mean (Benchmark):     0.0034        Trades:     578

Qs: Q1 2020: 0.00  |  Q2 2020: 0.00  |  Q3 2020: 0.00  |  Q4 2020: 0.25  |  Q1 2021: -0.47  |  Q2 2021: -0.27  |  Q3 2021: -0.39  |  Q4 2021: -0.12
Negative months:     11 (-2.19)
Negative quarters:   4 (-1.26)

Max_drawdown:        0.95           Avg_return:          -0.00
Calmar:              -0.83          Avg_loss:            -0.05
Sortino:             -0.67          Avg_win:             0.05
Sharpe:              -0.45              No_outliers:              -0.01164
CAGR:                -0.79              Geometric_mean:           -0.004
Win_ratio:           7.60           Volatility:          1.08
Win_rate:            0.47           Risk_return_ratio:   -0.03
Gain_to_pain_ratio:  -0.09          Outlier_loss_ratio:  3.30
```

-- NORMAL DISTRIBUTION OF RETURNS (alpha factor versus benchmark) --

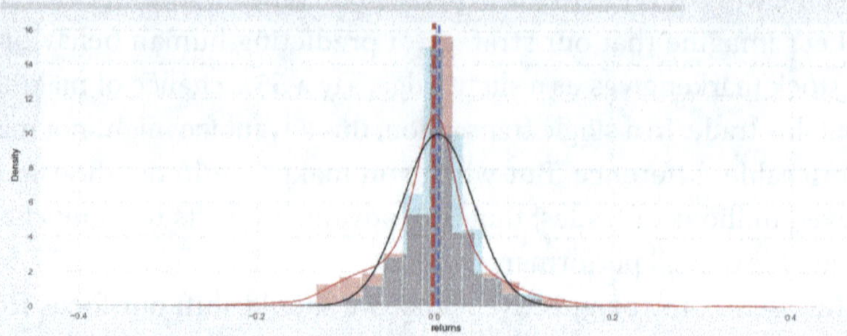

-- VISUALIZATION OF LOG RETURNS (identify max: 0.39 and min: -0.35 that will be removed) --

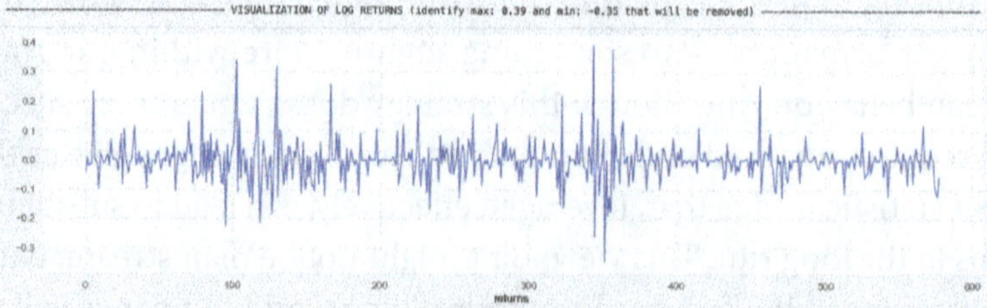

-- MONTHLY RETURNS (twenty five months, see drawdowns) --

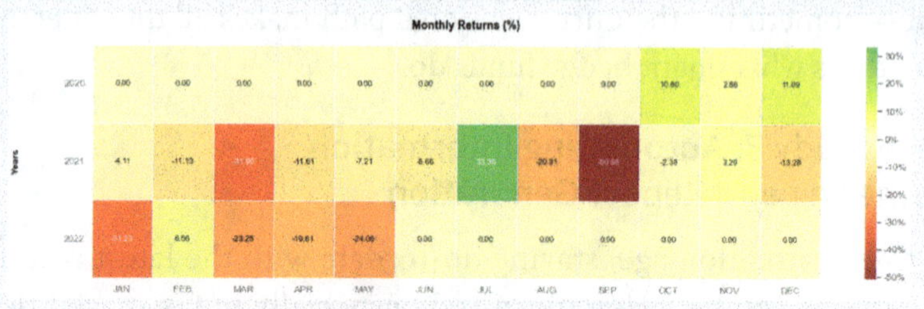

Rule #33: On Algorithmic Thinking

The age-old question "Can the stock market be predicted?" has sparked intense debates among economists and investors alike. As we delve into the arguments supporting both sides, it's important to begin with a disclaimer: This is not intended as financial advice. It merely provides an exploration of different viewpoints and theories.

- The Random Walk Theory, proposed by Burton Malkiel in his seminal book *A Random Walk Down Wall Street*, posits that stock prices change randomly, making them impossible to predict. This theory argues that the market's efficiency ensures all relevant information is quickly incorporated into a stock's price, meaning any future changes are the result of unforeseen events. Consequently, no amount of analysis can provide a guaranteed prediction of stock price movements.
- Detractors of this theory argue that while the market may be efficient, it is not perfectly so. They cite instances of market bubbles, anomalies, and behavioral biases as evidence of inefficiencies that could be exploited for predictive purposes.
- A tool often employed in the effort to predict market trends is Python, a high-level programming language prized for its simplicity and power. Python's extensive libraries and modules allow for the analysis and visualization of large datasets, making it a popular choice among financial analysts and quants. Through Python, analysts can implement machine learning models, backtest strategies, and conduct sentiment analysis on news articles and social media posts, among other tasks.
- However, when using tools like Python for predictive purposes, it is essential to understand the correct statistical distributions to apply. For example, the common assumption of using a Normal Distribution for stock returns often fails, as it underestimates the occurrence of extreme events. Empirical studies have shown that stock returns often follow a distribution with "fat tails" such as the Student's T distribution, which gives higher probabilities to extreme events.
- Another peril to beware of when predicting the stock market is the issue of "forward peeking" or "look-ahead bias." This occurs when a model unintentionally uses information that would not have been available or known during the period being analyzed, thus inflating its predictive accuracy. It's crucial to prevent such data leakage when backtesting predictive models to ensure reliable results.
- While the discussion around predicting the stock market is complex and fraught with challenges, it's hard to ignore the success of quant hedge funds. In fact, some of the most successful hedge funds in the United States are quant-focused, such as Renaissance Technologies and Two Sigma. These firms employ sophisticated quantitative models to identify and exploit market asymmetries, leveraging advanced machine learning techniques and vast amounts of data. Their success suggests that, despite its complexity and inherent uncertainties, the market may present patterns or asymmetries that, when accurately identified and interpreted, could be advantageous. While this approach certainly doesn't guarantee success and requires significant expertise and resources, the achievements of these quant hedge funds make a compelling case for the potential of algorithmic finance.
- In any case, it is a field where statistical understanding, sound computational skills, and financial acumen intertwine. As such, those venturing into this domain should do so with caution, a deep understanding of the underlying principles, and a healthy respect for the unpredictability of the market.

Figure 51. Value Creation Steps That Can Be Fed to AI

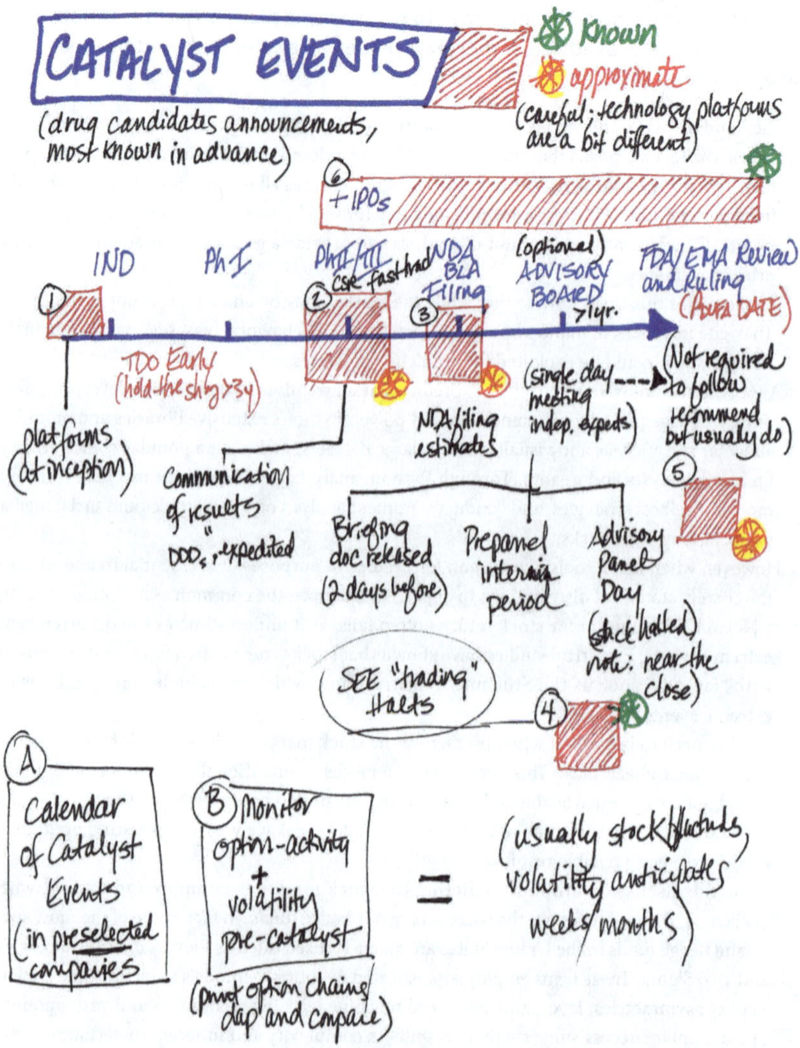

In the context of investing, catalyst events can provide valuable data points to feed into an artificial intelligence deep neural network (DNN).

- **A catalyst event,** often simply referred to as a catalyst, is an occurrence that causes a significant change in the price of a security (such as a stock or bond). Catalyst events can be a myriad of things and typically lead to more volatility, which can present both risks and opportunities for investors. Deep-tech and biotech companies exist in a dynamic environment, where they can choose to go public or initiate an initial public offering (IPO) at various stages of their life cycle. The decision depends on several factors, including their developmental progress, market conditions, and strategic considerations. A company may decide to go public even before filing an investigational new drug (IND) application, signaling the shift from preclinical to clinical development. Alternatively, they may opt for an IPO upon the completion of various clinical trial phases, such as phase 1 or phase 2.

- In the context of pharmaceutical or biotechnology companies, catalyst events can be related to drug development stages, for example:
  - **Clinical trial results:** The announcement of results from a clinical trial can cause a substantial change in a company's stock price. Positive results can lead to an increase in price, while negative results can cause a steep drop.
  - **Regulatory decisions:** The approval (or denial) of a drug by regulatory bodies like the U.S. Food and Drug Administration (FDA) can significantly impact a company's stock price.
  - **Patent decisions:** Gaining or losing a patent can impact a company's exclusive rights to manufacture and sell a drug, thereby impacting its stock price.
  - **Partnerships or M&A activity:** Announcement of a strategic partnership or a merger and acquisition event can also cause significant movement in stock price.
- For instance, a positive clinical trial result or a successful new drug application/biologics license application filing can lead to a surge in the company's stock price. Conversely, negative results or regulatory setbacks can trigger a drop. These catalyst events can serve as valuable data points for a deep neural network (DNN), aiding in understanding and predicting market trends.
- **DNNs,** as a subset of machine learning algorithms, are particularly well-suited for pattern-recognition tasks. In the context of biotech investing, they can utilize their capabilities to analyze and interpret catalyst events, with the goal of predicting potential market movements. Critical moments such as the new drug application (NDA), biologics license application (BLA) filing, or the Prescription Drug User Fee Act (PDUFA) date, when the FDA is set to complete its review, can significantly influence a company's stock price.
- However, to make the model's predictions more robust and informed, we can incorporate additional data points into the DNN. This could include the type of technology or field the company operates in — whether it's small molecules, biologics, advanced therapy medicinal products (ATMPs), or synthetic biology (synbio). The specific indication or disease the company's products target can also be a valuable data point. My own models include literally hundreds of other automatized data points. You will never run short of them to keep on experimenting by adding or subtracting elements to feed the AI.
- Furthermore, your subjective evaluation of a company's value, derived from your understanding and analysis of the company, can serve as an additional layer of information. This can capture aspects not necessarily reflected in public data but potentially influential in investment decisions, such as the management's competence, the robustness of the company's intellectual property, or the potential for its technology.
- By feeding these varied data points — catalyst events, technology type, indication, and subjective value perception — into a DNN, we aim to uncover hidden patterns or relationships that might be less apparent or too complex for manual analysis. This sophisticated AI tool can thereby assist in generating insights to inform investment decisions.
- However, as with all predictive models and particularly in the often volatile and unpredictable stock market, predictions made by these AI tools should be interpreted with caution. The goal is not to rely solely on these predictions but to use them as one among several tools in your decision-making arsenal. A well-rounded investment strategy should consider these AI-generated insights while also incorporating traditional financial analysis, sector knowledge, and common sense.

Figure 52. Deep Neural Networks Predictive Analysis

```
train_AI(
        EPOCHS = 1000,
        MINIBATCHES = True,
        BATCH_SIZE = 20000,
        MINIBATCHES_TEST = True,
        BATCH_TEST_SIZE = 100000,
        REGULARIZATION = None,
        STEPS = 50,
        SAVE_ABOVE = 10,
        SHOW_PLOT = False)
```

```
TRAINING REPORT:
--------------------------------------------------------------------------------
Model | Epochs: 1000
Model | Minibatches ||||| Train: (True, 20000) | Test: (True, 100000)
Model | Steps: 50
Model | Loss nn.L1Loss()
Model | Optimizer: torch.optim.AdamW(model.parameters(), lr=LEARNING_RATE)
Model | Learning rate: 0.005
Model | Regularization: None
Model | Total parameters: 82209
--------------------------------------------------------------------------------
--------------------------------------------------------------------------------
Time per epoch: 0.24 seconds
--------------------------------------------------------------------------------
--------------------------------------------------------------------------------
SAVED: 50/20000/100000 => T: 0.04810 | Te: 0.04537 | STRENGTH: 960.12 | 1Q: 16.7390 | LINEARITY: 57.35794 | Top: 1.75 | Five: 1.27 | Ten: 0.89 |
QUANTIZATION: 16.7390 | 1.69208 | -0.13461 | -1.85706 | -11.33375 | SCORE: nan | MINIBATCHES: True | BATCH SIZE: 20000 | STEPS: 50 | zero: 0.0000
NEGATIVES: First hundred: 0 | First thousand: 0 | First ten thousand: 1183 | First quant: 207 |
--------------------------------------------------------------------------------
--------------------------------------------------------------------------------
SAVED: 100/20000/100000 => T: 0.04461 | Te: 0.04440 | STRENGTH: 995.35 | 1Q: 16.6400 | LINEARITY: 59.81689 | Top: 1.51 | Five: 1.15 | Ten: 0.95 |
QUANTIZATION: 16.6400 | 1.96336 | -0.40349 | -2.02993 | -11.87862 | SCORE: nan | MINIBATCHES: True | BATCH SIZE: 20000 | STEPS: 50 | zero: 0.0000
NEGATIVES: First hundred: 0 | First thousand: 0 | First ten thousand: 1137 | First quant: 285 |
--------------------------------------------------------------------------------
150/20000/100000 ==>   T: 0.04291 | Te: 0.04362 | STRENGTH: 857.37 | 1Q: 14.7824 (0/54/1368) | LINEARITY: 57.99924 >>> Top: 1.40 | Five: 1.23 |
200/20000/100000 ==>   T: 0.04190 | Te: 0.04468 | STRENGTH: 923.25 | 1Q: 15.1270 (0/129/1663) | LINEARITY: 61.03291 >>> Top: 3.61 | Five: 1.77
250/20000/100000 ==>   T: 0.04083 | Te: 0.04354 | STRENGTH: 944.80 | 1Q: 15.5772 (0/55/1426) | LINEARITY: 60.65278 >>> Top: 4.97 | Five: 2.48 |
300/20000/100000 ==>   T: 0.03984 | Te: 0.04347 | STRENGTH: 861.47 | 1Q: 14.3365 (0/135/1578) | LINEARITY: 60.08937 >>> Top: 4.97 | Five: 2.05
350/20000/100000 ==>   T: 0.03977 | Te: 0.04353 | STRENGTH: 900.53 | 1Q: 14.6893 (0/149/1655) | LINEARITY: 61.30531 >>> Top: 1.25 | Five: 1.31
400/20000/100000 ==>   T: 0.03798 | Te: 0.04377 | STRENGTH: 950.68 | 1Q: 15.2633 (0/94/1564) | LINEARITY: 62.28531 >>> Top: 1.43 | Five: 1.08 |
450/20000/100000 ==>   T: 0.03846 | Te: 0.04310 | STRENGTH: 940.45 | 1Q: 15.2641 (0/121/1543) | LINEARITY: 61.61218 >>> Top: 1.64 | Five: 1.44
500/20000/100000 ==>   T: 0.03783 | Te: 0.04264 | STRENGTH: 968.37 | 1Q: 15.6530 (0/54/1402) | LINEARITY: 61.86471 >>> Top: 4.97 | Five: 2.06 |
550/20245/101000 ==>   T: 0.03804 | Te: 0.04333 | STRENGTH: 925.06 | 1Q: 14.9309 (1/119/1435) | LINEARITY: 61.95591 >>> Top: 1.17 | Five: 1.67
600/20495/102000 ==>   T: 0.03669 | Te: 0.04356 | STRENGTH: 957.00 | 1Q: 15.4777 (0/83/1500) | LINEARITY: 61.83090 >>> Top: 1.31 | Five: 1.42 |
650/20745/103000 ==>   T: 0.03682 | Te: 0.04289 | STRENGTH: 945.23 | 1Q: 15.3345 (0/78/1336) | LINEARITY: 61.64080 >>> Top: 3.39 | Five: 1.64 |
700/20995/104000 ==>   T: 0.03601 | Te: 0.04263 | STRENGTH: 989.35 | 1Q: 15.9115 (1/73/1346) | LINEARITY: 62.17805 >>> Top: 4.97 | Five: 3.16 |
750/21245/105000 ==>   T: 0.03477 | Te: 0.04433 | STRENGTH: 968.19 | 1Q: 15.6115 (0/125/1420) | LINEARITY: 62.01801 >>> Top: 3.61 | Five: 1.93
800/21495/106000 ==>   T: 0.03526 | Te: 0.04282 | STRENGTH: 975.75 | 1Q: 15.8472 (6/68/1330) | LINEARITY: 61.57227 >>> Top: 3.39 | Five: 2.36 |
850/21745/107000 ==>   T: 0.03504 | Te: 0.04404 | STRENGTH: 954.97 | 1Q: 15.7108 (2/67/1403) | LINEARITY: 60.78434 >>> Top: 3.61 | Five: 1.46 |
900/21995/108000 ==>   T: 0.03404 | Te: 0.04340 | STRENGTH: 906.82 | 1Q: 14.8607 (3/99/1587) | LINEARITY: 61.02147 >>> Top: 2.27 | Five: 1.46 |
950/22245/109000 ==>   T: 0.03406 | Te: 0.04401 | STRENGTH: 952.27 | 1Q: 15.5266 (2/72/1442) | LINEARITY: 61.33129 >>> Top: 2.03 | Five: 1.99 |
1000/22495/110000 ==>  T: 0.03428 | Te: 0.04386 | STRENGTH: 884.90 | 1Q: 14.5407 (4/105/1609) | LINEARITY: 60.85649 >>> Top: 3.39 | Five: 1.89
```

- The figure presented here illustrates a training session of an artificial intelligence (AI) model aimed at predicting stock market behaviors. As depicted in the upper graph, the loss — or error rate — decreases over each iteration, signifying the AI model's improving comprehension of the relationship between the parameters used to predict a company's performance and the company's actual performance.
- On the adjacent page to the right, a detailed report is showcased. The x-axis represents the performance of various stocks, while the y-axis represents the score assigned by the AI to each stock on any given day. Interestingly, the top 100 predictions are all profitable, depicted in green. The predictions ranked from 101 to 200 are predominantly also in the green, as symbolized by the area to the right of the red vertical line.
- As we move further down the graph, the last predictions are depicted in red, indicating a loss. A linear regression is used to emphasize the relationship in the graph, which **suggests that the AI system successfully detects a signal** amidst the stock market's substantial noise. Therefore, the AI model effectively separates valuable signals from background noise, offering predictions on company performance.

```
1 report()
2 stats_forward_backward_pass()
```

```
---------------------------------------------------------------------------------------------------------------
SAVED: T: 0.03428 | Te: 0.04386 | STRENGTH: 953.26 | 1Q: 16.2994 | LINEARITY: 58.48413109779358 | Hundred: 0.9613
QUANTIZATION: 16.29941314458847 | 1.8895693123340607 | -0.2020806772634387 | -2.0829519256949425 | -11.594319343566895 | lr= 0.005
---------------------------------------------------------------------------------------------------------------
```

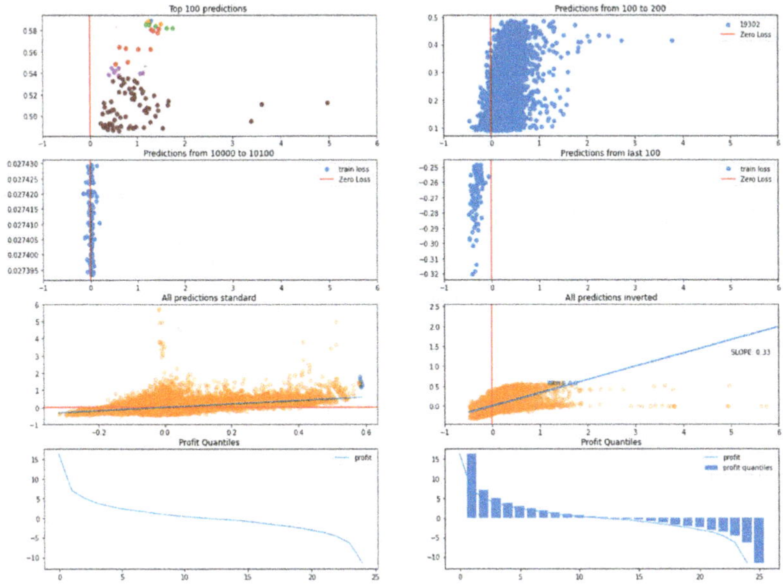


```
STATISTICS OF FORWARD PASS:
---------------------------------------------------------------------------------------------------------------
```

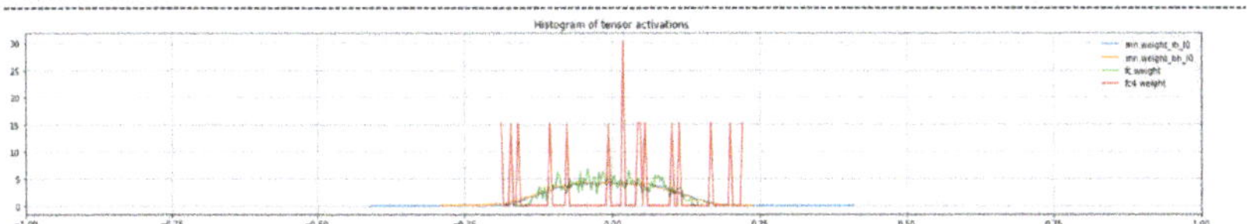


```
STATISTICS OF BACKWARD PASS:
---------------------------------------------------------------------------------------------------------------
```

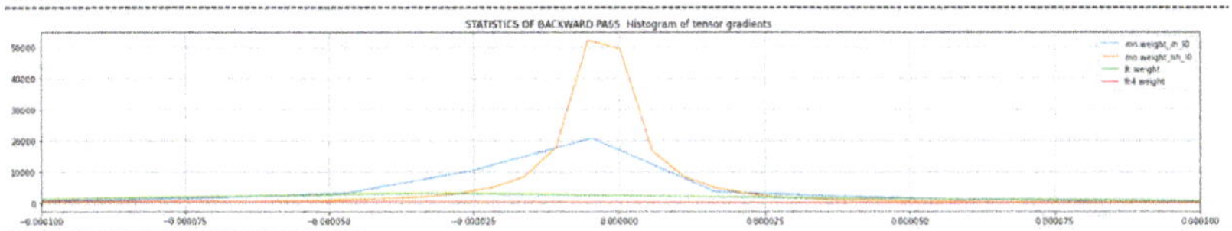


```
PERCENTAGE OF GRADIENT CHANGE USING THIS LEARNING RATE:
---------------------------------------------------------------------------------------------------------------
```

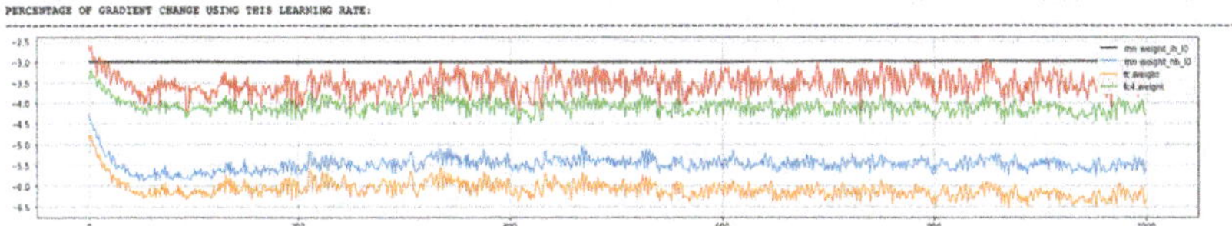

Figure 53. My Own Quant Architecture

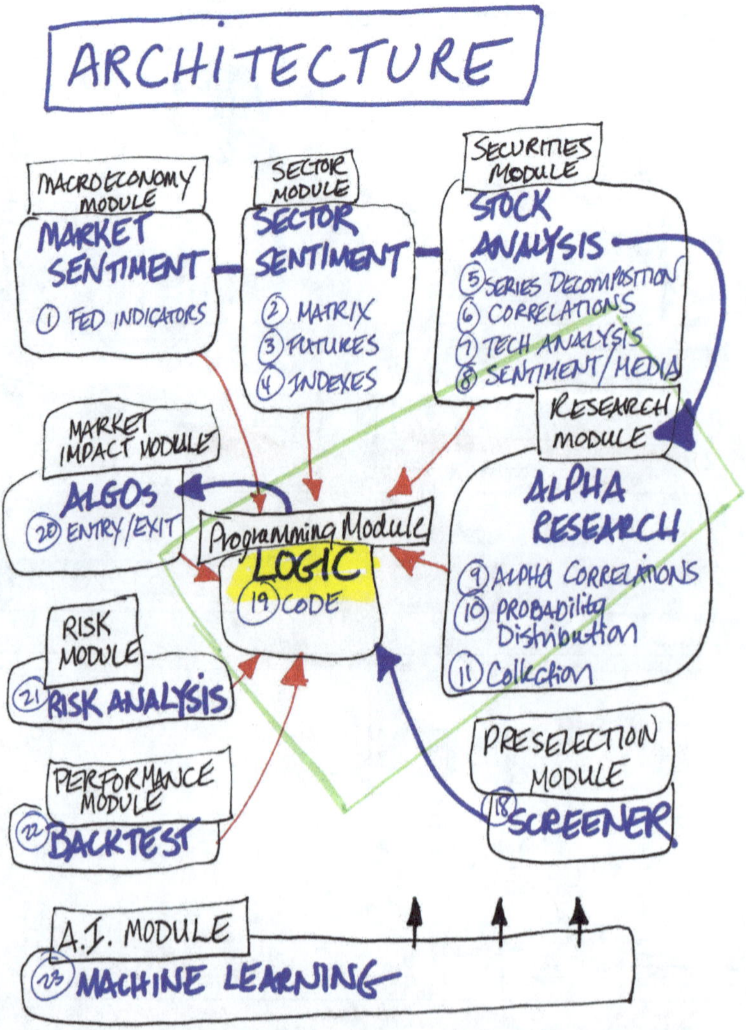

The figure represents a complex and modular architecture for quantitative trading strategy, inspired by numerous models observed over years of study. Each module has its distinct function, feeding into the overall trading strategy.

It's worth noting that while this model is built based on personal understanding and does not necessarily represent the exact architecture of any existing quant hedge fund, it provides a comprehensive overview of the factors involved in the operation of such funds.

- **General Architecture:** This architecture is complex and dynamic, encompassing a broad array of strategies and techniques. Despite this complexity, the central principle is simple: Any signal, no matter how imperfect, that gives a statistical edge over the market can lead to profitability over time due to the law of large numbers. This principle underpins the system, and each module is designed to help identify these beneficial signals amid the noise of the market.

- **Macro Economy Module:** The system begins with a Macro Economy Module that monitors overall market sentiment, using data from sources like Fed indicators or aggregated market trends. This provides a broad perspective on the general direction of the markets.
- **Sector Module:** The second module focuses more closely on the specific sector of interest. For instance, if investing in the biotech industry, one might study the NASDAQ Biotech Index, sector-specific ETFs or related futures.
- **Securities Module:** Moving further into specifics, the Securities Module allows for analysis on a stock-by-stock basis. This could include looking at price action, identifying correlations, employing technical analysis, or even scouring social media for sentiment related to particular stocks.
- **Research Module:** Next is the Research Module, where "alpha research" is conducted. An "alpha" in this context is any potential signal or strategy that might give an edge over the market. Various hypothetical scenarios are tested here, and these are backtested to verify their effectiveness.
- **The Pre-selection Module:** This module is akin to a stock screener, narrowing down the field of potential investments according to predetermined criteria, such as companies of a particular size or with high recent trading volume.
- **The Programming Module:** This module contains the code necessary to execute the strategies, taking into account the "market impact" of the fund's own buying or selling activity, to avoid disrupting normal market flow.
- **Risk Analysis Module:** Risk is managed by a dedicated Risk Analysis Module, which continuously assesses and monitors various types of risks associated with the investment strategies. The module uses advanced analytics and statistical models to predict potential risk scenarios and their impacts on the portfolio. It also sets risk thresholds and triggers alerts for proactive risk management.
- **The Performance Module:** This module tracks the effectiveness of the strategies in real time, allowing for constant re-evaluation and refinement.
- **AI Module:** Lastly, an AI underpins the entire system, enhancing each step with artificial intelligence's capability to decipher patterns from complex datasets and make predictions.

• **Alpha:** An "alpha" refers to a strategy or a signal that could potentially give an investor an edge over the market. Alpha is a term used in finance to describe a strategy's ability to beat the market, or its "edge." More specifically, it is also a measure of performance, indicating how much an investment has returned above or below its benchmark. A positive alpha indicates that an investment has outperformed its benchmark, while a negative alpha indicates underperformance. In the case of a quantitative hedge fund, an alpha could be a unique pattern or trend that has been identified through backtesting or other forms of analysis.

For instance, a strategy might suggest that buying a stock after it has dropped 30% in value and then selling it after a week could result in a profitable trade. The effectiveness of an alpha is typically tested through backtesting, where historical data is used to see how a strategy would have performed in the past. It's important to note that the effectiveness of an alpha might diminish over time as more traders become aware of it, or if market conditions change. So, it's crucial for investment strategies to evolve and adapt over time.

such as biotechnology. As the volume of data continues to explode, manual data gathering and report generation can become increasingly time-consuming and impractical. Recognizing this challenge, we can code a tool to automate these tasks, enhancing productivity and efficiency.

The tool I developed was designed to trawl through a multitude of published papers relevant to any field of interest. It extracts crucial data, interprets it, and compiles it into structured reports that are easy to digest. In other words, it transforms a mountain of complex data into manageable, actionable insights, essentially serving as a virtual research assistant.

What sets this tool apart is its ability to go beyond mere data extraction. It applies natural language processing (NLP), a subset of AI, to understand the context and relevance of the information it collects. This feature allows it to summarize complex scientific papers and highlight key findings accurately, thereby saving us a significant amount of time.

As a result, one can keep up with the latest trends and research in biotechnology without having to read through an overwhelming number of papers and articles. This tool has not only optimized our information-gathering process but also enriched our decision-making capabilities by ensuring we are always armed with the latest insights.

However, it's important to remember that while AI and machine learning can dramatically enhance our ability to process and understand information, they don't replace the need for careful reading, thoughtful analysis, and informed judgment. Rather, they complement these skills, providing us with an efficient way to navigate the vast scientific literature, identify promising opportunities or trends, and make data-driven decisions.

As we move forward, we can expect AI to play an increasingly significant role in helping us manage the deluge of data, extract valuable insights, and accelerate scientific discovery and innovation. Still, the human element — our ability to ask insightful questions, perceive subtle connections, and make strategic decisions — will remain essential. The goal, then, is not to replace human expertise with AI, but to leverage AI to enhance and extend our capabilities.

Case Study 4: Building an AI Analyst for Biotechnology

One of the most rewarding and exciting outcomes of my programming journey has been the creation of an artificial intelligence analyst, fondly nicknamed "AIA." AIA, a highly specialized tool, was conceived to help me and my team navigate the complex and rapidly evolving world of biotechnology more effectively.

AIA is a cutting-edge AI model, trained primarily on the GPT-3 architecture from OpenAI, but with a twist. Instead of being a general-purpose AI, AIA has been finetuned (trained) for biotechnology. She feeds on articles, papers from renowned journals like *Nature, Science, The New England Journal of Medicine,* and numerous other sources. She peruses news, books, and even the entire history of my email exchanges. She's a relentless learner, training 24/7, staying abreast of conferences, symposia, and other relevant events.

AIA's abilities transcend mere data gathering. She excels in complex problem solving, often discreetly assisting me during board meetings and other important gatherings via WhatsApp, providing quick, insightful responses to intricate issues. Her capacity to process and synthesize a wealth of information in real time has made her an invaluable asset to our team, significantly enhancing our decision-making prowess.

In an industry where being ahead of the curve can mean the difference between success and failure, having AIA on our side has proved to be a tremendous advantage. She epitomizes the power of coding, demonstrating how it can be leveraged to build tools that dramatically augment human capabilities in specialized domains.

Case Study 5: Monte Carlo Simulations for Decision-Making

In the realm of decision-making, particularly when dealing with complex problems or an environment rife with uncertainty,

Monte Carlo simulations have served as a powerful tool for me and my team. Named after the famous casino town, Monte Carlo simulations use randomness to solve problems that may be deterministic in principle but are too complex for a simple deterministic solution.

As an example, we've leveraged this technique in situations where we've needed to balance between exploration and exploitation — a common dilemma faced in the field of biotechnology. When we're

Figure 54. AI Reports

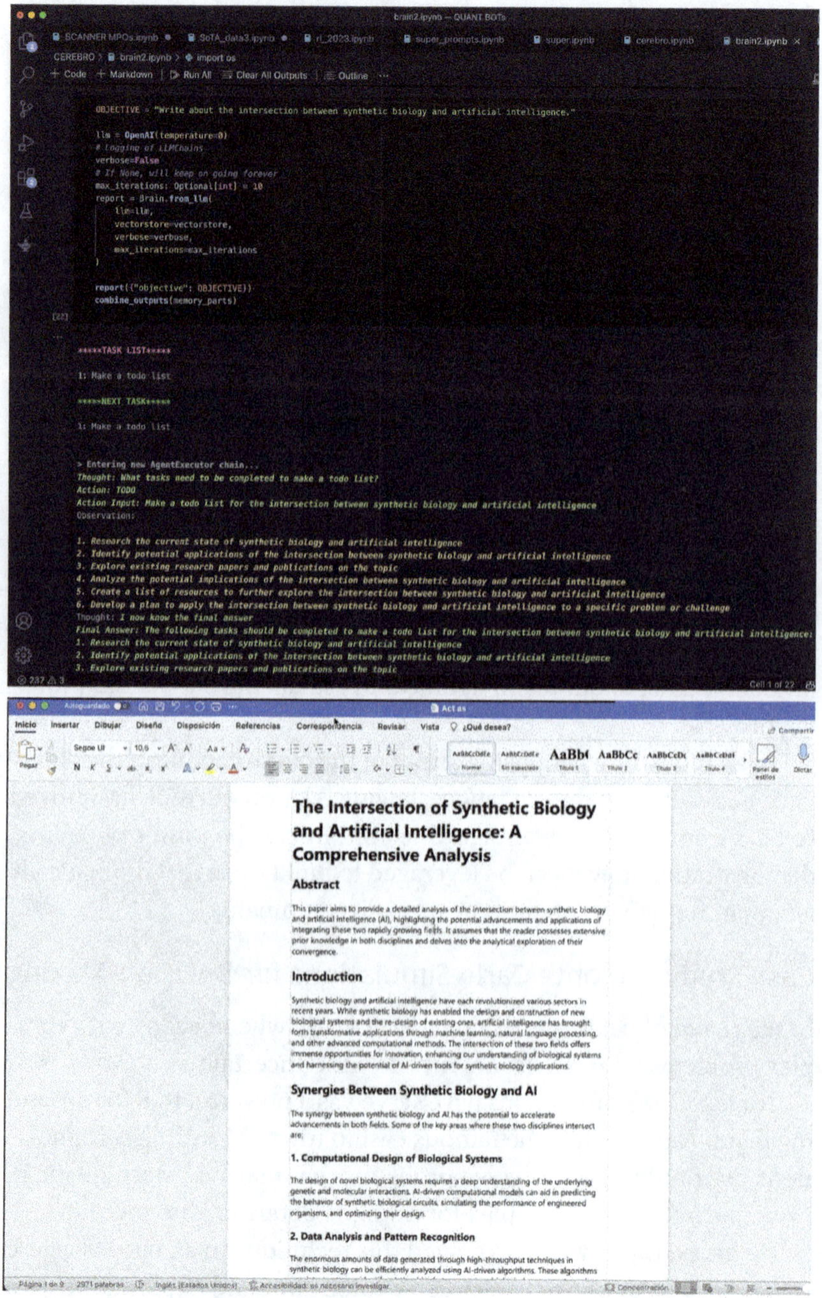

In our quest to build a powerful, collaborative AI, we aim to bring several instances of GPT chatbots to work together, engaging in a form of debate until the optimal solution for a given task is arrived at. This will involve a manager chatbot, a strategist, a solver, and a critic chatbot all collaborating in an iterative loop until the critic is satisfied.

- To ensure our chatbots can interact effectively, we need to set up the necessary building blocks. First, we set up the mechanism to call ChatGPT from within a line of code. Using Python, we imported the necessary libraries and created a structure that controls OpenAI, enabling us to pose questions to the model and receive responses.
- Given the fact that GPT was trained only up to the end of 2021, it lacks access to more recent information. To overcome this limitation, I coded a feature that allows the system to search Google for relevant information, thus allowing it to pull in up-to-date data as needed.
- To extend the working memory of the chatbots, I created a mechanism that ensures they remember everything discussed within their loop, regardless of the length or complexity of the conversation.
- Now with these building blocks in place, we proceeded to code the strategies, manager, and the "brain" that combines everything. The brain integrates memory, Google search, and all other components to make our AI system work in a coherent, synchronized manner.
- To test the system, we gave it a task of writing a report about the intersection between synthetic biology and artificial intelligence. This task required the system to utilize its search capabilities to find recent papers on the topic and then use its extended memory and analytic capabilities to compile a comprehensive report.
- The output was a six-page report detailing the current state of synthetic biology and artificial intelligence, the potential applications of their intersection, and key research papers in the field. While the formatting of the report needed some human intervention to make it more readable, the AI system was able to produce the content in less than three minutes.
- Despite the report not being perfect, it does provide a solid foundation for further exploration and understanding of the subject. More importantly, it demonstrates the potential of using AI to automate complex tasks, thus helping us navigate the vast and ever-expanding ocean of information in today's digital world.
- The potential uses of such sophisticated AI systems are vast. In this digital age, where the volume of available information is doubling every few years, the ability to quickly sift through vast data sets, analyze their content, and synthesize accurate and meaningful information will revolutionize numerous sectors. From academic research to corporate decision-making, medical diagnostics to personal assistance, such AI capabilities could tremendously enhance productivity, improve accuracy, and enable rapid, data-driven insights. Furthermore, the capacity of AI systems to interact and collaborate suggests the potential for more complex, multi-faceted problem-solving approaches, beyond the reach of any single human mind.

Figure 55. AIA (Artificial Intelligence Analyst)

PROJECT AIA.ipynb

Archivo Editar Ver Insertar Entorno de ejecución Herramientas Ayuda Última modificación: 2 de enero

Comentario Compa

+ Código + Texto

```
start = 34394959
abstracts = []
titles = []
good = 0

for x in range(5000):
    PMID = str(start+x)
    url="https://www.ncbi.nlm.nih.gov/pubmed/" + PMID
    try:
        r = requests.get(url)
    except:
        time.sleep(3)
        continue
    soup = BeautifulSoup(r.content, 'html.parser')
    tit = soup.find('title')
    citation = soup.find('div',{"class":"article-citation"})
    abst = soup.find_all('div',{"class":"abstract-content selected"})
    print(f'{x+12000} ({good}) \t| {tit.text[:150]}        ')
    #print(citation.text)
    #print(abst[0].text)
    try:
        if (50<len(abst[0].text.split())<500): # Only accept abstracts if the are between 50 and 500 words, exclude the rest
            if ("Nat" in citation.text) | ("Lancet" in citation.text) | ("JAMA" in citation.text) | ("N Engl" in citation.text) |
                #print(tit.text, citation.text)
                abstracts.append(abst[0].text.replace('\n',''))
                titles.append(tit.text.replace(' - PubMed',''))
                good = good + 1

    except:
        continue
```

```
12000 (0)     | Anti-Black racism in academia and what you can do about it - PubMed
12001 (0)     | Lipid nanoparticles for mRNA delivery - PubMed
12002 (1)     | Machine learning in combinatorial polymer chemistry - PubMed
12003 (1)     | Back pain in pregnant women attending an antenatal clinic in KwaZulu-Natal, South Africa - PubMed
12004 (1)     | Maternal experiences of caring for preterm infants in a vulnerable South African population - PubMed
12005 (1)     | South African pre-hospital emergency care personnel's lived experiences of managing paediatric emergencies: A qualitative research design utili
12006 (1)     | Erratum: Analysis of Patient Safety Incident reporting system as an indicator of quality nursing in critical care units in KwaZulu-Natal, South A
12007 (1)     | Erratum: Demographic and socio-economic predictors of physical activity among people living with HIV of low socio-economic status - PubMed
12008 (1)     | Healthcare workers' perceptions on collaborative capacity at a Referral Hospital in Malawi - PubMed
12009 (1)     | A nutritional profile of patients with tuberculosis at Standerton Tuberculosis Specialised Hospital, Mpumalanga, South Africa - PubMed
12010 (1)     | Chemotherapy-related subjective cognitive impairment in breast cancer patients in semi-rural South Africa - PubMed
12011 (1)     | Mental healthcare users' self-reported medication adherence and their perception of the nursing presence of registered nurses in primary healthc
12012 (1)     | Clinical, radiological, and laboratory predictors of a positive urine lipoarabinomannan test in sputum-scarce and sputum-negative patients with
12013 (1)     | Giant bacillary angiomatosis - PubMed
12014 (1)     | Maximum intensity projection aids in diagnosing acute appendicitis and mobile caecum: A case report and literature review - PubMed
12015 (1)     | Assessing the clinical utility of the severity dependence scale for benzodiazepine use disorder - PubMed
12016 (1)     | Theoretical understanding of contextual motivations for sustained adolescent marijuana use in South Africa - PubMed
12017 (1)     | Prevalence and correlates of psychological distress amongst healthcare workers during the COVID-19 pandemic: An online survey - PubMed
```

In this project, I've taken on the challenge of training an AI system using a Python notebook. The AI, called AIA (for Artificial Intelligence Analyst), is connected to my OpenAI account.

- To train AIA, we first need to gather relevant data, a process also known as data scraping. For this particular AI model, we source data from scientific publications such as *Nature*, *Science*,

The Lancet, and *The New England Journal of Medicine*, among others. Running the code initiates the data collection process, pulling in articles on various subjects from these journals.

- After scraping a considerable amount of articles, I halt the data collection process to illustrate the results. To keep things simple, I focus on the first article collected. Each article file is split into two: One file contains the article title and the other the abstract. The title is then fed into AIA, which is designed to learn the kind of responses we desire from it.
- Next, I convert the collected data into a tabular format. This is a preparatory step that makes the data ready for training.
- The actual training begins with fine-tuning the DaVinci model of AIA. This process has been ongoing for the past four months, during which AIA has been learning from scientific papers, my emails, and various books. The AI is set to train around the clock, learning from a wide range of subjects including CMC, regulatory pathways, intellectual property, and many others.
- The study involved the support of Laura Rodriguez and Gemma Guinart, two senior team members. They interacted with AIA by posing questions, to which AIA responded using three different models: an untrained model and two differently trained models. The trained models differed in their approach, with one being more creative and the other being more pragmatic and straightforward.
- The responses given by AIA were graded, and the results displayed for the first 15 responses. It's remarkable to note that the trained models achieved nearly a score of six, significantly outperforming the untrained model which managed only a score of around 2.5. The pragmatic and straightforward model was preferred by both evaluators.
- Finally, the grades of the different models were analyzed, further highlighting the significant performance improvement of the trained models over the untrained one. All in all, this demonstrates the potential of AI training and its impact on the AI's capability to deliver high-quality responses.
- The considerable performance improvement of the trained models underscores the critical role of quality data and iterative training in the development of AI capabilities. By feeding AIA with vast scientific knowledge and constantly refining its responses through evaluative grading, we are inching closer to creating an AI that can handle intricate research tasks, facilitate decision-making, and potentially contribute to the advancement of science and technology.
- The future of AI, as exemplified by AIA, is one filled with limitless possibilities. As AI continues to evolve, we are bound to see more powerful applications that will revolutionize various sectors of our society.

developing a new drug, for instance, we need to decide how much resource to allocate to test it against a wide range of conditions (exploration) versus using those resources to fine-tune the drug for conditions we already know it works against (exploitation).

By simulating thousands of different scenarios with varying degrees of exploration and exploitation, Monte Carlo simulations provide us with a range of potential outcomes and their associated probabilities. This insight allows us to make data-driven decisions that consider both the potential rewards and the inherent risks of our strategies.

Case Study 6: Summarizing Scientific Papers Using Code

Another significant use of coding skills I have found immensely valuable is the ability to summarize scientific papers efficiently. As you might imagine, the field of biotechnology is deeply intertwined with scientific research. Consequently, staying updated with the latest research and discoveries is of paramount importance. However, the sheer volume of scientific literature published daily makes it humanly impossible to read and digest it all.

To address this challenge, I developed a code that utilizes natural language processing (NLP) techniques to summarize scientific papers at the touch of a button. This code can scan through an entire scientific paper and extract the most relevant and essential information in just a few seconds. It has proved to be a great time saver, allowing us to keep up with the latest findings without spending countless hours reading through dense scientific text.

Further Applications of Coding

Beyond the specific case studies mentioned, coding has myriad applications that are revolutionizing the landscape of biotechnology and venture capital. It empowers one to build custom tools, enhances productivity, and enables creative problem-solving. In the ever-evolving landscape of cutting-edge technologies, coding skills are a catalyst for innovation.

- **Modeling and Simulation:** Coding allows us to build mathematical models of complex biological systems, conduct simulations, and predict system behavior under different conditions. This is particularly useful in drug discovery, where in silico models can drastically reduce the time and cost associated with laboratory experimentation.

- **Data Analysis and Visualization:** Coding facilitates the collection, analysis, and visualization of large and complex datasets. In the context of venture capital, this could be used to track market trends, analyze investment performance, and identify promising investment opportunities.
- **Automation:** Coding helps automate repetitive tasks, thereby freeing up valuable time for more complex decision-making tasks. For instance, we can automate email communications, data entry, and report generation.
- **Interdisciplinary Innovation:** Coding bridges the gap between different disciplines. It enables the integration of knowledge from fields like biology, physics, and economics, leading to interdisciplinary innovations. For instance, a venture capitalist with coding skills can leverage economic models to make better investment decisions in the biotechnology sector.
- **Competitive Advantage:** Ultimately, the ability to code offers a significant competitive advantage in the fast-paced world of cutting-edge technologies. It empowers one to keep up with the rapid pace of technological advancement and to capitalize on emerging opportunities.

Conclusion: The Intersection of Statistics, Bayes, Probabilistic Thinking, and Algorithmic Thinking

The previous four chapters laid out a comprehensive foundation of how we can think and act in the landscape of cutting-edge technology and venture capital. We began with a deep dive into statistics, revealing how it underpins the decision-making process and how it can be used to make sense of large amounts of data and derive actionable insights. Bayes' theorem then taught us to refine our predictions, continuously updating our beliefs and strategies as new information emerges. We took a step further into the realm of probabilistic thinking, learning to understand events not as certain outcomes but as probability distributions, and adopting a mindset that better navigates the inherent uncertainty of the cutting-edge tech industry.

Most recently, we've explored the transformative power of coding and algorithmic thinking. Coding not only provides us with an essential skill set for problem-solving and data manipulation, but it also shapes our thought process, pushing us to approach problems with a step-by-step, logical mentality.

Each of these topics — statistics, Bayesian thinking, probabilistic thinking, and algorithmic thinking — are powerful tools on their own. However, their real power is unleashed when they intersect and integrate, fostering a mindset that is well-equipped to thrive in the dynamic world of cutting-edge technology and venture capital. This mindset enables us to recognize patterns, to predict and adapt to change, to navigate uncertainty, and to make informed, data-driven decisions.

In the end, these chapters equip us with the theoretical underpinnings and practical tools necessary to become better thinkers and investors and, more importantly, to make a significant contribution to the advancement of science and technology. It is through the understanding and application of these fundamental principles that we can truly drive forward the frontiers of human knowledge and capability.

Rule #34
On Visual Thinking

"The truth is rarely pure and never simple."
Oscar Wilde in The Importance of Being Earnest

To complete this section on the right mindset to predict the future, I want to share a special tool. It's one that I've been using for many years, and this whole book spins from it. This tool has greatly helped me understand all kinds of landscapes and technologies.

Visual thinking is a powerful tool that enables a deep understanding and anticipation of future trends. It is through visual representation that we can condense complex systems into comprehensible formats, facilitating cognitive synthesis and driving insightful decision-making.

Visual thinking transcends the boundaries of conventional analysis. It allows us to grasp the bigger picture, identify patterns, perceive potential problems and solutions, and hence, construct informed predictions about what will come. By transforming information into visual formats, we can scrutinize data more effectively, identify trends, and discern connections that might otherwise remain obscured in textual or numeric representations.

At its core, it is the cognitive process of connecting disparate ideas and discerning patterns that can guide us toward informed decision-making. It is this ability, often referred to as "connecting the dots," that imbues visual thinking with profound value in our pursuit of innovative investment strategies. Furthermore, these visual tools guide us to prospective research areas.

Techniques for Visual Thinking

Visual thinking incorporates a variety of tools and techniques to make abstract concepts tangible. Schematics, diagrams, and mind maps are among the most popular methods used to visualize ideas and their interconnections.

- **Schematics** simplify complex systems into understandable representations, elucidating relationships and functions within the system. They strip down complexity to its essentials, providing clarity and promoting comprehensive understanding.
- **Diagrams**, on the other hand, highlight connections between different components. They can be used to represent hierarchies, flows, cycles, and more. Diagrams excel in communicating processes and pathways, providing a snapshot of how elements interact within a system.
- **Mind maps**, a favorite among visual thinkers, present a spiderweb of ideas emanating from a central concept. They allow us to see how various ideas branch out and interrelate, providing a high-level overview of a concept and its surrounding landscape.

Other visual thinking tools include concept maps, flowcharts, and infographics, each with its unique strengths and applications.

The Tree of Science: Bifurcations and Pruning

The landscape of knowledge and innovation can often feel like an organic, ever-evolving ecosystem. One helpful metaphor for visualizing this landscape is the "Tree of Science," a conceptual tool that offers unique insights into the growth and development of knowledge domains.

In the Tree of Science, each branch represents a different field or subfield of knowledge. Some branches may be old and sturdy, representing well-established disciplines. Others may be younger and more supple, symbolizing nascent areas of research. The branches' interconnections symbolize interdisciplinary work, showcasing how fields often draw from and influence each other.

This framework gives us a holistic view of the scientific landscape of, for example, a specific field or a specific indication, helping us comprehend the interconnectedness of diverse knowledge domains and the potential areas of disruptive innovation.

Figure 56. An Example of a Mind Map

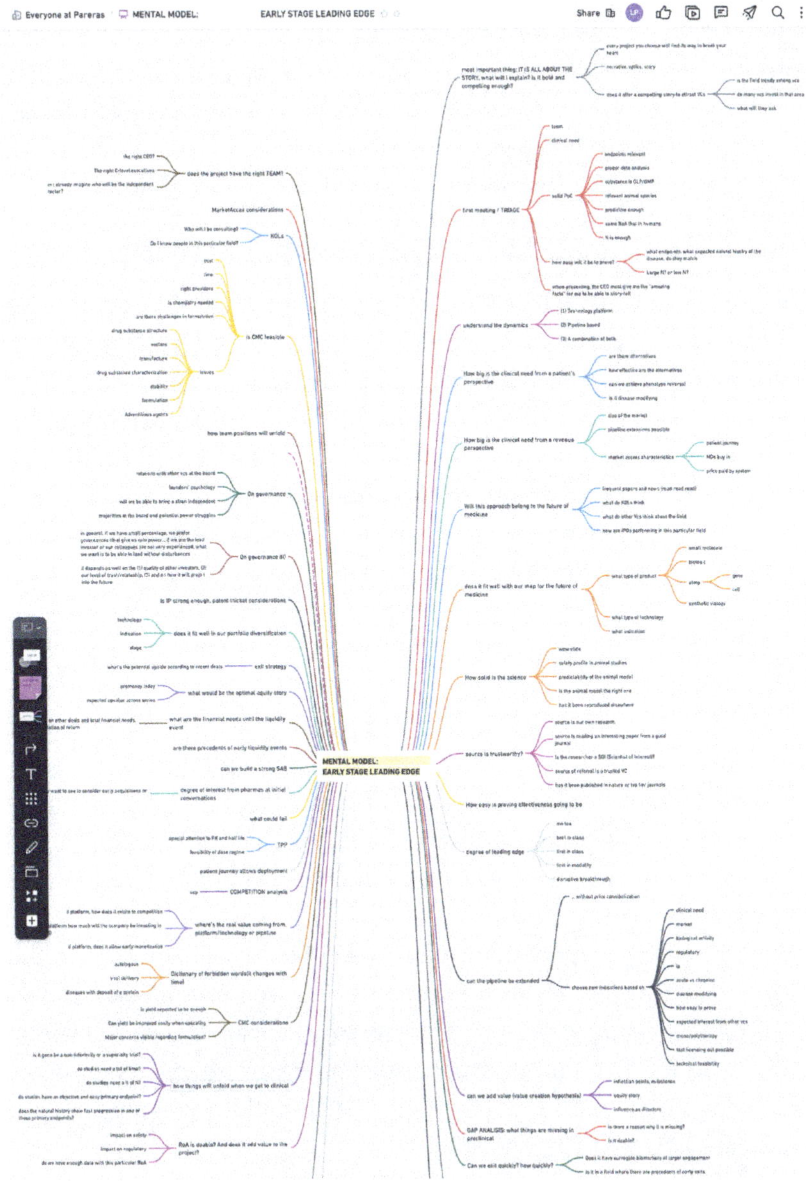

Here's a peek at one of my mind maps. It's a mental model I use when considering early-stage biotech companies. You don't need to dig into its contents, it's just a conceptual example to illustrate my process.

Bifurcations in the Tree of Science represent the emergence of new fields or subfields, typically spurred by breakthroughs or paradigm shifts. Understanding why bifurcations occur — why new branches sprout — can provide valuable insight into areas ripe for innovation. Similarly, comprehending why certain branches disappear or get pruned — whether due to lack of progress, relevance, or funding — can offer lessons on areas to avoid or reconsider.

The "X" on the Map: Identifying Promising Opportunities

The process of making investment decisions, especially in leading-edge fields, bears surprising similarities to creating a scientific diagram. Both involve visualizing a landscape of interconnected factors, and both require us to pinpoint specific areas of interest amid a vast array of data.

Just as a scientific diagram helps elucidate complex phenomena, a well-constructed investment map can illuminate the multifaceted landscape of investment opportunities. Such a map, whether it takes the form of a flowchart, a graph, or another kind of schematic, can illustrate the relationships between different investment opportunities, their potential returns, and the risks involved.

This visual approach allows for a clearer view of the investment landscape, making it easier to analyze and compare different opportunities. In the same way that a biologist might use a diagram to visualize a cellular process, an investor can use an investment map to understand the dynamics of the market and the potential trajectories of various ventures.

Using our investment map, we can begin to identify the "X" on the map — the next promising opportunity. This requires a deep understanding of the landscape and an ability to anticipate trends and shifts. Gaps in the market, unmet needs, and emerging trends often indicate promising investment opportunities. Visual thinking can help us spot these gaps and trends more effectively.

Other Potentially Useful Tools

Here are some concepts that can further enrich your thinking:

- **The Time Horizon Cone:** This visual tool helps anticipate the future by providing a structured way of looking at possibilities, probabilities, and certainties as they evolve over time. The cone widens as it extends into the future, representing increasing uncertainty and potential possibilities. Conversely, as you move back toward the present, the cone narrows, symbolizing a shrinking range of possibilities and an increase in certainties. This tool can be particularly useful when you're considering long-term investments in areas that involve considerable uncertainty, such as cutting-edge technology or scientific research.

- **SWOT Analysis:** SWOT (Strengths, Weaknesses, Opportunities, Threats) analysis is a classic strategic planning tool that can help visualize the internal and external factors affecting an investment opportunity. A SWOT matrix provides a comprehensive overview of the current landscape and can identify potential areas of growth, challenges to be addressed, and external factors that could impact the investment.
- **The Investment Lifecycle Diagram:** Similar to the life cycle diagrams used in biology, an investment lifecycle diagram visualizes the different stages an investment goes through, from inception to maturity and eventual exit. This tool can help an investor anticipate the challenges, risks, and returns associated with each stage, helping them plan their strategy more effectively.
- **Scenario Planning Diagrams:** These diagrams can help visualize different potential futures based on various factors and decisions. They are particularly useful in situations with a high degree of uncertainty, allowing for a comparison between the possible outcomes of a variety of strategic choices.
- **Technology Adoption Lifecycle:** This S-shaped curve, also known as the diffusion of innovations curve, helps visualize how a new technology or innovation is adopted within a market. By identifying where a particular technology is on this curve, investors can better understand its current market penetration and future growth potential.
- **Competitive Landscape Maps:** You'll find these maps throughout the book. They help visualize the competitive environment of an investment opportunity and can be based on factors such as product features, innovation level, etc. By plotting potential investments on such a map, investors can get a better understanding of each investment's competitive position and potential.

Figure 57. Visual Thinking for Future Anti-Ageing Therapies

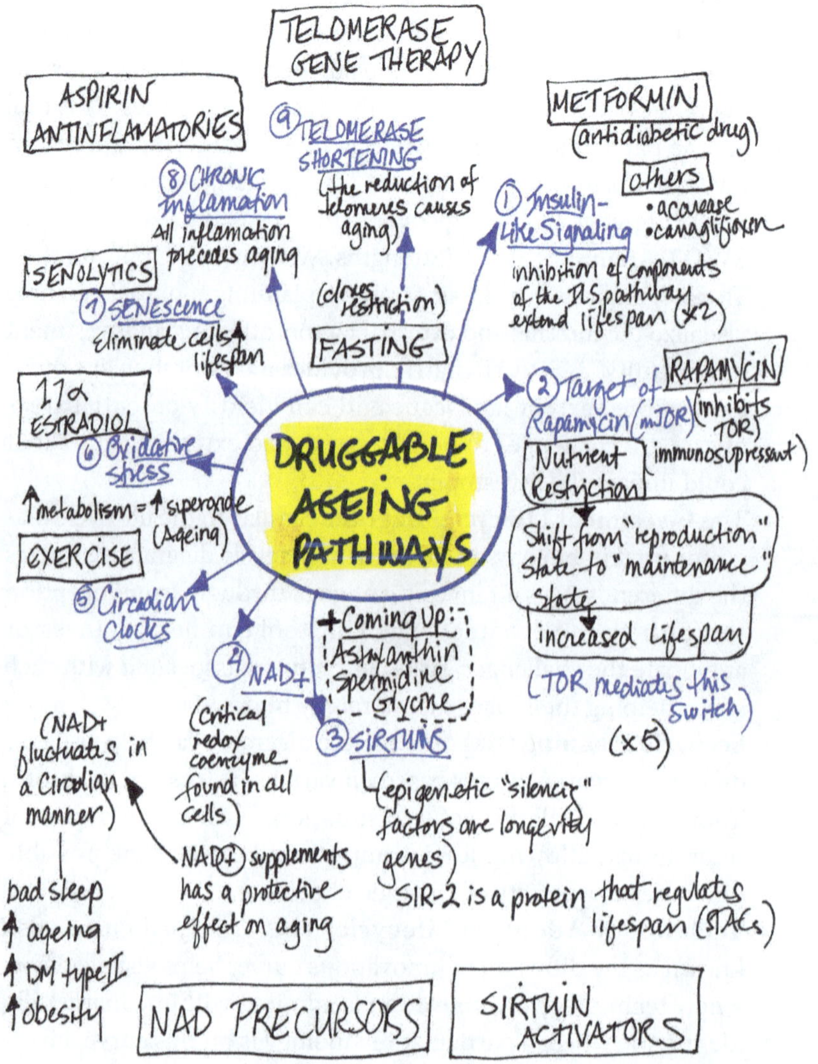

This visual representation provides an overview of the current and potential anti-aging therapies being explored in the field of longevity science. The strategies, represented in blue, are organized under broader categories of technological or methodological approaches, shown in red. This visual format facilitates a more cohesive understanding of these diverse anti-aging strategies and their interconnections.

- **Insulin-like signaling** pathways, which involve drugs such as metformin, an anti-diabetic medication known to extend lifespan in some organisms, are under active investigation.

- **Target of Rapamycin (mTOR)** strategy is centered on the Target of Rapamycin (mTOR) pathway, known for its role in cellular growth and metabolism. Rapamycin, an immunosuppressant drug, is known to inhibit mTOR, contributing to lifespan extension.
- **Sirtuins are** a family of proteins that play a role in aging by controlling cellular health. They are crucial for DNA repair and have been linked to the regulation of lifespan, leading to research on sirtuin-activating compounds.
- The NAD+ Pathway research indicates that supplements increasing NAD+ (Nicotinamide Adenine Dinucleotide) levels can offer protective effects against aging. Intriguingly, this pathway is also connected to the regulation of circadian clocks, underscoring the significance of lifestyle factors, such as exercise, in the biology of aging.
- **Oxidative stress** involves damage to cells from free radicals. Strategies are being explored to enhance the body's natural defenses against oxidative stress.
- **Cell senescence**, or the aging of cells, is another significant area of anti-aging research. Senolytics, drugs that selectively remove senescent cells, are believed to potentially enhance health and lifespan. Chronic inflammation, often a precursor to aging, is another area of focus, with potential therapies including anti-inflammatory drugs like aspirin.
- **Telomerase shortening** is addressed, as the reduction of telomeres, the protective caps on the end of our chromosomes, is a well-established cause of aging. Therapies here aim to extend telomeres and include promising pathways like telomerase gene therapy.
- The field of anti-aging pharmaceuticals is rapidly evolving and is anticipated to have far-reaching impacts on healthcare, society, and the economy. With the world's aging population growing at an unprecedented rate, the need to address age-related diseases and conditions has never been more significant. The consequences of aging extend beyond the individual, impacting healthcare systems, economies, and societies at large. Therefore, the development of effective anti-aging therapies could have transformative effects at multiple levels.
- On an **individual level**, anti-aging pharmaceuticals could fundamentally enhance the quality of life for older adults. These drugs aim not only to extend lifespan but also to extend the period of life spent in good health, known as healthspan. In doing so, they could reduce the incidence of multiple age-related diseases such as Alzheimer's, heart disease, and various forms of cancer, thus improving the overall well-being and life satisfaction of individuals as they age.
- At a **societal level,** the benefits of successful anti-aging pharmaceuticals are enormous. By reducing the burden of age-related diseases, we could significantly decrease healthcare costs, leading to more sustainable healthcare systems. With healthier older populations, societies could benefit from the continued contributions of these individuals, whether in the workforce, volunteering, or within their families and communities.
- Furthermore, anti-aging therapies could have **profound economic implications**. With extended healthspan, the costs associated with healthcare and social care could decrease. Simultaneously, economies could benefit from increased productivity as individuals remain healthier and active for longer.
- As we advance in this field, it's crucial to take a **holistic and ethical approach**, considering not only the scientific and medical aspects but also the social, economic, and ethical implications of these promising treatments.

Figure 58. Visual Thinking for Guiding Investment Decisions

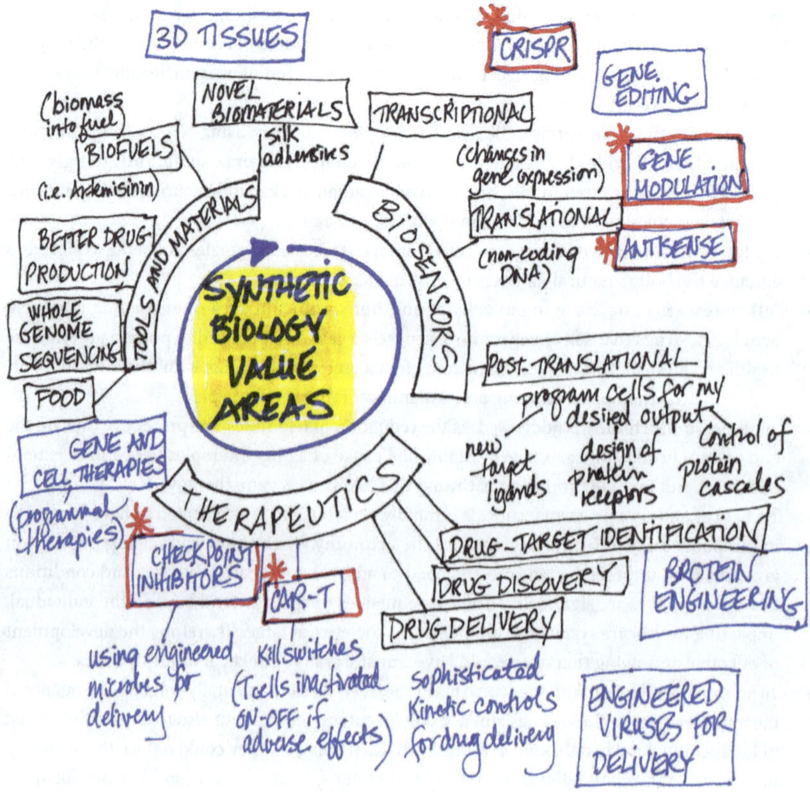

In this visualization, we're focusing on the potential reach of synthetic biology across various sectors. We've divided it into three broad categories: Biosensors, Therapeutics, and Tools and Materials, each capturing a different aspect of the field.

- **Biosensors sector** includes revolutionary areas such as CRISPR therapies and gene editing, gene modulation, and post-translational programming of cells. Post-translational programming, in particular, allows for the control of protein cascades and the design of novel protein receptors, demonstrating synthetic biology's transformative potential in understanding and manipulating cellular mechanisms.
- **Therapeutics sector** encompasses drug target identification, protein engineering, drug discovery, and innovative drug delivery methods. Synthetic biology offers sophisticated kinetic controls for drug delivery and the potential to enhance cell therapies like CAR-T with safety measures such as kill switches. This sector also includes the possibility of using engineered microbes for delivery in checkpoint inhibitors therapies and various gene and cell therapies more broadly.
- **Tools and Materials sector** involves diverse applications such as food production, drug production, biofuels, and the design of novel biomaterials. One classical example is the production of artemisinin, an antimalarial drug, showcasing one of synthetic biology's early

triumphs in drug manufacture. This sector also incorporates the potential of converting biomass into biofuel and creating new biomaterials, including fabrics like silk, adhesives, and even tissues.

Synthetic biology, an interdisciplinary blend of biology and engineering, is propelling us into an era of revolutionary scientific advancement. The discipline thrives on the design and construction of novel biological components, devices, and systems, promising transformative developments across various sectors. The first striking feature of synthetic biology is its capacity to enhance our comprehension of intricate biological systems.

At its core, synthetic biology aims to re-imagine and redesign biology, turning the complex language of life into a manageable, engineerable system. In doing so, it allows us to delve deeper into the mechanisms underlying biological functions, deciphering the genetic code that forms the basis of life itself. This knowledge serves as a powerful tool, enabling scientists to manipulate genes and design biological systems that operate with unprecedented precision and predictability. In essence, synthetic biology provides us with a granular understanding of the inner workings of life, opening up a realm of opportunities to leverage this knowledge for scientific advancement.

The application of synthetic biology in the health sector marks a significant breakthrough in disease diagnosis, prevention, and treatment. From the design of tailored therapeutic strategies using gene therapies to the development of biosensors for early and accurate detection of diseases, synthetic biology is rewriting the rules of medicine. For instance, the emergence of CRISPR-Cas9 gene-editing technology, a brainchild of synthetic biology, has revolutionized our approach towards genetic disorders, making precise, targeted treatment a tangible reality. Moreover, the potential to engineer microbes and other biological entities paves the way for innovative drug delivery systems, bringing forth a new era of personalized medicine.

Beyond healthcare, synthetic biology holds immense promise in addressing some of the world's most pressing energy challenges. By engineering microbes to convert biomass into biofuels, synthetic biology provides a sustainable and eco-friendly alternative to fossil fuels. This field extends beyond fuel production to the creation of bioplastics, biodegradable materials that could significantly reduce our reliance on petroleum-based plastics, thus contributing to environmental sustainability.

Furthermore, synthetic biology has the potential to address critical environmental issues. It offers innovative solutions to biodiversity conservation and restoration, such as the engineering of "super corals" to withstand rising sea temperatures or the use of gene drives to control invasive species. Moreover, the potential to design organisms that can absorb or break down environmental pollutants presents a novel approach to mitigate pollution and restore ecosystem health.

In conclusion, synthetic biology, with its convergence of biology and engineering, is propelling us into an era of unprecedented scientific and technological advancement. Its influence permeates various sectors, reshaping our understanding of life, revolutionizing healthcare, promoting sustainable energy solutions, and offering innovative strategies for environmental conservation.

- **The Risk-Reward Scatterplot:** This is a visual tool for assessing and comparing the potential risks and rewards of investment opportunities. Each opportunity is represented by a point on the plot, with its position determined by the estimated risk (usually represented on the x-axis) and estimated reward (represented on the y-axis). This can allow for a direct comparison of various opportunities based on their risk-reward profiles.

III

Choosing the Future

Rule #35

Sourcing Deal Flow

"Not all those who wander are lost."

J.R.R. Tolkien in The Fellowship of the Ring

Deal flow in venture capital is basically the business ideas or projects that entrepreneurs or startups looking for money present to a venture capitalist or a VC firm. The more projects a VC firm gets to look at, the better chance they have of finding a great business to invest in. This continuous flux of ideas is the lifeblood of the venture capital world, and its significance cannot be overstated.

We all invest in something: Investors put their money into promising ventures, while entrepreneurs pour their time and energy into cultivating their ideas and bringing them to life. Regardless of what's being invested, one thing holds true: the need to source and choose wisely.

The careful selection of what to invest in is crucial for both parties. Investors aim to allocate their capital efficiently, seeking out the most promising projects that offer the highest potential return. Similarly, entrepreneurs seek to invest their time and talent where they can make the most significant impact. Therefore, sourcing high-quality projects isn't just a routine task — it's a strategic move for both investors and entrepreneurs. In the following sections, we'll delve deeper into the ways to source and manage deal flow in the complex world of biotech and science.

The Investment Landscape

Venture capitalists, across the board, use a variety of strategies in sourcing deal flow, ranging from a passive, wait-and-see approach to an active, opportunity-seeking stance. Many VCs operate by reviewing the proposals they receive and selecting the best ones from this pool. Other VCs, actively venture out into the field to discover promising opportunities in addition to fielding incoming proposals.

One crucial element in the selection process is the alignment of potential projects with the strategic roadmap of the fund. For a venture to fit into our portfolio, for example, it must resonate with our vision of the future of medicine. In our case, the strategic roadmap, as we discussed in Chapter 3 around the forest and the trees, serves as our guiding principle, helping us evaluate whether a prospective venture aligns with our investment philosophy, focus areas, and risk tolerance.

To illustrate the various strategies of sourcing deal flow, we may draw parallels to fishing methods. The first scenario, where VCs passively receive proposals, is akin to casting a wide net. This approach captures a large volume of opportunities, yet lacks precision. The second scenario, where VCs actively scout for prospects, resembles hunting with a harpoon. Here, the focus is less on volume and more on the precise targeting of opportunities that align with the VC's strategic roadmap. As we move forward in this chapter, we will further explore these "fishing" methods and how they apply to the biotech investment landscape.

The Role of Strategic Alignment in Deal Sourcing

A strategic roadmap in the investment landscape is more than a plan; it is an informed, dynamic, crucial guide that outlines the path to potential investment opportunities. This roadmap lays out an investor's vision of where they see the future of biotech and medicine heading and which fields or technologies are likely to play a significant role in shaping that future. It represents a well-reasoned hypothesis of which sectors, technologies, or types of companies might produce the most impactful returns in the coming years.

A well-crafted strategic roadmap can serve multiple functions. It guides the investor in navigating the complex world of biotech, helping focus their attention on areas of most significant potential and saving time by narrowing down the scope of search. Furthermore, the roadmap helps align the portfolio with future trends, keeping the investments relevant in a rapidly evolving industry.

For venture capitalists, the strategic roadmap becomes an essential tool for sourcing deals. With a clear roadmap, investors can move beyond a reactive stance, where they merely respond to opportunities as they come. Instead, they can actively seek deals that align with their vision, their understanding of the market, and their anticipation of future trends. This alignment of deal sourcing with strategic roadmap not only increases the odds of successful investment but also helps build a cohesive portfolio that makes sense in the context of broader industry evolution.

Finding deals that perfectly align with a strategic roadmap is a task easier said than done. The inherent uncertainty of the biotech industry, marked by disruptive breakthroughs and swift changes in market dynamics, often challenges the foresight encapsulated in the roadmap. The truth is, I constantly change my mind, evolving with where science goes. Every quarter I realign my own expectations with the current status of the field and re-draw my maps of what interests me. This iterative process allows investors to stay attuned to the pulse of the industry, making them better equipped to source and manage deal flow wisely.

Deal Flow Sources

1. Incoming projects from entrepreneurs sending their decks

VCs often receive a plethora of proposals from entrepreneurs seeking investment. These inbound projects, akin to a fisherman's net, catch a variety of opportunities, some of which may have great potential. However, the sheer volume of these inbound projects presents its own challenge: finding the one that fits perfectly with the VC's strategic roadmap. It requires sifting through a multitude of proposals to spot the rare gem that aligns with the investor's vision and market prediction. Despite these challenges, inbound projects remain a source of deal flow, as they sometimes bring unexpected opportunities to light.

Entrepreneurs view this method as an opportunity to showcase their innovative ideas and gain the attention of potential investors. However, they may find it challenging to stand out amid the multitude of proposals received by venture capitalists. Tips for entrepreneurs include crafting a clear, compelling, and concise pitch deck that highlights the uniqueness of their project and aligns with the potential investor's strategic interests.

Venture capitalists may appreciate the diversity of opportunities this method presents but may be overwhelmed by the high volume of proposals. Their challenge lies in efficiently sifting through the decks to identify promising projects. While this method can lead to discovering unique opportunities, it also carries the risk of cognitive biases like the "halo effect" where an entrepreneur's presentation skills might overshadow the project's actual merit. I advise maintaining a disciplined evaluation process to mitigate such risks.

2. *Referrals from other funds*

Investing in biotech is not a solitary pursuit; it thrives on collaboration, shared insights, and collective wisdom. This principle underpins the strategy of sourcing deals from other venture capital firms. In this context, the importance of maintaining a strong network within the VC community cannot be overstated. Being trustworthy, humble, and committed with a strong track record of identifying winning investments and actively supporting portfolio companies can open doors to collaboration and co-investment opportunities. Upholding high ethical standards further enhances the VC's reputation, facilitating the flow of deals from peers in the industry.

Referring VCs utilize this method to diversify risk, gain access to additional resources, and benefit from shared due diligence and industry insights. However, they must carefully select who they invite to ensure compatibility in investment strategy and a commitment to shared goals. To maximize this strategy, referring VCs should maintain a well-curated network of reliable partners who bring complementary skills and resources. For the VC receiving referrals, this approach presents opportunities to gain access to curated deals, reducing the time and resources required for deal sourcing. Nevertheless, they must critically assess each opportunity to avoid potential groupthink and maintain alignment with their strategic roadmap. A healthy mix of trust in the referring VC's judgment and independent validation of the deal's merit is essential.

Sourcing deals through referrals brings together diverse perspectives and resources, enhances deal access, and fosters collaborative innovation. To be effective, it requires a robust due diligence process, clear communication, and well-defined co- investment agreements. This collaborative approach underscores the interconnectedness of the

VC ecosystem and the power of collective wisdom in driving biotech innovation.

3. Sourcing projects based on a map of strategically interesting fields

Like a hunter wielding a harpoon, a VC can actively seek out investment opportunities based on a well-charted map of the biotech ecosystem. This approach is proactive and highly targeted. It relies on a clear understanding of the state-of-the-art and emerging technologies, with a strategic selection of the areas that will shape the future of medicine. This method often involves creating a shortlist of the best companies in a chosen field and then deep-diving into these options to select the most promising one for investment.

The process of selecting the best companies in a particular field is a meticulous task. It involves extensive research, rigorous due diligence, and a keen understanding of the field's dynamics. Once the top contenders are identified, the selection process narrows down further. The final choice of investment is not a decision taken lightly; it reflects the VC's conviction in the company's potential and its fit with the strategic roadmap.

This proactive method enables VCs to align their investments with their strategic focus and vision for future trends in biotech. However, it requires extensive knowledge and foresight, and the success of such a strategy greatly depends on the accuracy of the VC's predictions about future trends. To be effective, VCs must stay abreast of developments in their focus areas, maintain flexible strategies to accommodate emerging trends, and be willing to invest the necessary time and resources into comprehensive due diligence.

Entrepreneurs might appreciate the targeted interest from VCs employing this strategy, as it implies a deeper understanding and commitment to their specific field. On the other hand, they may feel under greater scrutiny given the meticulous selection process. This proactive method is a more focused and calculated investment strategy, one that could yield higher returns given the careful selection process. Continuous learning, comprehensive due diligence, portfolio diversification, and collaboration with other

VCs can enhance the effectiveness of this strategy.

4. Academic publication-driven sourcing

Scientific journals such as *Nature* or *Science* serve as fertile grounds for sourcing potential investments. These publications cover cutting-edge research and innovative solutions, offering keen-eyed investors an early glimpse into the next big thing in biotech.

Spotting potential investments through these publications isn't just about early-stage investing; it often involves company creation. This route requires engaging with scientists to build a company around their groundbreaking research, offering a unique opportunity to shape the company's journey right from its inception. This method can provide early access to groundbreaking research and innovative ideas, offering potential high returns. However, it's labor-intensive, requiring an understanding of advanced scientific concepts and the ability to communicate with researchers effectively. For success, VCs should maintain close ties with the academic community, and keep up to date with the latest research publications.

Scientists may appreciate the interest and validation from the investment community and the opportunity to bring their research to the market. However, they might also be wary of the potential commercial pressures that could compromise scientific integrity. They should ensure that they partner with VCs who respect the balance between commercial success and scientific rigor and who can communicate effectively with them about their work.

Academic publication-driven sourcing is a highly specialized strategy that requires significant scientific understanding and a close relationship with the academic community. We cannot hide that this source might be perceived by everyone as high-risk, given the uncertainty associated with translating early-stage research into a commercially successful product. However, it can be also seen as high-reward, given the potential for breakthrough innovations. If you know how to do it well, it is, in my opinion, a great way of building your portfolio.

One of the first challenges in company creation is assembling a competent team. This includes hiring a CEO, a decision that's far from easy. In these early stages, the kind of seasoned CEO that a VC would ideally want on board often won't be interested. It's simply too early, and the company isn't yet stable or well-funded enough to attract top talent.

This is where the concept of an interim CEO comes into play. An interim CEO is a trusted individual from the VC firm, often an "Entrepreneur in Residence," who steps in to manage the company until it matures and can attract a long-term CEO. They can navigate the company through these delicate early stages, ensuring it gets off to a solid start.

Another key challenge lies in building a syndicate of investors. Your reputation as a VC plays a critical role here — it can make or break potential investment opportunities. Occasionally, a VC firm might decide to invest alone. While this can seem risky, the potential rewards are high if the company is properly structured and can hit key scientific milestones. If everything aligns, the company's upvalue at the next funding round could be significantly high.

Starting with a small board of directors is generally the best approach. As the company matures, you can bring in independent board members who offer diverse perspectives and expertise. A chairperson, who can provide effective leadership and direction for the company, is also essential. All of these elements need to be implemented step by step to professionalize the company gradually.

The process is by no means easy. The sheer number of decisions to be made can be overwhelming, and each one carries weight. However, the rewards are immense. Each company created by a VC contributes something new to the future: a ground-breaking technology, a life-saving therapy, a revolutionary product. Every successful company represents a step forward, and as a venture capitalist, you get to be a part of that progress. You've taken an idea, a mere possibility, and turned it into a reality — a company that wouldn't exist if not for your vision and efforts. It's a challenging yet fulfilling journey that contributes to the betterment of our future.

Building Bridges with Technology Transfer Offices

Maintaining a close relationship with technology transfer offices (TTOs) can provide invaluable insights and opportunities. These often-overlooked entities are a vital link between scientific research and commercialization, facilitating the translation of academic discoveries into tangible, market-ready technologies. By engaging with TTOs and listening closely to the scientists they work with, investors can gain early access to groundbreaking innovations that could define the future of medicine and healthcare.

To fully appreciate the importance of maintaining a close relationship with TTOs, it's essential first to understand their role. Technology transfer offices exist at many universities and research institutions worldwide. They are tasked with identifying research with potential commercial value, protecting intellectual property (IP) through patents, and transferring the technology to the market through licensing agreements or startup creation. In essence, they bridge the gap between the laboratory and the marketplace, making them a prime source of innovative, early-stage investment opportunities in the biotech sector.

Engaging with TTOs can provide a wealth of benefits for biotech investors. First, regular visits and communication can keep investors informed about the latest research and potential breakthroughs. This proactive approach can offer a competitive advantage, allowing investors to identify and seize investment opportunities before they become widely known in the marketplace.

Second, by understanding the strategic objectives and research focus of different institutions through their TTOs, investors can identify those that align with their own investment strategy and goals. This alignment can lead to more targeted, efficient deal sourcing, and potentially higher returns.

Finally, and perhaps most importantly, a close relationship with TTOs can provide investors with a deep understanding of the science behind potential investments. By listening to the basic science researchers involved in the projects, investors can better assess the true potential and risks of the technology, enabling more informed investment decisions.

These scientists are at the frontlines of innovation, often uncovering new insights that could have significant implications for healthcare and medicine. However, their work is often highly complex and specialized, meaning that its potential may not be immediately apparent to those outside the field. By taking the time to listen to these researchers, investors can gain an understanding of the science that underpins potential investments. This understanding can provide valuable context and clarity, helping investors to discern between truly groundbreaking innovations and promising but ultimately unfeasible ideas.

Furthermore, it can provide clues about the direction of the field and the "leading edge."

Beyond Sourcing: Scientists of Interest (SOIs)

Our team uses a specific term to describe scientists who are exceptional and pushing the boundaries in their fields. We call these individuals "Scientists of Interest," or "SOIs" for short. These SOIs are professionals we have identified as being at the forefront of their respective scientific areas. They consistently produce pioneering research, make significant discoveries, and have a reputation for high standards and innovation. They are leaders in the fields we are keenly interested in.

So, we maintain a database of those SOIs and we firmly believe that nurturing relationships with them will reap significant benefits in the future as these scientists create their companies. SOIs are not just accomplished researchers or academics; they are visionaries who are pushing the boundaries of their respective fields. These individuals are based worldwide and we keep an ongoing discussion with their labs.

Maintaining a database of SOIs is just the beginning; the real value lies in the continuous engagement with these scientists. Regular interaction not only fosters relationships but also allow us to stay updated with their latest research and developments. We strive to develop a relationship of mutual respect and trust. We believe that cultivating such a relationship is invaluable because these SOIs are likely to create companies based on their cutting-edge research in the future. When that happens, the established trust can lead to interesting investment opportunities.

However, convincing scientists to embark on this entrepreneurial journey presents unique challenges. Scientists are often primarily focused on their research, and the idea of transitioning their work into a commercial setting may seem daunting or distracting. As such, building relationships based on mutual understanding, respect, and a shared vision is crucial in persuading scientists to engage in company creation.

When forging partnerships with scientists, the importance of trust, humility, and commitment cannot be overstated. Trust is the foundation of any partnership. For scientists to entrust their life's work to an investor, they need to be confident in the investor's abilities, integrity, and vision. This trust is built not only through professional competence but also through open, transparent, and consistent communication.

Staying Updated

In the fast-paced world of biotech, knowledge quickly becomes outdated. Thus, continuous learning and staying abreast of the latest scientific literature, news, and books are crucial for successful deal sourcing. With a deeper understanding of recent advancements and breakthroughs, investors can better evaluate the potential of new ventures and anticipate the trajectory of the industry.

Regular immersion in the latest research findings allows investors to identify potential disruptors early and enables them to make informed investment decisions. As such, maintaining an up-to-date knowledge base is not merely a good-to-have skill, it's an essential strategy for success in the field.

Keeping a pulse on the state of the art and emerging technologies in biotech involves a multi-faceted approach. Regularly reading key scientific journals is one crucial tactic, providing a first-hand understanding of emerging trends and cutting-edge research.

Industry-specific news feeds can also provide a broad view of the current market dynamics and the major players in the field. Attending industry conferences and seminars is another valuable strategy. These gatherings offer an opportunity to hear directly from researchers and industry leaders, and also to network with other professionals in the field. Additionally, engaging in continuous dialogue with scientists, industry peers, and thought leaders can provide nuanced insights and expert perspectives.

Rule #36

Choosing the Future

"Your big opportunity may be right where you are now."
Napoleon Hill

Drafting this chapter has been a journey in itself, reflecting a 25-year-long quest for knowledge. Every word here carries the weight of my experiences, observations, victories, and failures. It is no exaggeration to say that I've been writing this chapter for the past two decades. Every day brought with it a new learning, a fresh perspective, shaping my understanding and molding my approach.

In the world of investing and entrepreneurship, one of the most critical decisions is choosing where to focus your energy, time, and capital. This chapter is dedicated to unraveling the complexities of that decision-making process, particularly when it comes to science-driven companies.

The term "choosing" here carries a broader connotation than just investing money. It also encapsulates the act of deciding which project to lead, which startup to establish, or even which problem to solve. You're investing, in essence, not just your money but also your time, skills, passion, and even your reputation.

As we venture into the specifics of this critical process, you'll see that the concepts and principles discussed in earlier chapters play a significant role here. The discussions about the forest and the trees, the need for broad knowledge, the focus on the critical path, the importance of game theory, the essence of algorithmic thinking — they all come into play when making a choice about where to invest or what company to start. If any of those concepts seem unclear, I recommend revisiting the relevant chapters to ensure a firm grasp of the ideas that will be integral to the discussions in this chapter.

Before we delve into the specifics of the choosing process, there are a few important caveats to keep in mind.

First, investing is a deeply personal endeavor. What works for one investor may not necessarily work for another. This is because investing, especially in the science-driven domain, is as much an art as it is a science. It relies on an intricate blend of knowledge, experience, intuition, and personal risk tolerance. So while the strategies and considerations presented in this chapter are informed by my years of experience and have proven effective for me, they are by no means the only way to approach investing. It's crucial to adapt these guidelines to your unique perspective, interests, and goals, and, over time, develop your distinct investing style.

Second, it's vital to acknowledge the stark differences between investing in early-stage and late-stage science-driven companies. Early-stage investing often involves betting on novel, unproven technologies, with a keen focus on the potential of the science and the capabilities of the team. It's a high-risk, high-reward landscape, often with longer time horizons before you see returns.

Late-stage investments, on the other hand, typically involve companies with more established technologies, proven track records, and clearer pathways to market. The risks are often lower, but so too are the potential returns. The focus here shifts from purely scientific potential to include commercial viability, market size, regulatory aspects, and competitive positioning.

In the context of science-driven companies, the landscape becomes even more nuanced. The nature of the science, the stage of technological development, the regulatory environment, and the competitive landscape all play significant roles in shaping the investment decision.

Throughout this chapter, you'll notice I frequently use biotechnology as the central theme or the prime example when discussing investment strategies and considerations. It's an industry I've spent a significant part of my professional life navigating, and it's where I've gained the insights and honed the investment strategies that I'll be sharing. The examples I use will naturally reflect this experience, offering you a first-hand perspective on how these strategies play out in real-life investment decisions.

More importantly, biotech embodies the core characteristics that define many deep- tech and science-driven fields. It involves complex, groundbreaking technologies that have the potential to revolutionize industries and impact lives. It operates in highly regulated environments and often involves long development timelines. And, the success of biotech ventures is tightly linked to both scientific validity and market realities.

Therefore, while I discuss specifics within the realm of biotech, the underlying principles and strategies are broadly applicable across different science-driven sectors. Whether you're considering an investment in AI, clean energy, quantum computing, or any other deep-tech field, you can extrapolate the framework and adapt it to fit the unique characteristics of these industries.

As we proceed, I encourage you to think critically about how the principles discussed can be applied to the specific sectors you're interested in. The power of this framework lies in its flexibility and adaptability, empowering you to make informed and strategic investment or startup decisions in a wide range of science-driven fields.

So, this chapter will tie together all the pieces, offering a comprehensive look at how all these elements interact in the real world of investing and entrepreneurship. It's about making informed, strategic decisions that align with your individual goals, strengths, and passion.

A Mental Frame for Choosing

The task of selecting a company for an investment or a project to lead may seem daunting due to the numerous variables in play. Over time, I have developed a mental frame to make this process more methodical, bringing a measure of clarity and structure to this complex decision-making process. This mental frame consists of a prologue, a triangle of fundamental characteristics, and an epilogue.

The **prologue** involves a general assessment of the company's technology or field. The prologue does not relate to the company itself, but involves a comprehensive evaluation of the field in which the company is working. This is where the questions arise: Will this field have a significant impact on the future of its industry? Is it in a position of potential growth and expansion — on the "sunny side of the forest" as I like to call it — or is it likely to be overtaken by competing technologies? In biotech, for example, is it a small molecule or an advanced therapy? Is it a classical antibiotic or a synthetic biology anti-infective? Is the field a trendy field with a lot of deal activity?

This requires you to have a well-defined understanding of the ecosystem around the specific technology, a map of sorts. Building this map involves reading extensively; interacting with colleagues, investors, and key opinion leaders in the field; and tracking trends. In a sense, it is like being a detective: gathering clues, analyzing patterns, and making informed predictions about the potential of the technology in question.

The **triangle** tries to analyze the fundamental initial characteristics to look for in a company. Once the general assessment of the technology has been completed, I delve deeper into the specifics of the company itself, examining it from three key angles.

1. **The first vertex concerns the solidity and impact of the scientific data:** How significant are the results compared to what others are doing? Is the science behind it robust and credible?
2. **The second vertex is the ease of proof:** How feasible is it to demonstrate the effectiveness of the technology or solution? This depends on several factors, as we will soon see, such as the expected sample size (N) that we'll need in a clinical trial, the standard of care currently in place, and the "straightforwardness" of the endpoints we are going to use, among other things.
3. **The third vertex is about the problem the company is trying to solve:** How important is it? How many people does it affect? Are there alternative solutions? What is the impact on those affected if a solution is not provided?

The final piece of my mental frame is what I term as the **epilogue**. This is where I imagine the narrative behind the investment or the startup, my investment thesis, so to speak. Is it a compelling story? Will it pique the interest of others, facilitating future fundraising efforts? Crafting this narrative and connecting with it on a personal level can provide a unique perspective on the potential of the investment or startup.

In essence, my mental frame is a dynamic process where all parts — the prologue, the triangle, and the epilogue — need to play in harmony to guide the decision-making process. Let's dig deeper.

Prologue: The Sunny Side of the Forest

In the journey of selecting a company to invest in or a project to lead, the first step is akin to a prologue — making a general assessment of the specific technology or science field that the company is using. This process I like to call "finding the sunny side of the forest." Reread the chapter on "the tree and the forest" to deep dive into the concept.

Using the analogy of a company as a tree, is the tree in the sunny side of the forest? This is to say, does the technology have the potential to flourish and grow, much like how plants in the sunny side of a forest have access to abundant light, facilitating their growth? Or is it planted in a dry rocky terrain with no water nearby?

Just as a botanist maps the distribution of different plant species in a forest to better understand the ecosystem, an investor or entrepreneur should map the ecosystem of the specific technology they're interested in. This mapping is a comprehensive process that involves collecting and analyzing a wide range of information about the technology, its current applications, its potential future uses, its competitors, and the overall market trends.

The goal is to build a detailed picture of the field/technology landscape. This includes understanding the current state of the technology, the trajectory of its development, and its potential impact on the industry. My question here always ends up in a resounding "Will this technology be in the future of medicine?" You may leverage numerous sources to achieve this, including scientific literature, patent databases, market reports, and conversations with other investors, industry professionals, and key opinion leaders.

The "sunny side" in this context refers to a position in the market where the technology is likely to thrive due to factors such as its novelty, its potential to solve significant problems, and its alignment with emerging industry trends. Conversely, technologies that are likely to be outcompeted or made obsolete by other, more advanced technologies, may be considered to be on the "shady side" of the forest.

There's a method in all this. Some advice to get to know the forest includes:

1. **Reading voraciously and continuously.** As an investor or entrepreneur in the field of deep tech, it's crucial to remain current with the latest research papers and news in your specific area of

interest. Knowledge, after all, is power. The more informed you are about current developments, the better equipped you are to anticipate where things are heading.

2. **Engaging in regular dialogue with the people who matter.** This includes key opinion leaders, top-notch scientists, colleagues, fellow venture capitalists, and entrepreneurs. These discussions often are a treasure trove of insights, helping you identify trends and opportunities that might otherwise have slipped under the radar. The power of collective wisdom and diversity of perspectives cannot be underestimated in the pursuit of trend detection.
3. **Looking for trends using algorithmic thinking.** Technological tools have democratized information and made it easier to identify and predict trends. Whether it's using machine learning algorithms, data analysis software, or AI-driven trend forecasting tools, leveraging technology is no longer optional in today's digital era. For a more in-depth exploration of this, I invite you to delve into the algorithmic thinking chapter.
4. **Meticulously and constantly monitoring the deal space.** All venture capital activities in your field, including acquisitions, financing rounds, licenses, and IPOs, should be on your radar. Maintaining a mental database of such events helps you understand market dynamics and predict future trends. The numbers often speak volumes; they can hint at which technologies are gaining momentum, which startups are attracting interest, and where investors are placing their bets.

Your mind requires a degree of foresight and an understanding of where the industry is headed. The goal is to invest in or lead projects that are built around technologies that will drive the future of their respective industries. Remember, being on the sunny side of the forest is not a guarantee of success, but it certainly increases the odds in your favor.

The Triangle

Criteria 1: How relevant is the science?

The first corner of the triangle used to evaluate potential investments or projects is what I call the "wow" slide (see the "wow slide" chapter). This is not merely an eye-catching slide in the pitch deck; it is a representation of the scientific data and evidence that substantiate the potential of the technology or solution the company offers.

A "wow" slide is crucial because it represents the groundbreaking nature of the science that a company is doing. It's the slide that makes you sit up, pay attention, and think, "Wow, this is something special." It's the slide that outlines the most impressive, most compelling data or results that a company has to offer. Essentially, it's the evidence that demonstrates that the company is achieving something truly remarkable in its field.

While considering the "wow" slide, look at how solid and good the results are compared to what others are doing in the field. The seriousness of the science, the magnitude of its effect on the patient population (the expected delta on the patient), and its comparative effectiveness against current standards of care are also significant. Keep in mind that the "wow" slide is not an abstract concept but a relative one. The efficacy of the technology or solution is not considered in isolation but relative to other solutions available in the market. Therefore, it's essential to know the field well enough to understand what the results presented truly signify.

The "wow" slide is usually related to scientific data, but in the context of deep- tech companies, this could also encapsulate unique technology breakthroughs or innovative solutions. Always remember that the "wow" slide should elicit excitement and anticipation about the potential of the technology. It should convince you that the technology has a strong scientific basis and holds great promise for the future.

Criteria 2: How easy will it be to prove?

The second corner of the investment decision triangle focuses on the ease of proof. Here, we evaluate how easy or hard it would be to demonstrate the effectiveness and feasibility of the solution or technology in question. The term "ease of proof" refers to the process and requirements necessary to validate the company's claims about its technology or product. In the field of deep tech, especially in biotech, this often involves rigorous scientific testing and validation, as well as regulatory approval.

Several factors can affect how easy it will be to prove that a therapy is effective. This could range from the size of the patient population (N), the standard of care that the solution will be compared to, and the specific endpoints that will be used in the testing or trial phase, among many others. These factors are deeply interconnected and can significantly influence the duration, cost, and complexity of the clinical trial.

Suppose the current common treatment (or "standard of care" — SoC) for a cancer we are trying to solve is already quite effective, helping 90% of patients survive for at least a year. If the regulatory authorities want us to prove that our new therapy works better than the current treatment, and we know that for ethical reasons they will force us to compare our treatment on top of the SoC versus the SoC as a standalone, we can anticipate we will need a large number of patients in our study to see a significant difference.

It's harder to prove that our drug increases survival to 95% when the current treatment already helps 90% of patients. It would be easier to show an effect if the standard treatment wasn't very effective to begin with. Easier here means we would need a lower "N" and therefore less money and less time.

This is also related to the natural history of the disease and the amount of time we'll need to spot an effect and wrap up the clinical trials.

Let's say we're testing a drug for pancreatic cancer, a disease where unfortunately patients usually pass away within a few months. If our drug is making a difference, we'll likely see that difference pretty quickly. But imagine we're dealing with a condition like muscular dystrophy, which progresses very slowly over many years. Spotting a change in that scenario would take a lot longer. Longer means more expensive, and less easy. You see? Everything is connected here, but what matters is understanding in advance how challenging it will be to prove that a treatment is effective.

Let's briefly look at some of these factors. However, keep in mind that every company is unique and may have additional factors to consider. So, you'll need to use your understanding of the specific indication and therapeutic modality to make an accurate analysis.

1. **Size of the Patient Population (N):** The size of the patient population, denoted as N, has a direct bearing on clinical trials. A larger patient population allows for a more robust statistical analysis, thereby lending more weight to the results, but it will need much more financing, more time. Conversely, a smaller N can make it challenging to draw significant conclusions, especially if

the condition being treated has a high degree of variability. This means less cost, less time. The accessibility and readiness of this patient population for recruitment to clinical trials also matters. A large patient population that is difficult to engage for trials presents its own challenges in proving the efficacy of a solution. Will we need in this project a low or a high N?

2. **The Standard of Care:** The standard of care refers to the current accepted treatment regimen for the condition in question. If the existing standard of care has a high efficacy rate, proving that a new solution is superior or at least non-inferior can be a daunting task (it will need a big N and therefore cost a lot of money). It necessitates demonstrating a noticeable improvement in outcomes, which can be challenging and time-consuming. On the other hand, if the current standard of care is ineffective or only moderately effective, there could be more room to demonstrate significant improvement. Is the standard of care already effective?
3. **The Natural History of the Disease:** This means how the disease usually progresses without treatment. This is crucial because it influences how long it will take to see if our drug is making a difference. If the condition progresses quickly, the timepoints at which we will assess the effect will be closer in time and therefore the duration of the trial could be short (let's say one year). For a slowly progressing condition, it could take many years to observe any changes. This means more time and higher costs.
4. **Choice of Endpoints:** The choice of endpoints in a clinical trial can significantly affect how easy it is to prove the claims of a deep-tech company. Some endpoints are more straightforward to measure, such as tumor size reduction in oncology trials, which can make the demonstration of efficacy more straightforward. In contrast, other endpoints can be more subjective or harder to measure reliably, such as pain reduction or an improvement in quality of life. The latter may require longer observation periods and larger sample sizes to show statistical significance, making the validation process more complicated. Are the endpoints for this condition objective and easily measurable?
5. **Regulatory Environment:** The ease of proving claims isn't just a scientific challenge; it's also a regulatory one. Different indications or therapeutic modalities may have varying requirements

Figure 59. Factors Affecting How Easy It Will Be to Prove

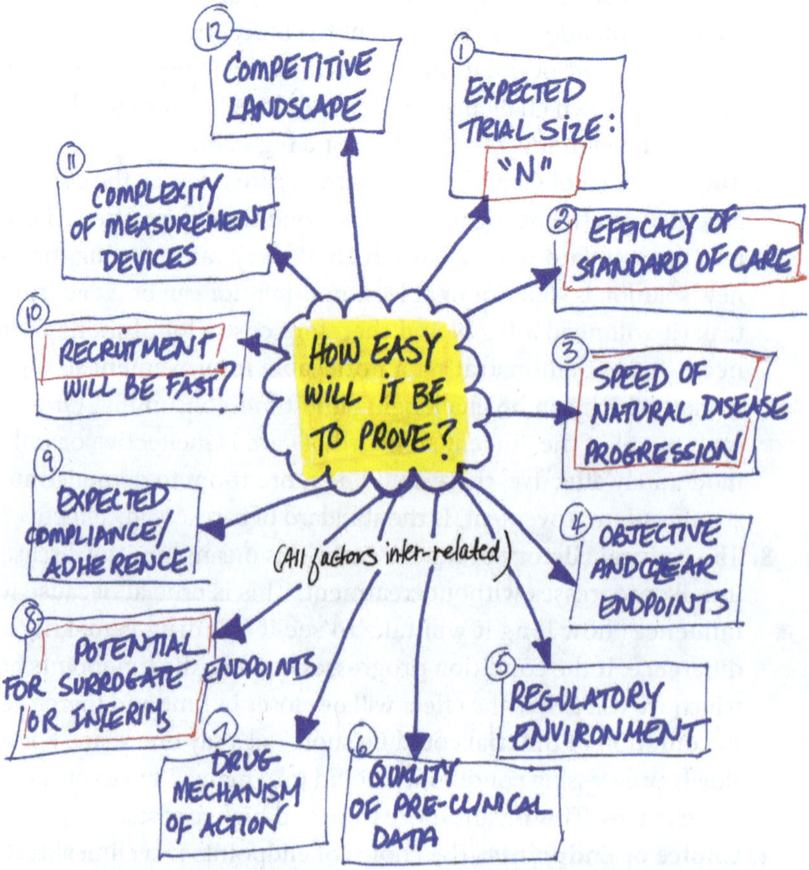

In evaluating the simplicity and feasibility of clinical trials, several factors come into play. These elements can significantly influence the time, cost, and likelihood of success of the clinical trial. Each case is unique, demanding an in-depth understanding of the disease and therapeutic strategy in question to conduct an accurate assessment. Let's review some of these influential factors (by no means a comprehensive list).

- **Patient Population Size (N):** The patient population size, or "N," directly impacts the clinical trials. A larger N facilitates more robust statistical analysis and lends credibility to results but requires more extensive financing and time. A smaller N, while less expensive and quicker, may present challenges in drawing significant conclusions, especially for variable conditions.
- **Existing Standard of Care:** The current accepted treatment or standard of care is a critical consideration. If the existing standard is highly effective, demonstrating superiority or non-inferiority of a new solution becomes challenging and potentially time-consuming. However, if the current standard is less effective, there's more room for significant improvement.

- **Natural Disease Progression:** Understanding the disease's natural progression without treatment is crucial, as it influences the timeframe for observing treatment effectiveness. Fast-progressing conditions may allow quicker evaluation periods, while slow-progressing conditions may require longer, potentially costlier trials.
- **Endpoint Selection:** The choice of endpoints in a clinical trial can significantly affect its simplicity. Some endpoints, like tumor size reduction in oncology trials, are relatively straightforward to measure, simplifying efficacy demonstration. However, more subjective or harder-to-measure endpoints, like pain reduction or quality of life improvement, may require larger sample sizes and longer observation periods, complicating the validation process.
- **Regulatory Environment:** Proving claims isn't solely a scientific challenge; it's also a regulatory one. Different indications or therapeutic modalities may have varying requirements for demonstrating safety, efficacy, and quality. Early engagement with regulatory bodies and adhering to their guidance throughout the development process can streamline the validation process.
- **Quality of Pre-clinical Data:** The robustness and reproducibility of pre-clinical data is a critical factor. Solid pre-clinical data can provide a strong foundation for clinical trials and increase the likelihood of positive outcomes.
- **Drug's Mechanism of Action:** Understanding the mechanism of action of a drug can significantly affect the design and interpretation of clinical trials. If the drug's mechanism of action is well-understood and can be reliably measured, it may be easier to prove its effectiveness.
- **Compliance and Adherence:** The level of patient compliance and adherence to treatment protocols can significantly affect the outcomes of clinical trials. Therapies that require complex administration or have severe side effects may have lower patient compliance, complicating the task of proving efficacy.
- **Measurement Technologies:** The availability and reliability of technologies to measure clinical outcomes can also impact how easily effectiveness can be proven. The more precise and reliable the measurement tools, the better the data quality, and thus the more convincing the evidence.
- **Competitive Landscape:** The presence of competing therapies in development can impact the ability to recruit patients for clinical trials and can influence regulatory standards, which might raise the bar for proving effectiveness and safety.
- **Clinical Trial Design Expertise:** A well-designed clinical trial can substantially increase the chances of proving a drug's effectiveness. Expertise in selecting appropriate patient populations, endpoints, control arms, and statistical analyses is crucial.
- **Safety Profile:** A drug with a good safety profile may require fewer patients or less time to demonstrate efficacy than a drug with notable side effects, since adverse events can complicate the interpretation of efficacy data and require larger sample sizes to demonstrate a favorable risk-benefit balance.

for demonstrating safety, efficacy, and quality. Understanding these regulatory nuances and planning for them can make the validation process smoother. It is crucial to engage early with regulatory bodies and follow their guidance throughout the development process.

The goal is to find a balance between ambition and feasibility. On the one hand, you want a company that's aiming to make a significant impact with its solution. On the other hand, the solution needs to be feasible and capable of being tested and validated within a reasonable time frame and budget. This consideration is crucial as it can affect the company's timeline for market entry, its financial needs, and ultimately its success or failure.

Remember, a solution with great potential but an extraordinarily complicated or costly proof of concept process may not be the best investment unless you're prepared for the long haul. Similarly, a solution with an easy proof-of-concept process but minimal impact may not be worth the investment either. It's all about finding the right balance based on your investment goals and risk tolerance.

Criteria 3: How big is the problem?

The third facet of the triangle is concerned with the gravity of the problem the company aims to address. Here, we assess the scope, magnitude, and implications of the issue the company's product or technology intends to solve.

This criterion questions the significance of the problem the company is trying to solve. It scrutinizes the need the company fills, the potential number of beneficiaries, the existence of alternative solutions, and the impact on those affected by the problem in the absence of a solution. This is the "why" behind the company — the compelling reason for its existence.

It's essential to gauge the scale of the problem. Is it a prevalent issue affecting many, or is it a niche concern impacting a smaller, albeit still important, group? Understanding the potential market size is crucial from a business perspective, but it's also essential from an impact standpoint. Solving a widespread problem has the potential to create more significant returns, but addressing a less common but nonetheless severe issue can also be impactful and profitable.

In biotech, the degree of unmet medical need can also play a role. For conditions with high unmet need, regulators may be willing to accept surrogate or intermediate endpoints, which can be demonstrated earlier than primary endpoints. This approach can expedite the proofing process. However, it requires careful negotiation with regulatory bodies.

There's an aphorism in the investment world: "Solving a problem will make you money, solving a very big problem will make you big, big, big money." This notion highlights the link between the size of the problem and the potential returns. The more important the problem addressed, the more underserved it is, the greater the potential returns. But remember, here the word "big" is not just about size — the severity of the problem, the lack of existing solutions, and the difference your investment can make are equally vital to consider.

Always start with the "why" — the problem the company aims to solve. It's the compass that guides everything else, including the company's strategy, its value proposition, and its potential for making a meaningful difference. A compelling "why" can often be a strong indicator of a company's potential for success.

Some final words of caution here. It's essential not to become overly fixated on the sheer number of people affected or the overall size of the market. Niche markets, which might at first seem small or exclusive, often present unique and potentially lucrative opportunities. So, again, "How big is the problem?" should read here as "How important is the problem?"

Let's consider a rare disease, for example. It might not affect a large number of people compared to more prevalent health conditions, but for those it does impact, the problem is incredibly significant. When the need is great, and there are few or no existing solutions, the importance of the problem is high, regardless of the size of the affected population. Regulatory authorities recognize the importance of addressing these significant health challenges, even when they are rare or affect smaller populations. For conditions with high unmet medical needs, regulatory bodies may be more willing to offer important advantages:

Regulatory authorities around the world, like the U.S. Food and Drug Administration (FDA) and the European Medicines Agency (EMA), understand the unique challenges involved in developing

Figure 60. Choosing the Right Indications

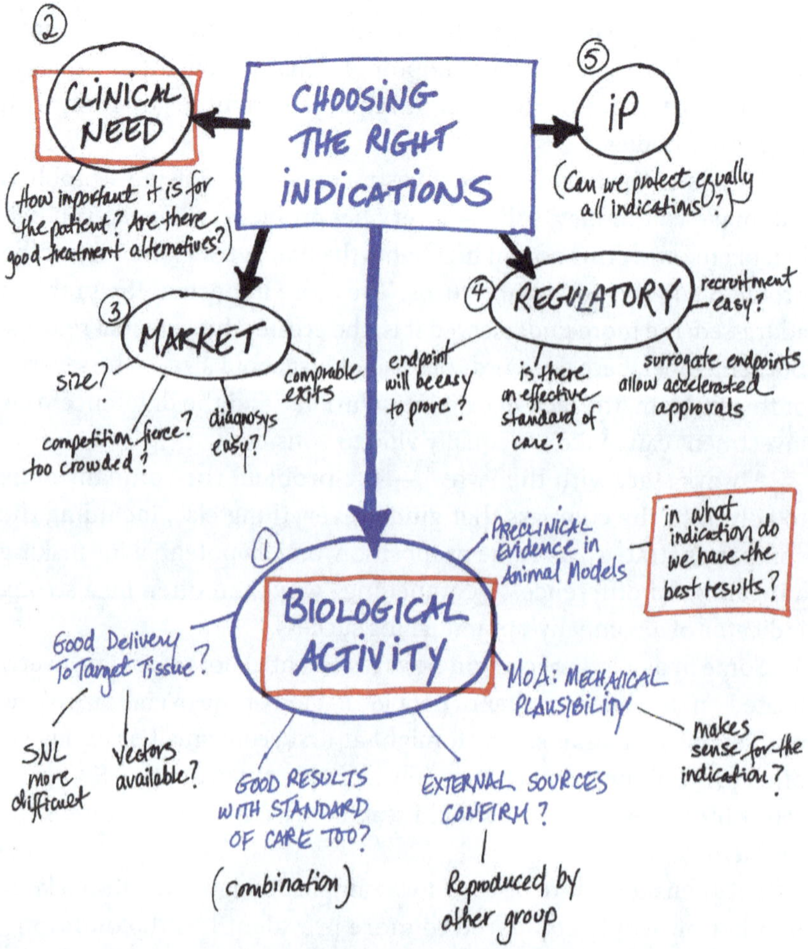

Investing in a company, particularly in the volatile biotech sector, requires thoughtful consideration and a degree of foresight. One pivotal decision in this process involves deciding the indications the company will target and navigating the company toward them. Understanding indications — the conditions that a drug is designed to treat — is crucial. Investors often enter at early stages when the most suitable indication may not yet be defined. Investors must hypothesize the best indication and steer the company toward it. How does one choose the "right" indications? Several factors come into play.

- **Biological activity:** Consider biological activity. Evaluate the clinical evidence from animal models and identify the indications where the experimental drug shows the most promise. Also consider the mechanism of action of the drug and its mechanistic plausibility for specific indications. Has the drug's effectiveness been validated by external sources? The necessity of the drug being used in conjunction with standard care and how well the drug works synergistically with it also needs consideration. The method of drug delivery to the target tissue or organ is another important aspect of biological activity. Certain areas, like the central nervous system, may pose specific challenges for drug delivery.

- **Clinical need:** Assess the clinical need. Is there a significant need for this treatment among patients? Are there already effective treatment alternatives available?
- **Market:** Evaluate the market size, competition, and ease of diagnosis for the chosen indication. Look at comparable exits or recent deals where pharmaceutical companies have acquired similar biotech companies.
- **Regulatory considerations:** Regulations can significantly impact the feasibility of an indication. Are the endpoints for this disease clear and objective? Does the therapy's effectiveness lend itself to easy demonstration? If an effective standard of care exists, will regulatory agencies require its use in clinical trials? Could surrogate endpoints permit accelerated approvals? Also consider potential challenges in patient recruitment for clinical trials.
- **Intellectual property (IP):** Are all indications equally protectable under IP law? Ensuring robust IP protection is crucial to maintain a competitive edge.
- **Patient Access and Recruitment:** This involves assessing the practicality of reaching the targeted patient population. Certain indications may be more common in remote or underserved regions, thus making it difficult to deliver the treatment.
- **Reimbursement Landscape:** Some indications might have a more favorable reimbursement environment, making them more attractive from a business standpoint. It's important to consider how likely insurance companies are to cover the cost of the therapy.
- **Technological advancements:** The rate of technological advancement related to the treatment of certain indications could make some more attractive than others. If an indication is being heavily researched and new technologies are being developed rapidly, it may be beneficial to ride that wave of innovation.
- **Public Interest and Funding Opportunities:** Some diseases garner more public attention and research funding than others, particularly those deemed public health crises or those championed by influential advocacy groups. This can lead to increased funding opportunities and public support for the biotech company and its mission.
- **Companion Diagnostics:** For some diseases, the development of effective diagnostics is as crucial as the development of therapeutics. If there is an opportunity to develop or partner with a company that produces companion diagnostics for a specific indication, it may improve the treatment's success chances.
- **Manufacturing Considerations:** Some treatments may require complex manufacturing processes or have stringent storage and transport requirements. This could make certain indications more appealing if they're compatible with more straightforward or cost-effective manufacturing and distribution processes.

therapies for rare diseases. Consequently, they put into place several programs and incentives aimed at promoting research and development in this area.

First, it's important to recognize what characterizes a disease as "rare."

Although the specific definition can vary by region, in the U.S., a disease is generally considered rare if it affects fewer than 200,000 people. In Europe, a disease is classified as rare if it affects fewer than five in 10,000 people.

- One of the significant benefits provided by regulatory authorities is expedited review and approval pathways. For instance, the FDA has established programs like the **Fast Track, Breakthrough Therapy, Accelerated Approval, and Priority Review designations** to speed the review and potential approval of drugs for serious conditions that fill an unmet medical need, including rare diseases. These programs aim to get treatments to patients more quickly by shortening the regulatory review and approval timelines.
- Another benefit is the **Orphan Drug Designation program**, which offers various incentives to encourage the development of drugs for rare diseases. These incentives can include tax credits for clinical testing, user fee waivers, and eligibility for seven years of market exclusivity upon approval.
- Financial incentives are another vital component of these benefits. Researching and developing new therapies is a costly and risky process, more so for rare diseases due to the smaller patient populations. To offset these risks, regulatory authorities provide **funding opportunities, grants, and fee reductions or waivers** to encourage companies to invest in the development of rare disease therapies.
- Regulatory authorities also provide **scientific advice and guidance** to companies developing therapies for rare diseases. This advice can help companies navigate the complex regulatory landscape, design appropriate clinical trials, and compile the necessary data for regulatory submissions.
- Another important but less tangible benefit is the **positive effect on a company's reputation**. Achieving regulatory designations like Orphan Drug status can raise a company's profile, attract

investment, and signal to stakeholders that the company is working to address an important unmet medical need.

In conclusion, the benefits offered by regulatory authorities play a vital role in promoting the development of therapies for rare diseases. By providing a supportive and incentivizing environment, they help lower barriers, speed up development timelines, and ultimately ensure that potentially life-changing therapies reach the patients who need them most. It's a testament to the recognition of the unique challenges and high unmet needs associated with rare diseases, and the shared commitment to addressing them.

The benefits provided by regulatory authorities for such conditions can significantly help companies bring these much-needed treatments to the market sooner. And all of this affects our criteria 2 and how easy it will be to prove. Again, as I've been saying all along, all factors here are interconnected.

Epilogue: Imagining the Story

We've delved into the framework of choosing a deep-tech company, covering everything from the sunny side of the forest to the "wow" slide, the ease of proof, and the magnitude of the problem that needs solving. However, at the heart of this all is the narrative, the story that binds these elements together.

Remember: These companies require significant funding after your investment, typically in the form of syndicates of investors joining you in the adventure. Choosing a deep-tech company to invest in is not just about scientific data or financial prospects. It's also about a genuine passion for the venture, a belief in its potential, and an excitement about its mission. Is the company's mission something that excites you? Does it inspire you and pique your interest? If the answer is yes, that's a good sign. The excitement you feel for the company can fuel your commitment to it and can be contagious, spreading to others involved in the venture.

Some questions to help you craft this story could be:

- Is the research being conducted by a reputable and well-known research lab?
- Are the researchers involved highly esteemed and easily recognizable in their field?

- Have their findings been published in a prestigious journal such as *Nature* or *Science*?
- Is the problem they're addressing currently trending in the media, or among venture capital circles?
- Can you find any anecdotes or interesting facts about the research that could make the story more engaging?
- Is there intense deal activity in this field?
- Are there past stories about Series A or Series B financing rounds involving reputable investors relevant to this field?
- Have there been recent and successful liquidity events in this field in terms of the number of deals and the amount of money involved?
- Have previous exits in this field provided substantial returns to investors?
- Do you firmly believe that this field will be a significant part of the future of medicine, and more importantly, how do you plan to communicate this potential to future new investors?

A crucial aspect of the narrative involves envisioning the entire "equity story" (see Chapter 20). This includes identifying the expected number of financing rounds. More importantly, for the narrative, we must determine the potential windows of opportunity for a liquidity event. Will we be required to remain invested in the company for an extended period? Or does a possibility for an early sale or IPO exist? This element is so critical that we will revisit it later.

A major part of a science-driven company's journey is securing sufficient funds to fuel its operations and growth. This typically requires significant fundraising efforts. When you are genuinely excited about the company and its mission, you will be much more effective in convincing others to support it financially.

Remember, a company's story is more than a marketing tool — it is the soul of the enterprise. It reflects the company's mission, the problem it seeks to solve, and the value it aims to bring to the world. Imagining this story, feeling a part of it, and being able to communicate it effectively to others, is a critical part of choosing a company to invest in.

Harmony of Prologue, Triangle, and Epilogue

Now that we've discussed the prologue (the sunny side of the forest), the triangle (the "wow" slide, ease of proof, and the importance of the problem), and the epilogue (imagining the story), it's important to highlight that these elements do not exist in isolation. They should play in concert, like an orchestra performing a symphony.

Each of these factors — whether it's the broader landscape of the technology, the specific attributes of the company, or the narrative that binds them together — has a unique role in the decision-making process. However, for a wise and informed choice, these factors should align and support each other. The technology should be promising (the sunny side), the company's scientific evidence should be compelling (the "wow" slide), the problem should be significant (the importance), and the potential to provide a solution should be clear and provable (ease of proof). Moreover, all these aspects should contribute to a powerful and convincing narrative (the story).

Striking a balance between these elements can be challenging.

A company might have a fantastic technology but lack the robust scientific evidence. Or, it might address a significant problem, but have trouble proving the potential solution. It's essential to weigh these factors against each other and strive for a balance. The company's story should reflect this balance and weave these elements into a cohesive narrative.

Remember, the decision to invest in a company isn't merely about ticking off boxes on a checklist. It's about assessing how these factors harmonize to form a promising, exciting venture. It's about feeling confident in the company's potential and being thrilled to become a part of its journey. When the prologue, triangle, and epilogue play in sync, that's when you know you're making a well-informed, considered choice.

Importance of the Team

You may have noticed that I haven't touched upon the aspect of "team" within the context of my prologue, triangle, and epilogue. This omission is deliberate and for two specific reasons.

First, the team's importance is so paramount that it precedes every other consideration. In a sense, the team is the lifeblood of the company; it's team members' combined skills, dedication, and passion that drive the venture forward. It's not enough for the technology to be promising or the problem to be significant; the team behind the company must be top-notch. They are the ones who will execute the vision, face the challenges, and steer the venture towards success. If the team lacks the necessary skills or drive, even the most promising company may falter. We don't invest in ideas; we invest in the execution of ideas and this needs a top-notch team.

However, in the context of early-stage investments, a team problem is usually "solvable." Sometimes the team is not even there and you need to create it. Furthermore, it's not uncommon for changes to occur within the team, especially with the position of CEO. If the company has potential but not the right CEO, maybe investors could find the right CEO and hire her or him. This fluidity is considered normal at this stage, thereby leading to its omission from the main framework of assessment, as it's a variable component that can be adjusted as necessary.

At early-stage investments, the focus is often on the science and the founder's or entrepreneur's vision. Here, the team needs to demonstrate a profound understanding of the science and technology and a clear roadmap of how to bring the concept to fruition. However, as the company grows and evolves, the requirements for the team change. When the venture transitions to later stages, where operational efficiency and business development become increasingly important, the team must adapt. This means augmenting the team with business savvy professionals or even considering a change in leadership.

The decision to change the CEO or bring in a professional CEO at a later stage is a common practice in science-driven companies. This change is typically planned transparently and in agreement with the founding team. The aim is to ensure that as the company scales and diversifies its operations, there is experienced leadership at the helm to guide it. However, any such decision should be made judiciously, respecting the unique culture and vision of the company.

So, choosing a company to invest in or lead isn't just about the promise of the technology or the size of the problem it aims to solve. It's also about the people who will turn that promise into reality as well. Investing your time or money in a company means investing in its team. Thus, the team's capabilities, adaptability, and harmony with the company's mission are key considerations in making your choice.

Understanding the S-Shaped Curve of Value

Investing in a science-driven company, particularly in the biotech field, often involves understanding an S-shaped curve of value. This curve represents the growth and value creation of a company over time. It starts flat, accelerates upwards (forming the S-shape), and then eventually flattens again.

For biotech companies, this S-shaped curve corresponds to well-defined development stages. The flat part represents the early conceptual phase and preliminary scientific experiments. Then comes the steep part of the curve, which usually starts with preclinical proof of concept — first in vitro, then in vivo in animals. This is followed by preclinical regulatory steps like safety and toxicity studies, then applying for an investigational new drug

(IND) application to regulatory agencies for the first in human trials. Subsequent stages — phase 1, 2, and 3 clinical trials — represent further upward progress along the curve. At each point along this trajectory, the company gains in value as it moves closer to potentially getting a product approved and on the market. Alongside these stages, factors like manufacturing the drug for the trial (CMC), IP strategy, and business development deals play out in parallel.

Depending on their development stage, companies might find themselves at different points along the S-curve. Some might be at the early flat stage, while others are at the steep part or approaching the plateau. Discerning where a company lies on this curve is an essential part of evaluating it as an investment.

Companies at the beginning of the curve or in the flat phase might be considered too early to invest in, particularly if there's a long road to significant value inflection points. On the other hand, those in the middle of the curve may offer faster opportunities for liquidity events, especially in more advanced fields where value can be captured earlier.

Pay close attention to the fact that the company's technology can significantly influence the shape or "shift-in-time" of its value trajectory. Advanced therapies like gene therapy, cell therapy, or synthetic biology (technologies regarded as more sophisticated) may exhibit a steeper curve and a leftward displacement. This means they could capture value earlier.

Understanding this S-shaped curve of value is vital for investors or entrepreneurs considering a biotech venture. It helps contextualize

Figure 61. The S-Shaped Curve of Value

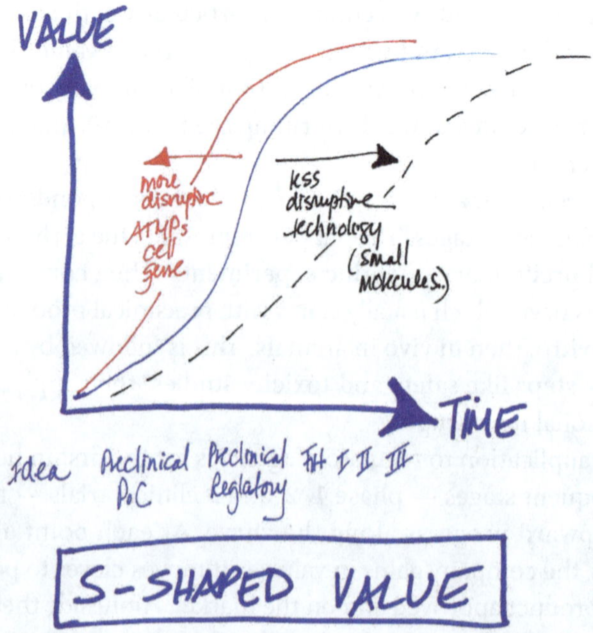

- **Exploration Phase** (The lower flat portion of the S curve): This phase represents the initial stages of a science-driven company's life, where basic research and discovery take place. Investment during this stage primarily funds experiments and data collection, with value creation being slow due to the high risk and uncertain outcomes associated with early-stage scientific research.
- **Acceleration Phase** (The steep upward portion of the S curve): As successful discoveries transition into the development phase, the value begins to accelerate. During this phase, the company focuses on refining and validating their technology or product. Positive results from preclinical and clinical trials, regulatory approvals, or partnerships can drive a significant increase in value. This phase is characterized by rapid value growth, but also high expenditure and risk, as failure in this phase can be costly.
- **Maturation Phase** (The upper flat portion of the S curve): In this phase, the product or technology has been commercialized and adopted by the market. The company's focus is on scaling up, optimizing operations, and expanding market share. Value creation continues but at a slower pace as the market becomes saturated.

where a company is in its development pathway and informs the expectations for its future value trajectory. In essence, it's a roadmap for the company's potential growth, helping you understand its present and foresee its future.

Opportunities for Liquidity Events

Will I be able to exit early? In the context of investing or leading a deep-tech company, liquidity events — such as a company's strategic sale or an initial public offering (IPO) — represent significant milestones where investors can potentially realize returns. However, the opportunities for these events can vary widely across different technologies, fields, or indications. Certain technological domains or fields can present more early opportunities for liquidity events. This could be due to the nature of the technology, the maturity of the field, or the urgency of the problem the technology is solving.

For example, certain areas of biotech addressing urgent, unmet medical needs with very novel technologies could present faster pathways to liquidity if the technology shows early promise. On the other hand, more old or crowded fields might require longer development and maturation periods before liquidity events can realistically occur.

In some advanced fields, there may be opportunities to capture value earlier. This could be due to the technology reaching market-readiness more quickly due to the appetite of potential buyers for cutting edge fields, or because there's a well-trodden path to liquidity events like acquisitions by larger, established companies.

Similarly, the indication, or the specific medical condition a technology is designed to treat, can also impact the speed to liquidity. Certain indications have a more established pathway to market, a larger patient population, or more urgent unmet needs, all of which can speed up development and adoption, and potentially lead to earlier liquidity events.

As an investor, it's crucial to take these timelines into account. Investing in deep- tech or science-driven companies is not just about understanding the technology, but also about understanding the field's maturity and its trajectory. It's about recognizing where the field is now, where it's likely to be in the future, and how quickly it can get there. This holistic understanding can then inform investment decisions, aligning expectations with the reality of the specific technology or field's development timeline.

And Now… the Due Diligence

Choosing a company to invest in or lead is just the beginning of a critical, more extensive process known as due diligence. This thorough investigation is vital to confirm and validate all the pertinent details about the company and its potential for success.

Conducting comprehensive due diligence helps to mitigate risks and uncover potential challenges or opportunities. It's an opportunity to verify the claims made by the company, inspect its operations and financials, and evaluate its strategic position within the marketplace. This process can be instrumental in avoiding costly mistakes or identifying unique value propositions that others might have overlooked. While due diligence will encompass many areas, some aspects warrant special attention in science-driven businesses. Among many other things, you'll focus on these areas:

- **The science:** Of course, this needs to be looked at again. The quality, breadth, and depth of a company's data are critical. It's important to carefully analyze all data generated by the company so far, considering the experimental design, statistical validity, and the robustness of the findings.
- **IP Strategy and Portfolio:** Intellectual property is often the lifeblood of deep-tech companies. It's therefore crucial to assess the strength and scope of the company's IP portfolio. This includes looking at existing patents, their geographical coverage, and the likelihood of them being upheld if challenged. The company's strategy for future IP development should also be evaluated.
- **CMC (Chemistry, Manufacturing, and Controls):** For companies in fields like biotech, the production of the product (drug, device, etc.) is a crucial element. Here, understanding the CMC considerations is important. This covers the procedures for manufacturing, the quality control processes, and the capability to scale production to meet potential demand.
- **Market Analysis:** Understanding the market is key. What is the size and growth rate of the potential market? Is it crowded with competitors, or does the company have a clear opportunity to

dominate? And importantly, what is the regulatory landscape for the product?

- **Financial Projections:** It's important to review the company's financial models and projections. Do they have a clear pathway to execute the preclinical and clinical trials? are their costs realistic?
- **Partnerships and Collaborations:** In the science and technology sector, partnerships can often play a critical role. Investigate any partnerships the company has, including academic collaborations, co-development agreements, and strategic partnerships.
- **Investor Base:** Who are the current investors in the company? Do they have a track record of supporting successful companies in this space? The quality of the investor base can often signal the potential of the startup.
- **Exit Strategy:** It's important to understand the company's exit strategy. Are they aiming for an IPO? A buyout? What other recent deals can offer some guidance and reassurance on the company's potential?

Remember, the goal of due diligence is to ensure that the company is a sound investment or a worthwhile project to lead. It is about knowing as much as possible, ensuring you've left no stone unturned.

When You Invest Very Early

Investing in cutting-edge technology and scientific innovations inherently involves being at the forefront of discovery. In the world of venture capital, this often translates to investing at the earliest stages of a company's life cycle, or even participating in company creation. The primary reason for this early investment is the sheer pace at which science and technology progress. Breakthroughs occur frequently and can rapidly shift the landscape of a given field. What is considered cutting-edge today might be outdated or mainstream tomorrow. This ever- volving landscape implies that by the time a company reaches the later stages of development, the leading edge of scientific discovery might have already moved on to newer ideas and technologies.

The focus on early-stage investments does not necessarily detract from the potential value or impact of later-stage companies. Still, in terms of accessing the latest scientific advancements and discoveries, early-stage companies often have the advantage. They are inherently closer to the research and are more likely to be working on the latest technological advancements.

Investing in these early-stage companies also allows for a more hands-on role in the shaping and direction of the company. It provides the opportunity to contribute to the development and implementation of the technology and potentially influence the company's strategic direction.

However, investing at such early stages also carries inherent risks. The technology may be unproven, the market uncertain, and the path to profitability unclear. This is why such investments should always be based on robust due diligence, a strong understanding of the scientific field, and an assessment of the commercial potential.

Despite these risks, the opportunity to invest in and shape the future of groundbreaking science and technology can be highly rewarding — not only in terms of potential financial returns (if you know how to choose well, early stage investments typically harvest the most profitable returns), but also in the impact on society. The most exciting scientific discoveries, after all, have the potential to revolutionize industries, transform our understanding of the world, and dramatically improve lives. It is, therefore, not surprising that many investors are drawn to the challenge and opportunity of

Investing in the field of deep tech often requires a proactive approach, far beyond the conventional methods of passively waiting for companies to present themselves. This is even more prominent in the realm of early-stage specialized funds, like the ones I had the privilege to found. The unique nature of our fund lies in its targeted investment strategy — focusing on preselected fields that we are convinced will shape the future of medicine. This precision requires us to delve deep into the research and development landscape, to unearth and catalyze the growth of nascent companies that are not yet on the mainstream radar. This active pursuit is an essential part of our investment process, not only enriching our portfolio but also playing a significant role in the technology transfer from academia into society.

The term "technology transfer" refers to the process of transferring scientific findings from one organization to real life for the purpose of further development and commercialization. This process is a crucial link between research and commercial environments, transforming scientific innovations into practical applications that benefit society at large.

Early-stage funds that actively seek out nascent companies play a crucial role in this technology transfer. We serve as a bridge between the world of scientific research and the market, identifying promising technologies within academic labs or small-scale research facilities and providing the necessary financial support and business guidance to bring these technologies to the public.

Often, the most transformative ideas are not found but sought. They exist in the realms of academic papers, lab experiments, and prototype development. As investors, our role extends beyond simply financing these ideas. We are part finders, part creators, identifying the technologies that carry the potential to revolutionize medicine and actively participating in their journey from concept to reality.

The importance of this step can't be overstated. It is the crucial pivot point that transforms a promising idea into a viable commercial entity. As investors, our proactive approach not only generates potential financial returns but also contributes significantly to societal growth. By facilitating the technology transfer process, we aid in turning scientific innovations into tangible solutions, leading to advancements in healthcare, improved patient outcomes, and overall societal progress.

Considerations for Portfolio Strategy

Selecting a portfolio for investment in science-driven companies demands deep thought, foresight, and a strategic understanding of the scientific landscape. Just as a symphony requires a balance of different instruments to create harmony, a diverse and complementary portfolio can create a well-balanced ecosystem that is resilient to the ever-changing dynamics of the scientific and investment worlds.

One of the most crucial considerations when building a portfolio is an understanding of the unique characteristics and trajectories of different scientific fields. Various sectors of science evolve at different paces and are subject to different market forces, regulatory environments, and technological developments. As such, diversification across different fields of science can provide a hedge against the inherent uncertainties and volatilities that can affect individual sectors.

Beyond diversification across different fields of science, the stage of development of the companies in your portfolio is another significant

Figure 62. Investments, Information, and Liquidity Events

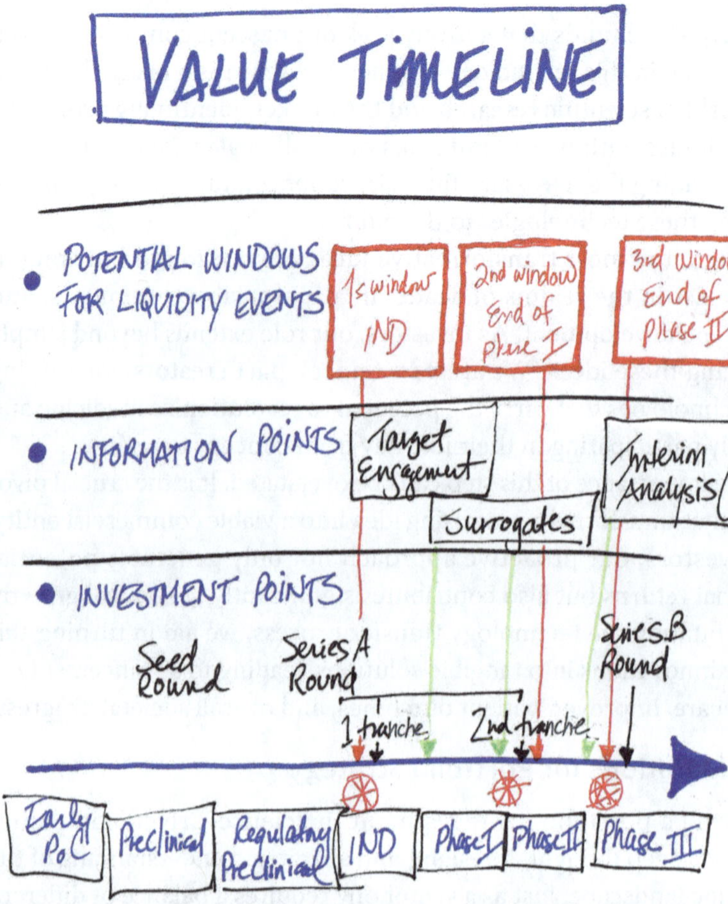

When choosing a company to invest in, you should look for multiple opportunities for information acquisition. Prioritize ventures that offer insights at various stages throughout the process. Success hinges on harnessing information at the right time, using it strategically to maintain leverage, manage risks, and potentially aim for an early liquidity event. Identify these windows for potential early liquidity events in advance and always keep them in mind. I suggest splitting the timeline into three parts: Investment Inflection Points, Information Inflection Points, and Potential Windows for Liquidity Events.

- **The crux of successful decision-making lies in the ability to gain leverage, maintain optionality, and effectively manage risks and rewards.** Venture capitalists strive to collate maximum information as early as possible. Critical junctures in the venture path require particular attention.

- **Target engagement.** Observing target engagement early on in the drug development process, such as at the end of phase 1 clinical trials, offers a wealth of advantages. First, it provides early evidence of the drug's potential effectiveness. A drug that shows strong target engagement is more likely to have a therapeutic effect, giving developers and investors alike confidence in the drug's potential success. Additionally, demonstrating target engagement early on allows for better decision-making in the drug development process. By knowing that a drug is engaging its target as intended, developers can make more informed decisions about how to proceed. This might include refining the drug formulation, optimizing the dosage, or progressing confidently into later stage trials. In the context of advanced therapies, such as gene and cell therapies, the importance of demonstrating target engagement is even greater. These therapies often involve complex mechanisms of action and can be more difficult to develop than traditional small molecule drugs.
- **The identification of the right surrogate endpoints**. These non-clinical markers are designed to predict clinical outcomes, providing an early indication of the likely success of a venture.
- **Interim analysis** presents another key opportunity for gaining early insights. However, they need to be approached with caution as premature termination of a trial could sometimes be unjustified. Nevertheless, with careful planning, interim analysis can provide valuable early information and maintain optionality.
- **Objective, clear-cut endpoints** reduce ambiguity and offer a concrete basis for evaluation. The potential to gain market authorization at an early stage, significantly boosts the venture's prospects, although this possibility hinges on a variety of factors.
- **Controlled blind studies versus open-label studies:** In a blind study, the participants, and many times even the investigators, do not know whether a participant is receiving the experimental treatment or a control (like a placebo). Its goal is to prevent bias, as knowledge of the treatment could influence the results. In contrast, an open-label study is one where both the investigators and the participants know what treatment is being administered. This type of study design might be necessary when the treatment being studied has visible side effects or when the study involves different types of treatments that are easily distinguishable. Open-label studies allow for real-time evaluation of data as it comes in. This is particularly valuable in rapidly developing fields, such as advanced therapies like cell therapies, where timely data can guide further research and development. Moreover, positive preliminary results from an open-label study could potentially trigger a liquidity event. However, there is a trade-off.

  Open-label studies may not provide the same level of statistical rigor as blind studies due to potential biases. Therefore, open-label studies might not be as effective in demonstrating a treatment's efficacy to the same degree of certainty as a blind study.

- **Prioritize ventures that offer potential for gathering insights early and throughout the process,** ensuring the capacity for informed decision-making is maintained. The essence of successful venture capitalism lies not in mere information acquisition but in the timeliness and strategic use of that information to maintain leverage, manage risks, and make the most of every opportunity. investing at the cutting edge of science and technology.

factor. Science-driven companies exist along a wide spectrum, from early-stage startups commercializing breakthrough research, to late-stage companies that are close to bringing products to market. Balancing investments across different stages of development can help mitigate the risks associated with early-stage investing, while still capturing the potentially high rewards of successful early-stage companies.

Next, consider the technological compatibility among the companies in your portfolio. While it may seem counterintuitive, investing in companies with overlapping technologies can create synergistic effects. For instance, advancements in one company can benefit others in the portfolio working with similar technologies or within the same field. Furthermore, having multiple investments in a particular technological space can deepen your understanding of that area, enhancing your ability to make informed investment decisions. However, while the benefits of synergies should not be overlooked, they should be balanced against the potential risks of overexposure to a particular technology or field. As a general rule, avoid having a portfolio that is so interdependent that the failure of one technology or adverse developments in one field could bring down multiple companies in the portfolio.

Final Thoughts and Advice

Investing in deep tech is a journey filled with uncertainties and exhilarations, with lessons drawn from successes and failures alike. Here is some distilled wisdom from my 20-year+ voyage in this field.

1. **The Inherent Inaccuracy of Decks and Business Plans:** Business plans and decks are indispensable guides, providing an initial roadmap for a company's journey. However, it is essential to remember that all business plans are flawed. They are predictions of an uncertain future based on a series of assumptions. The real question is not whether the business plan is right, but how wrong it could be and how prepared the team is to adjust and adapt. This understanding allows us to be flexible and resilient, to learn and adapt as we encounter the inevitable unforeseen circumstances.
2. **Recognizing the Fragility of Startups:** Startups, particularly in the deep-tech sector, are fragile entities. They operate on the precipice of possibility, taking ambitious leaps into the unknown. If one or two things go awry, they can be fixed, but if the problems

multiply, it might be wiser to consider other opportunities. An acute awareness of this fragility can instill prudence and caution, guiding us in making judicious decisions.

3. **Expectation of Ridicule for Innovative Ideas (Dator's Law):** As per futurist Jim Dator's law, any useful statement about the future should appear to be ridiculous. If your ideas are not at first seen as absurd, they may not be truly groundbreaking. Embrace this ridicule as an indication that you're pushing boundaries and remember that many transformative ideas were initially laughed at. This acceptance helps to fuel courage and resilience in the face of skepticism or cynicism.
4. **Embracing the Difficulty and Reward of Scientific Research:** The pursuit of science is not easy. It challenges our understanding, pushing us to the limits of our knowledge. Embrace the feeling of inadequacy that accompanies the pursuit of the unknown. It signifies that we are learning, growing, and contributing to the expansion of human knowledge. The reward lies not only in potential breakthroughs but in the very process of exploration and discovery.
5. **Balancing Options and Postponing Decisions:** The ability to balance multiple options without rushing to a decision is a vital skill in this field. Create optionality by considering different avenues without fully committing to any one of them prematurely. Only when you've thoroughly explored the alternatives, and when the time is ripe, should you make a definitive choice.
6. **Acceptance of Darwinism:** Not all projects are destined for success; some need to die quickly to allow resources to be channeled towards more promising endeavors. This Darwinian approach helps maintain focus on high potential projects, embracing failure as a natural part of the innovation process.
7. **The "Crossing the Rubicon" Mindset:** Once you commit to an investment or project, it's like crossing the Rubicon. There's no turning back, and the only way forward is to strive for success with unwavering dedication. In times of doubt, remember why you took the plunge and let that guide you through the journey, however tumultuous it may be.
8. **Know your biases:** Personal biases can influence every facet of our work in ways that are subtle and often overlooked. We bring

our past experiences, perceptions, and preconceived notions to the table every time we assess a startup or negotiate a deal. These biases can distort our vision, leading to flawed assessments and ultimately, misguided investments. As such, it is crucial to recognize and actively combat these biases in order to maintain strategic foresight and make sound investment decisions.

There are several types of biases that we commonly struggle with. Confirmation bias, for instance, compels us to seek out information that supports our existing beliefs and ignore information that contradicts them. The halo effect can cause us to overestimate the potential of a startup based on the charisma of its CEO. Conversely, the horn effect can make us undervalue a startup based on a single negative attribute. Availability bias, anchoring bias, overconfidence bias — the list goes on, each with its unique ability to warp our perception and judgement.

Understanding these biases and how they impact our decision-making process is only half the battle. The real challenge lies in actively mitigating their influence. This begins with a concerted effort toward self-awareness and introspection. Regularly questioning our own assumptions, inviting diverse perspectives, and fostering a culture of constructive criticism can help us keep our biases in check.

On the Right Way of Learning How to Choose

This final section is an essential guide for budding analysts, associates, and those who are beginning their journey in the venture capital world. It provides a roadmap of learning that I believe can significantly help navigate this multifaceted and complex industry. Embarking on the journey of choosing companies to invest in, especially within the realm of deep tech or biotech, is not a task to be undertaken lightly. It is a process that involves a significant learning curve. I propose a sequential five-step approach to mastering this complex task.

The first step is to become an adept **"bullshit detector."** The vernacular might seem crude, but it succinctly encapsulates the essence of this stage. Your initial focus should be on finding reasons to dismiss potential investments. Look for flaws in their scientific methodologies, the inadequacy of their research models, potential inaccuracies in their results, or suboptimal endpoints for their investigations. In essence, sharpen your skepticism and foster a meticulous attention to detail. This stage is crucial in building a critical perspective toward the plausibility and potential of companies.

The second stage involves transforming from a detector of falsehoods into a **"value detector."** At this stage, your objective is to discern the reasons that make a company worth investing in. This process necessitates a deep understanding of the ecosystem in which you are investing. It requires a clear conception of what constitutes value in a business and how different components of a company contribute to that value. Factors such as the company's stage of development, the field in which it operates, whether it is traditional or emerging, all influence its value proposition.

The third stage revolves around learning how to **contribute value** to companies. This involves identifying key experiments that should be conducted, performing a gap analysis to recognize what the company is missing to enhance its appeal, and influencing the team's behavior through insightful questioning. By this stage, you should be able to actively contribute to the development and growth of potential investments.

The fourth stage emphasizes **governance**. As you ascend to higher levels of seniority, you will have the opportunity to participate on company boards. Initially, you might serve as an observer, eventually graduating to the role of a board director, defending your fund's interests. This engagement provides a rich learning ground where you can absorb diverse viewpoints and nurture your intuition about the industry's workings.

The final stage, **choosing**, should not be ventured into until all the previous stages have been thoroughly mastered. Choosing a company to invest in, hence committing a substantial amount of capital, is a significant responsibility. It should be undertaken only when you are confident in your ability to fully discern the potential of a company.

Remember that choosing a company to invest in is not merely about identifying potential unicorns; it's about understanding the dynamics of the industry, the scientific credibility of the company, the potential of its products, and the ability of its team. Each step in this process is crucial, and the importance of mastering each cannot be overstated.

If you're young and passionate about this field, you may wonder where to direct your energy and focus for the greatest impact. While it's essential to master all the concepts covered in this book, if I were to choose just a few key factors that differentiate good from bad investors, I would emphasize three core components: understanding the future of technology, adding value to the companies invested in, and making wise investment choices.

1. **Mapping the Future of Medicine:** The first key factor is an intuitive grasp of what technologies will shape the future of medicine, getting to know well "the forest." This understanding doesn't come easily. It requires immersing oneself in the scientific ecosystem, consistently engaging with ongoing research, and having a clear sense of emerging trends. You must read extensively, cultivate deep relationships within the scientific community, and make effective use of sophisticated tools to analyze trends. The ultimate goal is to select the right scientific fields that have the potential for substantial future impact. Investing in technologies that will significantly shape the future of medicine is what can set a venture capital fund apart from others.
2. **Value-Add from the Board:** The second crucial factor is the ability and wisdom to provide meaningful help to portfolio companies from their boards. Venture capitalists aren't passive investors; their role extends beyond providing financial support. They are mentors, connectors, and sometimes troubleshooters. From connecting companies with the right partners and resources, offering guidance in strategic decisions, to assisting with management and leadership development, venture capitalists play a multifaceted role. The wisdom to offer impactful assistance comes from years of experience, a deep understanding of the field, and a genuine interest in seeing the companies succeed. The more hands-on and proactive a venture capitalist is in adding value, the higher the chances of a positive outcome.
3. **Choosing Wisely:** The third and perhaps the most elusive factor is the ability to choose wisely the right companies to invest in. This entails not only selecting companies that promise significant returns but also constructing a well-balanced portfolio. A good portfolio strategy involves diversification across stages of development, therapeutic areas, and risk profiles. Moreover, it's also about timing — knowing when to invest and when to divest. Each company within the portfolio should be chosen with the goal of

entering into a sale, IPO, or a liquidity event at some point in the future. The art of portfolio construction, therefore, lies in strategically combining everything mentioned in this book to make wise investment decisions.

IV

Epilogue: Science, Curiosity, Ethics, and Happiness

Rule #37

Understand Why Science Matters

"I am not afraid of tomorrow, for I have seen yesterday and I love today."
William Allen White

As we wrap up this book, let's think about the big picture, looking at how science, creativity, ethics, and happiness tie together. These four things are at the heart of projects that aim to change the world. Such projects are driven by scientific discoveries and bold new ideas. They often lead to big changes, shaking up whole industries.

As we move further into the 21st century, we can see that science and technology are key parts of our lives. They've taken us from understanding our own DNA to exploring the mysteries of quantum mechanics. Science has led us into a time of amazing potential. It changes the way we see the world. But science is also part of our everyday lives. It influences everything from the medicine we take to the smartphones we use all the time.

In the world of startups and investment, especially in cutting-edge areas like biotechnology, science is more than just a game-changer. It's a guide to what the future might hold. Here, we'll take a deep dive into why science is so important. We'll look at how it helps us understand the world, but also how it can help investors make good decisions. We'll explore the scientific method and show how it can help you find and manage investment opportunities. We'll compare the reliable facts of science with the unreliable ideas of superstition. By the end of this chapter, you'll understand why science is such a powerful tool.

The Scientific Method: Our Best Tool

A central pillar in the edifice of scientific achievement is the scientific method — a systematic, objective approach to understanding the universe and its workings. It is a four-step cycle that begins with observation, progresses to hypothesis, advances to experimentation, and finally leads to the refinement of theories or models based on the experimental results. This iterative process, underpinned by a staunch commitment to truth and verifiable evidence, has empowered us to continually expand the frontiers of human knowledge.

Observation sparks curiosity and questions, instigating the quest for understanding. It is through careful observation of phenomena that we discern patterns or anomalies, forming the bedrock upon which we build our hypotheses — tentative explanations that need testing. Experimentation then provides the crucible where these hypotheses are subjected to rigorous scrutiny, validated or refuted based on empirical data. The final step, refinement, allows us to modify our theories or models to better fit the observed facts, completing the cycle and setting the stage for further observations and hypotheses.

The scientific method is a testament to our relentless pursuit of knowledge, a tool that encourages us to challenge assumptions, validate claims, and continually strive for a more accurate understanding of reality. It fosters a culture of doubt and intellectual humility, recognizing that our grasp of the truth is always provisional, contingent on the latest evidence.

In the context of investment decisions, particularly in fields like biotech and disruptive innovations, the scientific method assumes a pivotal role. Assessing the potential of a new therapy or technology often involves testing hypotheses about its safety, efficacy, market acceptance, and impact on patients.

Rigorous analysis, evidence-based evaluations, and a willingness to revise investment theses in the light of new data mirror the principles of the scientific method. Thus, the scientific method, more than just a procedure for researchers, is a powerful decision-making tool, vital for navigating the uncertainties of groundbreaking investments.

It underlines the principle that sound investment decisions, like solid scientific theories, are not based on blind faith or untested assumptions, but on a careful, evidence-based assessment of the facts at hand. In the dynamic arena of leading-edge investments, it is our best tool for separating the wheat from the chaff and identifying truly transformative opportunities.

Science's Role in Leading-Edge Investments

Science acts as both the genesis of opportunity and the compass guiding investment decisions. It's a ceaseless fountain of possibilities, with each scientific breakthrough ushering in new territories to explore, like branches in a tree. Science and investment, in the modern context, have a symbiotic relationship. On one hand, advancements in scientific knowledge open new frontiers, fostering the development of innovative products, services, and technologies that hold the potential to disrupt established industries and market paradigms. These advancements embody opportunities for investors to capitalize on groundbreaking trends, supporting companies that are at the vanguard of progress.

On the other hand, understanding the science behind these advancements is crucial for investors to accurately gauge the potential and risks associated with their investments. The viability of a novel drug, the efficiency of a new renewable energy technology, the impact of a revolutionary data processing algorithm in AI — all these hinge on the underlying scientific principles. A robust scientific understanding aids investors in distinguishing between sound, evidence-based innovations and flashy but unsubstantiated claims. It equips them to ask pertinent questions, scrutinize the assumptions, and challenge the promises of investment prospects.

Moreover, the rigorous, skeptical mindset cultivated by the scientific method can be highly beneficial in investment decision- making. It encourages investors to challenge their biases, question their assumptions, and be open to revising their investment theses in light of new evidence. Such a mindset can be invaluable in avoiding pitfalls and steering investments toward truly transformative opportunities.

So, in the world of leading-edge investments, science is more than just the seed of opportunity — it's a critical lighthouse guiding investors through the often-tumultuous seas of decision-making.

Figure 63. How to Teach Science

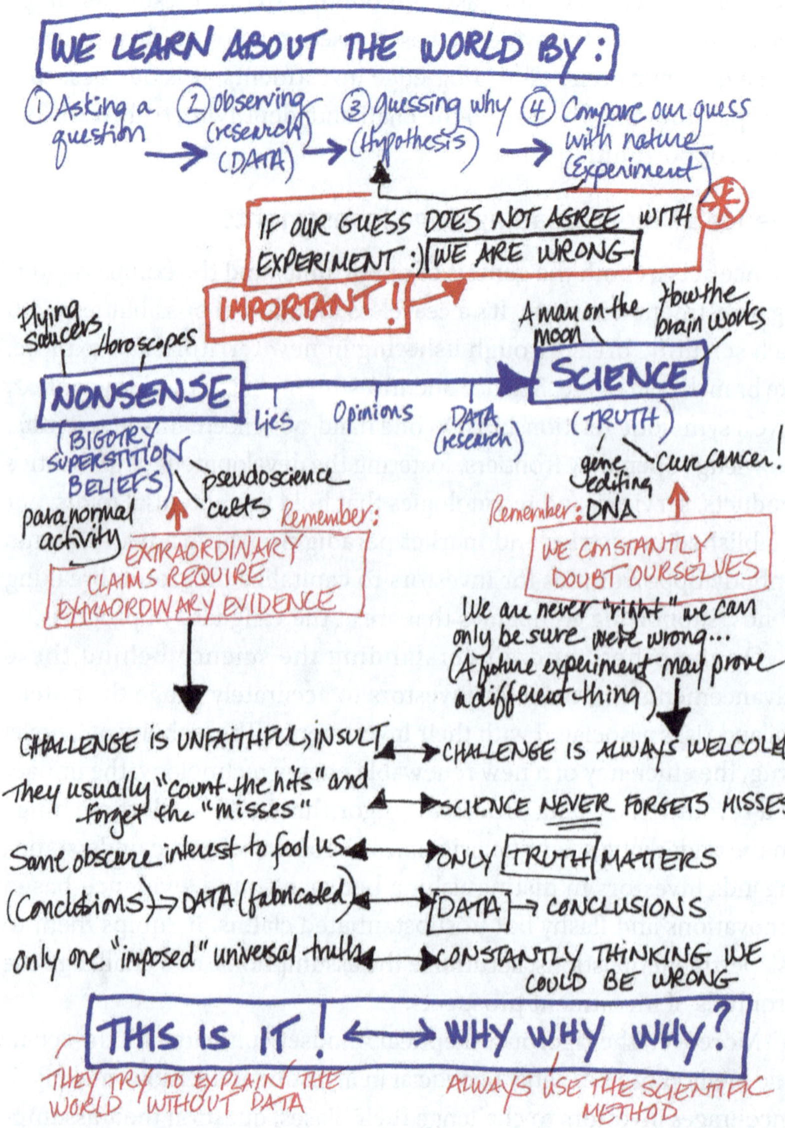

This figure delineates a critical contrast between superstition or false beliefs and science, two fundamentally disparate approaches to understanding the world. This representation aims to elucidate why science holds paramount importance in our contemporary world.

First, we must consider our **process of learning about the world**. It comprises four stages: (1) asking questions, (2) observing (via data collection and research), (3) guessing why (formulating hypotheses), and (4) comparing our hypotheses with nature (experimenting). A salient tenet of scientific inquiry is that if our hypotheses do not align with experimental results, they are incorrect. This rule is universally applicable and undeniably significant.

A continuum spans from nonsense, including superstitions, false beliefs, and pseudoscience, on the left, to rigorous scientific understanding on the right. It's important to discern between the baseless claims often seen in pseudosciences — like flying saucers, horoscopes, paranormal activities, and cults — and the empirical truth attainable through science, the same science that enabled humanity to land on the moon, cure diseases, and explore the workings of the brain.

From left to right, the continuum displays beliefs, lies, opinions, data, and finally truth. In navigating this spectrum, we should keep two axioms in mind. First, as Carl Sagan asserted, "extraordinary claims require extraordinary evidence" — a guiding principle for distinguishing between baseless beliefs and valid claims. Second, the scientific community's constant self-doubt is integral to the process of scientific inquiry. While we can never be definitively right — as future experiments might yield different results — we can be sure when we're wrong.

This figure also presents the dichotomy between the views of superstition and science:

- Superstition views challenges as unfaithful insults, while science welcomes and thrives on challenges.
- Superstition often focuses on "hits" and forgets the "misses," whereas science meticulously records both successes and failures.
- Superstition may succumb to obscure interests with the intent to deceive, while science values only truth.
- Superstition often proceeds from predetermined conclusions to selectively chosen data, while science bases conclusions on thorough data analysis.
- Superstition espouses a single, imposed universal truth, while science acknowledges the possibility of being wrong and constantly seeks to improve understanding.

In conclusion, the difference between nonsense and science fundamentally lies in their approach to knowledge acquisition. Nonsense often attempts to explain the world without data, demanding blind acceptance. In stark contrast, science always employs the scientific method, incessantly asking "why?" and seeking empirical evidence to support its conclusions. This constant pursuit of truth, however uncertain, is the essence of scientific inquiry.

Criticism and Skepticism: Essential Ingredients of Science

A vital aspect of the scientific method that translates directly into the realm of investment is the emphasis on criticism and skepticism. Science, by its nature, invites scrutiny and encourages skepticism. It thrives on critique and the testing of theories and hypotheses. No idea, regardless of its source or the reputation of its proponent, is above questioning or exempt from rigorous testing. This notion of constant questioning is central to the scientific process, serving as a quality control mechanism that separates the wheat from the chaff.

Applying this scientific skepticism to investment proves to be a valuable asset. Investors must have a healthy dose of skepticism, providing a safeguard against overly optimistic projections or unproven, high-risk opportunities. By promoting a thorough vetting of potential investments, criticism and skepticism protect investors from being swayed by hype and help them focus on sound, science-backed prospects.

In the realm of leading-edge investments, maintaining a science-literate approach is more than an asset — it's a necessity. Understanding the underlying science of potential investments enables discernment of truly innovative ideas and separates substantive, high-potential opportunities from the ones that merely shine on the surface.

To cultivate a science-literate investment mindset, investors can adopt a number of practical strategies. Keeping abreast of scientific developments in relevant fields through a steady diet of scientific literature, reputable publications, and scientific conferences is one. Engaging with scientific communities, either through networking events or online platforms, can also provide invaluable insights.

Beyond passive consumption, active learning strategies can also be beneficial. Consider enrolling in science courses or workshops that pertain to your investment interest. Seeking mentorship from scientists or more science-literate investors can also prove enlightening.

Finally, embody the essence of the scientific mindset in your approach: Be open to new information, be ready to question and scrutinize, and don't be afraid to revise your investment thesis in light of new evidence.

Science literacy in investment is not about becoming a scientific expert — it's about gaining the competency to appreciate the science behind the investments and harness it for informed decision-making. It is a means to navigate the complexities of today's leading-edge investments with greater confidence and acuity. I urge all investors and entrepreneurs to embrace the principles of scientific inquiry in their decision-making processes.

Just as the scientific method values observation, hypothesis formation, and rigorous testing, so should your investment strategy. This mindset, rooted in curiosity, skepticism, and evidence, will help you navigate the challenging terrain of disruptive innovation, distinguish genuine potential from mere hype, and ultimately, make more informed and successful decisions. The world of leading-edge investment is intricate and ever-evolving — a scientific approach can be your compass.

Rule #38

Surround Yourself with Curiosity-Driven Minds

"The world is full of magic things, patiently waiting for our senses to grow sharper."
W.B. Yeats

At its core, curiosity is an insatiable desire to learn and to understand. It's that spark that leads you to ask "why?" or "how?" when faced with something you don't yet comprehend. It's a relentless pursuit of knowledge and an openness to the unexpected. In the realm of business, especially in deep tech, curiosity isn't just important, it's essential. It paves the way for innovation, encourages risk-taking, and drives us to constantly seek better ways of doing things.

But curiosity isn't just about asking questions; it's a way of life for those of us enthralled by science. Science is essentially curiosity in action. It's about probing the mysteries of the universe, exploring the unknown, and constantly pushing the boundaries of our understanding. Just as curiosity sparks questions, science seeks answers.

If we take a moment to visualize a coin, with curiosity on one side and science on the other, we might soon realize that the two sides aren't entirely separate but are instead intricately connected. This interconnectedness is the cornerstone of the relationship between curiosity-driven and science-driven minds.

Curiosity as a Propeller of Scientific Inquiry

Curiosity is the fuel that powers scientific inquiry. It's what drives scientists to spend countless hours in the lab, conducting experiment after experiment in the quest for answers. It's what leads researchers to read through mountains of literature, eager to learn from the discoveries of those who came before them.

At their core, both curiosity and science are driven by a desire to answer fundamental questions about the world. They seek to unravel the mysteries of the universe, whether it's understanding the intricate web of life at a molecular level or probing the vast expanses of the cosmos. Each question answered opens the door to myriad new ones, keeping the cycle of curiosity and scientific inquiry perpetually in motion.

In the realm of deep tech, curiosity isn't just a valuable trait, it's a necessity. The complex, rapidly evolving nature of this field makes curiosity an essential tool for success. It's a world where the questions being asked are often as novel as the technologies being created to answer them. And in this ever-evolving landscape, those who can maintain their curiosity and harness it through rigorous scientific exploration will be the ones leading the way.

Connecting seemingly unrelated concepts and ideas to create innovative solutions is one of the magical facets of curiosity. This ability to "connect the dots" is central to innovation. It is what allows us to see opportunities where others see obstacles and to create unique solutions to complex problems.

In the realm of deep tech, where cutting-edge concepts often intersect, the ability to connect disparate ideas is crucial. Consider the world of artificial intelligence. AI draws upon diverse fields, from computer science and mathematics to psychology and philosophy. Without the ability to connect these varied dots, we wouldn't have the advancements we see today in machine learning, natural language processing, and robotics.

Science at the Frontiers

Think of frontier science as the edge of our collective understanding. It's where we've pushed the boundaries of our knowledge and stand poised to delve into the unknown. These frontiers represent not only the mysteries of our universe but also vast opportunities. Curiosity is what compels scientists to unravel the secrets of quantum mechanics, decode the intricacies of the human genome, or delve into the mysteries of dark matter. It encourages risk-taking, fosters innovative thinking, and cultivates resilience — qualities that are instrumental in pushing the frontiers of science further. This curiosity-led exploration, in turn, drives innovation, as the knowledge and insights gained pave the way for new technologies, applications, and solutions in deep tech.

The Need for a Broad Knowledge Base

The landscape of deep tech is complex and multifaceted, demanding a broad understanding of various fields and industries. This breadth of knowledge is an essential foundation for making informed decisions, whether you're an investor, an entrepreneur, or a CEO in the deep-tech realm.

Knowing a little bit about everything is necessary for investing wisely or being a successful entrepreneur or CEO in deep tech. It's not enough to be a specialist in just one area; you need to have a solid understanding of different fields to see the big picture and to anticipate how innovations in one area might impact or be impacted by developments in another.

This holistic perspective is particularly crucial for investors who need to assess the potential and risks of different ventures, for entrepreneurs who need to identify untapped opportunities, and for CEOs who must steer their companies through a rapidly evolving landscape.

Cultivating a broad knowledge base requires a strategic approach. Here are a few strategies:

- **Embrace Lifelong Learning:** Dedicate time for learning new things, whether through books, online courses, seminars, or podcasts. Diversify your learning resources and areas of study to broaden your perspective.
- **Engage with Different Disciplines:** Attend conferences and workshops outside your field. This can provide insights into different domains and foster interdisciplinary thinking.
- **Network Broadly:** Connect with professionals and experts from different fields. This can give you a window into the trends, challenges, and opportunities in various industries.

- **Question Everything:** Cultivate a habit of questioning and critical thinking. This can drive you to dig deeper and understand diverse subjects more thoroughly.
- **Stay Updated:** Regularly follow news and developments in different industries. This can keep you informed about the latest trends, innovations, and shifts in various sectors.

Surround Yourself with Giants, and You Will Become One

This isn't a tale of mythical creatures, but rather a metaphorical truth in the world of entrepreneurship and innovation. Giants, in this context, are those with expansive minds, relentless curiosity, and insatiable hunger for knowledge. They are the thought leaders, the disruptors, the agents of change, and the dreamers who dare to ask the challenging questions that propel industries forward.

The world of cutting-edge innovation is a complex landscape filled with ambiguity, uncertainty, and constant flux. It demands a unique breed of individuals who not only adapt but also thrive in such environments. As an entrepreneur or an investor, it is crucial to embed this spirit of curiosity within your team, your environment, and yourself. Prioritize curiosity when building your team. Seek out the individuals who ask thoughtful questions, who demonstrate an inherent interest in learning, and who express a genuine fascination for their field of work. Individuals who run out of questions run out of ideas, and in the world of innovation, ideas are the lifeblood of progress.

In an ecosystem that changes at an unfathomably fast pace, hiring curious minds is not just a desirable trait; it is an imperative. Curious people will keep you updated with the latest trends, the emerging technologies, the newest discoveries. They will be your eyes and ears, your think tanks, your problem solvers. The process of surrounding yourself with giants, that is to say, with the intensely curious, isn't merely a pursuit of knowledge; it's a journey of transformation. By surrounding yourself with these towering figures of curiosity, you invite their mindset, their worldview, their relentless questioning to influence your thinking. Their habits become your habits; their strengths become your strengths. And before you know it, you become a giant in your own right. It is the greatest privilege of what I do, to be surrounded by them at all times.

Ending on a Note That Pays Tribute to the Beauty and Awe-Inspiring Nature of Science

Ask questions, seek answers, venture into the unknown, and never stop learning. In the words of the great physicist Richard Feynman, "I have no special talent. I am only passionately curious." Allow your curiosity to guide your path, whether it leads you to decode the mysteries of the universe, create the next big thing in deep tech, or invest in a venture that could transform the future.

Science is a testament to our inherent curiosity and our relentless pursuit of knowledge. It's a tribute to our desire to understand the world around us, to make sense of the cosmos, and to harness this understanding to improve our lives. As we delve into the depths of the quantum world or gaze at the vastness of the universe, we're reminded of the beauty and wonder that lies at the heart of science. It's this awe-inspiring nature of science that captivates us, fuels our curiosity, and drives us to keep exploring, keep asking, and keep discovering. As a scientist, it's a privilege to be part of this grand endeavor, and as a reader, I hope you share in this sense of wonder and awe.

Rule #39

You Will Face Ethical Dilemmas

"We have to continually be jumping off cliffs and developing our wings on the way down."
Kurt Vonnegut

I love ethical dilemmas. They provide a framework to understand who we are, what really matters to us. In the fast-paced world of disruptive innovation and investment, a critical yet often overlooked aspect is the ethical dilemmas that emerge in the course of exploring the unknown. These quandaries not only challenge our pre-existing moral frameworks but are fundamental in revealing our true nature, our most deeply ingrained values, and our capacity for decision-making under uncertainty. From the biotech labs working on cutting-edge cancer research to the operating theaters of neurosurgery, these dilemmas are inescapable. They are inherent in our drive for advancement, our relentless pursuit of the next leap forward.

Understanding these ethical considerations is vital for managing innovation effectively. The choices we make, often between two seemingly undesirable outcomes, shape the trajectory of our ventures and, ultimately, the future of our society. Balancing the needs of the present with the potential benefits of the future, grappling with the tension between individual risk and collective advancement — these are the tasks that ethical dilemmas compel us to undertake. As we tread this uncharted territory, it is crucial to remember that while the dilemmas we encounter may be complex and uncomfortable, they are the crucibles in which our integrity as innovators, entrepreneurs, and investors is truly tested and refined.

In essence, ethical dilemmas are complex situations that often involve a decision-making process that tests our deepest moral and ethical convictions. They force us to choose between two or more conflicting values or principles, often resulting in an outcome that may not be entirely satisfactory or palatable (see advice #24 regarding trade-offs in Chapter 27). It is in the crucible of these dilemmas that our core values and fundamental beliefs are brought to the fore.

Ethical dilemmas, especially those emerging in the realm of innovation and advancement, often present themselves in an "unfair" light. It's in these unfair predicaments that the complexity and challenges of our field are most acutely felt, as we're often compelled to make decisions with far-reaching implications under conditions of considerable uncertainty.

Framework #1: The Many Over One

The journey into the heart of ethical dilemmas in innovation starts with a hypothetical scenario, which, despite its unrealistic nature, resonates deeply with the ethical quandaries inherent in leading-edge fields. Imagine you are a cancer researcher who has discovered a potential cure for pediatric cancer. However, you are aware that the first child treated with this new drug might die to the yet unknown appropriate dosage. Here's the unfair question: Do you proceed with the treatment, potentially saving millions of lives in the future, but gravely risking the life of one child now that could be trying a different form of therapy?

This dilemma opens up a Pandora's box of ethical considerations and moral tensions. There's a balance to be struck between the immediate harm that might befall one child and the future benefit that could potentially be realized for many others. Yet, it's essential to acknowledge that society already grapples with dilemmas of a similar nature. Clinical trials, for instance, entail a degree of risk for participants, yet they are critical for advancing medical science and potentially saving countless lives down the line.

Innovation, particularly in the leading-edge fields, inevitably gives rise to difficult ethical decisions. At times, the path toward advancement seems to demand a precarious balancing act, favoring the needs of the many over the immediate welfare of the individual.

This perspective, while challenging to navigate, is often necessary for propelling forward the boundaries of knowledge and technology.

However, this approach is not without its potential pitfalls. The ethical implications associated with prioritizing broader societal needs over those of the individual can be fraught with moral complexities and potential adverse consequences. It is here that a careful analysis is needed to weigh the balance between immediate harm and potential future benefits. It's within this balance that the true spirit of innovation lies.

Framework #2: The Future Over Today

Venturing into the realm of tangible, real-world ethical dilemmas, we turn to my former profession as a neurosurgeon. Here, a frequent ethical conundrum relates to the treatment of a condition known as brain aneurysm, an abnormally thin balloon-like structure extruding from an artery in the brain, posing a risk of rupture.

The dilemma arises during the surgical intervention, where a clip is placed in the neck of the aneurysm to prevent rupture. The task requires a high level of skill and precision, with significant risk involved. If the clip is placed by an experienced surgeon, the chances of successful treatment are high. However, if it is placed by a less experienced surgeon-in-training, the risk of rupture is elevated, potentially leading to detrimental patient outcomes.

On the surface, the decision seems straightforward: Allow only the most experienced surgeons to perform the procedure. But that perspective doesn't account for the future. If residents are never allowed to perform the procedure, their skills won't develop, and the future mortality rate of aneurysms would skyrocket.

This predicament is an embodiment of the ethical challenges that often accompany innovation. It illuminates the tension between immediate patient safety and long-term benefits to future patients, shedding light on the intricate balance that must be struck in our quest for advancement.

Hence, navigating the landscape of ethical dilemmas in innovation requires a distinct temporal lens. It necessitates looking beyond the immediacy of the present toward the possibilities and uncertainties of the future. The process of innovation inherently brings about change and challenges established norms. It demands the sacrifice of

Figure 64. Ethical Dilemmas in Genome Editing

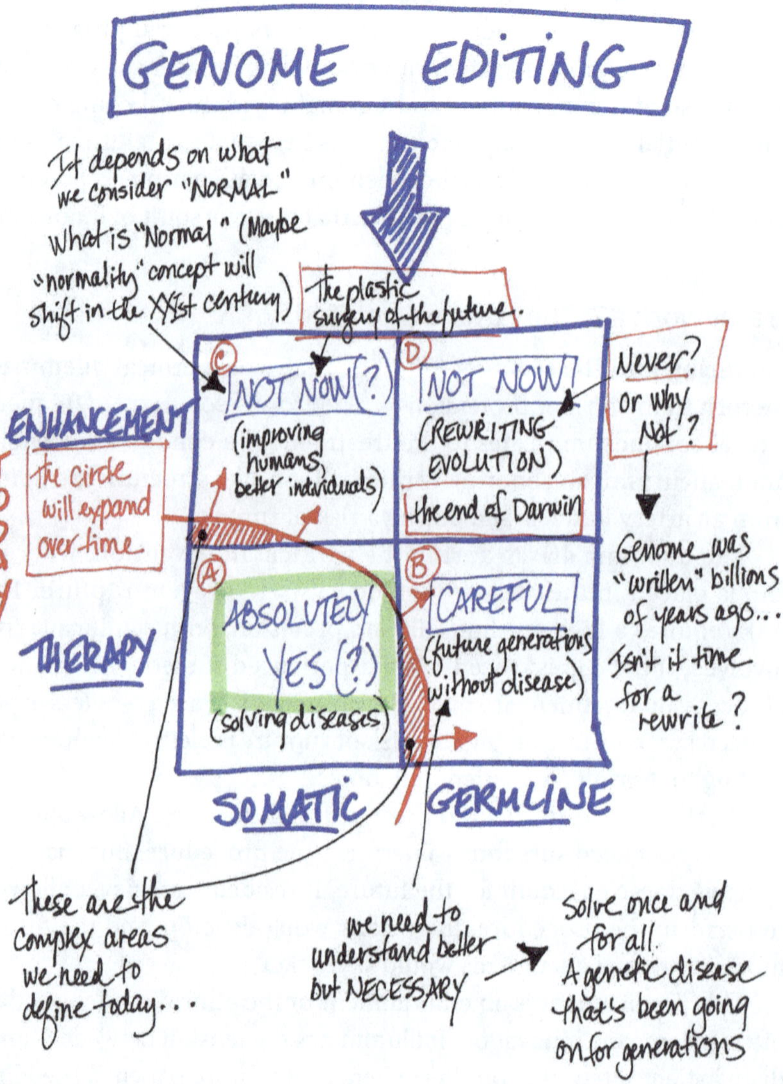

The 2x2 matrix presented in Figure 64 offers a roadmap for navigating the intricate ethical terrain in the realm of gene editing. The horizontal axis illustrates the types of cells subject to gene editing: somatic cells, wherein changes won't be transmitted to future generations, and germline cells, where alterations will pass down to the progeny. The vertical axis differentiates between the purpose of such modifications: therapeutic interventions aimed at correcting diseases, and enhancement, not just remedying diseases but also modifying traits of humans we deem preferable:

- **The bottom left quadrant embodies somatic cell therapy**, where specific diseases are targeted for a single patient. This quadrant is generally ethically unambiguous; it's about bettering individual lives by addressing specific health issues. As we move to other quadrants, ethical dilemmas become more complex.
- **The germline therapy quadrant** grapples with the balance between eradicating diseases for future generations and understanding the long-term implications of such gene edits. The benefit is apparent — generational freedom from genetic afflictions — but we must also proceed with caution, prioritizing safety.
- **When we explore enhancement in somatic cells**, we enter a domain of controversy. For instance, using gene editing to increase a child's height or physical traits invites debate akin to existing discourses surrounding plastic surgery. As we embrace human improvement, it raises questions about our shifting perceptions of "normal."
- The final, and arguably most contentious quadrant, concerns **germline enhancement**. This possibility is tantamount to assuming control over human evolution, opening the door to potentially dramatic changes to the human race. It sparks the question: Is it time for a "genetic rewrite," assuming we fully understand the repercussions?
- While our circle of acceptance may expand with time and advancements, it is crucial to tread with **caution**. The ethical terrain of gene editing is complex, and the consequences significant. Throughout this journey, the guiding principle must always be "Safety First."
- This figure not only visualizes the complexities and ethical dilemmas inherent in the field of gene editing, but it also underscores the **need for dialogue, regulation, and responsible innovation.** It encourages us to question how we define "normal" and whether our current notions of it are restrictive or liberating. The figure suggests that our understanding of normality might shift dramatically, redefining our ethical boundaries in gene editing.

This shift, however, must not come at the expense of safety and long-term societal good. The matrix highlights the importance of public engagement and understanding in shaping the future of gene editing. It is paramount that these discussions are not confined to the scientific community but extend to society at large. There is a need for inclusive dialogue that acknowledges the diversity of perspectives, ensures the equitable distribution of benefits, and addresses the potential risks. It challenges us to consider the profound implications of stepping into the shoes of "nature," of not just being subject to evolution, but becoming its architects. While this power brings the promise of immense benefits, it also comes with the potential for unforeseen consequences. It's a constant reminder that with great power comes great responsibility, and thus the importance of adhering to the principle of "Safety First."

As **we look forward to the horizon of possibilities**, the future in gene editing technology brims with hope, promise, and a touch of trepidation. If done correctly, we stand on the precipice of an era that could redefine our notions of health, longevity, and human potential. Illnesses that have plagued humanity for generations could become a thing of the past, and enhancements that seem like science fiction today might be within our reach. But in this radiant landscape of potential lies a slippery slope, a dystopian scenario where misuse of these technologies could have disastrous consequences, raising profound ethical and societal concerns. As entrepreneurs and investors, we are more than just bystanders in this unfolding drama of human evolution. We are the torchbearers of this transformative change, the navigators charting the course of this brave new world. We bear the tremendous responsibility of ensuring that these innovations serve the greater good, that they not only transform our lives but also uphold our shared values of equity, dignity, and respect for all life.

immediate comforts and certainties for the promise of future advancements and breakthroughs.

One key aspect of this temporal dimension is, again, the concept of delayed gratification. Innovation often requires the acceptance of short-term risks or sacrifices to achieve long-term gains. This principle applies not only to technical and economic aspects of innovation but also to ethical dilemmas. As seen in the neurosurgeon's dilemma, the decision to allow a less experienced resident to perform a risky procedure can lead to immediate harm but also to long-term benefits as the next generation of neurosurgeons becomes proficient in their skills.

Thus, in managing ethical dilemmas in innovation, one must always take into account this temporal dimension. Leaders in innovation must develop a forward-looking perspective, willing to make difficult decisions in the present that may prove beneficial in the future. This forward-looking perspective is not just a desirable attribute; it is an essential requirement for managing innovation effectively.

Ethical Dilemmas in Emerging Technologies

Emerging technologies often present new and complex ethical dilemmas. The potential of artificial intelligence (AI), for instance, is enormous. However, the ethical questions it raises are equally significant. On one hand, AI has the power to revolutionize society and usher in a golden age of humanity where scarcity is no longer a concern. On the other hand, unchecked AI development could potentially harm populations, creating widespread social and economic disparities. Investors, entrepreneurs, and innovators must grapple with these dilemmas to ensure responsible AI development.

Another potent example of technological advancement raising ethical questions is genome editing. This powerful tool could allow us to correct rare diseases, thereby improving the quality of life for many. However, it also presents the opportunity to alter human characteristics at will. Could we justify genome editing to make everyone taller simply because we want to? What about altering the genetic makeup of not just somatic cells, but the germline, thus affecting future generations? Navigating these ethical dilemmas is crucial for responsible innovation in this field.

Conclusion: Navigating Ethical Dilemmas in Innovation

Ethical dilemmas are not abstract intellectual exercises; they have real, tangible impacts on people and societies. They shape the very trajectory of innovation, influencing the development and application of technologies. They are like signposts in the journey of innovation. They tell us about our values, our choices, and our vision for the future. They force us to confront uncomfortable questions and make tough decisions. But they also guide us, helping us to innovate responsibly and effectively.

In the world of innovation, the ability to understand and navigate ethical dilemmas is not just a desirable skill, it's a necessity. You will face ethical dilemmas, rest assured. As we continue to push the boundaries of what's possible, we must remain cognizant of these ethical dilemmas and committed to navigating them responsibly. The future of innovation — and our collective future — depends on it.

Rule #40

On Happiness in Science: Finding Joy in Learning and Growth

"Happiness is a byproduct of function, purpose, and conflict; those who seek happiness for itself seek victory without war."
William S. Burroughs

You might be wondering, why is a chapter on happiness included in a book about investment strategies? The answer lies in understanding the price we pay for dedicating ourselves to significant pursuits. Such dedication often results in stress and relentless pressure to perform, with our value gauged by our latest achievements. How do we navigate through these challenges and maintain our sense of happiness? While this question seems straightforward, the answer is quite complex.

As we ascend our professional ladder, maintaining our position can be even more stressful. Let me clarify that I am no expert in happiness. Nor am I claiming that I've achieved a state of perpetual happiness. Rather, in alignment with Tal Ben-Shahar's philosophy, my goal has always been to aim for a state of "being happier" rather than being perfectly happy. Happiness, as I perceive it, is not a definitive state but a direction we strive for.

In this chapter, I share some ideas and tools that have brought me a measure of comfort over the years, particularly as my career responsibilities have increased. These are not meant to be life-changing prescriptions, but insights that I'm willing to share based on my personal experiences. From countering the impostor syndrome to the application of Stoicism, and from being in constant interaction with intelligent minds to the benefits of solitude, these insights will provide a foundation for a more sustainable, fulfilling journey in the realm of high-stakes investment.

The anecdote goes that Marcus Aurelius, the Roman emperor, employed a personal aide whose sole responsibility was to follow him around during his public appearances in the Roman squares. Each time Aurelius received accolades, the aide would lean in and whisper, "You are only a man, you're only a man." This humble reminder is integral to personal growth. When striving for self-improvement, we should surround ourselves with individuals who challenge our ideas and scrutinize our actions. If we ever find ourselves to be the most knowledgeable persons in the room, then it's time to switch rooms. We should aspire to be in the company of those who elevate our thought processes and expand our perspectives to horizons beyond our imaginations.

It's important to remember not to let praise inflate our ego, nor should we allow criticism to penetrate our hearts. By maintaining this balance, we can remain genuine and authentic in our endeavors. For Marcus Aurelius, the joy of learning and growth surpassed the allure of unquestioned authority. As an emperor, he had the power to surround himself with sycophants but chose, instead, the challenging path of self-improvement. In his personal quest for authenticity and truth, he navigated a delicate balance: never letting the chorus of praises inflate his ego, nor allowing the sting of criticism to wound his heart.

His legacy, thus, went beyond that of a wise emperor. Marcus Aurelius became a symbol of humility and ceaseless learning, his life an enduring testament to the pursuit of authenticity and growth. In a world governed by power and applause, he chose to remain, above all else, human.

This concept I refer to as a "rock personality" is particularly important in our volatile fields of entrepreneurship and venture capital investing. The nature of our business is akin to a rollercoaster ride, with the thrill of success one day and the pressure of poor decisions the next. Yet, it's essential to remember that we are neither geniuses nor failures; rather, we are human beings navigating a complex landscape. In this environment, striving for emotional stability is key. It means staying grounded, not getting excessively excited in the face of success, nor overly pessimistic when things don't go according to plan. This balanced approach cultivates a resilience that will keep you persevering through all kinds of challenges, and this perseverance is truly what matters most in our line of work.

Embracing this "rock personality" is not only beneficial professionally, but it also contributes to personal well-being. Knowing that you can weather the ups and downs, and continue to strive towards your goals, can provide a powerful sense of inner contentment and happiness.

Happiness Amplifies the Outcome

High-stakes investing is often seen as a world of cold calculation and relentless drive, a sphere that leaves little room for other considerations. This perception, while somewhat grounded in reality, overlooks a crucial aspect of the investment profession: the human element. Investment decisions, strategies, and the ability to weather the highs and lows of the market all fundamentally rely on the human capacity to cope, adapt, and maintain an overall sense of well-being. Happiness, or more precisely, the pursuit of happiness, therefore, is an essential yet underappreciated aspect of investment success.

Our understanding of happiness, however, needs redefining. The popular notion of happiness as a destination, a final state to be achieved, is not only unattainable but also misleading. Instead, as proposed by Tal Ben-Shahar, happiness should be viewed as a direction, a course of "being happier." It's about continual progress, constant adjustment, and the ability to find moments of contentment even amidst challenges.

This approach to happiness is particularly valuable in the high-pressure environment of leading-edge investment. Given the relentless stress and the rapidly changing dynamics of the investment landscape, a focus on "being happier" provides a resilient, adaptive framework for mental well-being.

Overcoming Impostor Syndrome

Impostor syndrome is a pervasive psychological pattern in which individuals doubt their skills, talents, or accomplishments and harbor an internalized fear of being exposed as a "fraud." It's particularly prevalent among high-achieving professionals and can profoundly undermine their confidence and performance.

The fear of being "found out" can lead to chronic stress, burnout, and even self-sabotage. Despite substantial evidence of their capabilities — successful investments, appreciation from peers, recognition in the industry — individuals suffering from impostor syndrome attribute their success to luck, timing, or deceiving others into thinking they are more intelligent and competent than they believe themselves to be. Overcoming impostor syndrome, therefore, is crucial in maintaining not just professional success, but also personal happiness. Here are some strategies to combat this undermining self-perception:

- **Acknowledge the Impostor Feelings:** Recognize and label your impostor thoughts when they occur. By simply acknowledging these thoughts as symptoms of impostor syndrome, you can begin to see them as irrational and separate from your true abilities.
- **Practice Self-Compassion:** Counter self-criticism with self-compassion. Treat yourself with the same kindness and understanding you would extend to a friend or colleague who doubts their abilities.
- **Challenge the "Perfectionist" Within:** Accept that mistakes and failures are part of the learning curve and not a reflection of your abilities or worth. Embrace the concept of "failing forward," which views each setback as an opportunity for growth and learning.
- **Celebrate Achievements:** Keep a record of your accomplishments, no matter how small they may seem. Regularly review this record to remind yourself of your capabilities and achievements.
- **Seek Support:** Share your feelings with trusted colleagues, mentors, or professional coaches. You'll often find that impostor syndrome is more common than you think, and sharing your experience can help alleviate the sense of isolation that often accompanies it.
- **Constructive Affirmations:** Develop a set of positive and realistic affirmations about your skills, abilities, and experiences. Use these affirmations regularly to counteract negative self-perceptions.

Aloneness Time

In the fast-paced, demanding world of biotech investing, the value of solitude, or "aloneness time," is often overlooked. Yet, it plays a crucial role in personal well-being, professional effectiveness, and yes, the pursuit of happiness. Solitude offers a respite from constant social engagement, providing space for reflection, and independent thought.

The importance of solitude lies in its ability to allow for introspection. It provides an opportunity to detach from the external world, facilitating a deepened understanding of oneself, one's values, and one's goals. Moreover, it's a space where new ideas and strategies can emerge, unimpeded by the noise of the outside world. For the deep science investor, solitude can be a fertile ground for creative investment strategies and innovative approaches.

However, cultivating "aloneness time" in today's hyperconnected society can be challenging. Here are a few strategies to ensure you get the solitude you need:

- **Schedule Solitude:** Dedicate specific periods for solitude in your daily or weekly schedule. This time should be non-negotiable and protected from other demands on your time.
- **Create a Solitude-friendly Environment:** Find a place that encourages quiet and reflection. It could be a home office, a secluded spot in a park, or even a favorite chair.
- **Disconnect:** Switch off your devices or put them on silent mode during your solitude time. This helps avoid distractions and ensures you fully engage with the process.
- **Engage in Solo Activities:** Reading, journaling, meditating, or walking are some activities you can do alone that promote reflection and rejuvenation.
- **Mindfulness:** Practicing mindfulness during your solitude time can enhance the benefits of solitude. It involves focusing on the present moment and accepting it without judgment.

The Happiness Equation

A fascinating approach to understanding happiness lies in this equation: "Happiness = Reality - Expectations." This model provides a clear, simple perspective on happiness that emphasizes the crucial relationship between our expectations and our reality.

The "Reality" component of the equation relates to our actual circumstances, actions, and abilities. This could include our personal capacities, professional skills, social relationships, physical health, and the various aspects of our tangible existence.

The "Expectations" component refers to the hopes, desires, and standards we set for ourselves. These expectations could be personal goals, societal norms, professional targets, or any desired state we aspire to attain.

The equation suggests that our happiness depends not on the absolute state of our reality, but on how this reality compares to our expectations. If our reality falls short of our expectations, we experience unhappiness. Conversely, if our reality exceeds our expectations, we experience happiness.

To increase happiness using this model, we have two primary strategies:

- **Enhance Reality:** The first method involves improving our actual circumstances. This could mean studying to acquire new skills, taking care of our physical health, fostering meaningful relationships, or investing time in pursuits we find fulfilling. In the context of biotech investing, enhancing reality might mean deepening industry knowledge, honing investment skills, or cultivating professional networks.
- **Manage Expectations:** The second strategy involves curbing our expectations to align better with our reality. This does not mean surrendering our dreams or settling for less. Instead, it's about setting realistic and attainable goals, acknowledging our limits, and being kind to ourselves when we fall short. It's about understanding that overthinking, constant comparison, and unrealistic standards can be significant sources of unhappiness.

Striking a balance between improving reality and managing expectations is essential for long-term happiness. In the high-pressure world of entrepreneurship or investing, where success is often measured by the latest achievement, maintaining this balance can serve as a vital tool for personal well-being and professional longevity. It can provide a direction for happiness, paving the way for a fulfilling and satisfying career in this dynamic industry.

Stoicism as an Operating System

Stoicism, an ancient philosophy founded in the early 3rd century BC, offers powerful mental models to sustain balance and resilience in high-stress environments. It centers around the notion that while we cannot control every situation's outcome, we can control our response and maintain our inner equilibrium.

Events can quickly swing from ecstatic highs to heartbreaking lows. To maintain emotional stability amid such fluctuations, adopting a Stoic approach can be invaluable. A stoic mindset, like the one we mentioned in our "rock personality" section, allows us to engage fully in our work without becoming excessively attached to particular outcomes, which are often outside our control.

One key Stoic lesson stems from my experience in neurosurgery. The success or failure of a complex surgical procedure can elicit intense emotions. However, for the sake of my mental well-being, I learned to manage these emotional swings. Whether celebrating a successful operation or mourning a patient's death, the Stoic principle of maintaining emotional balance was vital. The philosophy taught me to never be excessively jubilant or overly despondent.

In the realm of investing, this Stoic balance translates into not being overly exuberant with every investment that yields high returns, nor overly disheartened by each that doesn't perform as expected. It's about maintaining a sense of detachment and viewing successes and setbacks as part of the investing journey.

Stoicism also emphasizes the importance of focusing on the present moment, an idea that can be particularly helpful in the fast-paced, forward-looking world of biotech investing. By concentrating on the here and now, we can make more thoughtful decisions, avoid being swept away by temporary trends, and stay focused on our long-term investment strategies.

Thus, Stoicism serves as an effective "operating system" for navigating the high-stress environment of biotech investing. By helping maintain emotional equilibrium, fostering a focus on the present, and promoting detachment from outcomes, Stoicism equips us to better handle the inherent challenges of the investing world.

Engaging with Intelligent Minds

One of the most profound privileges is the opportunity to continually engage with intelligent, forward-thinking minds. The benefits of such interactions are multifaceted, not only contributing to professional growth but also fostering a unique form of happiness. Interacting with a diverse array of professionals — scientists, entrepreneurs, fellow investors, and others — provides access to a broad spectrum of ideas and perspectives. This intellectual diversity challenges us to think critically, stimulates innovative ideas, and promotes an enduring state of learning.

More than just a professional advantage, engaging with intelligent minds can be a source of inspiration and fulfillment. Witnessing the passion of a scientist explaining a new discovery, the enthusiasm of an entrepreneur pitching their latest innovation, or the wisdom of a seasoned investor sharing their insights, can stoke our own passion for the work we do.

These exchanges often bring about a sense of connectedness. Sharing knowledge, insights, and experiences fosters a unique bond, a shared understanding that transcends the immediate context of the conversation. This connection can foster a sense of belonging, a key component of emotional well-being and happiness. Moreover, these interactions can be a source of validation and encouragement. Discussing ideas with intelligent peers can provide reassurance, affirm our judgment, and strengthen our confidence.

To fully reap the benefits of engaging with intelligent minds, it's important to approach these interactions with openness and humility. Being open to new ideas, willing to question our assumptions, and ready to learn from others can enrich our understanding and expand our perspective.

The Struggle-Happiness Paradigm

Struggle is an integral part of the journey. But rather than being an impediment, that struggle can, in fact, contribute to happiness. Here, we'll examine the intriguing premise of "no struggle, no happiness" and explore how it dovetails with the concept of "flow."

The "no struggle, no happiness" theory posits that our happiness is closely tied to overcoming adversity and confronting challenges head-on. Struggle, in this context, is not merely a hindrance to be avoided, but a crucial element in our pursuit of happiness. Struggle compels us to grow, to improve, and to better ourselves. It breeds resilience, fosters creativity, and imbues our lives with a sense of purpose. Without it, our victories would feel hollow and our growth would stagnate.

Consider, for instance, the sense of accomplishment one feels after successfully closing a difficult deal, or the joy of watching a fledgling biotech startup thrive amid adversity. These victories are all the sweeter because of the struggle that preceded them.

Complementing this idea is the concept of "flow," proposed by psychologist Mihaly Csikszentmihalyi. Flow refers to a state of complete immersion in an activity, characterized by intense focus, creativity, and a distorted perception of time. It is often experienced when we are engaged in challenging tasks that match our skill level, thereby requiring us to be fully present and pushing us to our limits.

In the state of flow, struggle is not an impediment, but a pathway. It is in dealing with the struggle — the intricate puzzle of an investment decision, the complexity of an emerging biotech trend — that we find ourselves in this state of optimal experience. Flow thus provides a tangible connection between struggle and happiness, enhancing our capacity for resilience, joy, and ultimately, a fulfilling professional journey.

In essence, the "no struggle, no happiness" theory and flow theory present an alternative perspective on the role of struggle in our lives. They challenge the traditional view of happiness as a state devoid of struggle and introduce the idea that it is through embracing and navigating challenges that we find true satisfaction and joy.

Žižek's Theory on Happiness

The renowned philosopher and cultural critic Slavoj Žižek presents an unconventional perspective on happiness. He suggests that our perceived longing for happiness might not be our true desire and that our pursuit of it could be fundamentally misguided. Žižek argues that happiness is, in fact, a conformist concept — a notion ingrained in us by societal norms and expectations. It's a concept that is deeply rooted in our cultural consciousness, particularly since the "pursuit of happiness" was immortalized in the Declaration of Independence. However, Žižek suggests that our real desires may not be aligned with this pursuit. We may think we desire happiness, but our actions and choices often reveal a different story. This is most evident in creative or high-risk endeavors, where we willingly subject ourselves to stress, risk, and even potential suffering in the name of passion or discovery. The lure of groundbreaking discovery in the field of biotech, for example, often surpasses the quest for personal happiness.

Moreover, Žižek posits that our desires are often paradoxical. We tend to long for things that, once attained, lose their allure. The desire for a successful investment portfolio, for instance, might be motivated more by the process and the challenge than by the actual achievement. Once the goal is reached, it often loses its sheen, indicating that the desire was not for the end result, but rather for the journey, the struggle, and the anticipation.

Applying Žižek's theory to our professional lives invites us to reevaluate our motivations and our perceived goals. It's an opportunity to reassess whether we're seeking true satisfaction in our work or merely chasing a societal construct of happiness. And in doing so, we can realign our objectives to bring about a more fulfilling and meaningful professional journey.

The Pursuit of Meaning and Peace

As a potential alternative to the traditional pursuit of happiness, this chapter proposes a shift toward seeking meaning and peace in our personal and professional lives. This reorientation can provide a more profound sense of fulfillment and satisfaction. While happiness is often fleeting and dependent on external factors, finding meaning in our work provides a more lasting and deeply rooted sense of satisfaction. It allows us to perceive our professional challenges and achievements within a broader context, seeing them as contributing to a larger purpose.

Moreover, maintaining a sense of inner peace amid the volatility of the investment landscape can serve as a stabilizing force. This is not about eliminating stress entirely — a virtually impossible task in this field — but about learning to navigate it with a sense of calm and resilience. To facilitate this shift in focus, we can deploy various strategies and tools:

- **Mindfulness practices:** Techniques such as meditation and mindfulness can cultivate a greater sense of peace and resilience. By learning to stay present and grounded amid the turbulence, we can respond more effectively to challenges and stressors.
- **Meaningful work:** Seek opportunities that align with your personal values and interests. Finding meaning in your work can foster a deeper sense of satisfaction than chasing after fleeting moments of happiness.
- **Work-life balance:** Maintaining a healthy balance between your professional and personal life can contribute to a more profound sense of well-being. This includes ensuring that you allocate time for rest, recreation, and relationships.
- **Lifelong learning:** Embrace an attitude of lifelong learning. This not only enhances your professional skills but also contributes to your personal growth and satisfaction.
- **Reflective practices:** Regular self-reflection can help to clarify what truly matters to you, enabling you to align your professional pursuits with your personal values and goals.

Kotler's Theory of Flow

Steven Kotler's theory of flow serves as a powerful conceptual framework for understanding how we can achieve states of peak performance and happiness. Flow is characterized by a heightened state of consciousness that enables effortless action, deep focus, and a sense of time distortion. This state is often associated with a feeling of being completely immersed in an activity to the point where everything else seems to fade away.

Its motivators, as outlined by Kotler, include curiosity, passion, purpose, autonomy, and mastery. They operate in a particular sequence, each naturally leading to the next.

- **Curiosity:** This fundamental motivator fuels our desire to explore and understand. In the context of investing, it might be a fascination with biotech advancements, economic trends, or innovative business models.
- **Passion:** As our curiosity leads us deeper into a subject, we develop a passion for it. This passion propels us to invest our time, energy, and resources more intensively.

- **Purpose:** Over time, our passion can evolve into a sense of purpose. In the world of biotech investing, this purpose might be to contribute to advancements in healthcare, to support groundbreaking research, or to drive economic growth.
- **Autonomy:** With a clear sense of purpose, we seek the autonomy or the freedom to pursue this purpose. Autonomy in investing might involve making independent decisions based on our analysis and judgment.
- **Mastery:** Ultimately, our desire for mastery — the acquisition of skills and knowledge to pursue our purpose effectively — comes into play. In the investing world, this could mean continually learning about new technologies, studying market trends, or refining investment strategies.

On a personal note, this is what better works for me. This not only increases our potential for success in the field of investing but also enhances our personal satisfaction and happiness. Waking up eager to see what the day brings. This is happiness.

Conclusion

From understanding impostor syndrome to finding reasons to wake up every day excited with what's coming, from redefining happiness to embracing stoicism, we've examined a wide range of perspectives and strategies.

The key insights gleaned from this journey compel us to reconsider the traditional understanding of happiness. We've grappled with the realization that the pursuit of happiness may not necessarily align with our true desires, as suggested by Zizek's theory. We've also delved into the theory of flow, where happiness is found in the deep immersion and mastery of our work, as proposed by Steven Kotler.

The various theories and strategies presented in this chapter do not aim to provide a definitive answer to achieving happiness in high-stakes environments. Instead, they offer us an expanded repertoire of tools and perspectives to approach happiness in a more nuanced manner. As we move up the professional ladder, these insights may help us navigate the stress and challenges with greater equanimity and joy.

Ultimately, the pursuit of happiness in high-stakes professions is deeply personal and variable. Yet, this exploration invites us to find our unique path to happiness by aligning our professional pursuits with our deepest values, embracing challenges as opportunities for growth, and fostering a sense of curiosity and mastery in our work. By doing so, we may not only thrive in our professions but also cultivate a greater sense of fulfillment and well-being in our lives.

www.ingramcontent.com/pod-product-compliance
Lightning Source LLC
Chambersburg PA
CBHW071407230926
51846CB00001B/33
* 9 7 8 1 9 6 0 7 6 2 1 3 9 *